D1301540

A Shared Experience

A Shared Experience

Men, Women, and
the History of Gender

EDITED BY

Laura McCall and Donald Yacovone

FOREWORD BY

Mark C. Carnes

New York University Press

NEW YORK AND LONDON

NEW YORK UNIVERSITY PRESS
New York and London

Library of Congress Cataloging-in-Publication Data
A shared experience : men, women, and the history of gender / edited
by Laura McCall and Donald Yacovone ; foreword by Mark C. Carnes.
p. cm.
Includes bibliographical references and index.
ISBN 0-8147-9682-6. — ISBN 0-8147-9683-4 (pbk.)
1. Sex role—United States—History. 2. Men—United States—History.
3. Women—United States—History. 4. Family—United
States—History. 5. United States—Social life and customs.
6. United States—Social conditions. I. McCall, Laura, 1951–   .
II. Yacovone, Donald.
HQ1075.5.U6S48 1998
305.3'0973—dc21   98-6850
                  CIP

New York University Press books are printed on acid-free paper,
and their binding materials are chosen for strength and durability.

Manufactured in the United States of America

10 9 8 7 6 5 4 3 2 1

For my mother and father,
Corinne and Richard McCall,

and

For my daughter,
Natasha Logan Yacovone

Contents

Foreword

Mark C. Carnes

This book is in many respects a successor to the one I edited with Clyde Griffen nearly a decade ago. *Meanings for Manhood: Constructions of Masculinity in Victorian America* (1990) grew out of an exploratory conference on history and masculinity at Barnard College in January 1988. The conference was memorable for several reasons. On the eve of our first session a blizzard engulfed New York City, stranding some participants in distant airports and entombing everyone else in a conference room for the better part of two days. Barnard and Columbia students were away on winter break, and the emptiness of the campus was deepened by the silence of a snow-softened Morningside Heights. The eerie setting contributed to the intensity of the discussions, which proved far more stimulating than any I have witnessed in an academic setting.

Most of us were just embarking on our careers. Some were assistant professors; others were doctoral candidates in a wide range of specializations.[1] The academic job market was poor and we were anxious about our prospects. Yet as I recall, we seemed to share an almost giddy sense that just beyond the horizon lay a promising *terra nova*. Approaching it from different directions, each of us had caught a glimpse of this or that intriguing feature of the landscape. If our disparate perceptions could somehow be combined, we could map out, explore, and exploit this new academic terrain. As we trudged through the drifts blocking upper Broadway, we sensed that we were about to discover and lay claim to "men's history," thereby acquiring fame and riches of the academic kind: a job, perhaps, and even a chance to sip from that holy grail known as tenure.

There is, of course, no such thing as a new discovery. All explorers, academic or otherwise, follow paths at least partially blazed by pioneering predecessors. This was certainly true of "men's history" when we came upon it in 1988. One of the early works was G. J. Barker-Benfield's *The Horrors of the Half-Known Life: Male Attitudes toward Women and Sexuality in Nineteenth-Century America* (1976). Barker-Benfield revealed a pervasive and repellent misogyny among Victorian physicians, a characterization that neatly fit an early paradigm of women's history that emphasized men's victimization of women. In 1979 came two signal books: Peter N. Stearns's *Be a Man! Males in Modern Society* and Joe Dubbert's *A Man's Place: Masculinity in Transition,* ambitious syntheses that sought to show how industrialization and modernization altered and eventually led to a reconstitution of patriarchal institutions and values. Stearns and Dubbert conceded that they had undertaken these early attempts at synthesis before scholarly specialists had written the articles and detailed monographs on which historical narratives are customarily based. Their inspired deductions rested upon virtually nonexistent foundations.

At that time, however, there was little reason for anyone to undertake the requisite spadework in the historical archives. Young scholars in the 1970s and 1980s were attracted to new or newly invigorated specializations such as labor history, African-American history, and women's history, fields that promised to reclaim the voices of the dispossessed. There was no need to reclaim the history of men, whose words and documents had for centuries constituted the entire historical record. All history to that point, it had seemed, was "men's history."

The faultiness of this assumption was exposed in the 1980s, when one after another important books established women's history as indisputably the most exciting and fruitful field of contemporary historical inquiry. What became apparent to many readers of these new books, and certainly to those of us who met at Barnard, was that each new scholarly insight into the lives of women forced a reconsideration of the way we looked at men. The traditional history of men as subjects did not constitute a history of men as gendered beings.

My own experiences bore this out. I had for some time been puzzled by the lengthy, quasi-religious initiation rituals of the Freemasons, Odd Fellows, and scores of similar male-only fraternal orders. I could not explain why millions of middle-class men spent countless hours inventing, memorizing, and performing them; but these rituals became comprehensible when I looked at them in brilliant light provided by historians Nancy Cott, Ann Douglas, and Mary P. Ryan, among others, who had shown how evangelical women had attempted to mold the religious and moral behavior—the sense of manhood—of Victorian men. Fraternal rituals could be understood as a repudiation of these women's initiative. Thus, though women were pointedly absent from fraternal initiations, they were nevertheless central to an understanding of the phenomenon.[2]

These influential women's historians rejected the assumption of woman's victimization and passivity, emphasizing instead women's ability to break free from the constraints of patriarchy and reshape it according to their own lights. This insight greatly expanded both the topical range and causal significance of women's history. Women played an important role in even such seemingly male enterprises as war and party politics, areas that presumably had been exclusively men's realm. And if women's lives were bound up with men's, then the converse was equally valid, a truism that now seems numbingly obvious. The logical culmination of this line of thinking was to supplant both men's and women's history with an interactive history of gender. This observation surfaced repeatedly at the Barnard conference where Clyde and I, among others, advocated that this new enterprise—"men's history"—be subsumed into gender history from the outset.[3]

But this did not happen. Many women's historians, particularly those active in feminist causes, worried that "women's history" would lose its political edge if it were broadened to encompass men. For this reason all but a handful of job openings in gender history are still labeled as "women's history." And "men's history" did not wither away, as Clyde and I had proposed, but instead flourished in its own right. The term (and variants including "manhood" or "masculinity") now appears as a regular index category in many historical publications and reference volumes; papers on "men" and "manhood" have outnumbered those on "women" and "womanhood" at recent conferences of the major historical associations.

There is little indication that the persistence of "men's history" is linked to any of the current political movements associated with men. As many women as men are doing work in this field, and nearly everyone involved endorses feminism. The advance of men's history is more likely related to a heightened consciousness among all historians to issues of gender, and especially to the way gender has been implanted in *language*. Thus historians of medicine, science, law, diplomacy, politics, and countless other traditionally "masculine" fields have now spotted in the historical documents glaring hypermasculine rhetoric. Without intending to study gender, they realize they have happened upon it. Before they can return to their usual academic pursuits, they must come to terms with the men's arresting language.

As a result, much of this new work has been about men and their aggressive rhetoric rather than about the relation of men and women and the ways in which the rhetoric of gender resonates in their interactions. This was certainly true of *Meanings for Manhood;* most of the essays were about men: as boys, fraternal members, theologians, friends, professionals, and factory workers. Much of the recent research has similarly focused on men and manhood.

A Shared Experience: Men, Women, and the History of Gender, however, constitutes an essential and long overdue reshaping of gender scholarship. It makes a persuasive case for the integrated approach to a history of men and women that has long been advocated but rarely executed. We learn, for example, that

- while the Puritans censured men and women alike for belittling their betters, the resulting punishments were different for each sex;
- although Puritans imposed sharp gender distinctions in dress, language, and behavior, they nevertheless shared a belief that all that truly mattered was the soul, which had no gender;
- marriage in colonial New England, though theoretically based on men's dominance, in practice encouraged a partnership between husband and wife and allowed the latter recourse to various mechanisms to chastise abusive husbands;
- even in the patriarchal bastion of the antebellum South, women and men could forge relationships that subverted restrictive conventions;
- middle-class women played a major role in the formation of party politics, an arena from which they were supposedly excluded;
- despite the pervasive rhetoric of "separate spheres," Victorian authors, male and female alike, embraced an almost identical image of the domestic ideal;
- Victorian friendships, regardless of gender configuration, admitted a wide range of emotional behaviors;
- freed slave men and women together forged new gender conventions, as did Indian parents who had been forced onto reservations;

- the male and female leaders of settlement houses formed different types of personal sexual attachments, but together enshrined the brotherhood of man over the tribalism of the family;
- women and men together fought on behalf of woman suffrage, and employed similarly chivalric language to win the crusade;
- the "physical fitness" craze of the Eisenhower and Kennedy years had profound implications for the body images of both boys and girls;
- after World War II, men and women shared a similar ideal of what was expected of them as parents, one that men (then as now) found difficult to attain.

These essays do not cut to some self-evident truth about gender in the past. Rather, they contravene our earlier and simpler assumptions, forcing us to contend with complexity and nuance. It is easier to think of Puritan men as flinty patriarchs than as people who cherished a sexless vision of heaven; easier to assume that Victorian men and women inhabited separate physical and mental "spheres" than to see them working together to win political battles and build meaningful marriages, and so forth. But historical truths are always embedded in layers of complexity. This book—and the vision of an integrated gender history that it upholds—calls on us to dig deeper and think harder.

NOTES

1. There were two notable exceptions: Clyde Griffen, the Lucy Maynard Salmon Professor of History at Vassar, a distinguished practitioner and theorist of the new social history; and Nancy Cott, a young eminence in women's history at Yale. Those who attended, along with the books that I suspect were in germination at the time of the conference, included: Ava Baron, *Work Engendered: Toward a New History of American Labor* (1991); Gail Bederman, *Manliness and Civilization: A Cultural History of Gender and Race in the United States, 1880–1917* (1995); Mary H. Blewett, *The Last Generation: Work and Life in the Textile Mills of Lowell, Massachusetts, 1910–1960* (1990); Harry Brod, ed., *Theorizing Masculinities* (1994); George Chauncey, *Gay New York: Gender, Urban Culture and the Making of the Gay Male World, 1890–1950* (1994); Susan Curtis, *Consuming Faith: The Social Gospel and Modern American Culture* (1991); Timothy J. Gilfoyle, *City of Eros: New York City, Prostitution and the Commercialization of Sex, 1790–1920* (1992); Robert L. Griswold, *Fatherhood in America: A History* (1993); Michael Grossberg, *A Judgment for Solo-*

mon: *The d'Hauteville Case and Legal Experience in Antebellum America* (1996); John S. Hughes, ed., *The Letters of a Victorian Madwoman* (1993); Michael S. Kimmel, *Manhood in America: A Cultural History* (1996); Margaret Marsh, *Suburban Lives* (1990); Ted Ownby, *Subduing Satan: Religion, Recreation, and Manhood in the Rural South, 1865–1920* (1990); E. Anthony Rotundo, *American Manhood: Transformations in Masculinity from the Revolution to the Modern Era* (1993); and Mark C. Carnes, *Secret Ritual and Manhood in Victorian America* (1989).

2. See Carnes, *Secret Ritual and Manhood in Victorian America*.

3. Clyde Griffen and Mark C. Carnes, "Men's History: Whither and Whether," *Organization of American Historians Newsletter* (August 1988). On the importance of an integrated gender history, see also Gerda Lerner, "The Challenge of Women's History," in her *The Majority Finds Its Past: Placing Women in History* (1979); and Natalie Zemon Davis, who told the Berkshire Conference on Women's History that "we should now be interested in the history of both women and men. We should not be working on the subjected sex any more than a historian of class can focus exclusively on peasants" ("Women's History in Transition: The European Case," *Feminist Studies* 33 [1976]: 83–103).

Acknowledgments

Organizing a collection of essays is a difficult enterprise. Fortunately, we have been blessed with contributors whose patience, persistence, and professionalism allowed this book to happen. They deserve our deepest thanks. Few words, however, can express our gratitude to Niko Pfund, director and editor in chief of New York University Press. When this book was little more than an idea, he saw its potential. His enthusiasm and commitment convinced us that *A Shared Experience* would be safest in his hands. Niko's support never wavered and his encouragement came when we needed it most. We also wish to acknowledge the help of Conrad Wright and Mary Fabiszewski at the Massachusetts Historical Society, who read portions of the manuscript and offered invaluable suggestions. Joan Cashin offered timely advice and Mark Carnes provided sage wisdom based on a similar editorial experience.

We also thank Blackwell Publishers for permission to reprint Jane Kamensky's "Talk Like a Man: Speech, Power, and Masculinity in Early New England," *Gender and History* 8 (April 1996): 22–47; William M. Fowler, Jr., for Richard Godbeer's " 'Love Raptures': Marital, Romantic, and Erotic Images of Jesus Christ in Puritan New England, 1670–1730," *The New England Quarterly* 68 (September 1995): 355–84, copyright © 1995 by *The New England Quarterly*; the Organization of American Historians for Elizabeth R. Varon's "Tippecanoe and the Ladies, Too: Women and Party Politics in Antebellum Virginia," *Journal of American History* 82 (September 1995): 494–521; and the Society for Historians of the Early American Republic for permission to reprint material from Joan E. Cashin's "Black Families in the Old Northwest," *Journal of the Early Republic* 15 (Fall 1995): 449–75, copyright © 1995 by the Society for Historians of the Early Republic. Chapter 3 includes excerpts from materials held by the American Antiquarian Society and the Connecticut Historical Society, reprinted here by permission. Also included are excerpts from the Silliman Family Papers, Park Family Papers, Reeve Family Papers, and Thomas Clap Presidential Papers (YRG 2-A-5), from the Manuscripts and Archives, Yale University Library.

Introduction

> Of all the vulgar modes of escaping from the consideration of the effect of the social and moral influences upon the human mind, the most vulgar is that of attributing the diversities of conduct and character to inherent natural differences.
>
> —John Stuart Mill

A *Shared Experience* challenges our understanding of manhood, womanhood, and marriage in three hundred years of American history.[1] Since the rebirth of women's history scholarship in the 1960s, the notion that a vast chasm separated the historical experience of men and women has shaped our understanding of gender.[2] Men's and women's lives have been interpreted through the lens of strict gender segregation, epitomized by the nineteenth-century doctrine of separate spheres. Men, according to the standard litany, dominated a public sphere of economic and political life, while women were confined to a domestic sphere that demanded piety, purity, and submissiveness. Historians have begun to question this construct and the definitions of public and private spheres. Few, however, have been willing to reject the ideas of separate spheres or of "republican motherhood," a sister formulation that locates the origins of Victorian "true womanhood" in the popular republicanism of the Revolutionary era.[3]

The time has come to abandon these interpretive fictions, originally intended to create a coherent narrative of women's history from colonial times to the present. The history of masculinity, born appropriately enough out of the new women's history, is indispensable for formulating a new perspective on the personal lives and public meanings of manhood and womanhood.[4] As the essays in this collection make abundantly clear, male domination or patriarchy was anything but synonymous with rigid gender separation; the institution of marriage was more egalitarian than historians have been willing to admit; and men's and women's lives were far more interdependent than we ever imagined. More to the point, manhood and womanhood are not metaphorical polar opposites.

Severe social codes governing public behavior of the elite and middle classes, especially in the 1820s, did lead to segregation of the sexes in some circumstances.[5] In the everyday world of agriculture, fishing, commerce, industry, medicine, education, and politics, however, women assumed central, not marginal, roles. They helped forge the social, political, and economic life of the nation. Even the family, once seen as an isolated haven from the rigors of economic life, was in the mainstream of social and economic development.[6] Women were never confined exclusively to a domestic sphere and, given the demands of agricultural life (where the overwhelming majority of Americans labored), they never could have conformed to the stereotypes constructed by historians.

Our understanding of manhood and men's role in the family remain similarly clouded with clichés.[7] Too often, Puritans are depicted as impersonal, theocratic patriarchs. Jane Kamensky, Richard Godbeer, and Lisa Wilson put more appealing human faces on one of the most studied groups in all of American history.[8] Even when their primary interest is in the personal history of men, these authors understand that definitions of manhood developed in conjunction with ideas of womanhood, not in isolation.

Kamensky explores the "discourse of manhood," detailing the ways men enjoyed a freedom of speech largely unavailable to women. But such privilege, key to defining manhood, remained subject to rigorous discipline from the pulpit, in the courts, and on the town green. From childhood, boys and girls received identical training regarding class and social deference. A "respectful silence" was instilled in the untrained and untutored. Puritans demanded, at times ineffectually, that women's public demeanor should resemble a childlike silence. Within the family, however, women spoke on equal terms with men. The public nature of male expression gave the act of speaking immense importance, and gave manhood its privilege.

In speech, politics, and law, men ruled. While the patriarchal quality of colonial society remains unquestioned, simple characterizations cloud the real ambiguities that blunted male power and led to the gradual liberalization of American society.[9] Kamensky and Wilson help define the limits of male dominance and carve out realms where men and women enjoyed harmony, if not a semblance of equality. Wilson examines intimacy among men and women in colonial New England. Hierarchical ideas of politics and class shaped Puritan marriages, with men ruling the family as the king governed society. Nevertheless, no matter how much men were perceived as the dominant marriage partner, most unions were cooperative ventures founded upon love and respect. As one New Englander wrote, married partners were "mutually supporting, blessing & assisting Each other in the Ways of Duty." Puritan husbands and wives viewed each other as "helpmeets" who shared in life's "trouble & Afliction As Well As in Joy & prosperity."

Colonial communities, especially in New England, zealously regulated family life, intruding deeply into personal lives to guarantee order, stability, a town's reputation, and individual virtue.[10] When marriages broke down, as in any time or place, men and women often turned to the most disruptive weapons available to them. Wilson demonstrates that in such cases, men—through law, hectoring, or force—sought to preserve their privilege or regain dominance. Under most circumstances, however, a man could only resort to "an angry declaration of his right to rule." Women often turned to less violent and less official, yet equally effective, means to protect their interests and assert their authority. Damaging a man's reputation through gossip and slander, or subjecting him to ridicule through adultery, comprised reserve powers that tamed the extremes of male privilege. Men did not exercise absolute control.

Godbeer reinforces Kamensky's conclusions on the vital role of public speech in Puritan society and Wilson's emphasis on the positive qualities of Puritan marriages. The kind of speech Godbeer investigates establishes the rhetoric of marriage as a central metaphor of Puritanism. Perry Miller long ago explained that sermons written in the "Plain Style" favored the concrete and familiar over the abstract to rivet religious principles to both heart and mind. Puritans fashioned their metaphors from everyday life rather than from Latin or Greek phrases.[11] Thus, the institution of marriage and sexuality (sanctioned only in marriage) offered Puritan sermons fertile symbolic terrain.

Marriage became the Puritans' reigning metaphor to describe a man's and a woman's bond with Christ. Increase Mather reflected Puritan views when he spoke plainly about a man's or a woman's "marriage" with Christ as "the most desirable one that ever was or that possibly can be." For Puritans, the secular institution of marriage mimicked the marriage of God and his elect. Both unions fortified one another and allowed the faithful, as John Winthrop once proclaimed to his wife, to "delight in him as we do in each other."

Godbeer emphasizes the Puritans' use of gendered and sexually charged language to describe the individual's relationship to God. Puritans freely invoked erotic language, as Christians always had, to express the depth of their religious convictions. They perceived the reception of God's grace to be as powerful and as rapturous as sexual intercourse and invoked this imagery to communicate the wonders of salvation for the elect. For Puritans, salvation was the "fruit of sexual union with the savior."

The androgynous quality of Puritan rhetoric reflected a democratic element in Puritanism. Puritan divines emphasized that, ultimately, there was no male or female in Christ—all were equal. Whether man or woman, one could be a "bride of Christ." The willingness of Puritan men to situate themselves in this seemingly subordinate female role reveals their ambivalence over the culture's rigid social hierarchy. Such sentiments also parallel the sense of harmony and equity that Wilson finds in Puritan marriages. Equally important, Godbeer's work explores the influences that shaped later ideas of androgyny and the rhetorical framework that underpinned intimate male friendships in the nineteenth century.

Patricia Cleary captures a more secular moment in the creation of personal identity, revealing the expectations that guided childrearing in the Anglo-American world of the late eighteenth century. The Scottish Murray family, who apprenticed its female children to Elizabeth Murray Smith in colonial Boston, displayed surprising levels of flexibility in preparing girls for careers in commerce. The American colonies offered women business opportunities that were unavailable to them in Great Britain. In American cities such as Boston and Philadelphia, as many as 40 percent of shopkeepers were women, thereby propelling them into a very public realm. Business transactions with male merchants, for the acquisition of merchandise or credit, were inevitable and further expanded the sphere of activities available to women in the mercantile trade.[12]

For those women able to obtain formal schooling, curricula did not offer preparation for business or professional careers. Elizabeth Murray Smith sought informal apprenticeships for her nieces, not to make them into genteel ornaments, but to "improve" their minds and fortunes and make them "useful member[s] of society." Boys, on the other hand, studied traditional subjects, like math and geography, to prepare them for practical careers. Their moral education, however, lay in the hands of their fathers. Though we are accustomed to thinking of this aspect of child rearing as falling into a female-dominated domestic sphere, fathers held primary responsibility for their children's moral and ethical instruction until the twentieth century.[13] Young men with social aspirations learned that good conduct toward women was paramount and that proper relations with virtuous women were essential to a complete education. Rather than a message of gender segregation, young men learned that one may become "a scholar, a man of business, a Philosopher, and artist . . . [but that] ladies only can form the polite complete gentleman."

The fluidity of sexual roles, coupled with love and cooperation, are persistent themes in the marriages depicted in this book. From the language of the Puritans to the letters of early nineteenth-century spouses, men and women freely expressed their affectionate bonds. Anya Jabour disputes many of our assumptions about marriage in the early republic by examining the remarkable correspondence of William and Elizabeth Wirt. Though William Wirt's legal and political careers often kept the couple apart, they did not live in separate spheres. Their letters became the medium for working out their conflicts and strengthening their bonds. As correspondents, the two reversed stereotypical roles. William Wirt wrote letters of gushing sentimentality, while Elizabeth penned relatively brief missives that dwelled on practical affairs of home and business: overseeing ten children and as many slaves, maintaining plantation account books, and offering investment advice. The Wirts did not conform to familiar characterizations of marriage as a patriarchal prison or to gender roles based upon presumptions about domesticity.[14]

Marriage and family life among blacks and Native Americans also did not fit many current stereotypes. Joan E. Cashin and Katherine M. B. Osburn explore the painfully unique circumstances of black and Ute Indian families, respectively. Historians' debates over notions of "republican motherhood" or the "cult of true womanhood" have no relevance for these Americans. The black experience under Southern slavery, coupled with the ordeal of Northern discrimination, undermine assumptions that profound differences characterized the lives of black men and women. In slavery, both sexes performed the same arduous tasks and suffered together in an unimaginable list of torments inflicted by white masters. In freedom, they suffered relentless discrimination. With the exception of a few wealthy black elites, all worked to support their families. While men generally enjoyed a better-known public role in the black abolitionist movement, women possessed an equally important and energetic one. In dangerous circumstances they were as likely as men to employ violence for their own or others' survival. Whether delivering public addresses, raising funds, caring for fugitives, assisting in fugitive slave rescues, or as fugitives themselves, black women played an essential part in the campaign to end slavery.

Osburn details heart-wrenching stories of Ute Indian families' adjustment to assimilationist policies from the late nineteenth century to the early 1930s. Like African Americans in the Old Northwest, Utes suffered restricted opportunities and intense discrimination from white society. Ute fathers, denied their traditional position as hunters, found their role as public caretakers of their children a necessary but unsatisfying replacement. Using letters in student files in the former Office of Indian Affairs, Osburn chronicles Ute fathers' poignant efforts to conform to government mandates and protect the health and welfare of their children.

Collectively, the stories Osburn relates portray Ute fathers as intimately involved in the rearing of their children and record an image of Native Americans largely unknown in popular culture. Rather than stereotypical stoic warriors or broken alcoholics, the Indian men in Osburn's work are concerned and loving fathers who manage the education and care of their offspring. Ute children, sent to distant Office of Indian Affairs schools, occasioned the frequent and persistent involvement of their fathers, who stretched their limited power in the face of arrogant or indifferent white overseers.

Through the work of Osburn and Cashin we have a lively, compassionate, and necessary starting point for reconsidering the history of marriage and the family among minority groups in America.

Those who subscribe to the doctrine of separate spheres usually point to politics as uncontested evidence of the abyss that divided the historical experiences of men and women. Historians have assumed that because women were denied the vote they possessed no meaningful part in the nation's political life. Women presumably remained at home as republican mothers or Victorian domestic angels to raise good citizens, while men monopolized the aggressive public sphere of political power. Elizabeth R. Varon provides one of the most potent challenges to this principal tenet of separate spheres doctrine.[15]

According to Varon, the 1840 presidential campaign marked a pivotal change in women's political participation. No mere cheerleaders, Virginia Whig women employed the organizing and campaigning skills honed in benevolent reform movements to mobilize voters for their party. Women in Virginia and elsewhere reinforced the newfound democratic appeal of the Whigs and allowed the party to lay special claim to civic virtue. Wherever Whig party strength existed, in states like Virginia, Massachusetts, or Delaware, women organized voters, planned rallies, or signed public petitions in support of candidates. Their knowledge of political issues was as comprehensive as that of the average male voter, and their commitment to campaigning was equally unswerving. The wife of John Davis, candidate for Massachusetts governor, pledged "to do all in my power to change the rulers of the Country."[16] Other parties followed the Whigs' lead and rallied women to their political standard, thus bringing women farther into the mainstream of American life and into an ever-broadening sphere of shared experiences.

While Varon shows that the history of American politics fails to conform to traditional interpretations of gender, Laura McCall undercuts a principal foundation of separate spheres doctrine. Historians have relied heavily on didactic literature, including novels and ladies' magazines, to support their characterizations of gender, especially in the nineteenth century.[17] Rather than the traditional stark dichotomy of a male public sphere and a woman's private domestic sphere, McCall finds that male and female authors share similar concerns on a range of issues related to marriage and domesticity. Perhaps most surprising is McCall's discovery, after surveying 104 stories and novels published between 1820 and 1860, that both male *and* female authors emphasize marriage and the home as a source of joy and fulfillment for men.

The image of marriage that emerges from McCall's careful review of popular literature upsets facile assumptions about patriarchal domination and compels historians to reassess their rendering of the nineteenth-century social construction of gender. Contrary to expectations, neither men nor women endorsed male dominance. Instead, male and female authors envisioned marriage as a cooperative partnership founded on love, devotion, and companionship. If the era's literature is any guide, little distinguished the attitudes of men and women on issues of home and hearth.

The differences between manhood and womanhood in the nineteenth century are far less than we imagine. Donald Yacovone's reconsideration of masculinity and friendship warns against placing modern constructions of gender on the past and emphasizes the qualities that men share with women. Americans, until the early twentieth century, accepted no single definition of masculinity and permitted a variety of phases or styles of manhood. Thus, close male friendships cannot be explained by modern dichotomized categories of homosexuality or heterosexuality.[18] Before the era of Freud and the modernization of sex, men formed intense, affectionate relationships throughout their lives, free from guilt and homophobia. Whether businessmen, politicians, or ministers, rich or poor, Northerner or Southerner, white or black, men defined their manhood by the magnitude of their relations with other men.

The language of fraternal love, falling into centuries-old classical and Christian traditions, represents a pervasive cultural archetype. The "complete" man, prior to the modern era, combined elements customarily associated with women, constituting an androgynous ideal. Political leaders were valued for their strength and gentleness; soldiers for their bravery and tenderheartedness, their toughness and delicacy. Ralph Waldo Emerson epitomized this duality of manhood in mid-nineteenth-century America when he proclaimed that the "Hermaphrodite is then the symbol of the finished soul." The Civil War intensified, not diminished, such sentiments. Succeeding generations, symbolized by men like Theodore Roosevelt, formulated a new hypermasculine style that supplanted the androgyny of the antebellum era. The transformation of Anglo-American culture at the close of the nineteenth century and the "discovery" of homosexuality in the first decades of the twentieth destroyed the old order and gave rise to contemporary ideas of sexuality and gender identity.[19]

Kevin P. Murphy describes how the tradition of fraternal love merged with an urban and erotic homosociality. While not entirely homosexual in the modern sense, the homoerotics of New York settlement house reformers Charles B. Stover and John Lovejoy Elliot contested sexual identity at the turn of the century. Murphy's essay provides an arresting case study of the transition from a distinctly premodern sensibility to a more familiar sexual persona.

In collaboration with female settlement house reformers, most notably Jane Addams and Lillian Wald, Stover and Elliot sought a new social order, replacing the coercion of law and commerce with personal affection and compassion. For young reformers, the settlement house movement offered ideal laboratories for social and sexual experimentation. Well educated and from upper-middle-class families, Stover and Elliot formed alliances with lower-class boys to offer alternatives to the bourgeois family, defy the rising medical pathologizing of homoeroticism, and achieve social democracy.

In Murphy's inspired reconstruction of Stover's and Elliot's experiences, the intellectual and literary foundations of homosexuality assume prime importance. The writings of Socrates, Horatio Alger, Charles Loring Brace, and especially Walt Whitman proved critical to the "self-construction" of Stover and Elliot. Whitman, laying aside the contentious debate over his own sexuality, provided young male reformers with a model for the unification of homoerotics and politics.[20]

Whereas Varon places women near the center of American political history, Eric Dwyce Taylor finds that in the California of the early twentieth century, the politics of masculinity played a central role in the history of women. Too often ignored by Eastern-trained historians, California provides a compelling case study of how men voluntarily relinquished power and enfranchised women. Taylor explains how the 1911 vote on female enfranchisement exposed ingrained assumptions concerning definitions of gender, especially masculinity. By focusing on the rhetoric of chivalry, Taylor finds a common element linking pro-and anti-suffragist forces that exposes the difficulty men faced in imagining a public arena of political equality.

By adhering to notions of chivalry, most men viewed the debate over female enfranchisement as a search for the most effective means to guarantee the protection of women. Most pro-suffrage men maintained that only through the vote could women gain complete protection, while anti-suffragists asserted that enfranchisement threatened both female safety and male privilege. Extremists, like the future World War II general George S. Patton, saw politics as war by other means, a wholly inappropriate and impossible sphere of activity for women. The primary points of contention, as Taylor explains, had as much to do with competing definitions of masculinity as with the changing realities of the lives of American women. Ultimately, patriarchal privilege, not separate spheres, lost in the 1911 California election.

Anxiety over the state of masculinity in the post–World War II era assumes enormous importance in Robert L. Griswold's chapter. The absence of fathers during World War II created doubts over the next generation's manhood. Increasingly uneasy with the physical comfort that modern conveniences provided and threatened by the escalating tensions with the Communist bloc, Americans questioned their ability to endure physical hardship and guarantee democracy's survival. Anxiety over the "muscle gap" equaled the apprehension sparked by the "missile gap" with the Soviet Union.

The physical fitness crusade, begun under the Eisenhower administration, became a hallmark of John F. Kennedy's presidency. Kennedy's campaign sought to redeem male bodies and provide the necessary manly strength to assure global security. Although experts advanced physical fitness for girls and boys, the drive focused on male bodies. The national obsession with fitness, in the context of a thermonuclear arms race, intensified anxiety over the state of American manhood. Simultaneously, the postwar era witnessed unsettling revelations about the large number of homosexuals in American society. Griswold maintains that no mere coincidence can explain the heightened emphasis on masculine strength and the nation's most vociferous outburst of homophobia. With the end of the Cold War, however, distress over the physical state of American manhood subsided. Nevertheless American bodies—men's and women's—retain their formidable symbolism as repositories for our aspirations and doubts.[21]

In the same postwar era that developed the "muscle gap" and relegated many middle-class wives to the home, Jessica Weiss finds the origins of the "new father"—the true family man who shares child rearing responsibilities.[22] Ironically, the 1950s and early 1960s, rather than the mid-nineteenth century, saw the greatest divergence in the lives of married men and women. Surprisingly, even during this era of heightened sexual distinctions, as Weiss reveals, a new doctrine of domestic fatherhood emerged. A host of experts, professionals, and popular magazines urged fathers to take a greater role in raising their children.

Exploiting a source underutilized by historians, Weiss creatively mined the records of the Institute of Human Development (IHD) at the University of California, Berkeley. The interviews contained in the IHD archives exemplify the painful dilemma fathers faced in having to choose between the demands of the office and the home. Much like the dual meaning of chivalry in the California 1911 suffrage debate, the idea of the involved father rested on contradictory notions. The advocates of the new fatherhood popularized the idea, not as a matter of equity, but primarily as a method of rejuvenating men for the next day's work. As

Weiss deftly shows, the working fathers of the postwar era could not heed expert advice or even their wives' pleas and sometimes became strangers to their own families.

Weiss sketches out the origins of the "new fatherhood" in an era defined by "nuclear" families and a rigid division of family labor. As men and women continue striving to achieve parity in child-rearing responsibilities,[23] Weiss shows how current efforts depend on the postwar era men and women who struggled together to simultaneously defend and redefine their world.

The essays in *A Shared Experience* illustrate how far the field of gender history has advanced in such a remarkably short period of time. Still, much remains to be done. We know little about gender in the colonial Chesapeake, where high death rates, geographic mobility, and racial diversity made for some unconventional unions. Studies of rural, borderlands, and frontier life could significantly broaden our perspective. If the frontier served as a testing ground for American society, as has been theorized since the days of Frederick Jackson Turner, then historians need to fully analyze gender relations in the West. Far more attention needs to be given to Hispanics, Native Americans, African Americans, and Asians, and to the interplay among these groups and with whites.[24]

The essays in this book enhance our awareness of the social construction of gender. These explorations into the intimate lives of men and women reveal gender as a continuous process, subject to dramatic changes over time, rather than a static product of biologically determined traits. Equally important, they help reconceptualize how the history of gender should be written. Twenty years ago, Gerda Lerner, one of the great progenitors of women's history, called for a synthesis of the study of men and women into a "a new universal history, a holistic history."[25] Such a goal is only possible—and desirable—if we define this "new history" with flexibility, few presuppositions, and the awareness that men and women inhabited the same domestic and public spheres.

NOTES

1. The starting point for any study of gender is Joan Wallach Scott, *Gender and the Politics of History* (New York: Columbia University Press, 1988). See

also Judith Butler, *Gender Trouble: Gender and the Subversion of Identity* (New York: Routledge, 1990); and Anne Fausto-Sterling, *Myths of Gender: Biological Theories about Women and Men*, rev. ed. (New York: Basic Books, 1992).

2. Barbara Welter and Nancy Cott are the chief architects of the doctrine of separate spheres and the idea of true womanhood. See Nancy Cott, *The Bonds of Womanhood: "Woman's Sphere" in New England, 1780–1835* (New Haven: Yale University Press, 1977); and Barbara Welter, *Dimity Convictions: The American Woman in the Nineteenth Century* (Athens: Ohio University Press, 1976). More recent monographs that continue to accept the old models include Carolyn DeSwarte Gifford, ed., *The American Ideal of the "True Woman" as Reflected in Advice Books to Young Women* (New York: Garland Publishing, 1987); Ellen K. Rothman, *Hands and Hearts: A History of Courtship in America* (Cambridge: Harvard University Press, 1987); Stephen Mintz and Susan Kellogg, *Domestic Revolutions: A Social History of American Family Life* (New York: Free Press, 1988); Sara Evans, *Born for Liberty: A History of Women in America* (New York: Free Press, 1989); and Terri L. Premo, *Winter Friends: Women Growing Old in the New Republic, 1785–1835* (Urbana: University of Illinois Press, 1990). On republican motherhood, see Linda Kerber, *Women of the Republic: Intellect and Ideology in Revolutionary America* (New York: W. W. Norton, 1980); and Mary Beth Norton, *Liberty's Daughters: The Revolutionary Experience of American Women, 1750–1800* (New York: HarperCollins, 1980).

3. Challenges to the concepts of true womanhood and separate spheres can be found in Linda Kerber, "Separate Spheres, Female Worlds, Woman's Place: The Rhetoric of Women's History," *Journal of American History* 75 (1988–89): 9–39; Linda Kerber, Nancy F. Cott, Robert Gross, et al., "Beyond Roles, Beyond Spheres: Thinking about Gender in the Early Republic," *William and Mary Quarterly*, 3d ser., 46 (1989): 565–85; Susan Juster, " 'In a Different Voice': Male and Female Narratives of Religious Conversion in Post-Revolutionary America," *American Quarterly* 41 (March 1989): 34–62; and Karen Lystra, *Searching the Heart: Women, Men, and Romantic Love in Nineteenth-Century America* (New York: Oxford University Press, 1989), especially 20, 55. Margaret Nash, in "Rethinking Republican Motherhood: Benjamin Rush and the Young Ladies' Academy of Philadelphia," *Journal of the Early Republic* 17 (summer 1997): 171–91, provides the first sustained critique of "republican motherhood." Karen V. Hansen's *A Very Social Time: Crafting Community in Antebellum New England* (Berkeley: University of California Press, 1994) examines the lives of ordinary nineteenth-century New Englanders, revealing the integral nature of men's and women's lives and how they created a "social time" that defied categorization of activities into simple private and public arenas.

4. Mark C. Carnes and Clyde Griffen, eds., *Meanings for Manhood: Con-*

structions of Masculinity in Victorian America (Chicago: University of Chicago Press, 1990), 1–7. For other work on masculinity, see E. Anthony Rotundo, *American Manhood: Transformations in Masculinity from the Revolution to the Modern Era* (New York: Basic Books, 1993); Robert L. Griswold, *Fatherhood in America: A History* (New York: Basic Books, 1993); David D. Gilmore, *Manhood in the Making: Cultural Concepts of Masculinity* (New Haven: Yale University Press, 1990); and Mark Gerzon, *A Choice of Heroes: The Changing Faces of American Manhood* (Boston: Allen and Unwin, 1987).

5. The best illustration of these practices remains Francis Trollope, *Domestic Manners of the Americans,* ed. Donald Smalley (New York and London, 1832; reprint, New York: Vintage Books, 1949).

6. For examples, see Joan Jensen, *Loosening the Bonds: Mid-Atlantic Farm Women, 1750–1850* (New Haven: Yale University Press, 1986); Daniel Vickers, *Farmers and Fisherman: Two Centuries of Work in Essex County, Massachusetts, 1630–1850* (Chapel Hill: University of North Carolina Press, 1994); Elizabeth J. Tannenbaum, " 'What is Best to be Done for These Fevers': Elizabeth Davenport's Medical Practice in New Haven Colony," *New England Quarterly* 70 (June 1997): 265–84; Cornelia Hughes Dayton, *Women before the Bar: Gender, Law, and Society in Connecticut, 1639–1789* (Chapel Hill: University of North Carolina Press, 1995); and Lisa Wilson Waciega, "A 'Man of Business:' The Widow of Means in Southeastern Pennsylvania, 1750–1850," *William and Mary Quarterly,* 3d ser., 44 (January 1987): 40–64. For an older but still very useful analysis of the literature of family history, see Mary P. Ryan, "The Explosion of Family History," in *The Promise of American History: Progress and Prospects,* ed. Stanley I. Kutler and Stanley N. Katz (Baltimore: Johns Hopkins University Press, 1982), 181–95, especially 188.

7. Scholars have assumed that childbirth remained a female experience that wholly excluded men. Yet new research is showing a much greater role for men in limitation of family size, the care of pregnant wives, and assistance in the birthing room. See Shawn Johansen, "Before the Waiting Room: Northern Middle-Class Men, Pregnancy and Birth in Antebellum America," *Gender and History* 7 (July 1995): 183–200.

8. Colonial scholars remain indebted to the pioneering work of Edmund S. Morgan, *The Puritan Family: Religion and Domestic Relations in Seventeenth-Century New England* (New York: Harper and Row, 1966); and John Demos, *A Little Commonwealth: Family Life in Plymouth Colony* (New York: Oxford University Press, 1970).

9. For instance, see Mary Beth Norton, *Founding Mothers and Fathers: Gendered Power and the Forming of American Society* (New York: W. W. Norton, 1996); and Dayton, *Women before the Bar.*

10. Helena M. Wall, *Fierce Communion: Family and Community in Early America* (Cambridge: Harvard University Press, 1990), 7.

11. Perry Miller, *The New England Mind: The Seventeenth Century* (New York, 1939; reprint, Boston: Beacon Press, 1961), 300–362.

12. Patricia Cleary, " 'Who shall say we have not equal abilitys with Men when Girls of 18 years of age discover such great capacitys?' Women of Commerce in Boston, 1750–1776," in *Entrepreneurs: The Boston Business Community, 1700–1850,* ed. Conrad Edick Wright and Katheryn P. Viens Boston: Massachusetts Historical Society, 1997), 43.

13. John Demos, *Past, Present, and Personal: The Family and the Life Course in American History* (New York: Oxford University Press, 1986), 46–48.

14. Anya Jabour, " 'No Fetters but Such as Love Shall Forge': Elizabeth and William Wirt and Marriage in the Early Republic," *Virginia Magazine of History and Biography* 104 (spring 1996): 1–40. For the traditional view of nineteenth-century marriage, see Steven Mintz, *A Prison of Expectations: The Family in Victorian Culture* (New York: New York University Press, 1983).

15. A representative survey of the old literature on women and politics is Paula Baker, "The Domestication of Politics: Women and American Political Society, 1780–1920," *American Historical Review* 89 (June 1984): 620–47.

16. Ronald J. Zboray and Mary Saracino Zboray, "Whig Women, Politics, and Culture in the Campaign of 1840: Three Perspectives from Massachusetts," *Journal of the Early Republic* 17 (summer 1997): 277–315, 285 quoted; Whig Women to John M. Clayton, 2 August 1844, John M. Clayton papers, vol. 1, Library of Congress. See also Christopher J. Olsen, " 'Molly Pitcher' of the Mississippi Whigs: The Editorial Career of Mrs. Harriet N. Prewett," *Journal of Mississippi History* 58 (fall 1996): 237–54 and Rebecca Edwards, *Angels in the Machinery: Gender in American Party Politics from the Civil War to the Progressive Era,* (New York: Oxford University Press, 1997).

17. See also Laura McCall, " 'The Reign of Brute Force Is Now Over': A Content Analysis of *Godey's Lady's Book,* 1830–1860," *Journal of the Early Republic* 9 (summer 1989): 217–36.

18. The examples in Karen V. Hansen's remarkable " 'No Kisses Is Like Youres': An Erotic Friendship between Two African-American Women during the Mid-Nineteenth Century," *Gender and History* 7 (August 1995), reveal the impossibility of employing modern categories to comprehend nineteenth-century gender identity. See also Richard Godbeer, " 'The Cry of Sodom': Discourse, Intercourse, and Desire in Colonial New England," *William and Mary Quarterly,* 3d ser. 52 (April 1995): 259–86; and George E. Haggerty, " 'Olachryma-rum Fons' Tears, Poetry, and Desire in Gray," *Eighteenth Century Studies* 30 (fall 1996): 81–95.

19. Gail Bederman, *Manliness and Civilization: A Cultural History of Gender and Race in the United States, 1880–1917* (Chicago: University of Chicago Press, 1995); Kevin White, *The First Sexual Revolution: The Emergence of Male*

Heterosexuality in Modern America (New York: New York University Press, 1993).

20. On Whitman, see David S. Reynolds, *Walt Whitman's America: A Cultural Biography* (New York: Alfred A. Knopf, 1995); Geoffrey M. Still, ed., *Walt Whitman of Mickle Street: A Centennial Collection* (Knoxville: University of Tennessee Press, 1994); Harold Aspiz, *Walt Whitman and the Body Beautiful* (Urbana: University of Illinois Press, 1980); and Justin Kaplan, *Walt Whitman: A Life* (New York: Simon and Schuster, 1980).

21. For evidence of the contemporary, more psychologically driven wave of concern over the state of masculinity, see Robert Bly, *Iron John: A Book about Men* (Reading, Mass.: Addison-Wesley, 1990).

22. Stephanie Coontz, *The Way We Never Were: American Families and the Nostalgia Trap* (New York: Basic Books, 1992).

23. See Arlie Hochschild with Anne Machung, *The Second Shift: Working Parents and the Revolution at Home* (New York: Viking Penguin, 1989).

24. The best study of Hispanic gender relations remains Sarah Deutsch, *No Separate Refuge: Culture, Class, and Gender on an Anglo-Hispanic Frontier in the American Southwest, 1880–1940* (New York: Oxford University Press, 1987).

25. Gerda Lerner,*The Majority Finds Its Past: Placing Women in History* (New York: Oxford University Press, 1979), 168, 180.

Part I

Foundations of Gender

Chapter One

Talk Like a Man
Speech, Power, and Masculinity in Early New England

Jane Kamensky

The summer of 1681 found Cotton Mather on the brink of manhood. The son of one of New England's greatest theologians and the grandson, on his mother's side, of another, he seemed all but predestined to ascend to one of the more venerable pulpits in Massachusetts. But the road had proved surprisingly difficult. In addition to wrestling with the crippling doubts that plagued all devout Puritans, Mather had been forced to contend with a debilitating stutter that surfaced early in his childhood. These twin anxieties—worry over the state of his soul and panic about the quality and quantity of his speech—had all but consumed him in the years since 1678, when he graduated Harvard College at the age of fifteen.

By the middle of his eighteenth year, however, he had at least begun to find his voice. His first public sermon, delivered in the summer of 1680, was just a beginning. Now Mather was preaching oftener and better and to ever larger, more important audiences. Soon his words would reach even beyond New England; 1682 saw the publication of a brief verse that was the first drop in what would become a virtual flood of works printed in London as well as Boston. So it was with heartfelt gratitude that Mather retired to his prayer closet on the afternoon of 18 June 1681 to reflect upon the *"Kindesses* of God." "How *Miraculous* a Thing is the *Freedom of Speech*, conferred upon mee," he cried out (in full voice, I imagine). Surely, as he wrote in his diary, granting him the "necessary Supplies of *Speech* for my Ministry" had been among God's "most sensible [tangible] Answers to many Prayers."[1]

"Freedom of speech." A familiar concept, to be sure. But the meaning

Mather attached to the phrase is strange to our ears. The liberty for which he praised God was more somatic than ideological: the ability, quite literally, to make himself understood. Yet speaking was not merely instrumental, a means to an end, for Mather. In many ways it was an end in itself. "Freedom of speech" was the *sine qua non* of what he referred to as his *"Particular calling."*[2] Protestant reformers from Calvin's day forward had emphasized the extent to which a minister's authority was embodied in his ability to speak of and for God. As John Field and Thomas Wilcox had argued in the late sixteenth century, the godly minister distinguished himself *"by voice,* learning and doctrine" rather than by the "cap, gowne, [and] tippet" that marked his non-dissenting brethren. Thomas Cartwright, William Perkins, and others proclaimed that the regenerate preacher was "commaunded to cry out": to "lift up [his] voice like a trumpet."[3] For Mather, the implications were clear. Without the clarion call of "free" speaking there could be no preaching. No preaching meant no pulpit. And without a pulpit, Mather would have no public *name*, at least none worthy of his rhetorically gifted grandfathers, John Cotton and Richard Mather. It is not too great an exaggeration to say that without "free" speech, Cotton Mather could not have become, in the fullest sense, a Puritan man.

This essay is about the connection, made explicit in Mather's writings and remaining implicit in many other sources from early modern England and New England, between a certain kind of speech (the meaning of "free" demands further explication) and a certain understanding of what it was to be a man. Mather's case illustrates this link in particularly dramatic fashion. He demanded and eventually accrued great benefits from his tongue. To be sure, few men even among those of his elevated social standing ever claimed so wide an audience for their words. But to greater and lesser degrees, all white men in early New England could count on certain "freedoms of speech." The prerogative of public speaking reflected and, to a significant degree, constituted Puritan masculinity. Whether they were elevated preachers, middling merchants, or humble farmers, men in colonial New England trafficked in words. The "freedom" to do so was an essential part of what distinguished men from women and from boys. The *extent* of that masculine freedom, moreover, was one of the key elements separating those whom the Puritans knew as "men of parts" from those who found their rightful place among the "lesser sort."

*

Men, too, have gender, some of the most exciting new studies of the social relations of the sexes remind us. The first wave of feminist scholarship in the humanities and social sciences tended to cast women as the only gendered beings in the human drama. But as gender has come to be understood as an analytical category that covers more than simply women's experiences, researchers have begun to explore the many ways in which biological maleness has been translated, constructed, and distorted into the web of cultural understandings we call masculinity. In other words, manhood, once the invisible backdrop to almost all traditional studies, has become in recent years a "marked" entity, worthy of exploration in itself. Men have always had history. Now we are paying attention to the histories they have as *men*.[4]

Several important conclusions flow from the insight that masculinity, like femininity, is a cultural construction. The first is a call to historicize manhood, to recognize that understandings of what it means to be a man are time-bound, particular to given historical moments. Biological maleness may remain constant. (There is, of course, heated debate on this score, too.) But cultural *manhood* changes from age to age and from place to place. A second major finding of the new scholarship on men is more sociological. If historians remind us that masculinity is contingent upon time and place, sociologists and anthropologists point out that these various time-bound masculinities have meaning only in relation to other (sometimes overlapping) social categories, particularly understandings of childhood and of womanhood.[5] Becoming a man means learning to be, according to the lights of one's culture, not-woman and not-boy.

Put into practice, this theoretical insistence on the relational aspects of masculinity, upon the not-woman-ness of manhood, has resulted in a strong emphasis on the history of men's labor and, in turn, in a tendency to focus on the history of industrial and post-industrial societies. There is good reason for this. In some respects, manhood becomes most starkly visible in times and places where men's and women's lives diverge. For scholars of the early modern period, looking at men in places where women were not has meant paying special attention to the homosocial worlds of guild workers and merchants.[6] More typical are investigations of manhood that center around the ways in which men's labor cultures and practices dealt with the dislocating impacts of industrialism. Indeed, the story of the widening gulf between men's and women's working worlds, the ensuing debasement of traditionally male forms of labor, and the resultant need for workers to reformulate their notions of manhood forms something of a master narrative for historical studies of masculinity.

The master narrative has limited relevance to the world of Cotton Mather, his neighbors, and their forebears. Through its first century of white settlement, New England more closely resembled the agrarian world of the southern and eastern counties of England than the congested cityscape of seventeenth-century London, or even the urban villages of eighteenth-century Philadelphia and New York. With few exceptions, New England men did not derive the meanings of their manhood from such mercantile settings as counting houses, artisans' shops, workingmen's clubs, or shipyards. Yet we know, as Susan Amussen has recently demonstrated, that conceptions of manliness were very much in flux, and in contest, in the early modern English-speaking world.[7] Where did these conflicts play themselves out? What were the weapons of choice in the battle to reformulate manhood? If gender, as Judith Butler has theorized, is an "on-going discursive practice," we must be attentive to the scenes, stagings, and "locutionary acts" that comprise masculinity and femininity in particular communities. The New England town is no exception. In what kinds of venues and through what sorts of encounters was Puritan maleness constructed, bolstered, shored up—in short, *performed?*[8]

There are, to be sure, many answers: answers as disparate as the ranks and sorts of New England men, and as meandering as the pathways that took them through their daily lives. An elite few perfected the art of Puritan masculinity in specific, institutional settings. As men like Mather well knew, Harvard College and the ministry were filled with occasions for assembling, testing, and refining the components of maleness. So, too, New Englanders arranged ritual space in gendered ways. Seating assignments in Puritan meetinghouses, for example, physically incarnated the social gulf between men and women, between men and children, and, importantly, between some men and others.[9] But the work of performing gender roles did not stop at the meetinghouse door. In fact, it is scarcely an exaggeration to suggest that New Englanders were perpetually concerned with demarcating social cleavages of all kinds, gender included. Theirs was a world in which leading men imagined the natural "Condicion of mankinde" to be steeply vertical: in which some would always be male, some female; some "rich some poore, some highe and eminent in power and dignitie; others meane and in subjeccion." Virtually every occasion of social interaction represented a chance to craft personae that embodied these all-important hierarchies.[10] In ritualized settings such as college orations, church services, court days, and militia musters; in impromptu gatherings by firesides, in fields, or along fences: wherever people came together, Puritan men and women honed the vocabularies that pronounced their genders, ranks, and estates.

These vocabularies of social differentiation enlisted many elements, not all of them verbal. Then as now, people communicated status through a host of visual and somatic cues (facial expressions, postures, modes of dress) as well as through their words. Indeed, New England's Puritans needed no postmodern cultural theorists to explain the notion of embodied authority. As early as 1634, the General Court of Massachusetts (the colony's legislative body and its highest court) declared "some newe & immodest fashions" (ranging from metallic laces to "immoderate greate sleeves") to be "superfluities" that were "prejudiciall to the common good." The wearing of such lavish attire by any who could afford it threatened to blur supposedly inborn social distinctions. The "estate or qualitie of each person," the Court later ordained, should determine the "perticular rules" of proper dress. Those judged "to exceed their rankes & abilitie in the costlyness or fashion of their apparrill" were guilty of a form of lying: of using (visual) language to deceive onlookers.[11] Gender was central to this understanding of a person's rightful place and rightful face. As minister Nicholas Noyes made clear in an essay condemning the late seventeenth-century vogue for "periwigs," Puritans considered it abominable for men to toy with fashions which obscured the "visible distinction of sex." "The woman shall not wear that which pertaineth to a man," Noyes paraphrased from Deuteronomy, "neither shall a man put on a woman's garment." To do so was to "disguise," to "offend," indeed, to "degrade" the right ordering of society: the dominion of man over woman, preacher over hearer, magistrate over subject.[12]

Seating assignments, college rank, even hair styles, sleeve lengths, and the color of the trim edging one's collar: these were among the infinite number of infinitesimal signals which together added up to maleness and femaleness in early New England. In a world in which occupations were typically multiform and professional identities could hardly have been said to take the measure of a man, manhood was tested and renewed through the personal encounters that served as performances of status.[13] To a degree found in few other places and times, manhood in seventeenth-century Massachusetts was dramaturgic, interactional. And, although these dramas of manliness employed many "languages," considerable evidence shows that *speech* itself was a particularly important part of the mix.[14]

This is so, in part, simply because of the small scale of community life in early New England. In this respect, Mather and the two generations of Anglo-Americans who lived in Massachusetts before him inhabited a world that had much in common with villages in premodern Europe and, indeed, with many non-industrial societies even today: the world of the face-to-face. In this milieu the domestic and the civic could not easily be disentangled. Where private life was public business, gossip constituted a powerful form of authority, capable of making and unmaking personal fortunes. Theirs was, in short, a world in which the thickness and density of social networks made words into a kind of currency: a measure of character, a barometer of community membership, and, not least, a vital component of gender identity.[15]

If New England Puritans belonged, in a generic sense, to the world of the face-to-face, they also had to make sense of particular worlds in which speech took on heightened resonance. As colonials clinging to the far western edge of a metropolitan culture, New Englanders built their social edifice upon a foundation of severe and deeply felt information scarcity. Such a climate made speech both extraordinarily precious and extraordinarily powerful. The value of scarce words was further inflated by the fact that, at least in the early years of settlement in New England, other markers of status and power had limited purchase. Where the institutions of (male) authority—government, schools, and centers of economic power—remained in their infancy, verbally articulating one's place in the world was more essential than ever before. The records of the first years of Plymouth and Massachusetts Bay are filled with examples of fragile, newly constituted authority crumbling before the power of rumor.[16]

Adding to the turbulence in New England's communicative economy was the audible presence of ways of speaking wholly unfamiliar to English men. In New England and, indeed, throughout the colonial world, the speech of the native inhabitants of the Americas formed an ever-present backdrop to the construction of European settlements.[17] Scripture had promised, Puritan minister John Eliot wrote, that "He that walketh righteously, and speaketh uprightly" (as surely the Puritans did) would not encounter "a people of a deeper speech than thou canst perceive, of a stammering tongue, that thou canst not understand." But here did dwell such people; here resonated, indeed, *many* such tongues.[18] As English immigrants struggled to come to grips with the baffling diversity of native languages, they were forced to reexamine their own understandings of the relationship between speech and social order. They could grope for common ground between English ideals of manly verbal deportment and those of the American "Aberginians," emphasizing, as travel writer William Wood did, that "Garrulity is much condemned of [by] them" and praising Indian women for their reluctance to give out "cross words or reviling speeches."[19] But such comparisons must inevitably have felt strained. Confronted with sounds they heard as little more than "Ululation, Howling, [and] Yelling"—their ears ringing with expressions like " 'Hadree Hadree succomee succomee' (we come, we come to suck your blood)"—it seemed at times as if *"the English had lost their tongue."*[20]

An unsettling prospect for any good colonial, to be sure. How much more so for *godly* men! The reformed Protestant man linked his sense of self especially tightly to his words. If small societies and colonial enclaves shared a predisposition to value speech, Puritanism added the force of ideology to that of circumstance and thus imparted special powers to the spoken word in early New England. In their theology as well as in their social and spatial arrangements, New Englanders were not only people of words, but, more pointedly, people of the Word. An overly literal rendering of Calvin's translation of John emphasizes the primacy of voice at the dawn of the world: "In the beginning was Speech, and Speech was with God; and Speech was God." Scripture, for Calvin's English descendants, was not mere text; it was a form of speech, the vehicle through which God "opens his own most hallowed lips."[21] Intoning and hearing scripture were central acts of meaning in a culture that banished most other forms of ritual. Heartfelt, unscripted conversation with God—not feats of memory, not supplicant postures, not acts of priestly intervention—occupied the very center of personal piety. "Some foolishly imagine that praier is made either better or worse by the jesture of our bodyes," commented the sixteenth-century reformer, John Market. Privileging body over voice was, from Market's perspective, an inversion of the most dangerous kind. As he and others made clear, Puritan spirituality was an affair of the mouth and the ear.[22]

The reformers' logocentric worldview had profound, and somewhat contradictory, implications for Puritan masculinity. In some ways, Puritan thought collapsed the distinctions between the verbal prerogatives of men and those of women, presenting all layfolk with new opportunities for speaking to and of God without the intercession of priestly meddlers. In other respects, though, nonconformists' emphasis on words and on the Word invested speech with a new *gravitas*, effectively raising the standards by which every utterance would be judged. And, by making sermons the centerpiece of ritual life, Puritan thinkers demanded heightened respect for the voices of godly ministers, that is, for the voices of eminent men. This tension between verbal egalitarianism and verbal authoritarianism took on special significance amidst the fluidity of the North American colonies.

Small-scale communalism, colonialism, and Puritanism combined to give the medium of speech a certain pride of place among the multifold "discourses" of manliness in early New England. This is not to claim, of course, that the whole of masculinity in early New England was a tissue of words; we need to avoid reflexively privileging the verbal simply because other ways of performing gender do not make themselves heard as loudly in the evidence left to historians. Nor do I mean to suggest that the link between speech and masculinity was, in any sense, exclusive to Britain's New England colonies. Still, the relationship among words, power, and manliness did have a special intensity there. Words *mattered* to early New England men to a degree that is scarcely conceivable to us today, and in ways about which they were only too happy to testify.

Although they might have cringed at the postmodern idiom, early New Englanders well knew that gender was "socially constructed." Theirs, too, was a world in which men and women were made as much as born. As Susan Amussen has quipped, early modern English print culture suggests that "few men, apparently, knew how to be men"; they had to be carefully taught.[23] Learning how to talk like a man was a central ingredient of a seventeenth-century education in gender roles.

Almost from the cradle, pious New England children were schooled in the precise character of Mather's version of "free" speech, as well as in the gender and status conventions governing its appropriate uses. Proper speech, any child past infancy would have known, did not mean giving voice to one's every thought. Although (or because) the ability to speak was understood to be supremely natural, a facility granted by God and shared by all humans, following the impulses of the tongue could prove calamitous. So the first rule that delimited Mather's notion of verbal freedom required self-discipline. All words were to be carefully considered: in period parlance, "governed." As unformed social beings, children were considered especially prone to the sins of an ungoverned tongue. Sermons on family duties, textbooks teaching rhetoric, and manuals on deportment all schooled children to play their proper roles in the community's discourse.

That role, for young boys and girls alike, was one of respectful silence before their superiors at home and in the church, the school, and the commonwealth. Before they could learn the art of conversation, young people were instructed to "learne the art of silence." As one popular English authority put it, all young *"Discoursers, . . . should rather be given to heare than speake."* It was widely reported that "Silence" and "patience" were children's best maxims; *"swift to heare"* and *"slow to speake"* were compliments of the highest order. In an age that imagined the household as a miniature analogue of the state, one of the first principles children learned in the family—the "little commonwealth," so called—was that well-ordered conversation was vital to a well-ordered society.[24]

The lesson was subtly gendered as well. For girls, verbal modesty amounted to a life's work. Decorous female speech, the opposite of woman's natural tendency toward loquaciousness, was the cornerstone of the invisible boundary separating female spaces from civic spaces. The virtuous woman, according to one Italian humanist whose writings were popular in early modern England, disdained "to live among men and speak abroad," preferring to "hold her tongue demurely, and let few see her, and none at all hear her."[25] There were, to be sure, situations in which authorities *urged* pious women to speak. Protestant reformers idealized the godly household as a setting in which men and women might share "familiar conversation." William Whatley envisioned that pious husbands and wives would pray together, sing psalms together, and "reade the Word of God together"; they would "often talke together and be sorry together and be merry together, and communicate . . . each with other." New England ministers, too, praised the "vertuous woman" who lifted her modest voice in prayer.[26] Still, the verbal role recommended to adult women was in many ways closer to that of a young girl than to that of a grown man. Richard Brathwait made the connection explicit. What "is spoken of [young] Maids," he noted, is "properly applied . . . to all women: *They should be seene, and not heard.*"[27]

Just as this ideal of childlike silence linked girls with their mothers, it separated boys from men. Mute deference was but a temporary stopping point on the Puritan boy's road to a full adult voice. In the early modern world, boys had to learn when *to* speak as well as when *not* to. As one widely used Latin grammar reminded male pupils, "silence and modesty may become a man in its time," but he should also be "prepared upon all occasions [to] useth the ministery of the Tongue to unfold" his opinions.[28] The manner, frequency, and competency with which a man should make use of his voice hinged on status as well as gender. Young gentlemen of Cotton Mather's rank would cultivate a different balance of speech and silence than either their same-status sisters or lower-status boys. The privileged little tyke to whom Richard Brathwait directed *The English Gentleman* would learn the status-linked arts of rhetoric and Latin grammar as well as the sex-linked craft of writing, while his humbler peers received considerably less formal training in the speech ways of adult men.[29] But whether he was an aspiring Puritan divine schooled at Harvard or a common yeoman's son preparing to use his voice in the town meeting, a New England boy had to master language as well as to govern his tongue.

Indeed, where speech was concerned, the boy was father to the man. In encounters with their social betters, adult males were asked to employ the respectful speech they had learned in their youth. It was inappropriate (indeed, ungodly) for children to "answer their parents"—natural or metaphorical—"as if they were their equals; giving word for word."[30] But it was perfectly suitable (indeed, godly) for male children to speak "among Boys thy Equals . . . as *if thou wert a Man with Men*, and about Business of higher importance."[31] Regardless of his social status, the male child stood to inherit a substantial verbal patrimony. Preaching, voting, dissenting, publishing, contracting, promising, oath-taking, psalm-singing, even publicly professing faith: with few exceptions, these speech acts would be reserved for him alone.

But if the arena for his talk was large, it was not without limits; Mather's "freedom" was far from the expansive liberty that governs our own tongues. The paradoxical charge to New England boys can be summarized in a single maxim, intoned in a popular English conduct manual: "Speake freely, yet with reservation." Young men were cautioned that their speech should be "sober" and reminded that "moderation of the tongue is . . . an absolute virtue." At the same time, they were exhorted to develop mature public voices, both spoken and written.[32] The exemplar of right speaking whom the Anglican theologian George Webbe dubbed the "quiet man" carefully negotiated these seeming contradictions. Practicing the ethos of "quietnesse" in his family as in his community life, he avoided "unquiet" or "*Wanton words and speeches.*" As the Psalmist urged, his tongue was "milde . . . kept in as with a bridle." Kept in, but not cut out. The quiet man's watchwords were "First, *Meditation* before we speake: secondly, *Moderation*" in the quantity and manner of his speech.[33] The ethos of masculine "quietnesse" sought an Aristotelian mean between two feminine extremes: the child's prescribed silence, and the scold's infamous volubility.

It is simple enough to sketch the features of manly speaking in the ideal. But how do we "hear" it in practice? After all, the spoken word is evanescent by its very nature; 350-year-old utterances have long since faded to silence. It is far easier to see what Cotton Mather thought, wrote, and prayed about speech than to hear how he and other New England men actually *spoke.* Although the historian of Puritan New England lacks access to the ethnographer's video and audio tapes, extant speakers, and opportunity to become a "participant observer," the barriers between seventeenth-century words and twentieth-century ears are not quite so insurmountable as they might seem.

Episodes of "normal" speech are, for obvious reasons, the most difficult to reconstruct. Early New Englanders seldom recorded any spoken exchanges; those they did deem worthy of committing to paper tended, almost by definition, to stand out from the everyday. Still, by carefully mining diaries, court records, letters, memoirs, and the like, we can begin to sketch two important aspects of men's conversational milieu. The first, and easier to recover, is the social geography of speaking: the who, where and, sometimes, the what of their gendered verbal landscapes. By paying close attention to the casting of the innumerable scenes of day-to-day exchange (economic, social, legal, and domestic) described in the written record, we learn that the physical parameters of men's talk were much wider than those of their wives and sisters. Men chatted in mills and taverns, in shipyards and trading posts, in distant towns as well as beside their own hearths. This expansive spatial domain meant that men typically amassed what linguists would call broader "conversational competence" than the women in their families. They shared news from London as well as gossip from next door. They talked contracts and prices in addition to swapping stories about family and neighbors. On the small stage of early New England, male players had, in this sense, larger roles.[34]

We can also, on occasion, overhear encounters that hint at a gendered *style* for men's talk. Called to court to testify about a wide variety of suspected offenses, men often depicted themselves engaging in a playful sort of verbal rough-housing, bragging and exchanging pointed remarks with easy jocularity. Some men gloated about their social power, daring others to stand in their way. Thomas Johnson of Ipswich, for example, said that he carried a bottle of rum in his pocket and "hee car[e]d not, who knew it . . . wt was that to any man."[35] Such bragging tended to move fluidly from claims of economic clout to boasts of physical power. John Guppy taunted neighbors with talk about "what a Galant life [he] lived not wanting Pork Rum . . . Corn muton and other thing[s]." John Wolcott linked wealth and might when he gloated that his "father [had] a bigger bag of money" than John Atkinson, and that he would make life "hard enough for [Atkinson] with my foot and my fists."[36] Others linked status to sexual prowess. Some Ipswich men overheard Thomas Wells telling his sister-in-law that "there was such: vertue in his breeches yt if they were layd upon his bead" they "would doe the business" by themselves.[37]

Whether the topic was money, sex, or "small politics," the implied message of male braggadocio was the same: status. Boastful speech was one way New England men could define themselves as one-up from their peers. "I'm bigger, I'm richer, I'm stronger, I'm better," men's conversational style told all who would listen. Tough talk, a way to articulate or even to advance one's station, was a verbal gambit that sometimes backfired by landing men in court. Still, much of the boastful male speech that appears in legal records is peripheral to the charges under consideration in a given case, not itself an issue for the court's scrutiny. For the most part, bragging appears to have been a normal facet of male verbal style rather than a transgressive speech act.[38]

Despite the relatively expansive boundaries of acceptable male discourse, men sometimes *did* speak in ways that breached the limits of the permissible. In many ways, these instances of deviant speech, although they privilege the transgressive over the mundane, tell us more about the verbal dimension of Puritan masculinity than do other shards of surviving evidence. Listening to what Mather and his ilk deemed wrongful—indeed, criminal—words, we hear ordinary men testing and defining the outer limits of masculine possibility in their time and place. Examining the ways in which clerical and civil authorities plastered over such ruptures in the borders of male authority tells us still other things about the privileges of manhood in early New England.

Luckily for historians, authorities and common folk alike were deeply concerned with policing the boundaries of orderly speaking in early Massachusetts. The parameters of masculine "quietnesse"—the precarious balance between openness and restraint—were not just intoned from the pulpit; they were written into positive law. Magistrates, like ministers, worked to craft public voices that would articulate their authority. Their pronouncements "in public," as John Winthrop explained, were designed to "bear . . . as the voice of God."[39] Other men, the colony's laws dictated, were to treat the magistrate's verbal dignity as an example. The 1641 *Body of Liberties*, the first comprehensive code of laws in the Anglo-American world, virtually defined civic personhood by simultaneously expanding upon and delimiting a man's right to speak. "Every man whether Inhabitant or fforreinger, free or not free" was promised the "libertie to come to any publique Court, Councel, or Towne meeting" to ask "any lawfull, seasonable, and materiall question," or to "present any necessary motion, complaint, petition, Bill or information," so long as he did so "in convenient time, due order, and *respective manner . . . orderly and inofensively*." Subsequent bodies of local law mandated deferential speech to the colony's religious and civil leaders, prohibited blasphemy on pain of death, and invoked capital punishment for filial rebellion in word or deed.[40] These laws were not simply imposed from above; they were, the records make clear, as much a part of the consciousness of ordinary people as of their leaders. They were invoked, contested, expanded upon, and made real by litigants who might not have been able to define wrongful speech in legal terms, but who surely knew it when they heard it.[41]

The types of verbal offenses adjudicated in seventeenth-century New England were myriad, and the number of criminal presentments and civil trials over speech infractions positively legion.[42] Among this vast array, two types of verbal "deviance" cast especially bright light on the relationship between bounded-free speech and masculinity. The first is a criminal offense New Englanders often called "slighting," which was committed almost exclusively by men. The second is witchcraft, a capital crime with a substantial (perhaps even primary) verbal component and of which men were only rarely accused. The precise nature of these two offenses, along with the identities of the men who committed them and

the kinds of reparations they were made to enact, take us to the very
heart of the manly, verbal "freedom" for which Mather thanked God.

Slighting was a kind of verbal theft, the utterance of words that
enriched their speaker by stealing the reputation of their target.[43] The
offense thus encompassed sedition (words, thoughts, or actions against
the state) but also included much less overtly political offenses.[44] It was
not precisely sedition, for example, when a wealthy young Salem man
named John Porter, Jr., called his esteemed father "shittabed." But the
insult, with its connotations of bodily failure and lack of paternal control, did represent an assault on family government and was thus a
matter for public scrutiny. Indeed, it must have seemed only logical to
the Essex County magistrates when John, Jr., went on to unleash his
tongue upon other local authorities, calling the court's commissioners "a
coople of low-graded popes" and proclaiming that he would yield only
to "Better men then they be." For these and other *exclusively verbal*
offenses, the Massachusetts General Court termed Porter "the vilest of
malefactors" and prosecuted him all the way from the local magistrate's
parlor to an audience before the King's Commissioners.[45]

The case is in many ways emblematic, not least in the identity of its
main players. Like the elder Porter, the victims of slighting words were,
by definition, powerful men with reputations to lose. Like the younger
Porter, the speakers of slighting words also tended to be what the Puritans called "men of parts." I have identified 226 prosecutions for slighting words that came before the Essex County Courts and the higher
courts of Massachusetts between 1630 and 1692. Men were the targets
in all of these cases and the offenders in 200 (over 88 percent) of them.
The accused men were often prominent; honorific titles such as "Mr.,"
"Sargent," and "Gent." frequently preface their names. Delivered by
powerful men against other powerful men, slighting words represented
an abuse of social proximity, a breach of the relatively permeable boundaries separating rank and gender peers. Men, particularly respectable
men, were expected and even encouraged to engage their leaders in
dialogue. But as the Porter case demonstrated, when "fathers" talked
with their grown "sons," conversation might easily shade into contesta-
tion.[46]

Such verbal battles over authority loomed especially large in the public imagination at moments when fatherly power (in town and church as
well as at home) lacked clear definition. Here, too, the Porter case is
representative. Heard in the context of the widespread unease that fol-

lowed Charles II's Restoration, the younger Porter's words against an aging local patriarch took on frightening resonance. Throughout the seventeenth century, New England elites prosecuted slighting words most zealously at times when they felt most vulnerable, at those moments in which the prerogatives of male authority were least convincingly established. During the first decade of settlement, for example, civic fathers set themselves apart from the rest of their would-be brethren by dealing harshly with expressions of contempt for newly installed magistrates and ministers. In John Porter's day a generation later, and again during the crisis provoked by the dissolution of the first charter in the 1680s, New England courts proved unusually sensitive to derisive words.[47]

But the words of John Porter, Jr., and his ilk amounted to more than instances of bad timing. The settings in which slighting words took place magnified their threat to the faint boundaries between mis-speaking "sons" and their wounded "fathers." Slighting was not back-biting or tale-bearing (two other oft-lamented verbal evils); there was nothing secretive about it. Gossiping women might slink from house to house, trafficking in their husbands' secrets.[48] But slighting, like male talk more broadly, took place in the open, often in ceremonial spaces. A striking number of incidents were said to have unfolded "in a public place"— during "the [court] sessions," "at a town meeting," "in the time of public ordinances," or at militia muster.[49] The crime of slighting made manifest the outer limits of the talk that was permissible in male spaces. It was one thing for a man respectfully to "publish" his opinion in a town meeting, or to repair to a local ordinary and joust verbally with his neighbors.[50] It was quite another for him to abuse his access to the humble corridors of colonial power by speaking, as one wounded victim put it, "*in the face* of the country."[51]

What slighters said was the crowning element of their challenge to the expansive bounds of masculine verbal prerogative. Simply put, slighters spoke a language of inversion. In their words, high was low and up was down. Civil authorities were not paragons whose voices evoked the weightiness of God, but venial men who imposed draconian penalties for petty crimes. Speaking in just such an "insolent" manner, embodying his lack of deference by standing "with his armes on kembow," Thomas Dexter mocked the colony's nascent ruling stratum in 1632. The "best of them" sitting on the court, he said, "was but an atturney."[52] One Boston magistrate was, as his prominent detractor saw it, more of a "just ass" than a justice.[53] Leading men could drone on at great length about God's design for some men to walk while others rode on horseback above them. But such prescriptions would not hold up against the words of Thomas Wells, who proclaimed publicly in 1669 that he had never "crouched" before the likes of Simon Bradstreet: "I never stored my hat to him," Wells went on, "nor reverant him more than I would an Indgan."[54] Slighters dared to say that those in positions of leadership were not betters but peers, less fathers than bumbling younger brothers. "What understanding hadd [the Governor] more then himselfe?" John Leigh wondered out loud.[55] Those who heard his words must have wondered, as well: what kind of authority was it that provoked such public disrespect?

Even Puritan ministers, men who claimed in some respects the supreme spiritual *and verbal* authority in New England, became favored targets of slighters' opprobrium. Here, too, their message was inversion. Bay Colony churches, they said, were not incarnations of divine purity, but rather "a humane invention," gaudily painted up like "a whoare" or "a strumpet" to cover their inner corruption.[56] According to slighters, preachers of the Word, far from being the best men, were barely men at all. They could hardly *speak*, let alone use their voices to inspire. Henry Walton, for example, told the Salem congregation that "he had as Leeve to hear a Dogg Barke as to heare mr Cobbett Preach."[57] Instead of evoking in his listeners echoes of the prophets, a despised Essex County preacher was said to have "bawled like a bear."[58] To be a braying dog or a bawling bear in early New England was to lack precisely those qualities which defined ruling men: intellect, independence, godliness and, especially, *speech*.[59]

In a place in time where the structures, postures, and discourses of newly established authority were tenuous at best, the spectacle of prominent men verbally assaulting their would-be betters was indeed, as the General Court once put it, a "very evill example."[60] Slighters said, in essence, that hierarchy was not natural and immutable, but arbitrary and evanescent. Given the power of words on the small stage of colonial New England, their saying was a form of doing; uttering this message made it come true. The magistrates, arbiters of justice, became (in the mouths of their detractors) the most fundamentally unjust of men; ministers were transformed into the community's most grievous sinners and worst speakers. The most godly became the most "dog-ly," while those who deserved to be brought low claimed to "stand equall" (as the Court had said of John Porter) to the most high.[61] In short, the fathers of a community were made sons again as undutiful children usurped their rulers' rightful voices. The label "slighting" must, therefore, be understood quite literally. Words had the power to create big men; they also had the power to make big men small.

Witchcraft, of course, was an entirely different sort of "evil example." To roughly the same degree that slighting was marked male, it was, in elite and in folk definitions alike, a female failing.[62] It was also, to a significant degree, a *verbal* failing, a spectacular refusal (conscious or not) by some women to adhere to the conventions of feminine speech. Where the pious matrons whom Cotton Mather labeled "daughters of Zion" cultivated "silver tongues"—speech rare and pure, free of boastful "dross"—witches (and their possessed victims) ranted as if with the Devil's own voice.[63] The consequences for women who, in a forthright, almost masculine speaking style, cursed their neighbors, verbally assaulted their husbands, or menaced their preachers could be dire indeed; New England courts hanged twenty-eight women as witches between 1647 and 1693.[64]

Only a handful of New England men were ever rumored to be witches, let alone actually prosecuted for witchcraft. Fully half of those few were what scholars have called "secondary" suspects, accused because of family or social ties to "primary" female transgressors.[65] Male "witches" were thus decidedly exceptional. But they represent exceptions that further disclose the gendered rules of masculine speaking. For if kinship ties made certain men likely witches, verbal style amplified their suspiciousness; male "witches" sounded wicked. What this meant, in large part, was that they failed to sound (and thus to be) masculine.

With his forceful-but-governed tongue, the "quiet man" simultaneously deferred to his social superiors and governed those beneath him. As we have seen, the slighter audibly refused the mantle of verbal deference. But the male "witch" failed on both counts. Unable to curb the tongue of his cursing witch-wife, he appeared suspiciously, even diabolically weak. Paradoxically, his weakness was embodied by the very strength of his language. The male witch personified the scolding man who, as one contemporary proverb declared, "hath a woman's tongue in his head."[66] Being categorized as witches implicitly linked such men more closely to a figure of transgressive femininity than to their male peers.

The case of Hugh Parsons, tried and acquitted in Springfield, Massachusetts, in 1651 and 1652, points up the disparity between expectations for male speech and the speech of male witches. Parsons's wife, Mary, was the first in the family to be accused. Convicted years earlier as a slanderer, she had a longstanding reputation for scolding. As if to demonstrate her diabolically unfeminine speech, Mary Parsons also raised her voice against her husband, telling neighbors and local authorities that she "suspect[ed] him for a witch." Largely on his wife's insistent say-so, Hugh Parsons soon became the primary object of his neighbors' complaints to the court.[67]

Much of the evidence marshaled against him centered on his speech, both his anemic reaction to his wife's railing and his own muttering and cursing. At home, neighbors claimed, Parsons displayed a distinctly unmanly willingness to endure his wife's unwomanly tongue. George Colton told the court that Mary Parsons often "spake very harsh things" against her husband "before his face." If Hugh Parsons "had been innocent," Colton reasoned, "he would have . . . reproved her." But Parsons had done the opposite; as he told the magistrates, "he had such speeches from her daily" and "therefore he made the best of it." All too often, folks around him noticed, Parsons remained "wholly silent" in situations where it was his right—even his masculine duty—to speak out.[68]

Among his neighbors, though, he used a different kind of feminized speech. People who came into contact with Parsons often heard him "mutter and mumble," striking out at them with "threatening speeches." Dismayed over a bargain with Rice Bedortha, for example, Parsons had cautioned Bedortha's wife that he would "remember" her when she did "little think on it." He had menaced John Matthews with a variation on what neighbors called "his usual speech," vowing to "be even with him." With poetic flare, Parsons warned Samuel Marshfield, the plaintiff in a civil suit against him, that the judgment would rankle "as wild fire in this house and as a moth in [his] garment." Sure enough, Parsons's words did seem to rend the fabric of the Marshfields' daily life; Widow Marshfield reported that "shortly after" Parsons issued his "threatening speeches," her "daughter began to be taken with her fits."[69]

Such words were forceful stuff. Full of the promise of imminent harm, these threats were not lightly dismissed when uttered. They became more powerful still in retrospect when, as one of Parsons's neighbors put it, a victim fell to thinking about whether "evil might come upon me from the . . . threatening speech of" a witch.[70] Yet despite the real fear a cursing man like Parsons inspired in his neighbors, he wielded the weapons of the powerless. Unwilling or unable to claim the earthly verbal authority permitted him as a man in his society, the male "witch" fought his battles through what his accusers saw as occult means. His diabolic voice was the ally of his social impotence, a failure of masculinity.

People must have wondered why, for example, Parsons so often failed to negotiate a contract to his satisfaction. Such transactions fell firmly within the compass of a man's speaking role. And, if he felt himself unlucky in commerce, why did Parsons not seek redress in church or in court? Why, in short, did Parsons fail to find appropriate ways to speak (forcefully, respectfully) on his own behalf in a culture that gave men so many opportunities to do so? Men like Parsons puffed themselves up with curses. But this sort of strength bespoke underlying weakness. Cursing was the recourse of those from whom life demanded silence. Men had other speaking parts to play.

"Oh! Lord God, in Jesus Christ, help mee!" Cotton Mather implored in March 1683, "lett mee seek *Rules of right Speaking*." Released from the prison of his stammer, Mather was embarking on what would prove to be a life-long quest to cultivate speech that was not only unimpeded but exemplary. By praying devoutly and "*Reading . . .* profitable *Books*, which may teach mee, *the Government of the Tongue*," he sought to enhance what he often called his "usefullness." And so he did; just a decade later he would thank God for the related gifts of "my Free speech, my large Library, and my unblemished reputation." With "Free *Speech* and Fame," he rhapsodized in verse, he had at last claimed his patrimony.[71]

Mather went on to enumerate in his diary several of the "Rules for Speech" to which he credited his burgeoning "fame." The list elaborates a familiar mixture of freedom and restraint, with paeans to the virtues of reverence, moderation, and deliberation in everything one says.[72] Significantly, however, Mather failed to include a "rule" which was perhaps the first principle of manly speech. By 1683, when Mather made his list, it must have been abundantly evident to him and to other New England men that the overarching law of masculine verbal deportment was a certain elasticity in the way "rules of right speaking" were put into practice. Court records make clear that the speech codes Puritans wrote into law could be extraordinarily flexible when applied to male offenders. Particularly when compared to female mis-speakers, men accused of slighting (the verbal overmastery of the powerful) and "witchcraft" (the *lack* of verbal mastery among the powerless) could expect to be greeted with a measure of latitude.[73]

Despite their audible, public assaults on markers of male status slighters were often punished in a way that reasserted their gendered prerogatives. Indeed, the penalty which seventeenth-century Massachusetts courts most frequently levied upon slighting men may tell us more about the masculine prerogative for speech than does the crime itself. For in a seemingly libertarian streak rare in Puritan thought, the remedy prescribed for the ills wrought by this particular kind of wrongful speech was more speech, of a very special sort.[74] The ritual of court-mandated public apology, in which the offender stood on a stage constructed to mirror the site of his offense and metaphorically ate his words, was an unsaying, a perfect antidote to slighting. By intoning a script designed to deprive his wounding words of their sting, the apologizer accomplished a neat reinversion. Substituting the feminine language of the petitioner for the erstwhile over-mastering voice of the slighter, the unsayer reestablished the small distance between his male self and that of his ruler. I used words that were *"to[o] high* for mee," the unspeaker said. Now, made aware of my verbal misdeed, I *"Cast my selfe down."*[75] But down did not mean out. Apology was an optimistic ritual, a lottery in which mis-speaking men could embrace the dictates of well-ordered conversation and purchase another chance to speak manfully.[76] To "unsay" was to repent and live to speak (properly) another day. The notable absence of repentant slighters from the rolls of future mis-speakers suggests that many made good on their second chances.

Female speech offenders, including those few women convicted of slighting, likewise received punishments intended to restore them to their rightful places in the community of godly speakers. Yet the penances of male and female slighters were as different as gendered images of right speaking. For the "daughters of Zion," demonstrating repentant speech meant, for the most part, remaining silent. Although women frequently claimed the humble language of petition as their own, the courts rarely asked them to profess remorse publicly. In fact, punishments of female offenders often centered on displays of symbolic silence rather than upon performances of symbolic speech: New England variants on the scold's brank or bridle, such as the cleft-stick gag. Wearing rather than speaking her shame, the female mis-speaker might more readily be pinned with a paper which described her offense than asked to proclaim it herself.[77]

A pair of examples illustrates the point. Elizabeth Perkins of Ipswich was, in many ways, an archetypal female penitent. Convicted for a litany of slanderous words against various male authorities, she was sentenced to exhibit herself with a paper "pinned on her head . . . written in capital letters, FOR REPROACHING MINISTERS, PARENTS AND RELATIONS." The magistrates designed the penalty, they said, so that "due testimony *might be borne against* such a virulent, reproachful, and wicked-tongued woman."[78] The wicked-tongued man, in contrast, bore testimony against himself. John Allen read aloud his own confession for "notorious and barbarous speeches against authority," beginning his acknowledgment with words that neatly captured his gendered relationship to the ritual: "*I owne.*" Entitled, as a man, to "own" his voice, he owned his verbal misdeeds, too. Called before the magistrates, he articulated right order by speaking with a tamed tongue, not by displaying a silent one.[79]

Hanging, the punishment New England imposed on convicted "witches," offered no second chances. But where witching words were concerned, too, manhood purchased leniency. What happened to those men who, like Hugh Parsons, spoke in ways that would have been considered too masculine for women, but remained too feminine for Puritan men? The short answer is, not much. Male "witches" faced brighter prospects than their female counterparts at every stage of the judicial process, from informal suspicion through presentment to punishment. Only three men were formally convicted outside the Salem trials, and only two of those were executed.[80] The reason is simple. Ordinary folks and their leaders alike were manifestly unwilling to label men like Parsons witches, even when their crimes and their words directly paralleled the devilish expressions of their female counterparts. What was one to call a person who "set spelles & Rases the Diuell," who railed at magistrates and "over came" neighbors with "fayer smooth wordes," whose "cursing" and "swearing" revealed that the "devil" was "very frequent in [their] mouth"? The answer depended on the speaker's sex. This particular chronic mis-speaker, Thomas Wells of Ipswich, was branded a "very bad neighbor." It was a derogatory name, certainly; in early Massachusetts, it was even a criminal one. But it was, nonetheless, a label with wildly different meanings and consequences than "witch."[81]

Both slighters and male witches could resume speaking parts in the community's public discourse to a degree that women similarly accused often could not. In other words, the verbal prerogatives of masculinity trumped the disparity between the statuses of these two types of offenders. This is not to say that Puritan authorities rewarded or that ordinary New Englanders countenanced unbounded male speech; men who blurted out malign words were regularly convicted of lying, swearing, drunkenness, even of the serious crime of slighting. But if men were not *encouraged* to "publish" their discontent verbally, they were rarely silenced irrevocably for doing so.

Although masculine speech was less closely confined than its feminine equivalent, talking like a man in early New England was no easy task. In a world that believed in the precise classification of humanity into categories of rank and sort, gender and race, age and estate, capacious rules must only have fuelled the Puritan man's highly wrought sense of uncertainty. The difficulty involved in crafting a voice that bespoke manly authority stemmed from the very in-betweenness of early New England. Ruling men in early Massachusetts were caught between the old order they had rejected and a protean new one over which their power remained tenuous; between patriarchal notions of the family and emerging contractual ideas about the body politic; between a world of villages and subsistence farming and a nascent world of distant markets; between praising God and governing men.[82] Speech took center stage in this brave new world, never more so than for leading men. But what *kind* of speech? Unbridled self-expression was ill-suited to steer the body politic through these treacherous waters. No, manly deportment required a map, a guide in the form of Mather's internalized "rules of right speaking." Implicit, communally defined speech codes as well as laws or pronouncements from the pulpit attempted to mark the borders between masterful speaking and presumptuous slighting, between masculine commanding and feminine cursing. But the outer limits of manly propriety were not always easy to hear. In this sense, Mather's battle with stuttering mirrors the struggle of all men in colonial New England to invent voices of authority that would resonate in a place where men valued speech, freedom, and restraint in roughly equal measures.

NOTES

I would like to thank Sue Juster and Richard Godbeer for sharing their research on Puritan masculinity; Nancy Cott and two anonymous reviewers for *Gender and History* for their helpful suggestions; and Dennis Scannell for life lessons on the cultural construction of masculinity.

1. Worthington Chauncey Ford (ed.), *Diary of Cotton Mather*, 2 vols. (1912; repr. Frederick Ungar Publishing Co., New York, 1957), vol. 1, pp. 19–20, 2–3, emphasis original. I have retained original spellings and punctuation throughout, except when they impede clarity. The theme of speaking and impediments thereto is a frequent motif in the diary, which Mather began keeping in 1681. Kenneth Silverman, *The Life and Times of Cotton Mather* (Columbia University Press, New York, 1985); and David Levin, *Cotton Mather: The Young Life of the Lord's Remembrancer, 1663–1703* (Harvard University Press, Cambridge, 1978).

2. Mather, *Diary*, vol. 1, p. 19.

3. [John Field and Thomas Wilcox], *An Admonition to the Parliament* (1572), in *Puritan Manifestoes: A Study of the Origin of the Puritan Revolt*, ed. W. H. Frere and C. E. Douglas (Church Historical Society, London, 1954), pp. 11, 9, emphasis added; and [Thomas Cartwright], *A Second Admonition to the Parliament* (1572), in *Puritan Manifestoes*, p. 84, paraphrasing Jeremiah 1: 7 and 26:7–11. See also John T. MacNeill (ed.), *Calvin: Institutes of the Christian Religion*, trans. Ford Lewis Battles, 2 vols. (Westminster Press, Philadelphia, 1960); and Sandra Marie Gustafson, "Performing the Word: American Oratory, 1630–1860" (Ph.D. diss., University of California at Berkeley, 1993).

4. Michael Roper and John Tosh (eds) *Manful Assertions: Masculinities in Britain Since 1800* (Routledge, New York, 1991), pp. 1–24; E. Anthony Rotundo, *American Manhood: Transformations in Masculinity from the Revolution to the Modern Era* (Basic Books, New York, 1993); Mark C. Carnes and Clyde Griffen (eds.), *Meanings for Manhood: Constructions of Masculinity in Victorian America* (University of Chicago Press, Chicago, 1990).

5. Manhood is, of course, also defined against other social categories, including sexualities, races, and class identities.

6. See, for example, Merry E. Wiesner, "*Wandervogels* and Women: Journeymen's Concepts of Masculinity in Early Modern Germany," *Journal of Social History*, 24 (1991), pp. 767–82; Joan Pong Linton, "*Jack of Newbery* and Drake in California: Domestic and Colonial Narratives of English Cloth and Manhood," *ELH*, 59 (1992), pp. 23–51; and Lyndal Roper, "Stealing Manhood: Capitalism and Magic in Early Modern Germany," *Gender and History*, 3 (1991), pp. 4–22. On "homosocial" bonds, see Eve Kosofsky Sedgwick's *Between Men: English Literature and Male Homosocial Desire* (Columbia University Press, New York, 1985).

7. Susan Dwyer Amussen, " 'The Part of a Christian Man': The Cultural Politics of Manhood in Early Modern England," in *Political Culture and Cultural Politics in Early Modern England: Essays Presented to David Underdown*, ed. Susan D. Amussen and Mark A. Kishlansky (Manchester University Press, Manchester, 1995), pp. 213–33, esp. pp. 214, 227.

8. Judith Butler, *Gender Trouble: Feminism and the Subversion of Identity* (Routledge, New York, 1990), esp. pp. 33, 25, 141.

9. Robert J. Dinkin, "Seating in the Meetinghouse in Massachusetts," in *Material Life in America, 1600–1860*, ed. Robert B. St. George (Northeastern University Press, Boston, 1988), pp. 407–18.

10. John Winthrop, "A Modell of Christian Charity" (1630), in *Winthrop Papers*, 5 vols. (Massachusetts Historical Society, Boston, 1929–1947), vol. 2, p. 282. Because the family was so widely considered the crucible of both power and subjection, gender roles were arguably the most important symbols of "high" and "low" in early modern culture. See, e.g., William Gouge, *Of Domesticall Duties, Eight Treatises* (London, 1634); Susan Dwyer Amussen, *An Ordered Society: Gender and Class in Early Modern England* (Basil Blackwell, New York, 1988); and Anthony Fletcher and John Stevens (eds.), *Order and Disorder in Early Modern England* (Cambridge University Press, Cambridge, 1985).

11. For laws prohibiting the wearing of items of clothing unsuitable to people of lower ranks, see Nathaniel B. Shurtleff (ed.), *Records of the Governor and Company of the Massachusetts Bay in New England* [hereafter *Mass. Recs.*], 5 vols. in 6 (1854; repr. AMS Press, New York, 1968), vol. 1, pp. 126, 183, 274; vol. 3, pp. 243–44. Patricia Trautman, "Dress in Seventeenth-Century Cambridge, Massachusetts: An Inventory-Based Reconstruction," in *Early American Probate Inventories*, ed. Peter Benes (Boston University, Boston, 1987), pp. 51–73, argues that the courts were unsuccessful in enforcing a correlation between dress and wealth.

12. Noyes also descried the wigs for erasing distinctions *between* men by blurring the visual cues "distinguishing one man from another"; Nicholas Noyes, "An Essay against Periwigs," in *Remarkable Providences: Readings on Early American History*, ed. John Demos (Northeastern University Press, Boston, 1991), pp. 252–61, esp. pp. 253, 254.

13. On the hybrid character of men's working lives, even among those with artisanal skills, see Robert Blair St. George, "Fathers, Sons, and Identity: Woodworking Artisans in Southeastern New England, 1620–1700," in *The Craftsman in Early America*, ed. Ian M. G. Quimby (W. W. Norton, New York, 1984), esp. figure 2, p. 102.

14. See Toby L. Ditz, "Shipwrecked; or, Masculinity Imperiled: Mercantile Representations of Failure and the Gendered Self in Eighteenth-Century Philadelphia," *Journal of American History*, 81 (1994), pp. 51–80; Christopher Wal-

drep, "The Making of a Border State Society: James McGready, the Great Revival, and the Prosecution of Profanity in Kentucky," *American Historical Review*, 99 (1994), pp. 767–84; Rhys Isaac, *The Transformation of Virginia, 1740–1790* (University of North Carolina Press, Chapel Hill, 1982); and Jay Fliegelman, *Declaring Independence: Jefferson, Natural Language, and the Culture of Performance* (Stanford University Press, Stanford, 1993).

15. One of the best evocations of the social tensions nourished in face-to-face communities is John Putnam Demos, *Entertaining Satan: Witchcraft and the Culture of Early New England* (Oxford University Press, New York, 1982), ch. 9. See also Robert B. St. George, " 'Heated' Speech and Literacy in Seventeenth-Century New England," in *Seventeenth-Century New England*, ed. David D. Hall and David Grayson Allen (Colonial Society of Massachusetts, Boston, 1984), pp. 275–322; Mary Beth Norton, "Gender and Defamation in Seventeenth-Century Maryland," *William and Mary Quarterly* [hereafter *WMQ*], 3rd ser., 44 (1987), pp. 3–39; Richard Bauman, *Let Your Words Be Few: Symbolism of Speaking and Silence among Seventeenth-Century Quakers* (Cambridge University Press, New York, 1983); and J. A. Sharpe, *Defamation and Sexual Slander in Early Modern England: The Church Courts at York*, Borthwick Institute of Historical Research papers, no. 58 (University of York, York, 1980).

16. See Richard D. Brown, *Knowledge Is Power: The Diffusion of Information in Early America, 1700–1865* (Oxford University Press, New York, 1989); and Jane Kamensky, *Governing the Tongue: The Politics of Speaking in Early New England* (forthcoming from Oxford University Press), ch. 2.

17. See Stephen Greenblatt, "Learning to Curse: Aspects of Linguistic Colonialism in the Sixteenth Century," in *First Images of America*, ed. Fredi Chiapelli, Michael J. B. Allen, and Robert L. Benson, 2 vols. (University of California Press, Berkeley, 1976), vol. 2, pp. 561–80; Anthony Pagden, *The Fall of Natural Man: The American Indian and the Origins of Comparative Ethnology* (Cambridge University Press, New York, 1982), pp. 16, 20–22, 127–29; and Edward Gray, "Indian Languages in Anglo-American Thought, 1580–1820" (Ph.D. diss. in progress, Brown University).

18. The paraphrase is from Isaiah 33:15, 19–20. This passage forms the epigraph to John Eliot, *The Indian Grammar Begun; Or, An Essay to Bring the Indian Language into Rules . . .* (Cambridge, 1666), reprinted in *Old South Leaflets*, vol. 3, no. 52 (1894).

19. William Wood, *New England's Prospect* (1634), ed. Alden T. Vaughan (University of Massachusetts Press, Amherst, 1977), pp. 88, 81–92, 112–15. "Aberginian" was Wood's generic term for the natives living in what is now northern Massachusetts and southern New Hampshire.

20. Eliot, *Indian Grammar Begun*, p. 4; Wood, *New England's Prospect*, p. 77; [William Bradford and Edward Winslow], *Journal of the English Planta-*

tion at Plimoth, or *Mourt's Relation* (1622; facs. repr. University Microfilms, Ann Arbor, 1966), p. 53, emphasis added. Bradford and Winslow are referring to the sense of utter linguistic deprivation the Plymouth colonists felt at the death of the interpreter, Tisquantum (Squanto).

21. *"Au commencement estoit la Parole, et la Parole estoit avec Dieu; et icelle Parole estoit Dieu,"* John 1:1 as explicated in Jean Calvin, *Evangile selon Saint Jean,* vol. 2 of M. Reveillard (ed.), *Commentaires de Jean Calvin sur le Nouveau Testament* (Fontenay-Sous-Bois, Aix-en-Provence, 1967), pp. 12–15; Calvin, *Institutes,* vol. 1, pp. 75, 70, 81.

22. John Market, *A Book of Notes and Common Places* (London, 1581), p. 852, quoted in *A Cultural History of Gesture,* ed. Jan Bremmer and Herman Roodenberg (Cornell University Press, Ithaca, 1992), p. 6.

23. Amussen, " 'The Part of Christian Man,' " p. 214.

24. Gouge, *Of Domesticall Duties,* pp. 436–38. See also Cotton Mather, *A Family Well-Ordered* (Boston, 1699), pp. 60–61. Similar injunctions are found in English sources, including Richard Brathwait, *The English Gentleman . . . how to demeane or accommodate himself in the manage[ment] of publike or private affaires* (London, 1630), pp. 83, 13. On the theme of uncontrolled speaking in early modern English advice literature more broadly, see Jane Kamensky, "Governing the Tongue: Speech and Society in Early New England" (Ph.D. diss., Yale University, 1993), pp. 3–13.

25. Juan Luis Vives, *De Institutione Feminae Christianae* (1523), trans. Richard Hyrde as *Instruction of a Christian Woman* (1540), reprinted in *Vives and the Renascence Education of Women,* ed. Foster Watson (Edward Arnold, London, 1912), p. 55.

26. William Whatley, *A Bride-Bush, Or a Direction for Married Persons* (London, 1619), p. 44; see also Gouge, *Of Domestical Duties.* Laurel Thatcher Ulrich, "Vertuous Women Found: New England Ministerial Literature, 1668–1735," in *A Heritage of Her Own: Toward a New Social History of American Women,* ed. Nancy F. Cott and Elizabeth H. Pleck (Simon and Schuster, New York, 1979), pp. 58–80.

27. Richard Brathwait, *The English Gentlewoman . . . what habbiliments doe best attire her, what ornaments doe best adorne her, what complements doe best accomplish her* (London, 1631), pp. 41, 89–90, 170. See also Angeline Goreau, *The Whole Duty of a Woman: Female Writers in Seventeenth-Century England* (Dial Press, New York, 1985); Ian Maclean, *The Renaissance Notion of Woman* (Cambridge University Press, New York, 1980); David Underdown, "The Taming of the Scold: The Enforcement of Patriarchal Authority in Early Modern England," in Fletcher and Stevens (eds.) *Order and Disorder in Early Modern England,* pp. 116–36; and Lynda E. Boose, "Scolding Brides and Bridling Scolds: Taming the Woman's Unruly Member," *Shakespeare Quarterly,* 42 (1991), esp. pp. 185, 189, 195, 203.

28. John Hewes, *A Perfect Survey of the English Tongue* (1624; facs. repr. The Scolar Press, Menston, 1972), sig. X4.

29. The importance of classical eloquence to men's social standing is emphasized in Hewes, *Perfect Survey of the English Tongue*, sig. X4; and Owen Price, *The Vocal Organ* (1665; facs. rep. The Scolar Press, Menston, 1970), p. 47. See also E. Jennifer Monaghan, "Literacy Instruction and Gender in Colonial New England," in *Reading in America: Literature and Social History*, ed. Cathy M. Davidson (Johns Hopkins University Press, Baltimore, 1989), pp. 53–80.

30. Gouge, *Of Domesticall Duties*, pp. 437–38, 440.

31. [Anonymous], *The School of Good Manners* (1715; Boston, 1772), p. 25, emphasis added.

32. Brathwait, *English Gentleman*, pp. 13, 87–89. To gentlewomen, Brathwait also counsels "moderation," but he equates "moderate" speech with none at all, proclaiming that "Silence in a Woman is a moving Rhetoricke"; Brathwait, *The English Gentlewoman*, pp. 89–90, 170.

33. George Webbe, *The Practise of Quietnes: Directing a Christian How to Live Quietly in This Troblesome World*, 3rd ed. (London, 1618), esp. pp. 14, 100–101, 108–10, 257, 362. The injunction to bridle one's tongue, most frequently invoked for female audiences, comes from Psalms 39:1.

34. See Kamensky, "Governing the Tongue," pp. 104–54.

35. Presentment of Thomas Johnson, Ipswich, 1671, in *Verbatim Transcript of the File Papers of the Essex County Quarterly Courts, 1636–1692*, comp. Archie N. Frost, 75 vols. (typescript on deposit at the Essex Institute, Salem, Mass.; microfilm copy at Sterling Memorial Library, Yale University), vol. 17, case 47, sheet 1 (Josiah Ballard testimony), also case 47, sheet 2. Hereafter cited as *Essex File Papers*, vol.: case–sheet.

36. Presentment of John Guppy for theft, Salem, 1684, *Essex File Papers*, 42: 16–1 (William Godsoe testimony), also 16–2 through 16–3, see also George F. Dow (ed.), *Records and Files of the Quarterly Courts of Essex County, Massachusetts* [hereafter *ECR*], 9 vols. (Essex Institute, Salem, 1911–1978), vol. 9, p. 276; Woolcott v. Atkinson for debt, Ipswich, 1683, *Essex File Papers*, 39: 55–2 (Ephraim Wheeler testimony), also 50–1 through 55–4, *ECR*, vol. 9, pp. 9–11.

37. Wells v. Nelson for slander, Ipswich, 1669, *ECR*, vol. 4, pp. 104–5, *Essex File Papers*, 14: 22–6 (John Bear testimony). The only mention of female "boasting" in seventeenth-century Essex County is found in the fornication presentment of Barbara Clark and [illegible] Jones, Salem, 1639–40, *ECR*, vol. 1, p. 15; *Essex County Court Record Books* (mss. on deposit at the Essex Institute, Salem), vol. 1, p. 30 (case 25).

38. See Mary Beth Norton, "Gender, Crime, and Community in Seventeenth-Century Maryland," in *The Transformation of Early American History: Society, Authority and Ideology*, ed. James A. Henretta, Michael Kammen, and Stanley N. Katz (Alfred A. Knopf, New York, 1991), pp. 123–50, 286–94; and

Cornelia Hughes Dayton, "Taking the Trade: Abortion and Gender Relations in an Eighteenth-Century New England Village," *William and Mary Quarterly*, 3rd ser., 48 (1991), pp. 19–49.

39. James Kendall Hosmer (ed.), *Winthrop's Journal, "History of New England" 1630–1649*, 2 vols (Barnes & Noble, New York, 1959), vol. 1, p. 171.

40. The word "man" must be understood literally here; records make it clear that women did not possess such liberty. William H. Whitmore (ed.), *The Colonial Laws of Massachusetts, Reprinted from the Edition of 1660, With the supplements to 1672, Containing also the Body of Liberties of 1641* (Rockwell & Churchill, Boston, 1889), pp. 35, 45, 49, 55, 128–29, 143, 148, 154–56, 171.

41. See Hendrik Hartog, "The Public Law of a County Court; Judicial Government in Eighteenth-Century Massachusetts," *American Journal of Legal History*, 20 (1976), pp. 282–329; David T. Konig, *Law and Society in Puritan Massachusetts: Essex County, 1629–1692* (University of North Carolina Press, Chapel Hill, 1979); and Daniel R. Coquillette (ed.), *Law in Colonial Massachusetts, 1630–1800* (Colonial Society of Massachusetts, Boston, 1984).

42. See St. George, " 'Heated' Speech," pp. 288, 318–19.

43. See Demos, *Entertaining Satan*, pp. 78–79.

44. Slighting also included the English statutory offense of *scandalum magnatum*, words against the offices of the "great men" or peers of the realm. John Lassiter, "Defamation of Peers: The Rise and Decline of the Action for *Scandalum Magnatum*, 1497–1773," *American Journal of Legal History*, 22 (1978), pp. 216–36.

45. The Porter case played out in numerous episodes during the 1660s. See *Essex File Papers*, 7: 34–1 through 36–1; "Narrative of the Case of John Porter, Jr.," *Mass. Recs.*, vol. 4, part 2, pp. 216–18; *ECR*, vol. 2, pp. 335–38, and vol. 3, pp. 111, 117; and *Suffolk Court Files*, manuscript collection including papers submitted for trials before the Court of Assistants, on deposit at the Massachusetts State Archives at Columbia Point, case £608.

46. Significantly, male defendants predominate even more strongly among recidivist "slighters" (93.5 percent) and in cases tried before the higher courts (98 percent). Overall, women appeared in over 30 percent of civil suits over speech (chiefly slander and defamation) and in 22 percent of all categories of criminal speech prosecutions. Kamensky, "Governing the Tongue," pp. 346–51, 464–65. See also Eli Faber, "Puritan Criminals: The Economic, Social, and Intellectual Background to Crime in Seventeenth-Century Massachusetts," *Perspectives in American History*, 9 (1977–78), esp. pp. 120–22.

47. The incompleteness of the records involved (particularly at the county court level prior to 1640) and the shifts in population throughout the century make meaningful quantification of these trends difficult. The pattern is most pronounced in the proceedings of the General Court and Court of Assistants,

where the number of cases during the 1630s and the 1660s far exceeded the average number of cases per decade. The Essex Court Records show a marked peak around 1660.

48. The Pauline image of gossips "wandering about from house to house . . . speaking things which they ought not" (I Timothy 5:13) was a popular trope in early modern English writings on the scold.

49. See presentment of John Blood, Salem, 1647, *ECR*, vol. 1, p. 133; presentment of Samuel Moses, Ipswich, 1684, *Essex File Papers*, 41: 67–1; presentment of Thomas Wheeler, Salem, 1654, *ECR*, vol. 1, p. 360; presentment of Mr. Henry Sewall, Ipswich, 1651, *ECR*, vol. 1, pp. 200, 220–21.

50. The frequent use of "publish" to mean *verbally disseminate* itself illustrates the power of speech. See, e.g., presentment of Edward Lumas, Ipswich, 1672, *Essex File Papers*, 18: 91–1, sheet 3; presentment of Ruben Guppy, Salem, 1674, *ECR*, vol. 5, pp. 355–56; presentment of Henry Kenney, Salem, 1679, *ECR*, vol. 7, pp. 248–49. *The Diary of Samuel Sewall, 1674-1729*, ed. M. Halsey Thomas, 2 vols. (Farrar, Straus and Giroux, New York, 1973), mentions a case in which "publishing" remarks aloud was held to be more injurious than resigning them to paper; vol. 1, pp. 101–2.

51. Presentment of Eliakim Wardell, Hampton, 1663, *ECR*, vol. 3, p. 100, emphasis added; see also presentment of Samuel Shattock, Salem, 1663, *ECR*, vol. 3, p. 110; presentment of Ralph Fogge, Salem, 1649–50, *ECR*, vol. 1, pp. 185–86.

52. Presentment of Thomas Dexter, Boston, 1632–33, *Mass. Recs.*, vol. 1, p. 103; see also John Endecott to John Winthrop, April 1631, *Winthrop Papers*, vol. 2, pp. 25–26.

53. Presentment of Captain John Stone, Boston, 1633, *Mass. Recs.*, vol. 1, p. 108.

54. Thomas Wells v. William Nelson, Ipswich, 1669, *Essex File Papers*, 14: 22–6 (John Bear testimony); see also *ECR*, vol. 4, pp. 104–5. For a thoughtful consideration of Puritan images of high and low, and of the fragility of imagined authority in New England, see Darrett B. Rutman, "The Mirror of Puritan Authority," in *Law and Authority in Colonial America: Selected Essays*, ed. George A. Billias (Barre Publishers, Barre, Mass., 1965), pp. 149–67.

55. Presentment of John Leigh, Newtown, 1634, *Mass. Recs.*, vol. 1, pp. 132–33.

56. Presentment of Mr. Ambros Martin, Boston, 1638–39, *Mass. Recs.*, vol. 1, p. 252; presentment of Francis Hutchinson, Boston, 1641, *Mass. Recs.*, vol. 1, pp. 336, 340.

57. Presentment of Mr. Henry Walton, Salem, 1643, *ECR*, vol. 1, p. 59.

58. Presentment of Joseph Gatchell, Salem, 1680, *ECR*, vol. 7, pp. 406–8.

59. See St. George, " 'Heated' Speech," p. 294; and Edmund Leach, "An-

thropological Aspects of Language: Animal Categories and Verbal Abuse," in *New Directions in the Study of Language*, ed. Eric H. Lenneberg (MIT Press, Cambridge, 1964), pp. 23–63.

60. Presentment of Captain George Corwin, Boston, 1676, *Mass. Recs.*, vol. 5, p. 90.

61. *Mass. Recs.*, vol. 4, part 2, pp. 195–97, 210.

62. At least 80 percent of witchcraft suspects in the colonies were female; in early modern Europe, the proportion approached 90 percent. See Carol F. Karlsen, *The Devil in the Shape of a Woman: Witchcraft in Colonial New England* (W. W. Norton, New York, 1987), pp. 47–51: Demos, *Entertaining Satan*, pp. 60–62; Richard Godbeer, *The Devil's Dominion: Magic and Religion in Early New England* (Cambridge University Press, New York, 1992), pp. 20–21; and Brian P. Levack, *The Witch-Hunt in Early Modern Europe* (Longman, New York, 1987), p. 124.

63. Mather's praise for silver-tongued women (paraphrasing Psalms 39:1 and Proverbs 10:20) appears in Cotton Mather, *Ornaments for the Daughters of Zion* (Boston, 1692), pp. 49–51. Contrast with the descriptions of witches' ravings found in Cotton Mather, "A Brand Pluck'd Out of the Burning" (1693); Mather, "Memorable Providences, Relating to Witchcrafts and Possessions" (1689); and Mather, "Wonders of the Invisible World" (1693); all reprinted in George Lincoln Burr (ed.), *Narratives of the Witchcraft Cases, 1648–1706* (Charles Scribner, New York, 1914). On witchcraft as a speech crime see Jane Kamensky, "Words, Witches, and Woman Trouble: Witchcraft, Disorderly Speech, and Gender Boundaries in Puritan New England," *Essex Institute Historical Collections*, 128 (1992), pp. 286–307.

64. Godbeer, *Devil's Dominion*, pp. 238–42; Demos, *Entertaining Satan*, pp. 402–9; and Karlsen, *Devil in the Shape of a Woman*, pp. 51–52.

65. Demos identifies 22 male "witches" among the 114 people accused prior to the Salem outbreak, 9 of whom were husbands of female "witches" and 2 of whom were their "religious associates"; most of the others, he argues, became suspect in distinctly "limited" ways. Demos, *Entertaining Satan*, pp. 57, 60–62. Karlsen uses a base figure of 75 accused men including those suspected during the Salem trials (22 percent of the 342 suspects whose sex she has been able to identify conclusively), of whom nearly half (36) were "suspect by association." Karlsen, *Devil in the Shape of a Woman*, p. 47. Because documentation on these few male suspects is sparse, conclusions about the men who came under suspicion are speculative.

66. Thomas Adams, *The Taming of the Tongue*, in *The Works of Thomas Adams*, ed. Joseph Angus (1629; repr. James Nichol, Edinburgh, 1862), vol. 3, p. 17.

67. The documents relating to Mary and Hugh Parsons's case are reprinted in David D. Hall (ed.), *Witch-Hunting in Seventeenth-Century New England: A*

Documentary History, 1638–1692 (Northeastern University Press, Boston, 1991), pp. 25–27, 29–60.

68. Hall, *Witch-Hunting in New England*, pp. 43, 41.

69. Hall, *Witch-Hunting in New England*, pp. 32–33, 52–53, 35–37, 55. See similar accusations in the cases of William Graves (Hall, *Witch-Hunting in New England*, p. 168), and John Godfrey (Demos, *Entertaining Satan*, pp. 41–43, 52–56).

70. Hall, *Witch-Hunting in New England*, p. 36.

71. Mather, *Diary*, vol. 1, pp. 55, 154. Mather's massive published *oeuvre* is filled with disquisitions on the vicissitudes of speaking. See, e.g., *The Angel of Bethesda* (1724); *A Golden Curb for the Mouth, Which . . . Rushes into the SINS of Profane Swearing and Cursing* (Boston, 1709); and *The Right Way to Shake Off a Viper . . . What Shall Good Men Do, When They Are Evil Spoken Of?* (Boston, 1711).

72. Mather, *Diary*, vol. 1, pp. 55, 62.

73. In a recent article on male-male sexual relations, Richard Godbeer finds a similar pattern of lenience, but does not fully explore the extent to which such latitude reflects the gendered prerogatives of Puritan men; see Richard Godbeer, " 'The Cry of Sodom': Discourse, Intercourse, and Desire in Colonial New England," *WMQ*, 3rd ser., 52 (1995), pp. 259–86.

74. Almost all court-mandated apologies were connected to speech crimes, and, as with slighting, almost all those ordered to "acknowledge" wrongful words publicly were male. Jane Kamensky, "The Fine Art of Eating One's Words in Early New England," in *Possible Pasts: Becoming Colonial in Early America*, ed. Robert B. St. George (forthcoming from Cornell University Press).

75. Presentment of John Hoare for defaming authority, Boston, 1668–69, in *Records of the Court of Assistants of the Colony of Massachusetts Bay, 1630–1692*, ed. John Noble and John F. Cronin, 3 vols. [hereafter *Assts. Recs.*] (Rockwell and Churchill, Boston, 1901–1928), vol. 3, pp. 195–96, emphasis added; see also presentment of Nathaniel Hadlock, *ECR*, vol. 4, pp. 74–75; and Simon Tuttle's apology, *ECR*, vol. 3, pp. 141–43.

76. On the function of "reintegrative shaming" punishments, see John Braithwaite, *Crime, Shame and Reintegration* (Cambridge University Press, New York, 1989); Faber, "Puritan Criminals," esp. pp. 137–42; and George Lee Haskins, *Law and Authority in Early Massachusetts: A Study in Tradition and Design* (Macmillan, New York, 1960), pp. 210–11.

77. See, for example, the presentment of Elizabeth Due, Salem, 1654, *ECR*, vol. 1, pp. 361–62, 380. That such silent punishments were considered more ignominious than speaking one's own shame is borne out by the case of Ralph Fogge, who was threatened with having his offense written on a paper unless he acknowledged his mis-speaking aloud; presentment of Ralph Fogge, Salem, 1649–50, *ECR*, vol. 1, pp. 185–86.

78. Presentment of Elizabeth Perkins, Ipswich, 1681, *ECR*, vol. 8, pp. 89–90, emphasis added. Confirming the pattern of female penance, the punishment was remitted upon her private confession.

79. Presentment of John Allen for defaming authority, Salem, 1681, *ECR*, vol. 8, pp. 128–29. The record book notes that Allen's "free confession" procured him "much favor."

80. Karlsen, *Devil in the Shape of a Woman*, pp. 48–50; see also Godbeer, *Devil's Dominion*, pp. 20–21.

81. See Brandbrook v. Wells, Ipswich, 1668, *ECR*, vol. 4, pp. 49–50, 67, and *Essex File Papers*, 13:88–2, 88–6 through 89–1, 89–3, 89–4; Cross v. Wells, Salem, 1668, *ECR*, vol. 4, pp. 66–67, and *Essex File Papers*, 13: 104–2 through 104–4, 104–8; presentment of Wells et al., Salem, 1668, *ECR*, vol. 4, pp. 82, 99; Wells v. Nelson, Ipswich, 1669, *ECR*, vol. 4, pp. 104–5, and *Essex File Papers*, 14: 22–1 through 22–6; presentment of Wells, Ipswich, 1669, *ECR*, vol. 4, p. 142, and *Essex File Papers*, 14: 80–1 through 80–4. See also the cases of John Fuller, *Assts. Recs.*, vol. 1, pp. 228–29; John Broadstreet, *Essex File Papers*, 2: 46–2; and William Browne, *Essex File Papers*, 3: 108 through 113, and *ECR*, vol. 2, p. 36.

82. My thoughts on the liminality of Puritan manhood have been influenced by Susan Juster, "Orality and Sexuality in Early American Puritanism" (paper presented to the American Studies Association, November 1993). The paradoxical relationship between patriarchy and contractualism is the subject of Michael Warner's "New English Sodom," in *Queering the Renaissance*, ed. Jonathan Goldberg (Duke University Press, Durham, 1994), pp. 330–58. See also Jonathan Goldberg, "Bradford's 'Ancient Members' and 'A Case of Buggery . . . Amongst Them' " in *Nationalisms and Sexualities*, ed. Andrew Parker, et al. (Routledge, New York, 1992), pp. 60–77.

"Love Raptures"

Marital, Romantic, and Erotic Images of Jesus Christ in Puritan New England, 1670–1730

Richard Godbeer

On 19 October 1717, Samuel Sewall's first wife, Hannah Hull, died at the age of fifty-nine. God, Sewall wrote in his diary, would now teach him "a new lesson; to live a widower's life." By February 1718, though, Sewall was already contemplating another loving union. The prospective spouse about whom he enthused in his diary was not, however, one of the Bostonian widows before whom he would later lay his suit.

> I had a sweet and very affectionate meditation concerning the Lord Jesus; nothing was to be objected against his person, parentage, relations, estate, house, home! Why did I not resolutely, presently close with him! And I cried mightily to God that he would help me so to do.[1]

During the same year in which Sewall was contemplating Christ's un-impeachable qualifications as a spouse, Increase Mather published his *Practical Truths Plainly Delivered* wherein he described a "marriage" with Christ as "the most desirable one that ever was or that possibly can be." No "greater dignity" was imaginable than marrying "the only son of the King of Heaven," no "greater felicity" than to have as a husband "the wisest and richest that can be thought of." The bride of such a groom would be "made happy for ever."[2] That June, Mather's son Cotton preached "to the flock on [how] the marriage of our saviour unto his people may be attended with many happy consequences," a sermon he published under the title *A Glorious Espousal* in 1719.[3]

The marital imagery evident in New England Puritan literature of the early seventeenth century grew lusher and more widespread by the last quarter of that and the first quarter of the eighteenth century. By examining marital, romantic, and erotic conceptions of Jesus Christ as well as how they changed over time, we can learn a great deal not only about Puritan religious culture as it evolved in early New England but also about attitudes toward family, gender, and sexuality. Contemporary thinkers realized that the "glorious espousal" had potentially troublesome aspects. Since a union with Christ was deemed infinitely superior to that between husband and wife, pointed comparisons of the two estates might damage, perhaps even undermine, a significant Puritan goal: to rehabilitate human marriage. An additional difficulty, one identified more by recent than contemporary scholars, is that designating believers as brides of Christ might have alienated male sensibilities and, indeed, may well have been linked to the increasing preponderance of women in New England congregations. The latter part of this essay shows how these problems resolved themselves in the context of Puritan culture and, more specifically, of attitudes toward gender in Puritan society.

The sources upon which I base my examination were written exclusively by ministers and lay males who belonged to the social elite. These voices represent, to use David D. Hall's term, the "committed core" of Puritan society as opposed to those whose religiosity was more limited and intermittent. Thus, I am describing conditions of cultural transmission rather than reception. I suspect, however, that the motifs and attitudes conveyed by the elite of the godly Puritan community were also significant in the lives of the less powerful and meditative.[4] While I am not unaware of the limitations inherent in the extant sources, I am also convinced that they reveal evidence sufficiently provocative to challenge some of our current beliefs about Puritan society.

When Puritans evoked scriptural images of Christ as bridegroom and lover, they drew upon a tradition well established in Christian devotional literature, both Catholic and Protestant. Yet, as Amanda Porterfield has shown, such imagery took on new meaning in the context of Puritan attitudes toward marriage. Medieval mystics had described union with Christ in terms of feelings and relationships that they shunned in an earthly setting. Members of the religious orders yearned for marriage with their savior and yet committed themselves to celibacy as a prerequisite for sanctity. The joyful anticipation of ecstatic union with Christ by men and women who had taken, or at least revered, vows of chastity affirmed their opposition of physical and spiritual realms as well as their belief that devotion necessarily involved transcendence of the body.[5]

The Reformation's emphasis on a believer's personal relationship with God gave renewed significance to marital imagery among Protestants in general. But Puritans went further: their unusually positive attitude toward marriage, and sex within marriage, transformed the notion of espousal to Christ. That more benign view of the relationship between husband and wife was bound up with the Puritan reaffirmation of family life as a primary agent of grace and social order. Like other Englishmen, Puritans worried about the disorder and godless behavior pervading their society. But whereas most of their contemporaries favored reforming and reinforcing agencies of church and state to meet this crisis of authority, Puritans advocated a more fundamental shift from external to internal discipline. Individuals, they proclaimed, should be trained to control themselves at an early age. In the society envisaged by Puritans, this task could best be accomplished within the virtuous family, which would lovingly but firmly break the willful impulses of its children and teach them self-discipline.[6]

The relationship between husband and wife, the cornerstone of family stability, was to be not only a spiritual but also a physical partnership. Ministers taught that God had ordained sexual relations within marriage both as a means to procreation and as an expression of marital affection. "Conjugal love," declared Samuel Willard, should be expressed through "conjugal union, by which [husband and wife] become one flesh." This "oneness" was "the nearest relative conjunction in the world . . . follow[ing] from a preference that these have each of other in their hearts above all the world." Ministers enabled married partners to remain pure within the context of a physical relationship by redefining chastity not as abstinence but as "a moderation, whereby we are to keep ourselves within due bounds, in whatsoever hath any respect to natural generation." Marital vows set those "due bounds."[7] According to Puritans, then, sex between husband and wife was not a necessary evil but a desirable good.[8]

This affirmation of marital sex had important implications for Puritans' use of spousal imagery. Instead of depicting union with Christ in mystical terms that eschewed the impurities of physical desire, Puritans used concrete, earthy language to draw direct parallels between human marriage and the soul's espousal. Christ's marriage with believers now provided a model for husband and wife as they sought to build and sustain their relationship. "[T]he ground and pattern of our love," wrote John Winthrop to his third wife Margaret Tyndal just before their marriage in 1618, "is no other but that between Christ and his dear spouse." Human marriage would, in turn, inspire believers to strive for union with their other, greater spouse. Winthrop hoped that his and Margaret's "consideration" of their love for one another "could make us raise up our spirits to a like conformity of sincerity and fervency in the love of Christ our lord and heavenly husband; that we could delight in him as we do in each other."[9] Heavenly and terrestrial marriages thus became symbiotic, their similarities as striking and instructive as their differences.

Spousal imagery peppered New England sermons, devotional texts, diaries, and personal correspondence throughout the seventeenth and early eighteenth centuries, but there was a dramatic shift in the meanings ministers ascribed to it. The first and second generations of New England pastors often evoked the bride's adulterous tendencies to signify estrangement from Christ, a concern that reflected the spiritual disillusionment many Puritans felt after arriving in New England as well as the ministers' growing fears of declension.[10] Thomas Shepard was far more inclined to bemoan his "widow-like separation and disunion" from his savior than to celebrate their union, just as Michael Wigglesworth constantly berated himself for "going awhoring . . . after vanities" and wounding his "head and husband," Jesus Christ, "by not loving and delighting in his presence, by . . . liking other loves more than him."[11]

The emphasis in both public and private writings during the first forty years of settlement lay on the failure of the bride to remain faithful and the reciprocal act either of Christ's forbearance or God's righteous anger.[12] But by the last quarter of the century, images of Christ as a wronged husband and of God as a vengeful father were eclipsed by those of Christ the supportive lover and God the welcoming parent. Emory Elliot has shown that between the 1660s and 1690s, New England ministers "helped to alleviate the spiritual malaise of the second generation and to prepare its members for assertive action" through "a new message of assurance" and "the exchange of one dominant archetype— the image of the angry and wrathful God the Father—for another archetype—the figure of the gentle, loving, and protective Christ."[13] As clerics began to reconceptualize the believer's relationship to divinity to privilege nurturing love over inspirational terrorism, so they recast spousal imagery to support their new message. Instead of threatening their flocks with punishment for their infidelities, ministers now sought to seduce them with promises of a loving and fruitful relationship with Christ. The prospect of imminent doom in the hands of a father outraged by the harlotry of his prospective daughter-in-law was exchanged for that of ravishment in the bosom of a smiling husband.

Clerical references to divine espousal became more frequent, more extensive, and more positive in tone.[14] During the last quarter of the seventeenth century and the first quarter of the eighteenth, pastors such as Samuel Willard and Cotton Mather described the soul's marriage to Christ in ever more elaborate detail, occasionally devoting entire sermons to the subject.[15] In doing so, they acted not only as teachers whose duty it was to explicate a recurring scriptural metaphor but also as self-styled "friends of the bridegroom" who courted on Christ's behalf.[16] The days on which ministers preached became Christ's "wooing days," when the savior would "deck and array himself with all his glory and beauty," like a suitor hoping to bedazzle the object of his love.[17] Since pastors were also prospective brides in their own right, they served simultaneously as interpreters, advocates, and potential recipients of the redeemer's advances.

The ministers' use of marital imagery in these turn-of-the-century sermons was literal minded, often downright prosaic, and appealed blatantly to self-interest. According to their descriptions of "marriage" with Christ, the souls of the redeemed and their savior were united through "a regular procedure" that bore a close resemblance to earthly marital arrangements.[18] First, God the Father consented to the match and so became "firmly engaged" to adopt his son's brides and "to carry to us in all things, as a father."[19] Next Christ would approach the soul and make his offer of marriage. His clerical advocates encouraged acceptance by detailing both the personal felicity and the "unsearchable riches" to be derived from the "transcendent match." In addition to securing a partner who was "altogether lovely," the bride would "wear the name of her husband," would share "in the glory of the person of Christ, as the wife is honoured by the dignity which her husband enjoys," and would become joint heir "with him who is the heir of all things."[20] Union with Christ began to sound like a social climber's dream as the groom's advocate exclaimed, almost salivating as he did so, "What a vast jointure hast thou!" But ministers recognized that the prospect of so unequal a match, between "a miserable sinner" and "the only begotten son of God," might be more intimidating than enticing. They urged the prospective bride not to back away because of her "want of a dowry." Christ had laid down "an honourable preferment" in its place, covenanting "his estate to redeem her, to pay her debt, to purchase her her freedom, her furniture, and her felicity." Like any husband, Christ assumed responsibility for his wife's debts: "He has suffered to make satisfaction to God for all our sins, which are our debts."[21]

Presented with this humbling yet aggrandizing proposal, the soul had only to utter one word of compliance and the betrothal would become "unquestionable." As in earthly marriage, betrothal was followed by a period of waiting. The "contraction" between soul and savior occurred "in this world," but "consummation" took place in "the world to come." In the interim, believers would suffer all the frustrations of those engaged couples who declined to swell the ranks of pregnant brides. They "could but now and then steal a sight of him, or obtain a kiss from him" in brief "interviews" between which they "pined away with love-sickness." Their consolation was that once married, their "caresses" would be "both full and uninterrupted."[22] Meanwhile, God had ordained the Lord's Supper as a prenuptial celebration during which the betrothed could regularly and "solemnly renew" their marital covenant.[23] When the nuptial day itself arrived, an occasion coincident with the Day of Judgment, the righteousness imparted by Christ would appear as the bride's wedding garment, "an embroidery with grace inlaid, of sanctuary white most fair." Thus "drest in heavens fashion rare," the souls of the saved would ascend to "the holy court," where their bridegroom would greet them "with widened arms," present them to his father, and then take them away to "his own home," where they would live together in "eternal cohabitation" and "joy unspeakable."[24]

In addition to shedding its earlier monitory tone, marital imagery became more intimate and familial. The individual believer was not only a bride in his or her own right but also a constituent part of the collective spouse, the sum of the elect; ministers sometimes used the word "bride" or "spouse" to signify the redeemed as a collective singular. Earlier descriptions had tended to use impersonal terms such as "the church" to define the larger bridal group into which believers would be incorporated. But during the last quarter of the century, clerics began to characterize the spousal community in more personal terms. They referred with increasing frequency to the extended family of which the redeemed soul would become a member once in heaven.

The redeemed would join with each other, their mutual husband, the angelic host, and the father of all to constitute the "family of God." Whereas Michael Wigglesworth had claimed that the elect would forsake family ties to embrace their new relationship with God the father and Christ the husband, ministers such as Cotton Mather and John Davenport now claimed that in heaven, the saints were "each of them as dear to another, as if all relations of husbands and wives, of parents, and children, and friends, were in every one of them."[25] Edward Taylor treated the subject at length. This close-knit family had "all one father" and were "all children of one mother Jerusalem that is above." They had "all one nature, the New Man" and were "all of one spirit and temper." They were "all one family, the household of God"; they were "all brethren and sisters." They lived "all the same life," were "maintained all by the same food," were "employed in the same service, walking in the same path, making to the same mark." They were "all arrayed in the same apparel, viz., the wedden garment, and all guests at the same wedden, and discumbitants at the same table." Thus, Taylor concluded, "they are all alike excellent, as to the sort of excellency, and knit together in the same bond of love." Their "distinct love" for each other arose from the fact that they were "brethren" and "love[d] as brethren."[26]

Images such as those arrayed by Taylor comport well with the tribalism Edmund Morgan first identified as "growing at the heart of New England Puritanism" during the second half of the seventeenth century. As pastors became disheartened by the spiritual intransigence they discovered among most New Englanders, they directed their efforts more pointedly toward church members and their children rather than the entire community. Meanwhile, half-way membership was granted to the unregenerate children of full members, and with more of these families intermarrying, the covenanted community began to resemble a tribal network. Ministers sought to justify these developments by arguing that most of the elect were descended from godly parents, as "a defensive, tribal attitude" took hold within the covenanted community.[27] Late seventeenth-and early eighteenth-century descriptions of spiritual marriage now stressed "the privileges of the children of God" and "eternal inheritance" achieved through "a covenant of espousals."[28] Edward Taylor clearly expressed that sense of tribal entitlement:

> I being grafft in thee am graffted here
> Into thy family, and kindred claim
> To all in heaven, God, saints, and angels there.
> I thy relations my relations name.

> Thy father's mine, thy God my God, and I
> With saints, and angels draw affinity.[29]

When Samuel Willard declared of the redeemed, "we are the children of one father, the spouse of the same Christ, the temple of the same spirit," he too invoked an extended family of fellow saints, a consummation of the closed community from which brides of Christ were destined to emerge.[30]

Descriptions of espousal late in the century focused much more than previously not only on an exclusive sense of familial community but also on the romantic, sensual, and even sexual connotations of Christ's union with the souls of the elect.[31] Ministers encouraged their flocks to feel Christ's love as a romantic, voluptuous experience. "Here he comes," rhapsodized Willard, "to give us the caresses of his love, and lay us in his bosom and embraces. And now, oh my soul! Hast thou ever experienced the love of a saviour?" Contemplating Christ's bestowal of grace often occasioned sexual and reproductive metaphors. The soul would "receive him," declared Cotton Mather, and "bring forth fruit unto him." References to grace as "a seed that is sown within us" invoked rich symbols of human and agricultural fecundity. Thomas Foxcroft's 1722 vision of redemption is particularly graphic:

> As Christ that pure prolific corn of wheat fell into the ground and died, and rose again; so (the grave being made fertile by his dead body lying in it) the saints shall be impregnated, and spring up; sprout upon his stalk, and (being ripe to the harvest of glory) be gathered into the garner of paradise.[32]

Just as Foxcroft's saints became "impregnated," so Christ's "excitation" of grace after its "infusion . . . into the soul" was often referred to as "quickening," a word also used to describe the first stirrings of new life in the womb. The process of "excitation," explained Samuel Willard, was both "moral" and "physical": "He invites, and useth arguments with the man, and so it is moral; but he withall puts in his finger, and makes a powerful impression."[33]

The reproductive emphasis in sexual imagery used by ministers may also have been prompted by Puritan tribalism. Once the half-way covenant transformed church membership into a familial prerogative and ministers began encouraging their congregations to hope that grace was hereditary, so physical procreation and spiritual fecundity became closely related in Puritan minds. Just as future church members were to spring from the loins of godly parents, so believers envisaged regeneration as the fruit of sexual union with their savior. The salvation of the individual soul as well as of the Puritan community on earth was now perceived in terms of the reproductive imperative intrinsic to the tribal ethos.

Samuel Willard suggested in a 1699 sermon that allusions to sexual relations with Christ were not entirely metaphorical. Although the union between savior and believer was "not carnal, but spiritual and mystical," nevertheless it "comprehend[ed] not the souls only, but also the bodies of the children of God." Not even the body's death and its separation from the soul could break the bond between body and Christ. This was not to suggest that a literal union would occur—it was, after all, "spiritual and mystical"—but the rather ambiguous implication of the body in the union did lend an earthy resonance to the imagery in which Willard and his colleagues delighted. Willard refused to "meddle with nice and curious enquiries about this union, which have no footing in the Word of God, and no way serve to edification," but Cotton Mather, admittedly idiosyncratic in many regards, confided to his diary the extravagantly sensual experiences he underwent during spiritual exercise. He dwelt on "the rapturous praelibations of the heavenly world" in which he was "swallowed up with the ecstasies of [Christ's] love." So "inexpressably irradiated from on high" was Mather on some occasions that he was "not able to bear the ecstasies of the divine love, into which [he] was raptured": "they exhausted my spirits; they made me faint and sick; they were insupportable; I was forced even to withdraw from them, lest I should have swooned away under the raptures."[34]

Edward Taylor's poetry, written between the 1680s and 1720s, contains the most eloquent expressions of romantic and erotic yearning for Christ within Puritan culture. Taylor envisaged the savior as "a spotless male in prime." He addressed him in language of utter infatuation:

> Thou art the loveli'st object over spread
> With brightest beauty object ever wore
> Of purest flushes of pure white and red
> That ever did or could the love allure.
> Lord make my love and thee its object meet
> And me in folds of such love raptures keep.

The bridegroom Taylor imagined for himself was a tender and compassionate lover, who offered affectionate solace and protection to his soulmate:

> Peace, peace, my honey, do not cry,
> My little darling, wipe thine eye,
> Oh cheer, cheer up, come see.
> Is anything too dear, my dove
> Is anything too good, my love
> To get or give for thee?[35]

The bride's heart was a bed in which the couple would find peace together. Faith would prepare the heart as a "feather-bed . . . with gospel pillows, sheets, and sweet perfumes" to better welcome Christ the lover. Taylor's yearning for divine arousal of his spiritual "fancy" was vividly sexual: "Yea, with thy holy oil make thou it slick till like a flash of lightning it grow quick." The poems leave no room for doubt that Taylor anticipated union with his savior through the ecstatic experience of orgasm and penetration.

> O let thy lovely streams of love distill
> Upon myself and spout their spirits pure
> Into my viall, and my vessel fill
> With liveliness[36]

According to Taylor, the soul was "the womb," Christ "the spermadote," and "saving grace the seed cast thereinto." Once "impregnate[d]" by Christ, the soul was "with child" and in due course would produce "the babe of life." That infant, Taylor's poems make abundantly clear, was the fruit of matchless love, conceived "in folds of such love raptures" as only Christ could provide.[37]

Only Christ: there lay the rub. It was, ministers argued, impossible to find complete happiness and fulfillment other than through Christ. "The whole creation," declared Samuel Willard, "affords no such object, the fruition whereof can make a man happy."[38] Recognizing the limitations of the relationship between husband and wife was an important requirement of Puritan piety, even as Puritans sought to rehabilitate marriage. An uneasy dynamic between human and divine espousal surfaces in Puritan writings throughout the seventeenth century, but meeting the demands of both became potentially more problematic as marital imagery grew increasingly prominent and celebratory. The dual shift of emphasis from cuckolded to loving savior and from the sins of the community to the promising future of a tribal family sharpened the tension between the imperatives of human marriage on the one hand

and primary espousal to Christ on the other. How could the godly portray marriage as the key to an orderly society and yet categorize that marriage as secondary? How could they succeed at one marriage without compromising the other?

Puritans had always insisted that spousal affection be tempered by commitment to another and superior union, that between Christ and the believer. John Winthrop, writing to his prospective wife in 1618, compared himself disparagingly to "Christ thy best husband." Edward Taylor subordinated earthly love to divine in a 1674 letter to his intended, Elizabeth Fitch: "I send you not my heart: for that I hope is sent to heaven long since and (unless it hath utterly deceived me) it hath not taken up its lodgen in any one's bosom on this side the royal city of the great King."[39]

A similar ambivalence characterized Puritan attitudes toward sexual relations. The celebration of sex between husband and wife as the expression of covenanted love was limited and partly undercut by lingering distrust of earthly relations, physical as well as emotional. As Willard stressed in 1703, "conjugal union" was ordained by God and signified the "preference" that husband and wife had for each other "in their hearts above all the world." But the act of generation was also associated with the curse placed on Adam and Eve, so that both the sexual act itself and the children emerging from it were compromised morally by the legacy of original sin. Cotton Mather confessed to his diary in 1711 that he was "continually crying to God" on his children's behalf, lamenting the "inexpressible circumstances of meanness relating to their origin, their production and conception."[40] Carnal impulses also threatened to distract men and women from spiritual strivings, a recurrent theme in Puritan literature, both public and private. Although God could be glorified through the body, its appetites more often seemed directed toward less exalted priorities. Diarists such as Increase and Cotton Mather, Peter Thacher, and Josiah Sewall often condemned their "fleshly" instincts as leading them to spiritual "barrenness" and "unfruitfulness." Cotton Mather bemoaned his "barren soul" and "barren life," pledging himself to extinguish his "filthy lusts," thus liberating himself to experience the raptures of "ineffable union" with Christ which would "bring forth fruit to God."[41]

The only union that was not tainted in any way was that between the regenerate soul and its savior. Christ was conceived "immaterially" rather than through physical intercourse and so did not inherit original sin. Because he was "born of the virgin," he escaped "vileness of that nature." As Edward Taylor put it, Christ's "love was ne'er adulterate, e're pure." Sexual union was also pathetically inadequate when compared with Christ's embrace. As Willard explained in 1688, earthly delights could never satisfy man's voracious appetite:

> The reaches of man's soul are so vast, that they can grasp in the whole creation, and scarce feel it: the desire of man, that horseleeches daughter, is still crying, Give, Give: the bed is too narrow and the covering too short: the world looks bulky, but it is empty, void, and waste.

Willard's image of a narrow, ill-covered bed on which man's desire must ultimately be frustrated contrasts dramatically with Taylor's vision of the heart as a "feather-bed . . . with gospel pillows, sheets, and sweet perfumes," where the soul would receive its savior, characterized by Increase Mather in 1718 as "the most desirable one that ever was or that possibly can be."[42] Here was a form of sensual, even sexual, experience about which the godly need harbor no guilty doubts. Erotic images of Jesus Christ provided a wholly positive outlet for physical impulses that Puritans could not welcome unequivocally elsewhere.

Portraying human marriage and sexual relations between husband and wife as secondary and imperfect may strike modern sensibilities as unfortunate but it was not necessarily problematic for godly Puritans. Their earthly relationships, they assured themselves, although inferior to the divine, offered all the joy and comfort that could be expected in this life. When Winthrop wrote in 1620, "My sweet spouse, let us delight in the love of each other as the chief of all earthly comforts," his recognition of the limitations of marriage did not minimize the joy he took in it. Fifty years later, after telling Elizabeth Fitch that his heart was already pledged to Christ, Taylor nonetheless assured her, "the most of it that is allowed to be laid out upon any creature, doth solely, and singly fall to your share."[43] Human and divine marriage were, ideally, symbiotic. John Cotton had rejoiced in his earthly wedding day as "a day of double marriage." Winthrop had hoped that the "blessings" of marriage would enhance his "estimation" of what was to follow, "our better and only ever[−]during happiness in heaven." Yet Winthrop also worried that his love for Margaret might distance him from Christ: "the love of this present world, how it bewitcheth us and steals away our hearts from him who is our only life and felicity."[44]

Winthrop's fears echoed throughout the seventeenth century and beyond. Pastors warned that earthly love was valuable only because it was ordained by God and only insofar as it served him. John Cotton condemned those couples "so transported with affection" that they conceived of "no higher end than marriage itself," and he urged men to think of their relationships with their wives "not for their own ends, but to be better fitted for God's service." In 1718, Cotton Mather determined to be "temperate" in his "conversation" with his wife. "I do not apprehend," he wrote in his diary, "that heaven requires me utterly to lay aside my fondness for my lovely consort." Nevertheless, he continued, "I must always propose a good end and a higher end in it, something that may be an expression or an evidence of my obedience to God."[45]

Like Winthrop, Mather anticipated competition between his mundane and divine commitments. He hoped that his earthly marriage would "exhibit in it a conformity to the good one, and a pattern to all observers," yet he feared "inordinate affection as may grieve the holy spirit of God."[46] On at least two separate occasions, Mather urged his congregants to delay marriage until they had betrothed themselves to Christ. The intent of that injunction, which bore eloquent testimony to Mather's own anxieties, was to secure the believer's primary affections in Christ against all earthly temptations. "How well it would be for thousands of souls," Mather declared, "if they would order it for themselves, never to marry anyone until they are first espoused unto their saviour!"[47]

The double espousal in which Puritans engaged was thus potentially insidious, even destructive. Rivalry, whether implicit or explicit, between human and divine marriages might cast into doubt the wisdom of invoking marital images so frequently. As we have seen, Cotton Mather, one of the prime exponents of such imagery, was clearly disturbed by his sense of the competition between earthly and spiritual affections. Not all Puritans were as assiduous as he in seeking out spiritual contradictions and likely scenarios for crises of conscience, but Mather was certainly not alone in feeling troubled about this issue. Its ramifications extended beyond private concerns and into major social considerations. As pastors increasingly invoked spousal imagery, their consequent emphasis upon the inferiority of human marriage threatened to compromise, at least rhetorically, the very institution that lay at the heart of a well-ordered Puritan society. Aware of this dilemma, ministers were anxious to defend their use of spousal metaphors.

First, they explained, marriage had been ordained by God "through frequent use . . . in the holy scriptures" as the most appropriate of earthly relations through which to understand the union between redeemer and redeemed. Although "carnal similitudes" were inherently "defective" and so must be applied "warily" to "spiritual" phenomena, God's "dressing up of heavenly matter in earthly language, and thus accommodating himself to our capacity," revealed his commitment to communicating effectively with humankind. Marriage was "the figure" that God had chosen to portray his "affection . . . unto his chosen children," and it was by far the least inadequate of the metaphorical options available. In meeting one of their fundamental challenges as pastors, to evoke the nature of union with Christ in all its wonder, ministers could not afford to neglect the rhetorical tool God had placed in their hands, no matter what their reservations.[48]

Puritan pastors also strove to neutralize the possible negative effects of spousal imagery by emphasizing its potential for elevating human marriage. Christ's relationship to the individual believer and also the church as a whole was held up as a model for marital relations. In 1716, as Benjamin Colman urged husbands to give virtuous wives "a singular respect, and the most honourable treatment in the world," he drew his congregation's attention to the example set by Christ the bridegroom:

> The expressions of the love of Christ to his church in the Book of Canticles is the best account how the husband ought to regard her and treat her. . . . As the holy soul, and as the purchased church is fair and lovely in the eyes of God, and dignified by him; so let the deserving wife be esteemed by her happy spouse."

When clerics advised their flocks to think of human marriage as "a lively emblem of what passes between the Lord Jesus Christ and his church," they considered double espousal in terms of the relationship between the Fall and Redemption. In doing so, they offered a means of easing the tension between their exaltation of marriage and continued distrust of carnal relations. Just as Christ's sacrifice eclipsed Adam and Eve's lapse, so the savior's promised espousal with his elect enabled human marriage to rise above its association with the primal couple's sinfulness. Such was the philosophy that underlay John Winthrop's hope that his and Margaret's love would form "into the similitude of the love of Christ and his church." Rather than seeking to transcend his corrupted flesh, Winthrop wanted to resanctify it through a form of typological regimen. Instead of seeing marriage primarily as a corrupt legacy of human history's origins, Winthrop could treat it as a presage of the joys accompanying that history's culmination.[49]

A prospective instead of retrospective view of marriage proved particularly important as divine espousal became more visible in the language of Puritan piety toward the end of the seventeenth century. Laying emphasis upon the emblematic nature of human marriage either precluded fears of rivalry between the two relationships or helped resolve such fears as they arose. It was Cotton Mather who explicated most clearly the value of that perspective for those, including himself, who remained troubled by the tension between spousal imagery and human love, as well as the social imperative to exalt human marriage. Couples who modeled their marriages on that of Christ the second Adam would, he argued, cleanse their relationships of the taint left by the first:

> A marriage carried on with such a regard unto the second Adam in it; what a rare course is herein taken, to abate, and prevent, much of the curse, which every marriage in this world, is likely to be more or less encumbered and embittered withall!

Mather's next remark was particularly revealing:

> What a rare course is taken, that instead of cause to have it said, "It is good that a man should not touch a marriage," it shall still hold good, "It is not good for man to be alone."[50]

Worries about the conflicting demands of human and divine espousal, as well as the "vileness" of the sexual act through which husband and wife consummated their marriage, might, Mather conceded, drive some believers to have second thoughts about their rejection of celibacy. But by elaborating the similarities between the two forms of union in earthy detail, by domesticating the savior, and by seeing human marriage as a "lively emblem" of its divine equivalent, ministers pulled human marriage out of its base beginnings. Furthermore, by describing the saints in familial language, thus imputing tribalism to the invisible as well as visible church, Puritan clerics bolstered their claim that marital relations on earth were complementary, not antagonistic, to those in heaven.

Such strategies forwarded the Puritans' program to rehabilitate human marriage, even as they recognized its contingency in light of greater commitments and prospects. For God to dispense grace through "the heart of a son" was thus a "special providence" for both this world and the next.[51] It offered a resolution of sorts to a potentially crippling struggle between the spirit and the flesh. That resolution was, of course, never complete. The complex dialectic between human and divine espousals, along with the combination of positive and negative sentiments attached to the relationship between husband and wife on earth, illustrates with particular vividness the ambivalence that lay at the heart of Puritan spirituality as the godly sought to negotiate between a comprehensive social vision that centered on the family and their preoccupation with the spiritual family that awaited them in the world beyond. But the dedication of marriage to the second Adam did ensure that the relationship between divine and earthly espousals was largely constructive; it salvaged marriage as the locus of Puritan aspirations.

Historians have recently been struck by another aspect of marital imagery and its implications for religious culture in early New England. Spousal metaphors envisaged all believers, male and female, as the brides of Christ. Men as well as women were to yearn for "the caresses of his love" and prepare their wedding gowns for the nuptial celebration after which their "glorious espousal" would be consummated. Such images provoke intriguing questions about the gendering of roles in early New England culture and the willingness of men to adopt seemingly "feminine" qualities.[52] Mary Maples Dunn, Gerald Moran, and Amanda Porterfield have argued that increasing use of spousal imagery was linked to changes in the sexual composition of church membership as women came to out-number men in most congregations by the late seventeenth century. According to Dunn, bridal images "validated" the transformation of congregations into largely female bodies. Moran argues that the use of spousal language reinforced the skewed sex ratio because "wives could easily identify with marriage and humiliation to Christ in regeneration, while for dominant fathers and husbands, the achievement of true piety demanded an abrupt reversal in roles."[53] Both Dunn and Moran assume, the former implicitly and the latter more explicitly, that many men would have found spousal imagery disconcerting when applied to themselves. However, while it is certainly the case, as Amanda Porterfield has remarked, that "the image of the bride of Christ became increasingly realistic in an empirical, social sense" as the composition of New England congregations altered, to argue for a causal link between membership sex ratios and the use of marital imagery is problematic on two counts.[54]

First, as Margaret Masson and Laurel Thatcher Ulrich have pointed out, the increasing use of spousal language during the 1670s and 1680s coincided not with a decline but a rise in male church membership. Moran has shown convincingly that the long-term trend was toward female majorities, but his own numbers demonstrate that that movement was temporarily reversed during the very period in which clerics multiplied their marital and romantic images. Such imagery, therefore, did not immediately encourage or confirm changes in the sexual composition of church membership.[55] The larger trend did resume during the last decade of the century, so one could argue for a gradual or delayed impact. But there is a second, more significant problem with the attempt to link marital imagery to the feminization of church congregations. That problem concerns the automatic assumption that Puritan men would have felt uncomfortable in the role of submissive bride.

Puritan men who truly understood their theology had no reason to believe that their masculinity would be threatened by their union as brides to Christ. The son of God was to marry not men and women but the souls of men and women. The distinction was important since souls did not adopt the sex of the bodies they inhabited. Ministers generally characterized the soul as either sexual indeterminate or female. Whereas they used the generic masculine to describe human beings non-specifically or collectively, they preferred neutral and feminine pronouns when referring to the soul. "It is now entertained by Christ as his spouse, the marriage completed," declared Willard expectantly, "it is with him at his own home . . . God the Father receives it, with the most inlarged expressions of his divine love to it." "The soul hence gives itself," Shepard explained, "like one espoused to her husband, to the Lord Jesus."[56]

The combination of neutral and feminine signification reflected the two gendered perspectives from which ministers viewed the spiritual realm. On the one hand, biological differences between men and women, although crucial in this world, were irrelevant in discussions of the soul, which was immortal and transcended carnal identity. In that sense, the soul need not be referred to in gendered terms and, indeed, to avoid doing so would underline its transcendence of earthly bounds. On the other hand, "carnal similitudes" involving sexual identity were best able to convey the union of redeemed and redeemer. Thus, the soul could appropriately become feminine when discussing its union to Christ. The soul was represented only rarely as a male entity, even when the human being it inhabited was male.[57]

Even men who were not punctilious about such distinctions would have had little cause for discomfort in assuming a bride-like posture before Christ since this was a role men were trained to adopt in other contexts as well. Social and political order in New England rested just as firmly on male as on female submission to those placed above them. Winthrop equated a citizen's "subjection to authority" with a wife's "subjection to her husband's authority" and that of "the church under the authority of Christ, her king and husband."[58] That last phrase was telling in its equation of spiritual, political, and bridal comportment. The use of graphic spousal imagery to describe relations between savior and saved surely reinforced gender hierarchy within the family, but Christ was much more than a masculine role model for men: they developed a range of social capacities by relating to him as brides as well as emulating him in the role of bridegroom. On the other hand, while men were expected to become bride-like as citizens and Christians, though Christ-like as husbands, women wielded considerable moral and practical authority, albeit informally, both in the household and the larger community. Their very willingness to fulfill expectations of them as obedient wives enabled them to exercise power as "deputy husbands" and church members.[59] A virtuous woman as much as any man had "the image of Christ and God upon her," and on the Day of Judgment, her soul would "be marvellously changed into the likeness of the Lord Jesus Christ himself."[60]

Historians who focus on male hegemony and female subjugation in Puritan New England overlook the complex interplay between power and powerlessness within both Puritan theology and social experience. Believers of whichever gender could become potent only through recognizing their own spiritual impotence and reliance upon their savior: just as Christ became the agent of God's power by serving him, so ministers assured their flocks that the redeemed would become "members of Christ," dedicated to his service and empowered by their regeneration.[61] The word "member" was used in early modern English to denote a penis, as clergymen and their audiences would have been well aware. Indeed, ministers often made use of phallic imagery in their evocations of redemption. Cotton Mather imagined God as "a sacred root," Christ as "a trunk issuing from it," the Holy Spirit as "sap running through it," and the redeemed as "branches thereto belonging." Taylor anticipated that redemption would turn his "sorry quill" into "a golden trumpet." In 1654, John Norton had combined male and female sexual imagery in his description of regeneration:

> if thou beest a sincere member of this body, thou art a growing member
> . . . a full member is an honour to Christ, when you come empty to the
> worship of God but go away full, they shall bring forth fruit.[62]

On the one hand, the regenerate soul came "empty" but went away
"full," grew thereafter, and bore "fruit" to Christ, an image that evoked
impregnation. On the other, Norton's prediction that the believer would
embody "a growing member" and "bring forth fruit" after becoming
aroused by divine worship suggests phallic stimulation and ejaculation.
While the awakened souls of both men and women surrendered themselves to be penetrated and fertilized by their savior, they also became
phallic extensions of Christ. Thus, sexual imagery in clerical discourse
reinforced the polymorphous qualities required of the ideal Christian,
although the repeated use of phallic images to denote spiritual power
reminds us of the limits to gender fluidity within Puritan culture.[63]

Nonetheless, to delimit submissive behavior and humiliation as "feminine" or power and assertiveness as "masculine" is to misrepresent
gender roles in Puritan culture. Laurel Thatcher Ulrich is right to insist
that there was "no such thing as female piety in early New England,"
for the same "qualities" were demanded of both men and women. Although ministers argued that the hazards of childbirth especially inclined
women toward religion, they "stressed the experience of childbirth,
rather than the nature of the childbearer," and so "upheld the spiritual
oneness of the sexes."[64] A new emphasis on women's worth at the end
of the seventeenth century, especially in the sermons of Cotton Mather,
was not accompanied by an identification of sex-related qualities. Distinct views of masculine and feminine personalities would develop during the course of the eighteenth century, but meanwhile images of piety
represented, in Porterfield's words, "the humanity that men and women
held in common."[65] As Benjamin Wadsworth put it, there was "no
difference between men and women" in a spiritual sense: they "equally
need[ed] Christ."[66] The bridal image evoked not femininity as such but
instead a role that both men and women were expected to assume in
various contexts. From that perspective, it was neither surprising nor
problematic that "manhood" in its sex-specific as well as generic sense
should become Christ's "bride."

Just as gender roles in early New England were much more flexible than
has often been assumed, the same can be said of gender identity. Marital
and romantic imagery in Puritan piety did not pose a problem for male

New Englanders because notions of gender were in other respects extremely fluid.[67] Nor did spousal metaphors undermine the Puritan rehabilitation of marriage through their denigration of earthly relations in comparison to those with Christ. In fact, affirming the importance of divine espousal as a model for its human equivalent helped ministers and their flocks to rid marriage of its primal taint through its resanctification in the second Adam. Marital, romantic, and erotic conceptions of Jesus Christ could thus assume a positive and significant role as part of the New England clergy's reinvention of their faith toward the end of the seventeenth century. A more hopeful, albeit also more exclusive, assertion of spiritual life drowned out the threats and forebodings of the jeremiad. That reformulation focused on the prospects of the tribal elect instead of the manifest failings of those who surrounded them. It anticipated in joyous tones the "love raptures" that the saved would experience as they rested at last in the embrace of their divine husband.

The Puritans' commitment to order and their frank hostility toward "disorderly" relations of any kind should not blind us to the permeability and reciprocity that characterized many of the roles and categories through which they made sense of their lives. Just as spiritual assurance and doubt were locked in a symbiotic embrace, anxiety and relief prompting each other in a redemptive cycle of death and rebirth, so the gendering of Puritan culture depended on a series of identities that, although self-consciously structured, were neither rigid nor mutually exclusive. Theirs was a world in which earthly bridegrooms could anticipate eagerly becoming brides in heaven; in which human and divine marriages were to be understood as qualitatively and substantively different yet would flourish largely through each other's example; in which both men and women embraced a polymorphous sexuality through which they would bear "the babe of life" even as they rejoiced in their phallic credentials as "members of Christ"; in which the godly became potent through their very impotence; in which social power and powerlessness were contingent upon each other in everyone. Such was the ambivalent, sometimes ambiguous, world that Puritans constructed for themselves.

NOTES

1. *The Diary of Samuel Sewall,* ed. M. Halsey Thomas, 2 vols. (New York: Farrar, Straus and Giroux, 1973), 2:864, 882.

2. Increase Mather, *Practical Truths Plainly Delivered* (Boston, 1718), pp. 59–60.

3. Cotton Mather, *Diary,* ed. Worthington C. Ford, 2 vols. (1911; reprinted, New York: Ungar, 1957), 2:540; *A Glorious Espousal* (Boston, 1719).

4. David D. Hall, *Worlds of Wonder, Days of Judgment: Popular Religious Belief in Early New England* (New York: Knopf, 1989), p. 15.

5. Amanda Porterfield, *Female Piety in Puritan New England: The Emergence of Religious Humanism* (New York: Oxford University Press, 1992), chap. 1. See also E. Ann Matter, *The Voice of My Beloved: The Song of Songs in Western Medieval Christianity* (Philadelphia: University of Pennsylvania Press, 1990).

6. See Carol Karlsen, *The Devil in the Shape of a Woman: Witchcraft in Colonial New England* (New York: W. W. Norton, 1987), pp. 160–66; and Larzer Ziff, *Puritanism in America: New Culture in a New World* (New York: Viking, 1973), p. 14. The family would also provide a spiritually nurturing environment in which the young could identify their "calling" within godly society. It served, furthermore, as a model of hierarchical relations in society as a whole, so that the careful articulation of domestic relations would train children to perform effectively in the larger world as adults.

7. Samuel Willard, *A Complete Body of Divinity* (Boston, 1726), pp. 609, 669.

8. See Edmund Morgan, "The Puritans and Sex," *New England Quarterly* 15 (1942): 591–93, and *The Puritan Family: Religion and Domestic Relations in Seventeenth-Century New England* (1944; reprinted, New York: Harper and Row, 1966), p. 41.

9. *The Life and Letters of John Winthrop,* ed. Robert C. Winthrop, 2 vols. (Boston, 1864–67), 1:136, 193.

10. See Emory Elliott, *Power and the Pulpit in Puritan New England* (Princeton, N.J.: Princeton University Press, 1975), chap. 3; Patricia Caldwell, *The Puritan Conversion Narrative: The Beginnings of American Expression* (New York: Cambridge University Press, 1983), chap. 3; and David Cressy, *Coming Over: Migration and Communication between England and New England in the Seventeenth Century* (New York: Cambridge University Press, 1987), chap. 8.

11. *God's Plot: The Paradoxes of Puritan Piety, Being the Autobiography and Journal of Thomas Shepard,* ed. Michael McGiffert (Amherst: University of Massachusetts Press, 1972), p. 98; and Michael Wigglesworth, "Diary," ed. Edmund Morgan, in *Transactions of the Colonial Society of Massachu-*

setts, vol. 35 (Boston, 1946), pp. 332, 401; see also pp. 332–33, 336, 344, 425–26.

12. In two case studies, Porterfield shows that Thomas Hooker and Thomas Shepard "most often used the analogy between Christian life and wifely devotion in negative terms, defining sin against God in terms of the failure of wifely affection." John Cotton's use of spousal imagery was much more positive and seductive, but he was atypical of his generation in that regard (*Female Piety in Puritan New England,* pp. 55, 66–79).

13. Elliott, *Power and the Pulpit,* pp. 13–14, 175.

14. The printing explosion toward the end of the century played a role in increasing the number of references to espousal, but they grew proportionately more prominent as well.

15. As Elliott has pointed out, Samuel Willard's works "best demonstrate the message of assurance and hope that emerged from the conflicts and tension of the difficult transition years." Yet "the real virtuoso of the new themes and language of the sermons of the last decades of the century was the vigorous young minister Cotton Mather" (*Power and the Pulpit,* pp. 158, 186). Not surprisingly, their sermons explore spousal imagery to a greater degree than their colleagues'.

16. Cotton Mather, *Ornaments for the Daughters of Zion* (Cambridge, 1692), p. 64; *A Glorious Espousal,* p. 12; *A Union with the Son of God by Faith* (Boston, 1692), pp. 13–15; *The Mystical Marriage* (Boston, 1728), p. 6.

17. Joshua Moodey, *A Practical Discourse Concerning the Choice Benefit of Communion with God in His House* (Boston, 1685), pp. 24–25.

18. Cotton Mather, *A Glorious Espousal,* pp. 14–20.

19. Willard, *A Complete Body of Divinity,* p. 489. See also Cotton Mather, *Bethiah* (Boston, 1722), p. 11.

20. Cotton Mather, *Ornaments for the Daughters of Zion,* pp. 64–65; *A Union with the Son of God by Faith,* pp. 15, 21; Willard, *A Complete Body of Divinity,* pp. 488, 557. See also Increase Mather, *Practical Truths,* pp. 59–60.

21. Cotton Mather, *The Mystical Marriage,* pp. 13, 1, and *Ornaments for the Daughters of Zion,* p. 69; Edward Taylor, *Treatise Concerning the Lord's Supper,* ed. Norman S. Grabo (East Lansing: Michigan State University Press, 1966), p. 185; Increase Mather, *Practical Truths,* p. 60.

22. Cotton Mather, *A Glorious Espousal,* pp. 20 (see also *Bethiah,* p. 23), 9; Willard, *A Complete Body of Divinity,* p. 557.

23. Willard, *Treatise Concerning the Lord's Supper,* p. 17. See also Moodey, *A Practical Discourse,* pp. 24–25. Ministers, like Solomon Stoddard, who were eager to broaden access to the Lord's Supper, accordingly refused to equate it with a wedding feast since doing so would discourage from participation those less confident of their betrothal. See, e.g., Stoddard, *An Appeal to the Learned* (Boston, 1709), pp. 3–5.

24. Edward Taylor, "God's Determinations," *The Poems of Edward Taylor,* ed. Donald E. Stanford (New Haven: Yale University Press, 1960), p. 453; Willard, *A Complete Body of Divinity,* pp. 534, 556; Cotton Mather, *Bethiah,* p. 30.

25. *The Poems of Michael Wigglesworth,* ed. Ronald A. Bosco (New York: University Press of America, 1989), pp. 60, 229; Cotton Mather, *Ornaments for the Daughters of Zion,* p. 99; John Davenport, *The Saint's Anchor-Hold* (London, 1682), p. 28. To be sure, the saints would not engage in "conjugal union" with each other. Such relations would "cease and be useless" because the saints now found themselves in a more fulfilling "union" with Christ. (See Willard, *A Complete Body of Divinity,* p. 546.)

26. Taylor, *Treatise Concerning the Lord's Supper,* pp. 170–71. Such language could also be applied to the diabolical community: the confession of faith that Taylor penned for his flock spoke of leaving "Satan's family" before joining Christ's "own household." (See *The Unpublished Writings of Edward Taylor,* ed. Thomas M. and Virginia L. Davis, 3 vols. [Boston: Twayne, 1981], 1: 51.)

27. Morgan, *The Puritan Family,* p. 173.

28. Willard, *A Complete Body of Divinity,* pp. 488, 489.

29. Taylor, "Preparatory Meditations," in *Poems,* p. 47.

30. Willard, *A Complete Body of Divinity,* p. 879.

31. John Cotton, who differed from most of his first-generation colleagues in using marital imagery primarily to seduce rather than to chastise, had invited his audience in 1651 to contemplate redemption in sexual terms: "Have you a strong and hearty desire to meet him in the bed of loves, whenever you come to the congregation, and desire you to have the seeds of his grace shed abroad in your hearts, and bring forth the fruits of grace to him[?]" (*Christ the Fountain of Life* [London, 1651], pp. 36–37).

32. Willard, *Some Brief Sacramental Meditations* (Boston, 1711), p. 4; Cotton Mather, *Ornaments for the Daughters of Zion,* p. 68; Willard, *A Complete Body of Divinity,* p. 821; Thomas Foxcroft, *A Funeral Sermon Occasioned by Several Mournful Deaths* (Boston, 1722), p. 27. The brides of Christ, declared Willard in a similar vein, were "made to partake in his sap and virtue, and thereby receive grace from him" (*A Complete Body of Divinity,* pp. 849–50).

33. Cotton Mather, *A Glorious Espousal,* p. 23, *Bethiah,* pp. 42, 46, *A Union with the Son of God by Faith,* p. 17, *Divine Afflations* (New London, 1722), p. 9, and *Diary,* 1:222; Taylor, *Treatise Concerning the Lord's Supper,* p. 210; Willard, *A Complete Body of Divinity,* p. 459.

34. Willard, *A Complete Body of Divinity,* p. 536; Cotton Mather, *Diary,* 1:98, 426, 471, 483.

35. Taylor, "Preparatory Meditations," pp. 212, 295, and "God's Determinations," p. 414.

36. Taylor, "Preparatory Meditations," pp. 228 (see also p. 57), 362–63, 248, 142 (see also pp. 176, 292, and 340).

37. Taylor, "Preparatory Meditations," pp. 230, 164, 259, 295, and "God's Determinations," p. 448. John Winthrop had invoked Christ in 1630 as "my love, my dove, my undefiled" and prayed that he might be "possesse[d]" by his savior in "the love of marriage," but his language lacked the overtly erotic tone of Taylor's poetry and other late seventeenth-century writings (*Life and Letters,* 1:397).

38. Willard, *A Complete Body of Divinity,* p. 7.

39. Winthrop, *Life and Letters,* 1:138; Taylor, *Unpublished Writings,* 3:37.

40. Cotton Mather, *Diary,* 2:118. See Kathleen Verduin, " 'Our Cursed Natures': Sexuality and the Puritan Conscience," *New England Quarterly* 56 (1983): 220–37.

41. Cotton Mather, *Diary,* 1:270, 302, 304, 551, and 2:111, 119, 523; and various references throughout the diaries of Increase Mather, Joseph Sewall, and Peter Thacher, all located at the Massachusetts Historical Society, Boston. See also Willard, *A Complete Body of Divinity,* pp. 567, 755, 756, 759, 760, 764, 778, 779, 811, 825, 912.

42. Willard, *A Complete Body of Divinity,* p. 299; Cotton Mather, *Diary,* 2:118; Taylor, "Preparatory Meditations," pp. 199 (see also p. 139: "There is no sin can touch this lovely love. /It's holy, with a perfect holiness"), 8; Increase Mather, *Practical Truths,* p. 59. John Cotton had been confident that Christ's allure could rescue unmarried young men from illicit desires. He urged those who were "troubled with lust after women" to "turn the strength of [their] affection to another, that is white and ruddy, the fairest of ten thousand." Once they realized Christ's love for them, they would "find little content in any other thing besides" (*A Practical Commentary* [London, 1658], p. 131).

43. Winthrop, *Life and Letters,* 1:161 (see also pp. 135, 159, 193, 290, 297); Taylor, *Unpublished Writings,* 3:37.

44. Cotton Mather, *Magnalia Christi Americana,* ed. Thomas Robbins, 2 vols. (1852; reprinted, New York: Russell & Russell, 1967), 1:258; Winthrop, *Life and Letters,* 1:159, 193.

45. John Cotton, *A Practical Commentary,* pp. 126, 200; Cotton Mather, *Diary,* 2:523.

46. Cotton Mather, *Diary,* 2:727. See also Wigglesworth, "Diary," pp. 390–91.

47. Cotton Mather, *A Glorious Espousal,* pp. 37–38, and *Bethiah,* p. 24.

48. Willard, *A Complete Body of Divinity,* 429–30, and *Heavenly Merchandize* (Boston, 1686), p. 2; Cotton Mather, *A Glorious Espousal,* p. 3. One of the most basic defects in the metaphor, Cotton Mather pointed out, was that "the nearest conjugal union" was "dissolved by death, whereas our union with our Lord is everlastingly indissoluble" (*Union with the Son of God by Faith,* p. 22).

Mather also emphasized that whereas an earthly husband was unlikely to forgive and forget repeated "violations of the covenant," Christ was "willing to marry a soul that ha[d] been fearfully vitiated and prostituted" (*Ornaments for the Daughters of Zion*, pp. 67–68, and *A Glorious Espousal*, p. 4). Yet marriage was, insisted Willard, an appropriate metaphor, not least because it was "a rational union" and "founded in mutual consent, from whence proceeds that bond by which they are tyed one to the other inseparably" (*A Complete Body of Divinity*, p. 430).

49. Benjamin Colman, *The Honour and Happiness of the Virtuous Woman* (Boston, 1716), p. 26; Cotton Mather, *The Mystical Marriage*, p. 15; Winthrop, *Life and Letters*, 1:161.

50. Cotton Mather, *A Glorious Espousal*, p. 46.

51. Samuel Willard, *The Child's Portion* (Boston, 1684), p. 11.

52. The challenge to gender identity posed by scriptural images of Christ as a bridegroom has been met in various ways by different Christian cultures. In the high Middle Ages, for example, it was not unusual for the devout to address Jesus as a mother and to use feminine imagery in their descriptions of Christ and God. (See Caroline Walker Bynum, *Jesus as Mother: Studies in the Spirituality of the High Middle Ages* [Berkeley: University of California Press, 1982], pp. 110–69.)

53. Mary Maples Dunn, "Saints and Sisters: Congregational and Quaker Women in the Early Colonial Period," in *Women in American Religion*, ed. Janet Wilson James (Philadelphia: University of Pennsylvania Press, 1980), p. 593; Gerald F. Moran, " 'Sisters' in Christ: Women and the Church in Seventeenth-Century New England," also in *Women in American Religion*, p. 61. See also Porterfield, *Female Piety in Puritan New England*, p. 7.

54. Porterfield, *Female Piety in Puritan New England*, p. 8. Possible causes for the sex ratio shift are discussed by Moran, " 'Sisters' in Christ," pp. 57–64; Dunn, "Saints and Sisters," pp. 592–93; and Margaret W. Masson, "The Typology of the Female as a Model for the Regenerate: Puritan Preaching, 1690–1730," *Signs* 2 (1976): 314–15.

55. Masson, "The Typology of the Female," p. 315; Laurel Thatcher Ulrich, " 'Vertuous Women Found': New England Ministerial Literature, 1668–1735," in *Women in American Religion*, p. 84 n. 65; Moran, " 'Sister's in Christ," p. 51, fig. 1.

Of course I do not deny that marital imagery would have been appealing to women, but I am not convinced that it was crucial in attracting them or deterring males from church membership. Laurel Thatcher Ulrich's position that "church membership was one of the few public distinctions available to women" and that religious involvement gave women a measure of power seems to me a much more promising explanation of why women of the second and third generations flocked to church in disproportionate numbers. (See Ulrich's *Good Wives: Image and Reality in the Lives of Women in Northern New England, 1650–1750* [New York: Oxford University Press, 1980], pp. 216–26.) One would not expect first-generation settlers to fit this pattern, since so many of the men as well as women migrated specifically to become part of a covenanted community.

56. Willard, *A Complete Body of Divinity,* p. 534; Thomas Shepard, *Works,* ed. John A. Albro, 3 vols. (Boston, 1853), 2:31. Jonathan Mitchell referred to the soul as "it" repeatedly in his "Continuation of Sermons upon ye Body of Divinity" (see, e.g., 213: 7 Feb 1657, Massachusetts Historical Society). For discussion of the soul as a female entity, see Elizabeth Reis, "Satan's Familiars: Sinners, Witches, and Conflicting Covenants in Early New England" (Ph.D. diss., University of California, Berkeley, 1991), chap. 3. Reis argues that ministers presented the soul as a consistently female entity so that the souls of men as well as a women could engage in what she describes as "heterosexual intercourse" with Christ.

57. For an exception, see Willard, *A Complete Body of Divinity,* p. 533.

58. John Winthrop, *The History of New England from 1630 to 1649,* ed. James Savage, 2 vols. (Boston, 1825–26), 2: 281.

59. See Ulrich, *Good Wives,* chap. 2; Porterfield, *Female Piety in Puritan New England,* chap. 3. This is not to deny that female power was much more circumscribed and conditional than was male authority.

60. Cotton Mather, *Ornaments for the Daughters of Zion,* pp. 39, 42.

61. See, e.g., Willard, *A Complete Body of Divinity,* pp. 543–47.

62. Cotton Mather, *Union with the Son of God by Faith,* p. 5; Taylor, "Preparatory Meditations," p. 175; Jonathan Mitchell, "Notes on Sermons by John Norton," 28 December 1654, Massachusetts Historical Society. Similarly, when Increase Mather, Joseph Sewall, and Peter Thacher referred in their diaries to being "enlarged" in spiritual exercise, they invoked the phallic arousal provoked by Christ's presence as well as the spiritual pregnancy that would end their "barrenness" and "unfruitfulness."

63. Just as the redeemed exhibited both masculine and feminine sexual qualities, so God the Father sometimes became a maternal and reproductive figure in clerical writings. Willard referred to "the womb of providence" and spoke of the world as "a sucking infant depending on the breasts of divine providence" (*A Complete Body of Divinity,* pp. 131, 145). See also Shepard, *The Sincere Convert* (London, 1664), p. 119. For an extended discussion of maternal imagery in Puritan literature, see David Leverenz. *The Language of Puritan Feeling: An Exploration in Literature, Psychology, and Social History* (New Brunswick, N.J.: Rutgers University Press, 1980).

64. Ulrich, " 'Vertuous Women Found,' " pp. 75, 79. See also Masson, "The Typology of the Female," pp. 312–13, and Emory Elliott, "The Development of the Puritan Funeral Sermon and Elegy: 1660–1750," *Early American Literature* 15 (1980): 154–55.

65. Porterfield, *Female Piety in Puritan New England,* p. 156. See also
p. 153; Lonna M. Malmsheimer, "Daughters of Zion: New England Roots of
American Feminism,"*New England Quarterly* 50 (1977): 491; and Ulrich,
" 'Vertuous Women Found,' " p. 87.

For Porterfield to characterize Puritan piety as "female" strikes me as contradictory since she recognizes that that "piety functioned similarly for men and
women" (*Female Piety in Puritan New England,* p. 7). Masson's claim that
"men were expected to play a female role in conversion" is troublesome for the
same reason; she herself argues that there were no "fixed or mutually exclusive"
sex roles among New Englanders ("The Typology of the Female," p. 305).

Philip Greven argues that male believers, in submitting to God, "had to
subdue those parts of their being that seemed to be 'masculine' and to enhance
those aspects of their being that seemed to be 'feminine,' " Greven identifies "a
persistent inner conflict" within men between "masculine and feminine impulses." But it is not clear that Puritans saw these "impulses" as contradictory
or even that they identified them specifically as "masculine" and "feminine"
(Philip Greven, *The Protestant Temperament: Patterns of Child-Rearing, Religious Experience, and the Self in Early America* [Chicago: University of Chicago
Press, 1977], pp. 125–26).

66. Benjamin Wadsworth, *Unchast[e] Practices Procure Divine Judgments*
(Boston, 1716), pp. 5–6.

67. Walter Hughes offers a deconstructive interpretation of references to
union with Christ in " 'Meat out of the Eater': Panic and Desire in American
Puritan Poetry," in *Engendering Men: The Question of Male Feminist Criticism,*
ed. Joseph A. Boone and Michael Cadden (New York: Routledge, 1990),
pp. 102–21. Making use of contemporary theoretical frameworks that explore
the relationship between language and the subconscious, Hughes argues that a
"figurative homosexuality within the religious lives of Puritan males" provoked
a "homosexual panic" that surfaces in the writings of Michael Wigglesworth
and Edward Taylor (pp. 103, 107). I would agree that such expressions offered
some resolution to repressed and guilt-ridden sexual desires, although I am not
convinced that the desires in question were specifically homosexual. The polymorphous gendering described above would have made it possible for godly men
as well as women to adopt a potent male figure as a totem without any sense of
its being inappropriate. This flexibility, it should be emphasized, did not extend
to actual sex between men (or between women), for a discussion of which see
my " 'The Cry of Sodom': Discourse, Intercourse, and Desire in Colonial New
England," *William and Mary Quarterly* 52 (April 1995): 259–86.

Chapter Three

A Marriage "Well-Ordered"
Love, Power, and Partnership in Colonial New England

Lisa Wilson

Benjamin Wadsworth, in his 1712 sermon *The Well-Ordered Family*, concluded "the Husband is ever to be esteem'd the Superior, the Head, and to be reverenc'd and obey'd as such."[1] So powerful are such declarations to modern sensibilities that other, equally common colonial New England representations of marriage as a partnership seem impossibly hypocritical. Men who recorded their feelings, however, felt that female subordination and affection were essential and complementary parts of a successful marriage.[2] In both the seventeenth and eighteenth centuries, a husband was part of an interdependent family system that required mutual support to function successfully.[3] Cooperation, not simply coercion, kept a family "well-ordered." Although the words came more freely by the end of the colonial period, the tender language of love marked the writings of men in both centuries.[4] For these men, maintaining the delicate balance between household head and loving husband was the key to domestic bliss as well as social acceptance.

Partnership in marriage was both an ideal and a reality in colonial New England. This is not to suggest that men and women were equal. Rather, both had a stake in their household and their children. Often their daily routines and duties were different, but both worked toward common goals. Men counted on their wives not only to handle their own responsibilities, but to assist the men in their duties if needed.[5] In a happy union, the mutual support of marriage and the well being of the family were central.

John Winthrop, like many husbands, described his third wife, Margaret, as his "yokefellowe."[6] G. Selleck Silliman and his wife, Mary, referred to each other in their correspondence as "dear partner."[7] In marriage a man entered a partnership that provided support for both husband and wife. In describing his vision of marital bliss to his betrothed, Silliman pictured them passing "through all the Scenes of this Life mutually supporting, blessing & assisting Each other in the Ways of Duty."[8] On the eve of his marriage, Minister John Walley, of Ipswich and later Bolton, Massachusetts, hoped that he and his wife "might be Helpers to each other."[9] Together, husband and wife shared the joys and sorrows of life. William Dawes, in defending his new wife to his doubting friend, Stephen Salisbury of Worcester, declared that with her he could "Share Equily in trouble & Afliction As Well As in Joy & prosperty both is Equall."[10]

Walley spoke of his approaching marriage to his "dear Friend" in 1748.[11] Cotton Mather lamented the loss of his wife in 1713, "My dear, dear, dear Friend."[12] The mother of Mary Silliman stayed with her daughter while her "best Friend" remained in the army during the Revolution.[13] Like friendly companions, husband and wife chatted with one another, supported each other, and asked each other's advice.

The newly married Eliphalet Pearson wrote to his "friend" as he struggled to get his home ready for her arrival.

> You will excuse my just hinting at, the happiness your friend would enjoy in the company & converse of his other *Self*. However, if you should, upon a full view of all reasons & circumstances, think it expedient to come next week, I shall readily acquiesce in your opinion. I never wished so much to see my friend. Shall have many matters to communicate, on which I shall wish for your advice.[14]

Silliman, a Fairfield, Connecticut, lawyer and Revolutionary general, consulted his best friend often about decisions great and small. Because of economic difficulties brought on by his imprisonment during the Revolutionary War, he contemplated leaving public life.

> What shall I do my Love?—My late expensive Absence has cost me a great Deal of Mony,—should I again fall into the Enemy's Hands it would hurt me irreparably almost,—To reduce myself to a private Character would be my best Means of Safety, as the Enemy would make no Efforts after a Private,—[section deleted], were it not for the Advice of some great Characters, and for Fear that the People of my own County would be disgusted at it, I should most certainly do this,—What shall I do My

Dearest? I wish I had Your Advice,—I am at a great Loss how to conduct.[15]

Deep friendship characterized these marriages. Tapping Reeve, founder of Litchfield Law School, wrote to his "lovely Sally" about his "Pleasure of reflecting that I have one friend in you that will be ever an unshaken friend."[16] A man could gain a rare kind of friend in a successful marriage, one whose faithfulness and loyalty surpassed all others.

Winthrop wrote to his wife while waiting for the *Arabella* to set sail for New England. He began, "My Love, My Joy, My Faithful One." He also christened her "dear heart," "my Most Sweet Heart," and "My Sweet Wife."[17] Likewise, a few months after signing the Declaration of Independence, William Williams of Lebanon, Connecticut, member of the Continental Congress, addressed his wife, Mary, as "my Dear Love" and "my dear Child."[18] Reeve called his "lovely Sally" "my Sweet girl" and "innocent chicken."[19] Silliman, in a letter to his father-in-law with news of his homecoming from the army, sent his love "to that Dear, Beloved Woman, whose uniformly endearing & Vertuous Conduct, deserves all the Tenderness that can possess a human Heart."[20]

These men, despite the patriarchal realities of New England society, loved their wives with great intensity.[21] Williams assured his wife Mary that he loved her as his "own soul."[22] Similarly, Winthrop addressed one of his loving letters to "Mine Own Sweet Self" and often referred to his wife, Margaret, as "more dear to me than all earthly things."[23] He read and reread his wife's letters aboard the *Arabella*. "I am never satisfied with reading, nor can read them without tears; but whether they proceed from joy, sorrow, or desire, or from that consent of affection, which I always hold with thee, I cannot conceive."[24] Walley thanked God before his wedding in 1748 "that I have such abundant Reason to think that we have a sincere & fervent Love to each other."[25] Soon after his marriage, Mather Byles confided to his father: "I enjoy all that full Satisfaction, which results from the tendrest Connexion of humane Life." He claimed to have "no romantic Ideas of visionary, unattainable Bliss: I really possess much more than I thought possible."[26]

Husbands also freely wrote of their passion. The bed was a private place where a couple shared warmth, quiet conversation, and lovemaking. William Henshaw wrote to his wife, Phebe, during his sojourn in the Continental Army, "these Cold Nights I am Sensible of the want of a Bed fellow, I know not how long it will be before I enjoy the satisfaction of having you by my side."[27] Benjamin Bangs, a Harwich, Massachusetts, trader, noted in his diary that his wife tended her sick mother all night with the sad notation, "I sleep alone."[28] Reeve cautioned his beloved Sally to "not abuse my sweet Lips with your savage little teeth."[29] Winthrop often ended his letters to Margaret with phrases like "I kisse my sweet wife," "kiss me my sweet wife," or "with many kisses and embraces."[30] Finally, Silliman assured his lonesome wife that her passionate letters did not make her "a fond Hussey." He thanked her for "being so particular in your Letters the more prolix the better; are You not a married Woman my Dearest, may You not delight your Husband with saying to him just what you please?"[31]

Men spoke most eloquently and passionately about their love for their wives on their wedding anniversaries, at the birth of a child, and when separated by the exigencies of war. An anniversary prompted a tender husband to thank God for his good fortune. When the fear and joy of childbirth loomed, a man again examined his heart. When war threatened his life, he recorded his most intimate thoughts about husbandly love and duty. These events made a man take pause and describe his deepest feelings.

Ezra Stiles, for example, reminisced in his diary in 1775: "This day 1757 I and my Wife were married. She has been a great Blessing to me; may the blessed God continue her a Blessing." The next entry in Stiles's diary acknowledged, "My wife very ill."[32] A husband marked an anniversary when the happiness of his marriage day contrasted with the less happy present. John Tudor observed in 1748: "This day we have been Marred 16 Years, and by the goodness of God to our Famaly and Us, we have not had one Death in it til Yesterday Died our Negro Man Named Town."[33] Although focusing on God's mercy, Tudor feared the separation that death brought. Samuel Sewall recorded in 1711: "This being my Marriage-day, and having now liv'd in a married Estate Five and Thirty years," celebrated the event by retreating into his "Closet" for "Meditation and Prayer" and later attending a friend's funeral. The previous week he had lamented the recent deaths of "ancient Friends."[34] His own successful life and marriage made his anniversary a time of solemn thankfulness. The unfortunate Cotton Mather marked his anniversary with the sorrow of impending loss: "When I had been married unto her just sixteen Years, (and as near as I can recollect, on that very Week, sixteen Years, that I was married unto her) God began to take her from me."[35] His wife languished and later died from the complications of a miscarriage.

When husband and wife were apart on an anniversary, written expressions of love replaced private conversation. In September 1746, Ebenezer Parkman lamented the "Foul Weather" and the absence of his wife. Visiting her parents, she left him "dull without my Dear Consort." He reminisced,

> But how Ardent and United were we this Day Nine Year ago! when our Nuptials were Celebrated at Mr. Pierpoints at Boston. The Lord has pleas'd to overlook the many miscarriages and Defects which we have been chargeable with since, especially my own! and make us Mutually Blessings, and Helps to the Kin of God! O how soon the Time will come when there will be neither marrying nor giving in Marriage, but the Saints shall be as the Angels of God![36]

Silliman also found himself away from home on his wedding anniversary. He wrote to his disappointed wife:

> I am sorry to inform You, that I have no Prospect of keeping our happy Anniversary with You,—I hope You will have a Pleasure in observing it, in the Company of our Dear Sons, & Friends that I expect will be with You Each of whom I hope will think it an Anniversary that deserves Commemoration. My Love & Compliments to them respectively,—I regret the Occasion that keeps me from my Dearest at such a Time,—A Time ever to be observed by me with Delight & Pleasure.[37]

An anniversary was properly shared and celebrated together. Separation left many a disappointed husband to record his private feelings alone.

Among the fortunate few, Tudor enjoyed his "beloved Wife of my Youth" for fifty years. On his anniversary in 1782, he recorded in his diary that "we have lived the whole time very comfortably and at this Day are so." He marked the dear legacies of their long life together: "In our Youthfull Days had Six Children, 3 Sons and 3 Daughters, but our two Eldest Sons died at Sea." His surviving children provided him with "12 Grandsons and 4 Granddaughters, but we have lost by Death 6 Grandsons" and one granddaughter. In fifty years this loving couple had "never, in all that Time, been absent from each other more than 5 Weeks at one time." They marked the day with "an Entertainment for our Children, and their Children, and a lovely Sight and Day we had of it."[38]

Childbirth provided a husband with a fearful reminder of his love for his wife.[39] A man remained strangely removed from the stage of this human drama, although his risk of loss was great. Childbirth was ultimately a female-centered experience; on most occasions, a woman had her friends and midwife, not her husband, by her side.[40] The husband waited anxiously, often close by, listening to his wife's groans, awaiting the outcome. Men, although absent from the actual event, knew about pregnancy, childbirth, and its complications. Left on the periphery, however, a husband felt fragile.

A common hope expressed by both men and women was that a pregnant woman would become a "Living mother of a Living Child."[41] Michael Wigglesworth received the news of his daughter's birth after his wife's thirty hours of hard labor. "After about midnight he [the Lord] sent me the glad tidings of a daughter that an the mother both living."[42] Ebenezer Parkman recorded in his diary that "About 7 o'Clock a.m. a Fourth living Son was born, and my wife liv'd through it and becomes Comfortable through the tender Mercy and Goodness of God."[43]

Women appreciated only too well that childbirth meant potential death. Husbands also feared a wife's death, dreading the possible loss of their dearly beloved. Benjamin Bangs lay in bed with his wife in the spring of 1760. Husband and wife shared the same fears, and both had trouble sleeping.

> [M]y Dearest friend is much Concern'd being in and near a time of Dificulty & Dreamd a Dream that troubl'd Her much I put it off Slightly for fear of Disheartning Her but Directly upon it Dream'd much ye Same my Self of Being Bereft of Her & Seeing my Little motherless Children about me which when I awoke was Cutting to think of.[44]

Many husbands coordinated the assemblage of birth assistants. When Parkman's wife went into labor, he went to get the midwife and the women who would attend her. Confronted with a snowstorm on his mission to "fetch Granny Forbush," the midwife, he found the snow so deep that it was "extraordinary difficult passing." When he found himself floundering in front of a neighbors' house, he enlisted the aid of two men of the house who "rode before me, by which means I succeeded." Local men brought their wives and a load of wood to help with the snowbound birth.[45] Parkman, at another birth, summoned the midwife and other women when his wife "call'd Me up by her extreme pains prevailing upon her and changing into signs of Travail." The women came and stayed "all Day and Night." The following morning "the Women Scattered away to their several Homes" except the midwife, who stayed behind. Late that night he was again "call'd . . . with great earnestness to gather some women together." He "ran on foot," through bitter weather, to assemble the women.[46] Peter Thatcher realized his wife "was very ill" and sent a neighbor for the midwife. The midwife was attending another birth, and it took two hours for her to arrive. When "shee came shee sent for ye women."[47] The young Samuel Sewall awoke at two in the morning and "perceived my wife ill." He lit a candle and raked the fire. At five, when his in-laws awoke, he informed his mother-in-law of his wife's condition. She "bad[e] me call the Midwife."[48]

With the women assembled, the husband waited and prayed. As Parkman put it, "I resign my Dear Spouse to the infinite Compassions, allsufficiency and soverign pleasure of God and under God to the good Women that are with her, waiting Humbly the Event."[49] Although peripheral, he remained aware of the delivery's progress. The overly sympathetic Michael Wigglesworth suffered mightily:

> The nearnes of my bed to hers made me hear all the nois. her pangs pained my heart, broke my sleep the most off that night, I lay sighing, sweating, praying, almost fainting through wearines before morning. The next day. the spleen much enfeebled me, and setting in with grief took away my strength, my heart was smitten within me, and as sleep departed from myne eyes so my stomack abhorred meat. I was brought very low and knew not how to pass away another night; For so long as my love lay crying I lay sweating, and groaning.

This was their first child. If childbirth was so painful he pondered, "then how dreadful are the pangs of eternal death."[50]

Sewall stayed with his mother-in-law in the kitchen during one birthing. She had joined his male vigil because "my wife was in great and more than ordinary Extremity, so that she was not able to endure the Chamber."[51] At a previous birth, Sewall and his father-in-law waited in the "great Hall," where they "heard the child cry."[52] The ever-industrious Cotton Mather tried to sleep through his wife's labor so that he could attend to his sabbath business the next day. He awoke "with a Concern upon my Spirit" and felt compelled to pray in his study. "While my Faith was pleading, that the Saviour *who was born of a Woman*, would send His good Angel to releeve my Consort, the People ran to my Study-door with Tidings, *that a Son was born unto mee*."[53]

With the child born, the women settled down to a repast organized by the grateful husband. Sewall feasted his wife's attendants with "rost

Beef and minc'd Pyes, good Cheese and Tarts."[54] The women assisting Parkman's wife finished eating before dark "tho some of them tarry'd in the Evening."[55] Slowly, the women went home either by foot or by horse. Sewall "Went home with the Midwife about 2 o'clock, carrying her Stool, whoes parts were included in a Bagg. Met with the Watch at Mr. Rocks Brew house, who bad us stand, enquired what we were. I told the Woman's occupation, so they bad God bless our labours, and let us pass."[56]

Even for a couple blessed with a strong union, conflicts proved disruptive. Arguments followed gender specific patterns. The worst that a disgruntled wife could do was to challenge a man's authority as family head. If he was cuckolded or beaten, the husband's mental anguish was severe because a wife took aim at his most valued commodity, his reputation. The sullying of his good name would lead to social humiliation. His livelihood, so dependent on personal networks, suffered if an ugly familial conflict became public.[57] When men were challenged, they turned to the familiar rhetoric of male authority. Rather than suffer such humiliation, they tried to reassert their right to rule.

For men, an ideal wife did not disturb the peace of a household. Mather Byles informed his spinster sister, Mary, about the "Peace & Tranquility" of his new wife and home. If only she could be so happy in her marriage, "That your Husband may say of you, as I can of your Sister *Byles,* that he never saw your Brows wrinkled into a disagreeable Frown, or your Lips polluted by a peevish Syllable."[58] Silliman listed the wonderful qualities of his first wife to the father of his second. Among her valued gifts was "a most happy, mild & calm Temper." With such a disposition "she never gave her Husband any Uneasiness by any Excess of her own Temper." He wanted to assure his new father-in-law that he had been happily married and that his new wife, miraculously, compensated him for his loss.[59] On recalling the many merits of his recently deceased wife, Thomas Clap remembered that not "so much as Short Word ever pass between us upon any Occasion whatsoever." If they disagreed "about any lesser matters, we used to Discourse upon it with a Perfect Calmness & Pleasancy."[60] Any expression of temper in a woman was a sign of trouble, and men, if Clap is any indication, diligently sought to avoid confrontation.

An angry wife, however, challenged a husband's right to rule. John Adams of Braintree, Massachusetts, Revolutionary leader and future president of the United States, recorded a "conjugal Spat" between his father and mother which caused such a ruckus that he was forced to leave the room and take "up Tully [Marcus Tullius Cicero, Roman statesman and author] to compose myself." The point of contention was the boarding of a young girl, Judah, in the household. The real issue was that John Adams the elder had made a commitment that increased Susanna Adams's workload but brought little to the family coffers. After heated discussion "My P[apa]. continued cool and pleasant a good while, but had his Temper roused at last, tho he uttered not a rash Word, but resolutely asserted his Right to govern." Mrs. Adams's response was less then deferential.

> My Mamma was determined to know what my P. charged a Week for the Girls Board. P. said he had not determined what to charge but would have her say what it was worth. She absolutely refused to say. But "I will know if I live and breath. I can read yet. Why dont you tell me, what you charge? You do it on purpose to teaze me. You are mighty arch this morning. I wont have all the Towns Poor brought here, stark naked, for me to clothe for nothing. I wont be a slave to other folks folk for nothing."—And after the 2 Girls cryed.—"I must not speak a Word [to] your Girls, Wenches, Drabbs. I'le kick both their fathers, presently. [You] want to put your Girls over me, to make me a slave to your Wenches."

Asserting his right to rule did little to diffuse the situation. According to John Adams the younger, this was the normal course of their disagreements—she raged and he remained cool. "Cool Reasoning upon the Point with my Father, would soon bring her to his mind or him to hers."[61]

Richard Prey [or Pray] of Ipswich, Massachusetts, appeared in a Salem court in 1647/8 to answer charges that he had beaten his wife. Among the witnesses was Jabisch Hackett, who had seen him try to hit her with a large stick, kick her across a room, and throw a "porridge dish" at her. The provocation for this abusive outburst had been her public contradiction of him, declaring that he had, despite denials, profaned the Lord's Day with his swearing and cursing. This enraged Prey. One brave soul tried to intervene:

> Some one present told Prey that the court would not allow him to abuse his wife so, and he answered that he did not care for the court and if the court hanged him for it he would do it. It was said to him that the court would make him care, for they had tamed as stout hearts as his, and Prey

answered that if ever he had trouble about abusing his wife, he would cripple her and make her sit on a stool, and there he would keep her.

His justification for his behavior was "that he would beat her twenty times a day before she would be his master." The court fined him "10s. for swearing, 10s. for cursing, 20s. for beating his wife, and 40s. for contempt of court, or to be whipped at the Iron works."[62] Contempt of court, curiously, seemed the more serious charge.

Money and power lay at the center of the maelstrom that surrounded the marriage of Edward and Betteris Berry. Married previously, Betteris negotiated a prenuptial agreement with her new husband, Edward. He assured her at the time that he "desired nothing of my estate he desired nothing but my person." After the ceremony, Edward apparently changed his mind and sought to void the agreement. She refused and he began a campaign to force her compliance. He told a friend "that if I would not give up ye writings that were made between us he would make me weary of my life & so indeed I found it." She left the house with his consent in 1676 because she could not "liue with such a Tyrant." The court ordered them to "live together according to God's ordinance" or face a five-pound fine. She complied, but appeared in court a year later to obtain relief from his drunken rages. She had tried to persuade him to "live in Love & unity as other Folks doe." He responded by calling her an "old cheating Rogue" and hoped "The Divell take thee." Edward Berry enlisted the help of his son, who threatened to throw his stepmother down the stairs and then destroyed a chest of drawers she had brought to the marriage. In Berry's view, the treatment visited upon his wife was fully justified; "she should have nothing of him because he had nothing of hers."[63] He could not abide his wife's power over his financial future: this was a husband's prerogative. He had relinquished his patriarchal power before marriage and now wanted it back.

The difficult third marriage of the compulsive Cotton Mather to Lydia Lee George floundered in part because of his inflexible devotion to work. He often spent his entire day in his study, emerging only to pray with the family and to eat. His wife finally left him in the midst of an argument.[64] Her rage seemed to Mather like a "Satanical Possession."

> After a thousand unrepeatable Invectives, compelling me to rise at Midnight, and retire to my Study that I might there pour out my Soul unto the Lord; she also gott up in a horrid Rage, protesting that she would

never live or stay with me; and calling up her wicked Niece and Maid, she went over to a Neighbour's House for Lodging.

His children joined him in a "Vigil" of songs and prayers until the house finally went to bed as the sun rose. Mather used his work for the Lord as a shield against intimacy. When his wife's frustrations reached their zenith, she took aim at her enemy's weak point. She exposed their differences to public scrutiny, thereby attacking his "Esteem in the World" and threatening the "Success" of his "Ministry."[65]

Jacob Eliot found himself in a similarly contentious marriage when he approached the altar at the age of sixty with his young bride, Ann Blackleach.[66] This Lebanon, Connecticut, minister discovered his wife had little patience for his devotion to spiritual work. Her anger flared when he refused to allow her to enter his study because he was "Engaged deeply in Devotion." She aimed to wound. "You are no more fit to go into a Pulpit than the Devil Himself." After one battle, he angrily threatened to "Complain to her Friends & expose Her." Her equivalent threat was to "expose" him "to all the Parish."[67]

Domestic disputes tested the limits of a husband's power, leaving him frustrated, and with an angry declaration of his right to rule as his only recourse. The elder Adams knew he could not take in boarders unless his wife agreed to provide the domestic service necessary for their support. Prey understood that nothing short of crippling his wife could assure her dependence and his control. Berry belatedly discovered that he could not overturn a prenuptial contract without his wife's approval, and reduced himself to coercion and cruelty. When marital relations deteriorated, gendered patterns of power emerged. Men demanded their prerogative as patriarchs, and women reached for the familiar weapon of gossip.

Women could upset the balance of power in a household most dramatically by sexual betrayal. A promiscuous wife not only publicly humiliated her husband, but threatened the legitimacy of his children. Cuckolded men were considered aberrant and despised.[68] The law also considered a woman's sexual misconduct more heinous than a man's. The penalties applied to an adulterous woman exceeded the punishment meted out to her male counterpart. In the early laws of Massachusetts, for example, a woman who had sex with a man other than her husband was considered an adulteress, a crime punishable by death. For a man, such sexual impropriety was labeled simply fornication, penalized by a fine or whipping.[69] Women were told that philandering husbands should be ignored or at least tolerated.[70] A cuckold, however, received scolding rather than sympathy from his community. He was regarded as a fallen man unable to control his wife's behavior. Among the European elite, such a husband was unfit for public office. In villages, he was subject to public shaming rituals.[71] Men who suffered from their wive's adultery endured public ridicule as well as private pain.

Laurence Turner of Ipswich, Massachusetts, struggled to regain his honor in the face of his adulterous wife's flagrant behavior. He came to court in 1650 to try and end the gossip, if not her sexual betrayals. John Chackswell, a boarder in the Turner home, recounted a sexual dalliance that occurred in the husband's absence. Sarah Turner "in a sporting way, throw water at one Tobias Saunders," also a boarder in the Turner household. "Saunders, who was looking in at the window, ran into the house and took said Sarah in his arms and assaulted her." A female neighbor came to the door and was also assaulted by Saunders and John Smith. Thomas Billings "came in from the forge" and was pushed into the sexual fray. Chackswell "being troubled, rebuked them saying, 'Heere is good doeings, take heed wt you doe' and went to an upper chamber, not countenancing their lascivious acts."

Sarah Turner was also reported to have enticed Roger Tyler with her carnal language. She called to him as he left his house, "Tyler you have eaten Turnopps." He replied "Thou Lyest Turners Wife." She challenged him "Come hethr & let mee kisse thee & then I'le tell yee." Laurence Turner challenged his neighbors' testimony in court. He sought to redeem his reputation, if not his marriage.[72]

William Beale went to court in Ipswich, Massachusetts, to end the gossip about his wife and their servant, Benjamin Chandler. Beale's wife went to a neighbor's house asking for Chandler after her husband "warned" him out of their house because "her husband was jealous of him." In his rage, Beale accusingly declared that "all her children were bastards save one." When Beale found his former servant, "he took an ax and beat down Benjamin Chandler's cabin to try to expel him." The court case, however, involved not adultery or assault, but slander and defamation. Beale brought William Hollingworth to court "in behalf of his wife" because Mary Doninge heard from Alexander Giligan that Mrs. Hollingworth "said to Beale's wife that her husband would not join the church so long as such as she was in it." Beale's concern was that his domestic difficulties had become a town scandal. He did not want the reputation of being a cuckold.[73] The damage of the town rumormongers threatened these men as much if not more than their wive's alleged infidelities.

Not unlike a cuckolded husband, a man beaten by his wife suffered public ridicule. In early modern France and England, it was common to make such a man, like his cuckold counterpart, ride backward on a donkey holding its tail. Like his backward ride, the man who endured such treatment reversed the natural order of things. The woman who did the beating rarely received social censure. To go to court to stop such abuse or even to acknowledge publicly such treatment was not an option for most men in early New England, either.[74] Jacob Eliot suffered at the hands of his tormented and abusive wife, Ann. "She flew into the most Violent passion imaginable, & with her fist doubled, fell upon me & struck me with all her might, upon my Head & Breast, arm & shoulder, half a Dozen times or more." A similar outburst demanded his reaction, when his wife "flew into the utmost Rage & fury again, Calling me a Cursed Devil Kicked at Me, & struck me with her Fist again, & took up a Powder Horn, to strike me over the Head with, but defending my self, I warded off the blow."[75] At the height of a confrontation that ended with her attempted suicide, Ann "Strook me with her Fist as hard as She could in the face, & about my Head & Belly several times & hurt me very much (especially with one Stroke in my face which I felt very sore for several Days after)." She even tried to kill him when she "took me by the throat, got both her hands into the handkerchief about my Neck, & try'd, with all her might, to twist it round to Choak me." Trying to contort the situation to her advantage, Ann Eliot threatened to tell neighbors about "my abuse to Her, twitching & halling her about to kill her, when only to defend my self & prevent Her runing away to destroy her Self, I, as gently as I could Sometimes took hold of her Arms or Cloaths."[76]

Ann relentlessly found fault in her husband: "I can't Speak loud to a Servant, or so much as mend the fire, but Snubbed and reproved Sharply."[77] To Jacob, her railings were "all for nothing, or for the least trifle in the world."[78] Eliot described what he considered the ridiculous circumstances that roused his wife's ire:

> my Singing to the Child to get him to sleep (being mad before) cry'd out with great Vehemence & Spight, o don't don't don't don't Mr. Eliot make that noise! I am almost killed with it already &c—Soon after She letting a rousing Fart, I pleasingly & Jocosely Said that was as bad a Noise I

thought as my Singing, at which She flew into a prodigious Rage, & wished She had dy'd in her Cradle, before She had been bro't into so much Trouble &c.[79]

Of course, her real provocations even the long-suffering Jacob knew only too well. From her cutting remarks, she clearly resented his absorption in his religious studies and his ministerial condescension toward her. She often vented her anger by "trifling, Jesting & playing with Sacred things" to provoke a response. He would quote scriptures during their confrontations "by way of Caution or advice, with a design to expound upon it—[she] not staying to hear me out, but turning quick & in great rage replying—Shitt on the Text."[80]

In fact, Ann justifiably worried about her financial status and that of her child. Eliot had two children from his first marriage who would share part of their father's estate. Married in 1760, Ann and Jacob had two sons: Joseph, born in 1762, and John, born in 1764. Ann urged her elderly husband, who died in 1766, to rewrite his will to include his second family. After the birth of her first son, she became consumed with worry that "her & Jose [would be] . . . left destitute." Jacob dismissed her concerns saying, "I intended to take Care about [you] . . . as soon as I could Conveniently." But Jacob ignored her long-standing request, throwing Ann into a "most Violent & uncurbed passion."[81] She protested that his son Jacob, by his first wife, "might be content with what he had got, for he should have no more. . . . He had much more than his part already, & She would Say it to all the World."[82]

Jacob's fury was directed not only at his wife's violence, but also at his own weakness. He thundered back at her, but he considered even these responses as a defeat: "I shew'd some heat & anger (God forgive me)."[83] When he answered her with "some Zeal," he justified himself with the aside, "it is marvellous I have born so much."[84] He berated himself for giving in to her demands. When she refused to sleep with him he "(like a Fool for Peace Sake) Consented & Submitted."[85] He preferred silence and Christian forbearance to confrontation, which may account for Ann's rage. After ordering him not to touch her in bed, saying he "Stank so Devilishly she could not bare me," he responded with cutting kindness:

I bore all with invincible patience & for the most part Silence—at last without the least Ruffle I faced my Dear—if by a few words you will say what will pacify you, & put an end to the Controversy, that we might go to Sleep in peace & love—otherwise, I was resolved by the Grace of Heaven, to Disappoint the Devil & Her, by not being Mad, let her say what She would.[86]

Donning the mantle of God's servant, he could make sense out of his situation. He turned the other cheek because he was strong. But his Christian forbearance also left the martyred Jacob feeling that he was little more than "a page, or Servant" in his own home.[87] After one of their bedchamber quarrels, Ann "with Sovereign Authority said, I command you to go & lie up Chamber." He "laugh'd, & reply'd, that she had expressly inverted the Sacred Text. . . . Husbands obay your Wives." His laughter was soon replaced by a "profound silence," which he broke by begging her "to admit me to bed."[88] A furious wife could threaten the natural order. An abused man's shame could lead to silence and private humiliation.

When a man married, he risked his heart and his reputation. Marriages, particularly for the men examined here, were based on both a loving partnership and male dominance. The question of whether one or the other dictated marriage patterns in a given place and time overshadows the obvious: both were always present. For the men studied here, these two imperatives did not seem contradictory. By the end of the eighteenth century, more open expression of sentiment was certainly encouraged, but loving expressions characterized male writings throughout the colonial period.

NOTES

1. Benjamin Wadsworth, *The Well-Ordered Family* (Boston: G. Green, 1712).

2. Historians of early modern Europe have made this observation. See Keith Wrightson, *English Society, 1580–1680* (New Brunswick, N.J.: Rutgers University Press, 1982), 90–104; Ralph A. Houlbrooke, *The English Family, 1450–1700* (London: Longman, 1984), 119; Magdalena Balthasar Paumgartner, *Magdalena and Balthasar: An Intimate Portrait of Life in Sixteenth-Century Europe Revealed in the Letters of a Nuremberg Husband and Wife, and Illuminated by Steven Ozment* (New York: Simon and Schuster, 1986), 163.

3. Recently, Daniel Vickers has refined the notion of "interdependent" families in colonial New England. See *Farmers and Fishermen: Two Centuries of Work in Essex County, Massachusetts, 1630–1850* (Chapel Hill: University of

North Carolina Press, 1994). For early modern England and France, consult Louise A. Tilly and Joan W. Scott, *Women, Work, and Family* (New York: Holt, Rinehart, and Winston, 1978), part I.

4. Like many recent scholars of British and French history, I have found more continuity than change in the way affection was expressed in colonial New England marriages in both the seventeenth and eighteenth centuries. See Martine Segalen, *Love and Power in the Peasant Family: Rural France and the Nineteenth Century* (Chicago: University of Chicago Press, 1983); Houlbrooke, *The English Family;* John R. Gillis, *For Better, For Worse: British Marriages, 1600 to the Present* (New York: Oxford University Press, 1985); Alan Macfarlane, *Marriage and Love in England: Modes of Reproduction, 1300–1840* (Oxford: Basil Blackwell, 1986); Paumgartner, *Magdalena and Balthasar;* Martin Ingram, *Church Courts, Sex and Marriage in England, 1570–1640* (Cambridge: Cambridge University Press, 1987); Carol Z. Stearns and Peter N. Stearns, eds., *Emotion and Social Change: Toward a New Psychohistory* (New York: Holmes and Meiers, 1988); Jeffrey R. Watt, *The Making of Modern Marriage: Matrimonial Control and the Rise of Sentiment in Neuchâtel, 1550–1800* (Ithaca: Cornell University Press, 1992).

5. Laurel Thatcher Ulrich, *Good Wives: Image and Reality in the Lives of Women in Northern New England, 1650–1750* (New York: Alfred A. Knopf, 1982), chap. 2.

6. John Winthrop to Margaret Winthrop, 10 May 1621, in Robert C. Winthrop, *Life and Letters of John Winthrop,* 2 vols. (Boston, 1864–1867; reprint, New York: Da Capo Press, 1971), 1:164.

7. G. Selleck Silliman and Mary Silliman to Joseph Fish, 12 December 1776; G. S. Silliman to [Joseph Fish], 7 December 1777; both in Silliman Family Papers, Manuscripts and Archives, Yale University Library.

8. G. Selleck Silliman to Mary Noyes, 19 April 1775, Silliman Family Papers, Manuscripts and Archives, Yale University Library.

9. John Walley Diary, 17 October 1748, John Walley Papers, Massachusetts Historical Society (hereafter MHS).

10. William Dawes to Stephen Salisbury, 1 April 1773, Salisbury Family Papers, American Antiquarian Society (hereafter AAS).

11. John Walley Diary, 18 September 1748, John Walley Papers, MHS.

12. Cotton Mather, *Diary of Cotton Mather,* ed. Worthington Chauncey Ford, 2 vols. (New York: Frederick Ungar Publishing Co., 1911), 2:255.

13. Joseph Fish to Rebecca Fish, 13 October 1777, Silliman Family Papers, Manuscripts and Archives, Yale University Library.

14. Eliphalet Pearson to Mrs. Pearson [Sarah Bromfield], 15 October 1785, Park Family Papers, Manuscripts and Archives, Yale University Library.

15. G. Selleck Silliman to Mary Silliman, 22 May 1780, Silliman Family Papers, Manuscripts and Archives, Yale University Library.

16. [Tapping Reeve] to Sarah Reeve, 25 September 1773, Reeve Family Papers, Manuscripts and Archives, Yale University Library.

17. John Winthrop to Margaret Winthrop, 3 April 1630, 30 October 1624, and 26 November 1624, in Winthrop, *Life and Letters of John Winthrop*, 1: 390–91, 196–97.

18. William Williams to Mrs. Mary Williams, 3 September 1776, Williams Papers, Connecticut Historical Society (hereafter CHS).

19. [Tapping Reeve] to Sarah Reeve, 25 September 1773, Reeve Family Papers, Manuscripts and Archives, Yale University Library.

20. G. Selleck Silliman to Joseph Fish, 12 December 1776, Silliman Family Papers, Manuscripts and Archives, Yale University Library.

21. For a recent discussion of the relationship between gender and patriarchy in early New England, see Mary Beth Norton, *Founding Mothers and Fathers: Gendered Power and the Forming of American Society* (New York: Alfred A. Knopf, 1996).

22. William Williams to Mary Williams, 3 September 1776, Williams Papers, CHS.

23. John Winthrop to Margaret Winthrop, 28 April 1629 and n.d., in Winthrop, *Life and Letters of John Winthrop*, 1:290, 380.

24. John Winthrop to Margaret Winthrop, 3 April 1630, in Winthrop, *Life and Letters of John Winthrop*, 1:391.

25. John Walley Diary, 17 October 1748, John Walley Papers, MHS.

26. Mather Byles [Jr.] to Mather Byles [Sr.], 22 July 1761, Byles Family Papers, MHS.

27. William Henshaw to Phebe Henshaw, 30 January 1776, Henshaw Family Papers, AAS.

28. Benjamin Bangs Diary, 27 January 1764, Bangs Collection, MHS.

29. [Tapping Reeve] to Sarah Reeve, 25 September 1773, Reeve Family Papers, Manuscripts and Archives, Yale University Library.

30. John Winthrop to Margaret Winthrop, 22 January 1628, n.d., and 14 March 1629, in Winthrop, *Life and Letters of John Winthrop*, 1:283, 381–85.

31. G. Selleck Silliman to Mary Silliman, 21 August 1776, Silliman Family Papers, Manuscripts and Archives, Yale University Library.

32. Ezra Stiles, *The Literary Diary of Ezra Stiles*, ed. Franklin Bowditch Dexter, 3 vols. (New York: Charles Scribner's Sons, 1901), 1:517.

33. Diary of John Tudor, 1732–1793, John Tudor Papers, MHS, 4.

34. Samuel Sewall, *The Diary of Samuel Sewall, 1674–1729*, 2 vols. (New York: Farrar, Straus and Giroux, 1973), 2:654–55.

35. Mather, *Diary of Cotton Mather*, 1:449.

36. Ebenezer Parkman, *The Diary of Ebenezer Parkman, 1703–1782*, ed. Francis G. Walett (Worcester, Mass.: American Antiquarian Society, 1974), 141.

37. G. Selleck Silliman to Mary Silliman, 22 May 1780, Silliman Family Papers, Manuscripts and Archives, Yale University Library.

38. Diary of John Tudor, 1732–1793, John Tudor Papers, MHS, 40.

39. John Demos, *A Little Commonwealth: Family Life in Plymouth Colony* (New York: Oxford University Press, 1970), 66, 192–93; Catherine M. Scholten, *Childbearing in American Society, 1650–1850* (New York: New York University Press, 1985), 21–22. Women died in childbirth during the colonial period, though the fear of mortality outstripped the reality. See Maris A. Vinovskis, "Mortality Rates and Trends in Massachusetts before 1860," *Journal of Economic History* 32 (March 1972): 201–14; Daniel Scott Smith and J. David Hacker, "Cultural Demography: New England Deaths and the Puritan Perception of Risk," *Journal of Interdisciplinary History* 26 (winter 1996): 381. Edward Shorter argues that fertile women died earlier than men because of the dangers of childbirth. But more important causes were "overwork" and "undernutrition." See Shorter, *A History of Women's Bodies* (New York: Basic Books, 1982), 241.

40. Scholten, *Childbearing in American Society;* Laurel Thatcher Ulrich, *A Midwife's Tale: The Life of Martha Ballard Based on Her Diary, 1785–1812* (New York: Alfred A. Knopf, 1990).

41. Elisha James to Sarah James, 3 June 1777, James Family Papers, MHS.

42. Michael Wigglesworth, *The Diary of Michael Wigglesworth, 1653–1657: The Conscience of a Puritan,* ed. Edmund S. Morgan (New York: Harper and Row, 1946), 96.

43. Parkman, *Diary of Ebenezer Parkman,* 150.

44. Benjamin Bangs Diary, 25 April 1760, Bangs Collection, MHS.

45. Parkman, *Diary of Ebenezer Parkman,* 87.

46. Ibid., 56.

47. Diary of Peter Thatcher, 28 February 1682/3, Thatcher I Collection, MHS.

48. Sewall, *Diary of Samuel Sewall,* 1:41.

49. Parkman, *Diary of Ebenezer Parkman,* 150.

50. Wigglesworth, *Diary of Michael Wigglesworth,* 96.

51. Sewall, *Diary of Samuel Sewall,* 1:324.

52. Ibid., 1:41.

53. Mather, *Diary of Cotton Mather,* 1:307.

54. Sewall, *Diary of Samuel Sewall,* 1:324.

55. Parkman, *Diary of Ebenezer Parkman,* 113.

56. Sewall, *Diary of Samuel Sewall,* 1:41.

57. Toby L. Ditz, "Shipwrecked; or, Masculinity Imperiled: Mercantile Representations of Failure and the Gendered Self in Eighteenth-Century Philadelphia," *Journal of American History* 81 (June 1994): 51–80.

58. M. Byles to Mary Byles, 4 October 1762, Byles Family Papers, MHS.

59. G. Selleck Silliman to Joseph Fish, 12 July 1775, Silliman Family Papers, Manuscripts and Archives, Yale University Library.

60. Thomas Clap, "Meditations upon the Death of my Wife," 9 August 1736, in "Memoirs of some Remarkable Occurances of Divine Providence ...," Thomas Clap Presidential Papers (YRG 2-A-5), Manuscripts and Archives, Yale University Library.

61. John Adams, *Diary and Autobiography of John Adams,* ed. Lyman H. Butterfield, 4 vols. (Cambridge: Belknap Press of Harvard University Press, 1961), 1:65–66.

62. *Records and Files of the Quarterly Courts of Essex County, Massachusetts,* 8 vols. (Salem, Mass.: Essex Institute, 1912), 1:136. For more detail on the history of this unhappy couple, see Norton, *Founding Mothers and Fathers,* 79, 426 n. 59.

63. *Records and Files of the Quarterly Courts of Essex County, Massachusetts,* 6:195, 297–98.

64. Mather's brooding over his failure to be appointed president of Harvard caused a final argument and leave-taking. Lydia returned when news came that her husband's oldest son had died at sea. Kenneth Silverman, *The Life and Times of Cotton Mather* (New York: Harper and Row, 1984), 382–89.

65. Mather, *Diary of Cotton Mather,* 2:749–52.

66. I have been unable to determine her exact age, but because she had children during their marriage, and because her sister married Eliot's son, I have assumed her to be at least twenty years his junior. See Clifford K. Shipton, *Sibley's Harvard Graduates,* 17 vols. (Cambridge: Harvard University Press, 1942), 6:382.

67. Jacob Eliot Diary, 1762–1764, Ms. 56663, CHS, 3–8.

68. Lawrence Stone, *Family, Sex and Marriage in England, 1500–1800,* abridged edition (New York: Harper and Row, 1979), 316–17; Segalen, *Love and Power,* 45; Roderick Phillips, *Putting Asunder: A History of Divorce in Western Society* (New York: Cambridge University Press, 1988), 351; Richard P. Gildrie, *The Profane, the Civil and the Godly: The Reformation of Manners in Orthodox New England, 1679–1749* (University Park: Pennsylvania State University Press, 1994), 129.

69. Ulrich, *Good Wives,* 94; Roger Thompson, *Sex in Middlesex: Popular Mores in a Massachusetts County, 1649–1699* (Amherst: University of Massachusetts Press, 1986), 128–29, 141–42.

70. Thompson, *Sex in Middlesex,* chaps. 8 and 9; Lyle Koehler, *A Search for Power: The "Weaker Sex" in Seventeenth-Century New England* (Urbana: University of Illinois Press, 1980), 149, 453–59.

71. Stone, *Family, Sex and Marriage,* 316–17; Jean-Louis Flandrin, *Families in Former Times: Kinship, Household and Sexuality* (Cambridge: Cambridge University Press, 1979), 124–25; Segalen, *Love and Power,* 45–46; Thompson,

Sex in Middlesex, 142; Phillips, *Putting Asunder,* 350–51; G. R. Quaife, *Wanton Wenches and Wayward Wives: Peasants and Illicit Sex in Early Seventeenth Century England* (New Brunswick, N.J.: Rutgers University Press, 1979).

72. *Records and Files of the Quarterly Courts of Essex County, Massachusetts,* 1:198–99.

73. Ibid., 3:280–82.

74. Segalen, *Love and Power,* 43–45; Edward Shorter, *The Making of the Modern Family* (New York: Basic Books, 1975), 222–24; Phillips, *Putting Asunder,* 334; Merril D. Smith, *Breaking the Bonds: Marital Discord in Pennsylvania, 1730–1830* (New York: New York University Press, 1991), 116–17.

75. Jacob Eliot Diary, 1762–1764, Ms. 56663, CHS, 6–8.

76. Ibid., 18.

77. Ibid., 2.

78. Ibid., 3.

79. Ibid., 4.

80. Ibid., 1–3.

81. Ibid., 9–10.

82. Ibid., 13.

83. Ibid., 7.

84. Ibid., 9.

85. Ibid., 11.

86. Ibid., 16.

87. Ibid., 2.

88. Ibid., 11.

Chapter Four

Making Men and Women in the 1770s
Culture, Class, and Commerce in the Anglo-American World

Patricia Cleary

In the spring of 1770, sixteen-year-old Polly Murray and her fourteen-year-old brother Jack faced the most abrupt and dramatic change of their young lives, bidding farewell to their parents, eight younger siblings, and home in Norwich, England, to sail unfamiliar seas and settle in the remote colonial town of Boston. There, separated from their nearest relations by thousands of miles, they would be under the care of their aunt, Elizabeth Murray Smith, a former shopkeeper and wealthy widow with no children of her own. Under her auspices and with her direct encouragement, the two would seek their fortunes, Polly as a shopkeeper and Jack as a merchant.

The willingness of Polly and Jack's parents and aunt to subject them to the trauma of such upheaval to seek their livelihoods in the colonies offers a window into class attitudes, cultural beliefs, and commercial aspirations of the 1770s. This forced migration clearly reveals that the elder Murrays considered geographic mobility to be a viable, if not necessary, means for both sexes to achieve economic mobility. Among the older generation of Murrays, several had emigrated from the family home in the Scottish borderlands in the 1730s, to pursue livelihoods elsewhere in the empire, setting a historic pattern of emigration that would repeat across the centuries.

The Murrays' experiences reveal that raising children involved complex planning and careful calculations. Reconstructing their efforts to train the young and their debates over the best way to do so, shows how genteel ideals of manhood and womanhood inspired the non-elite to emulation, but not unthinking imitation. Like many others with genteel aspirations and less-than-genteel income, the Murrays sought to modify prescribed models of behavior to fit their economic situation. In particular, they turned to industry and commercial activity as the means both to earn a living and to offset what they saw as the corrupt tendencies of an elite education.

Although possessed of substantial financial resources, the senior branch of the Murray family did not hold property in Scotland. Almost the entire county of Dumfries, where they were tenants, belonged to one great laird (lord). While not landowners themselves, the Murrays counted many of the gentry among their relatives. In Scotland, where land was concentrated in the hands of a few, tenancy "was an economic relationship more than a social status" and tenants not infrequently had their own subtenants as well as servants.[1] Economic opportunities, however, were limited. Accordingly, like many other Scots who took advantage of the freedom of movement ushered in by the 1707 Act of Union with England, the Murrays left the land of their birth: three moved to America, one settled in England, and one adopted the perpetual motion of a military career. Not surprisingly, a few decades later, they considered migration as a means of promoting the commercial interests of the rising generation.

Yet the decision to send the two young people to America was fraught with anxiety, generated in part by their age, educational training, and background. Preparing Polly and Jack for adulthood entailed more than providing them with the means to earn a living. The Murrays wanted to "make" their children into men and women who would be "useful members of society." The process of educating someone, male or female, to be a "useful" person who also embodied ideal gender traits was neither simple nor straightforward. Education consisted of much more than formal schooling, embracing rigorous instruction in life skills as well. Young people needed to master not only academic subjects, but complex rules of appropriate behavior. On both sides of the Atlantic, men and women debated what constituted appropriate education for their children. Educational practices and behavioral ideals were in a state of flux, especially for people like the Murrays, whose own social position was not entirely fixed and was in part a product of their own efforts. The Murrays were not alone in the quandaries they faced. British pundits and colonial American writers alike grappled with the multiple meanings, goals, and avenues of educating the young.

The gendered aims of education, for those of genteel status and for the many who aspired to be gentlemen or ladies, translated into distinctive curricula. The direction and purpose of childrearing depended on class as well as gender. For young men, training in subjects such as geography or arithmetic would help lay the basis for a mercantile career. With an emphasis on fine handwriting and solid Latin, this education marked men of commerce and culture. With proficiency in these subjects, they gained the vocational and social skills to negotiate the business deal as well as the drawing room.

For the ideal gentlewoman, in contrast, ornamental accomplishments predominated. Desirable refinements included the ability to speak French and play a musical instrument.[2] These skills, which lacked the obvious commercial applicability of those men acquired, nonetheless had an economic value, one grounded in the marriage market. There, a woman possessed of numerous decorative accomplishments could compete well. A dowry alone could not guarantee the acquisition of the most desirable mate. For girls of lower social status, in contrast, even acquiring literacy skills could prove difficult.[3] While knowing how to read would enable girls to peruse the Scriptures, it was less important than the housewifery skills that would enable them to do domestic work and eventually take care of their own households.

Education could, however, blur hierarchies and disrupt social relations, as individuals endeavored to use it to transcend the rank of birth. The idea that one could aspire to a higher status through adopting genteel behavior, manners, and dress disturbed those of lofty social position. "The fundamental issue in the eighteenth-century concept of gentility," one historian concluded, "was the claim of legitimacy that separated those with a recognized right to position from those who consciously set out to acquire it."[4] Thus, education became a highly contested subject in a colonial society that seemed far more democratic than its British antecedents.[5]

Class conditioned the precise educational formulae that people used to assert upward social mobility. Hence, educating young people had to involve an appraisal of their talents and aspirations, as well as their financial resources. What was appropriate to the elite could not be readily embraced by non-elite families like the Murrays. Presumption could mean disaster for their children. As they attempted to model their offspring upon the widespread cultural ideals of genteel manhood and womanhood articulated in a range of prescriptive texts, they had to remember the social and economic realities of their situation.

With branches in New England and Great Britain, members of the Murray family endeavored to address the issues of managing the young in a rapidly changing society. Familiar with life on either side of the Atlantic, they had firsthand experience with metropolitan London as well as provincial Boston. Like thousands of other geographically mobile families, the Murrays relied on fruitful webs of interdependence that linked colonists with the economy and culture of the mother country.[6] Their story sheds light on important and interrelated phenomena: how members of a middling family with gentry connections, genteel aspirations, but limited resources educated their children; how this education embodied shifting and uncertain criteria that nonetheless defined manhood and womanhood; and, finally, how Anglo-American commercial developments fostered geographic, social, and economic mobility.

Examining the guidelines set out in conduct manuals and educational treatises in the context of the practices of particular readers lays bare the conflicts encountered and ideals espoused by middle-class seekers of gentility. While the elder Murrays wanted their youngsters to be genteel, they also expected that they would be able to support themselves, a goal potentially incompatible with some aspects of "gentle" education. There was much contention over whether the ends of genteel education were valid for young men and women, whether they were appropriate to either England or the colonies, and even whether they were achievable.

For the Murrays, as for many of their contemporaries, these educational expectations raised multiple problems, particularly in their potentially corrupting and enervating effects. The pursuit of genteel culture could involve young people in dissipating conduct. Following the prescribed norms created tension; a thin line could separate those who embraced only the positive attributes of genteel behavior—the polite manners and self-presentation—from those who were corrupted by its superficiality, potential for immorality, and standards of consumption. Luxury and indulgence were frequently decried as the markers of the genteel.

Given the peregrinations and economic history of the Murrays born in Scotland, it is not surprising that they viewed "industry" as the key to redressing the imbalances of excessively polite education. Although far from penniless after their father's death in 1728, neither were the male members of the elder generation destined for lives as landed gentle-men. The oldest sibling, James, left Scotland when quite young, to pur-sue a mercantile career in London, then immigrated to North Carolina in the 1730s to develop a plantation and pursue commerce as a sideline.[7] Barbara, closest to James in age, accompanied him when he sailed for the colonies; within a few years, she had married and set up her own household. The youngest of the Murray offspring, Elizabeth followed her older siblings to North Carolina in her early teens, acting for a time as James's housekeeper. Several years later, in 1749, just before her twenty-third birthday, Elizabeth decided to establish herself as a shop-keeper in Boston. Unlike these siblings, John Murray chose not to cross the Atlantic, settling instead in Norwich, where he attempted to support a family, which eventually included ten children, on a sometimes inade-quate physician's income.[8] Over the years, as his family grew, John told his brother James that if he were unable to amass a fortune for his children, he hoped to "be able to enable them by a proper Education to earn their own bread with credit and industry."[9] In his view, earning a living was a fallback position, not the life course that he would choose for his offspring.

The early loss of both of their parents underscored for the Murrays the importance of thinking about and preparing for the future from a very young age. These Scottish-born siblings certainly did not hesitate to give each other advice. Even as a young man, James had counseled his mother on how his younger brothers and sisters should be educated. As early as 1733, James urged his mother to move the family to a town where the children could be better educated than at home. Education, he told her, "would do them more Service than to put double the money" into their pockets that she would save by country living.[10] James offered the most detailed advice regarding his brothers.[11]

In assigning responsibilities for the young, the Murrays believed it proper for men to oversee the education of boys, "making Men" of them, and for women to supervise the training of girls. In the decades after she moved to Boston, Elizabeth Murray personally supervised the education of several of her nieces; the family delegated responsibility for young men to other adult males.[12] Although Jack, for example, came to the colonies to enter trade, a profession that she knew well in some respects, he was instructed by a man.[13]

Perhaps the most mobile of the Scottish-born Murrays, Elizabeth Murray Smith—who, in 1760 married James Smith, her second spouse

4.1 *Mrs. James Smith (Elizabeth Murray)*, 1769, by John Singleton Copley. Gift of Joseph W. R. and Mary C. Rogers. Courtesy of the Museum of Fine Arts, Boston.

and a seventy-year-old sugar merchant—first urged the plan of colonial migration for her niece and nephew. Her own experiences as a Boston shopkeeper and frequent transatlantic journeys made her an ideal mentor. Smith's efforts to install the youngsters in the colonies, her siblings' and friends' reactions to her scheme, and the conduct of the migrating youths themselves provide the framework for this analysis.

When she first offered to help her brother by taking charge of his oldest children, Elizabeth Murray Smith did so with a belief that her niece Polly had been educated injudiciously. At the age of sixteen, Polly "had finished her education and must have appeared the fine lady, if she had stayed with her acquaintance."[14] She had not the "fortune to support the appearance she must make." With no productive employment at hand, explained her aunt, "if Polly stay[ed] she must enter all the gayitys of Norwich."[15] These "gayitys" posed problems for Polly. The frivolous diversions of the gentlefolk could endanger Polly's character if she spent too much time in their pursuit; moreover, she could not afford the requisite apparel. Elizabeth Murray Smith's more practical plans for her niece, which she recommended to her brother, would enable her to develop "some way of providing for herself."[16]

This solution to the problem of a young woman educated to expectations of cultural and material consumption that exceeded her income had its roots in Elizabeth's own youthful experiences as a retailer. She decided to save Polly by sending her to Boston to become a shopkeeper. In short order, she provided her niece with credit, supervised the selection of her initial stock, and arranged for her to work in the shop of two women shopkeepers in Boston, where Polly would gain firsthand experience with commerce before going into business for herself. In embracing commercial endeavor as a corrective, Elizabeth Murray Smith's aspirations for her niece reflect a modification of the ideals of gentility. In effect, she, like many other critics, rejected the current of contemporary thought that depicted women of a particular status as removed from practical economic concerns and as embodiments of cultural consumption. She turned the tables by transforming her niece from a buyer into a purveyor of consumer goods.

At the center of Elizabeth Murray Smith's criticisms was ambivalence about cultural consumption. She wanted to remove Polly from the decadent influences of polite culture, which, while beneficial in small doses, could prove destructive if consumed in excess. As she put it: "I hope going among strangers will rouse her facultys and made her industrious, which to me is more agreeable than the fine delicate creatures that fly about for amusement." The existence of such "fine delicate creatures," whose decorative accomplishments served to attract male admirers of feminine gentility, depended upon display and disposable income. To avoid this kind of life, Elizabeth Murray Smith sought to help her young niece by offering Polly the opportunity to become financially independent, and thereby enable her, as the "eldest of ten helpless Children," to assist her younger siblings if she did well. Yet when Elizabeth first arranged for Polly and Jack to make their way in the colonies, the action troubled her. "Poor things," she mused, "they part early from their fond parents & family[;] perhaps I am to blame."[17]

When her niece and nephew sailed, Elizabeth Murray Smith defended her decision to bring them to the colonies. Reminding a friend of their frequent discussions "on the education of youth," she argued that she followed her ideal in having Polly sent abroad. That ideal was "to give a young Lady an usefull education[;] so soon as she has finished that to put her upon some scheme to improve her mind time & fortune." This approach to raising a young woman could help her become what Elizabeth preferred: "an usefull member of society" as opposed "to all the fine delicate creatures of the age."[18] She wanted women to be more than ornamental fixtures in gentlemen's drawing rooms. Instead, she aimed for them to transcend such gender-prescribed behavior and to contribute to society as individuals distinguished by their intellect, industry, and income.

After Jack and Polly sailed in 1770, Elizabeth Murray Smith decided that another of her brother's children could benefit similarly from working in the colonies. Accordingly, Anne Murray joined her siblings in New England in the summer of 1771, working with her sister and another young woman in their Boston shop. For the next few years, the young women stayed busy selling fashionable imported wares. Their successes encouraged the Murrays to consider shopkeeping for Polly and Anne's younger sister Charlotte as well. In 1773, John Murray informed his sister Elizabeth that "agreeable to [her] desire [he had] pushed Charlotte forward in her Arithmetic," adding that as soon as she was fit for bookkeeping, she would be instructed in it.[19]

While Polly Murray seemed to thrive, proving a capable shopkeeper, Anne Murray found the experience to be a humiliating one and pleaded with her parents not to subject Charlotte to it. Anne believed that shopkeeping did not suit someone of her education and background. In later years, she remembered her Boston sojourn with bitterness and herself as "a childish girl of sixteen taken from a boarding school."[20] Indeed, she saw herself as "a perfect Child in mind and manner" when she left her parents.[21] Describing her life in New England, she recalled unpleasantness and "painful scenes." "The great part of *my* residence in Boston was one of most severe mortification; a plan of life for which from Nature and education I was totally unfit, was marked out for me by those whose will had ever governed my conduct. . . . Never was a Girl of 16 so much a Child as myself in person and mind; yet with this childishness I was not insensible to the consequences of loss of Caste." Although despondent about her lot, Anne did not disobey. She recalled only one complaint to her parents: "This resulted from the proposal to send our Sister Charlotte to us. I then begged that no more of the family might be placed in the state of degradation I experienced."[22]

Anne Murray's reaction emphasizes the importance of class in education and training: she thought shopkeeping inappropriate for a female of her background. Whether it was Anne's pleading or the disruption of the war that prevented the Murrays from sending Charlotte to Boston is unknown; the business began to decline after Polly went home for a visit in 1774 and fell apart altogether when Anne eloped in 1775.

With his offspring reaching adulthood far from his parental eye, John Murray attempted to give his children epistolary advice. His concern that they become "useful" and "genteel" young men and women underpins a lengthy birthday letter addressed to Jack. This thirty-three-page letter, which John Murray wrote for his eighteen-year-old son four years after the boy left England for America, clarifies the Murrays' views on education in the Anglo-American context. Detailing the elder Murray's views on education and deportment for young men, this document offers one of the most insightful eighteenth-century perspectives on the meaning of manhood. Written in part as a critical response to the most popular prescriptive tract of the 1770s, Lord Chesterfield's *Letters to His Son on the Fine Art of Becoming a Man of the World and a Gentleman,* John Murray's letter also enables us to gauge public reactions to advice literature. While historians have largely focused on prescriptions, Murray's letter provides rare insight into readers' reactions.[23]

John Murray began by informing his son that he recollected feeling "all the man" at the same age. He positioned himself as one who, upon the mature reflection of many years, realized that as a youth of eighteen he had not fully achieved adulthood and still had need of parental advice. In opening his letter this way, Murray simultaneously recognized his son's putative maturity and declared that the young man remained an adolescent. While considerable historical debate surrounds the timing and invention of adolescence as a developmental stage, significant evidence places an awareness of it in the eighteenth century.[24] By the late 1700s, Scottish literati viewed the period from fourteen or fifteen to full adulthood as a distinctive one of intellectual and emotional growth.[25] Thus, in 1770, when Jack Murray left his father at fourteen to travel to Boston and then to Providence, Rhode Island, where he became acquainted with trade under the auspices of his cousin John Clark, his childhood was at an end. Four years later, Jack was making the transition from youth to adulthood.

John Murray clearly modeled his letter upon advice literature. In summarizing the common traits of conduct books, one scholar characterized these didactic texts as providing the young with gender instruction from an authorial persona that stood "as the voice of society" and as "in loco parentis."[26] Murray's missive fulfills this definition precisely. In his parental role, he wrote the letter as a guide and a legacy for his young son. Apologizing for the detailed, lengthy text, Murray hoped that Jack would excuse him. "As it is the first family letter I ever wrote and may be the last," he declared, "I shall endeavour to give such hints as may be useful in every line of life, and enable you to improve upon the parental task before or after I fall asleep."[27]

After opening with birthday congratulations and an invocation "to follow the footsteps" of great men in the family's past, Murray dispensed briefly with personal news and explained his choice of birthday present. Wanting to "improve" his son's mind and "amuse" him at the same time, he sent a set of Shakespeare's plays. He also intended to send Lord Chesterfield's *Letters,* but at the last minute changed his mind.

Like many other readers in England and America, John Murray eagerly sought out this text, an exemplar of advice literature that consumers hoped would "guide them through the growing labyrinth of genteel taste and etiquette."[28] Lord Chesterfield's *Letters,* first printed in 1774, promised to do just that.[29] Soon thereafter, they were published in the colonies as well. The first edition appeared in New York in 1775; numerous reprints followed.[30]

Just before sending his son the *Letters,* John Murray decided to read the work; he found its contents immoral and shocking. In condemning Chesterfield, Murray was far from alone; indeed, Chesterfield's fame endures partly as a result of the censure his correspondence inspired.[31] Murray, like Chesterfield's many other critics, accused the earl of moral expediency: of using polished manners to manipulate others, and most egregiously, to maneuver virtuous women into compromising liaisons.[32]

Rather than send his son the offensive publication, John Murray summarized it, criticized it, and offered in its stead his own guidelines for turning his son into an ideal man. In his overview of Lord Chesterfield's plan for his son, Murray expressed some approbation of the rigorous curriculum Philip Stanhope, the earl's "natural" son, followed. While Chesterfield's educational program for his son was arduous, Murray's was not insubstantial either. Sprinkling his letter with Latin, he indicated that his son possessed familiarity with that language. In addition, the elder Murray, like Chesterfield, urged the study of politics, geography, and history as requisite attainments. John could not, however, countenance the morality behind the manners his lordship attempted to inculcate in his offspring. Once Philip Stanhope had completed his academic instruction, his father sent him to Italy to learn Italian and become a ladies' man. At the age of eighteen, Philip landed in Paris, where his father, "thinking him old enough to guide himself under his Lordship's own occasional directions," dismissed the young man's tutor and gave him "free command of money" in a town where, according to John Murray, "every Vice may be said to be fashionable." Industrious application to studies, an admirable and appropriate endeavor for a young gentleman, gave way to indulgence, excess, and dissipation.

John Murray viewed Lord Chesterfield's writings on women as reprehensible. Murray emphasized how his own precepts regarding women differed dramatically from the earl's, which he saw as undermining and corrupting genteel womanhood. The earl had ordered his son "to be gay and gallant, to indulge a passion for the sex whether he had [one] or not." In Murray's opinion, seeking out female companionship itself did not present the difficulty. Rather, the earl instructed his son, as Murray recounted the counsel, not to seek out "girls of the town or demireps," women "of too easy purchase, low and unsafe." Nor did Chesterfield encourage his son to find amusement "with young ladies of character." The target of the young man's affections ought to be "no other and no less than married women . . . of the most distinguished virtue." To underline the horror of this practice, Murray invoked the image of a personal tragedy: "What would you think of, what would you do to that Villain who should dare to make an attempt upon your Mother's Honour?"

In Murray's view, then, a gentleman made himself known in part by his conduct toward ladies. The ideal traits of each sex were respected, supported, and defined by the appropriate interaction between them. Indeed, Murray saw gentlewomen as essential to the identity of genteel men. "A man may be a scholar, a man of business, a Philosopher, and artist, but ladies only can form the polite complete gentleman," he declared. Gentility, in this construct, could be achieved only in the sphere in which men and women, who embodied contrasting and complementary aspects of appropriate behavior, interacted with decorum.

Where Chesterfield's dictates on female companionship subverted socially ordained gender roles by undermining the sanctity of marriage and encouraging sexual licentiousness, John Murray supported the status quo by limiting sexual access and controlling passion. Murray recommended that his son spend some of his leisure hours among virtuous women in a chaperoned setting, suggesting that Jack take "tea in a respectable genteel private family, where there [were] some agreeable young ladies under the eyes of a prudent Mother and Grandmother." In his associations with women, Jack must be wary of dangers, of excessive high spirits, of libertinism. "At all events," urged his father, "avoid mischievous intrigues, low amours and adulterous connexions." Sexual contact of the kind Chesterfield urged could prove a moral contagion, just as much as "low" liaisons might foster the spread of venereal disease.

In offering Jack this guidance, John Murray attempted not only to insure that his son would become a genteel man, but to provide him with some practical economic advice.[33] Behavior and reputation held singular importance for young men without titles or legacies. In a sense, John Murray's son Jack and Lord Chesterfield's natural son Stanhope faced similar difficulties. In his distance from his father, Jack shared the lack of direct parental patronage and reputation; moreover, he had far less financial support than Stanhope. While Jack might receive advantage from the stature and connections of his aunt, once a well-known and highly respected businesswoman, and his elder cousin John Clark, to whom he was apprenticed to learn the mercantile trade, he would still have to prove himself a man of business in his own right.

Jack was fatherless not by the circumstances of his birth, but by the choices that placed an ocean between him and his father's hearth. For his part, John Murray also saw his children as "orphaned." In 1771, when his sister Elizabeth married for the third time, John worried that his offspring would suffer from the change in her status, writing: "Oh my Children! Orphans in a Strange Land! what will become of you, if Providence should remove your Aunt or any Cause alienate her Affection?"[34]

In different ways, both John Murray and Chesterfield attempted to educate their offspring according to individual standards and likely saw themselves as failing their sons to some degree. Both young men rejected at least a part of the paternal legacy.[35] Jack Murray, leaving home while still quite young, never developed the ties of loyalty to king and country that his father cherished. Indeed, during the Revolution, Jack simultaneously rebelled against parents and monarch by joining the Continental Army. After the war, he continued to pursue commerce and remained in the United States, while his sisters Polly and Anne, who both left Boston before the Revolution, never returned to shopkeeping. John Murray's hopes—that Jack would mature to become "an ornament" to his family, country, and human nature—were at least in part disappointed.

While the Murrays' verdicts on the success of sending Polly, Jack, and Anne to America were mixed, the economic and educational outcome of one experiment in childrearing garnered consistent praise. In addition to transporting her brother John's children to the colonies for a time, Elizabeth took another niece, raised under her tutelage, to England and Scotland for polish. Thirteen-year-old Betsy, the daughter of James Murray, spent several months in boarding schools in Norwich and Edinburgh in 1770, where she studied music and attended many plays.

Apparently, Betsy's education did not have the negative effects that Polly's and Anne's had, perhaps in part because it offered no conflict with a model of genteel womanhood that eschewed economic endeavor. Betsy Murray's friends and family offered generally positive assessments of her progress. One described her as improving "prodigiously" in her writing.[36] James Murray also praised his youngest daughter, telling his oldest daughter Dolly that her sister had "been much improved" and had learned "to sing & play on the guitar."[37] Elizabeth, who thought of educating youth from an economic perspective, took delight in Betsy's boarding school stint partly because it would offer a grand return on a small capital investment. She was pleased with her niece's accomplishments, concluding that "her visit to Scotland has been of great service to her [;] they say the improvement she had there is & will be of more use than three thousand pound wou'd ha[ve] been."[38] This comment neatly captures Elizabeth Murray Smith's view of education as a means to a social and economic end, in this case marriage; her strong opinions on women's education; and her view on the financial repercussions of her plans. In this instance, she defined Betsy's cultural improvement by the size of a dowry.

The relative ease with which the Murray cousins participated in the societies they encountered on opposite sides of the Atlantic points toward broad cultural sharing, rather than to an inferior and self-consciously backward America contending with a sophisticated and superior England.[39] As Richard Bushman and others have argued, imitation on the colonial side simply signified "American participation in an Anglo-American cultural system."[40] What comes into focus is the similar subordinate status shared by cities such as Norwich, Edinburgh, and Boston in relation to London.

In choosing each locale for its specific educational opportunities, the elder Murrays simultaneously challenged and affirmed different aspects of contemporary mores. In the context of the colonies, they incorporated "industry" into the educational formula for both young women and men, implicitly undermining some of the aims of traditional British genteel education. Elizabeth mentored her nieces and nephews according to the lessons learned through her firsthand experiences with the business and economic opportunities available in Boston. John Murray attempted to fulfill his parental responsibilities to his son from the distance of several thousand miles. In doing so, he sought advice and inspiration from a published source of authority, which ultimately proved unacceptable.

In his reaction to Chesterfield's best-selling *Letters to His Son,* John Murray expressed the difficulty that the Murrays and their contemporaries had with models of gentility and ideals of manhood and womanhood. Even as they sought social mobility through their pursuit of education, the Murrays endeavored to design a model of gentility for young men and women that allowed them to embrace economic activities *and* preserve their sense of morality. In surveying the prescriptive literature that presents idealized behavior, one scholar concluded that although some early texts appealed primarily to aristocratic audiences, the bulk of such material can be characterized as "solidly middle class" and as reflecting "questions about gentility, right-doing, and manners, but more importantly, questions about social identity and roles and how to live good and successful lives."[41] The key concerns had to do with how to act while getting ahead.

Those who sought success tried to achieve higher status partly through emulating the manners of the elite gentlefolk. After goods that were formerly luxuries within the reach only of the wealthy few became widely available and affordable, subtleties in manners and carriage assumed more importance in distinguishing social status. Regarding England's middle classes, "gentility was the most prized possession of all in a society obsessed with the pursuit of property and wealth. It could be purchased, but only if the code of genteel conduct was sufficiently flexible to fit the diverse social and educational circumstances of the purchasers."[42] The effects of the Murrays' efforts to manipulate this code to meet the needs of young women and men demonstrates both its malleability and limits: while Polly Murray became a notable shopkeeper, her younger sister Anne could never transcend her initial, internalized sense of proper behavior for a young gentlewoman.

NOTES

1. Ned C. Landsman, *Scotland and Its First American Colony, 1683–1765* (Princeton: Princeton University Press, 1985), 21–22, 30.

2. For a survey of such skills valued in the colonies see Julia Cherry Spruill, *Women's Life and Work in the Southern Colonies* (1938; reprint, New York: W. W. Norton, 1972), 193–205, 217–23. Laurel Thatcher Ulrich explored distinctions between "pretty gentlewomen" and good housewives in *Good Wives: Image and Reality in the Lives of Women in Northern New England, 1650–1750* (New York: Oxford University Press, 1980), 68–83.

3. Although there is considerable evidence demonstrating that literacy rates among women improved dramatically in the late eighteenth and early nineteenth centuries, scholars disagree about the exact timing of and impetus for the improvement. Various factors served as likely indicators of whether a community invested in education for girls as well as boys. Kathryn Kish Sklar found that an entrenched male elite, a skewed distribution of wealth in favor of a rich minority, and centralized religious authority tended to inhibit the elimination of gender inequities and expenditures in the educational system. Sklar, "The Schooling of Girls and Changing Community Values in Massachusetts Town, 1750–1820," *History of Education Quarterly* 33 (Winter 1993): 537.

4. Karin Calvert, "The Function of Fashion in Eighteenth-Century America," in Cary Carson, Ronald Hoffman, Peter J. Albert, eds., *Of Consuming Interests:*

The Style of Life in the Eighteenth Century (Charlottesville: University Press of Virginia, 1994), 270.

5. Most scholarly treatments of early educational practices focus on the last quarter of the eighteenth century, when Americans invented new political reasons for educating boys and girls in particular ways. In those years, as Linda Kerber has argued, the overriding issues were whether education would produce the virtuous men needed for the survival of the republic and how and whether women should be trained for the political task of educating future citizens. See Kerber, *Women of the Republic: Intellect and Ideology in Revolutionary America* (Chapel Hill, 1980; reprint, New York: W. W. Norton, 1986).

6. Mary Sumner Benson argued that the views of British and French authors who discussed women's abilities and training were widely adopted in the colonies. Benson, *Women in Eighteenth-Century America: A Study of Opinion and Social Usage* (New York, 1935; reprint, Port Washington, N.Y.: Kennikat Press, 1962), 11.

7. James Murray's letterbooks are in the James Murray Papers, Massachusetts Historical Society (hereafter MHS). Some of his letters have been published in Nina Moore Tiffany, ed., *Letters of James Murray, Loyalist,* with a new introduction and preface by George Athan Billias (Boston: Gregg Press, 1972).

8. Boston and Norwich shared characteristics of urban centers in provincial relationships to the metropolis of London. A seat of worsted manufacturing, Norwich remained the second or third largest city in England until the 1770s. Paul Langford, *A Polite and Commercial People: England, 1727–1783* (New York: Oxford University Press, 1992), 74, 418.

9. John Murray to James Murray, 14 April 1764, Murray Papers, box 3, New-York Historical Society (hereafter NYHS), New York.

10. James Murray, 6 October 1733, Murray Papers, box 5, typescripts, NYHS.

11. A more detailed discussion of James Murray's advice and actions appears in "A Family in Motion," chap. 2 in Patricia Cleary, " 'A Spirit of Independence': Elizabeth Murray and Public Roles and Private Lives in Eighteenth-Century America" (manuscript in author's possession).

12. James Murray to John Murray, 5 August 1760, J. M. Robbins Papers, box 1, 1732–1774, typescripts, MHS.

13. One of Elizabeth's experiences with a male protégé ended badly. After she had installed the youngster in her second husband's sugarhouse, she "was so indulgent," in her brother's critical view, "as not to press him against his inclination to the trade." As a result, the young man, whom James Murray described as "a compound of folly, family pride, insolence, and ingratitude," simply "would not apply to the business." James Murray to John Murray, 7 August 1765, J. M. Robbins Papers, typescripts, box 1, 1732–1744, MHS.

14. Elizabeth [Murray] Smith to Christian Barnes, 24 April 1770, J. M. Robbins Papers, MHS.

15. Elizabeth [Murray] Smith to [unknown], January 1770, J. M. Robbins Papers, MHS.

16. Elizabeth [Murray] Smith to Christian Barnes, 24 April 1770, J. M. Robbins Papers, MHS.

17. Ibid.

18. All quotations in this paragraph from Elizabeth [Murray] Smith to Mrs. Deblois, 13 April 1770, J. M. Robbins Papers, MHS.

19. John Murray to Elizabeth [Murray] Inman, 12 July 1773, J. M. Robbins Papers, MHS.

20. Anne Murray Powell to George Murray, 1 August 1838, William Dummer Powell Papers, Mrs. Powell's Letters, 1803–1844, box 4, A97, Metropolitan Library of Toronto.

21. Anne Murray Powell to George Murray, 16 October 1838, William Dummer Powell Papers, Mrs. Powell's Letters, 1803–1844, box 4, A97, Metropolitan Library of Toronto.

22. Anne Murray Powell to George Murray, January 2, 1840, Mrs. Powell's Letters, 1803–1844, box 5, A98, William Dummer Powell Papers, Metropolitan Library of Toronto.

23. In addressing prescriptive literature, Cary Carson laments the lack of information about how readers actually responded to such texts. Carson, "The Consumer Revolution in Colonial British America: Why Demand?" in Carson, Hoffman, and Albert, eds., *Of Consuming Interests,* 642, 643 n. 243, 644, 648–49.

24. For a summary review of this literature, see John Dwyer, *Virtuous Discourse: Sensibility and Community in Late Eighteenth-Century Scotland* (Edinburgh: John Donald Publishers Ltd., 1987), 72–94.

25. Ibid., 74.

26. Sarah E. Newton, *Learning to Behave: A Guide to American Conduct Books before 1900* (Westport, Conn.: Greenwood Press, 1994), 9–10.

27. John Murray to John B. [Jack] Murray, 31 July 1774, box 5, Murray Papers, NYHS. All quotations from correspondence between John Murray and his son refer to this letter unless otherwise noted.

28. Calvert, "The Function of Fashion in Eighteenth-Century America," 271.

29. Chesterfield's letters proved an instant success in England, inspiring reactions from such celebrated figures as King George III and writer Fanny Burney and selling perhaps as many as ten thousand copies within a year. Sidney L. Gulick, ed., *Two Burlesques of Lord Chesterfield's Letters,* publication no. 81 of the Augustan Reprint Society (Los Angeles: William Andrews Clark Memorial Library, UCLA, 1960), i; Sidney L. Gulick, Jr., *A Chesterfield Bibliography to 1800* (Chicago: University of Chicago Press, 1935), 4.

30. Chesterfield's letters, with the most aristocratic elements as well as some infamous improprieties edited out, became the basis for the earliest conduct books for men printed in the colonies and remained a staple of advice literature collections for decades. They were often printed with Benjamin Franklin's *Way to Wealth,* another popular guide to social and economic success. Between 1775 and 1800, Chesterfield's letters were reprinted at least thirty-one times; the edited form, *The Principles of Politeness,* became the most popular advice manual. See Arthur M. Schlesinger, *Learning How to Behave: A Historical Study of American Etiquette Books* (New York: Macmillan, 1947), 9, 12, for details of popularity of various conduct manual. See Gulick, *A Chesterfield Bibliography to 1800,* 63, for details of publication of Chesterfield's letters.

31. Like John Murray, Mercy Otis Warren objected to Chesterfield's views of women, targeting his misogyny in a letter to her own son. Mercy Otis Warren to Winslow Warren, 24 December 1779, reprinted in Edmund M. Hayes, "Mercy Otis Warren versus Lord Chesterfield, 1779," *William and Mary Quarterly,* 3d Ser., 40 (1983): 619–20. Abigail Adams, who was partially responsible for the publication of Warren's letter in a Boston newspaper in 1781, agreed with her friend's view and described the earl as "inculcating the most immoral, pernicious and Libertine principals." Adams's comments are cited in Schlesinger, *Learning How to Behave,* 12.

32. See Michael Curtin, "A Question of Manners: Status and Gender in Etiquette and Courtesy," *Journal of Modern History* 57 (September 1985): 403. For another view of courtesy literature, see Nancy Armstrong and Leonard Tennenhouse, "The Literature of Conduct, the Conduct of Literature, and the Politics of Desire: An Introduction," in Armstrong and Tennenhouse, eds., *The Ideology of Conduct: Essays on Literature and the History of Sexuality* (New York: Methuen, 1987), 15.

33. Manners, even stripped of their moral context and compass, could help an individual achieve worldly success. As Samuel Shellabarager explains, the plan of travel and behavior that the earl outlined for his son would provide a "process of infinitely shifting contacts which would polish him to the desired smoothness of worldly address." Shellabarager, *Lord Chesterfield and His World* (Boston: Little, Brown, 1951), 318. Charles Pullen argues that the earl endeavored not to inculcate immoral codes of conduct but rather to prepare his son to compete and succeed in a world where appearances mattered sometimes as much as realities and where knowing the rules of the game was key. Pullen, "Lord Chesterfield and Eighteenth-Century Appearance and Reality," *Studies in English Literature, 1500–1900* 8 (Summer 1968): 501–15.

34. John Murray to Elizabeth [Murray] Smith, 9 November 1771, Murray Papers, box 3, NYHS.

35. Bereft of his father's title and estate, Philip Stanhope could never have what might have been his birthright had his father been married to his mother.

The training he received did not translate into a phenomenally successful career. In his interactions with women, Philip diverged from his father's precepts dramatically by embracing domesticity and secretly marrying the woman of his choice.

36. Jacobina Day to [Elizabeth Murray Smith], 13 February 1771, J. M. Robbins Papers, MHS.

37. James Murray to Dolly [Murray] Forbes, 21 June 1771, J. M. Robbins Papers, MHS.

38. Elizabeth [Murray] Inman to Lady Don, [1772], J. M. Robbins Papers, MHS.

39. Richard Bushman surveyed accounts of colonial cultural history and their biases in "American High-Style and Vernacular Cultures," in Jack P. Greene and J. R. Pole, eds., *Colonial British America: Essays in the New History of the Early Modern Era* (Baltimore: Johns Hopkins University Press, 1984), 345–83.

40. Ibid, 348. Bushman took this approach of assessing American imitation and exceptionalism in the context of Anglo-American provinciality to explore how English cultural patterns influenced what he termed the distinct subjects of high and vernacular culture.

41. Newton, *Learning to Behave*, 3.

42. Langford, *A Polite and Commercial People*, 464.

Part II

Gender before the Fall

Chapter Five

"The Language of Love"
The Letters of Elizabeth and William Wirt, 1802–1834

Anya Jabour

In 1803 a young lawyer wrote a passionate letter to his bride: "The language of love can never grow old. . . . It will always be new and fresh and sweet—Your dear letters, those effusions of the best of hearts, what a rich repast will they form[.]" This letter was only one of hundreds exchanged by William and Elizabeth Wirt over the next three decades. William Wirt (1772–1834) was U.S. attorney general from 1817 to 1829 and a literary figure who contributed to the legend of the Old South. Elizabeth Gamble Wirt (1784–1857), also an author, wrote America's first book on the "language of flowers." Although both Elizabeth and William Wirt wrote for publication, their most prolific writings were personal and family correspondence. William Wirt's law practice in Virginia, Washington, D.C., and Maryland separated the couple for many months each year. While apart, the Wirts exchanged letters every week, every other day, or every day, depending on the mails. Their private correspondence is an unusually rich source for the study of marriage and gender roles in the early nineteenth century.[1]

Scholarly descriptions of relations between men and women in nineteenth-century America emphasize the differences between the sexes. American women inherited English common law's civil death. No woman could vote. Married women suffered from coverture: under common law, the wife surrendered to her husband her right to her property and to any money she might earn in return for his obligation to support her and her children and provide a dower (usually one-third of their joint estate and personal property) for her support after his death. These inequities may have been exacerbated in the Old South, where women's legal and economic powerlessness was compounded by the fact that husbands usually outpaced their wives in age, education, knowledge of the world, and physical strength.[2]

Despite these harsh realities, a modern idea of marriage as an affectionate partnership was increasingly in vogue among middle-and upper-class Americans in the early nineteenth century. "Companionate marriage," a set of ideals found on both sides of the Atlantic between 1680 and 1850, replaced older conceptions of the family as patriarchal and under the rightful dominance of the male head of the household. Ideally, companionate marriage permitted individual choice in unions based on romantic love and encouraged affectionate, rather than authoritarian, marital relationships.[3]

Of course, a new ideal of companionate marriage did not eliminate the differences between men and women in nineteenth-century America. Studies of married couples in the South have demonstrated that some men and women who adopted the new ideal of companionship experienced their union differently because of their unequal standing in marriage and society. Others simultaneously celebrated romantic love and patriarchy. Studies of Northern women also note that although women gained a certain amount of status within marriage by holding sway over the home, men retained power in the male-dominated workplace. As a result, the ideology of separate spheres developed, conceding men's dominance in the public sphere while celebrating women's role in their own, separate, "woman's sphere." The new ideal of companionate marriage, therefore, encountered significant obstacles in the form of prevailing models for gender relations—domestic patriarchalism in the South, and separate spheres in the North—that accepted and even celebrated different positions for men and women both inside and outside of marriage.[4]

Elizabeth and William Wirt's letters to each other offer another possible clue to the dynamics of relations between women and men in nineteenth-century America. The Wirts moved in a circle of well-to-do Southerners and had ties both to the planter class and to the South's urban professionals. In addition, the Wirts achieved national recognition during their years in the nation's capital. William Wirt gained fame as a popular lawyer and as U.S. attorney general, but the Wirts also attained a reputation together as a model couple. In 1828, Margaret Bayard Smith, a Washington resident and a popular domestic author who wrote for both Northern and Southern publications, paid the couple her highest compliment. The Wirts, she told her son, were her "beau-ideal." Smith was so impressed that she modeled the characters in one of her novels, *A Winter in Washington,* on the Wirts.[5]

The best glimpses into the Wirts' marriage, however, come from their own correspondence. Like many couples in the antebellum South and elsewhere in the nation, Elizabeth and William Wirt were often separated. It was through their correspondence that they, like other well-to-do Southerners, relayed the details of their daily lives, exchanged advice, and explored issues of the greatest personal importance.[6]

The Wirts' correspondence reveals that through the "language of love," this husband and wife articulated an ideal of mutual affection, respect, and companionship. Their vision of companionate marriage helped them to resist both the inequalities inherent in marriage in nineteenth-century America—particularly in the Old South—and the division of men's and women's lives into the separate spheres of home and work commonly attributed to couples in the antebellum Northeast. The Wirts created their own model for marriage. Using the language of love, they crafted an ideal that emphasized the qualities and goals that men and women shared. They did not always live up to their own vision of marriage, but neither did they accept rigid gender roles as an ideal. The more their lives seemed to resemble either patriarchy or separate spheres, the more unhappy they were. Far from celebrating the distinctions between men and women, the Wirts strived for a union of mutuality and reciprocity.

Elizabeth and William Wirt saw marriage as a shared experience. Their correspondence indicates that gender conventions such as patriarchy and separate spheres were perhaps less binding for women and men in the nineteenth century than they are for historians today. Their writings make a strong case for the need to take another look at the history of gender roles. Elizabeth and William Wirt did not always achieve the high standards they set for themselves, but their letters deepen our understanding of men and women in nineteenth-century America.

Although the Wirts struggled to maintain their ideal of mutual affection throughout their three decades of marriage, their letters reflect the changes in their relationship over time. In their early love letters, Elizabeth and William Wirt adopted a "language of love" that transcended definitions of masculinity and femininity. Through this language, the Wirts expressed their emotions candidly and demonstrated their goal of shared love and intimacy. As the Wirt family grew, Elizabeth's obligations to their ten living children and William's commitment to his law practice increased. At one point in their relationship, the couple lived together only two months out of every twelve. The disparity between the reality of the Wirts' separate lives and their ideal of mutuality created tension, and Elizabeth and William's letters took on the tone of lovers' quarrels. Yet, while the Wirts suffered what Elizabeth once called "an almost compleat divorcement," they attempted to maintain the love-letter form in their correspondence with each other. This device allowed them to preserve their ideal of shared love. In the last few years of their marriage, the Wirts revived the language of love. Their final letters detailed their reconciliation and continuous efforts to make their dream of togetherness a reality.[7]

The Wirts used their correspondence to communicate their desires, to express dissatisfaction with their prolonged separation, and finally to resolve their conflicts. Throughout their married life, they articulated an ideal of marriage that was in stark contrast to both the Northern ideological construction of separate spheres and the Southern ideal of domestic patriarchy. Although not fully successful in living up to their own ideal, the Wirts nevertheless suggest that separate spheres and patriarchy were not the only options for nineteenth-century couples.

William Wirt and Elizabeth Gamble met in Richmond in 1799. William was the son of immigrant tavernkeepers in Maryland. He studied law privately in his home state and obtained his license in 1791 in Virginia. With the help of well-placed benefactors, he began his practice in Culpeper and Albemarle counties. He rose to the upper echelon of Virginia society with his marriage in 1795 to Mildred Gilmer, the eldest child of revolutionary veteran and physician George Gilmer. Little is known of Mildred or of her relationship with William. When she died childless in 1799, William moved to Richmond to accept a position as clerk of the House of Delegates. There he met Elizabeth Washington Gamble. Elizabeth was the youngest daughter of one of Richmond's leading families. Her father, Robert, had achieved wealth and prominence as a colonel in the American Revolution and had gained success as a merchant, first in Staunton and then in Richmond. Although only fifteen years old when she first met the twenty-seven-year-old widower, Elizabeth was a witty conversationalist who did not hesitate to discuss politics with her suitors. She had attended a private female academy in Richmond and, according to William, she possessed "vigorous intelligence and solid judgment."[8]

Following a lengthy and sometimes stormy courtship, in the summer of 1802 eighteen-year-old Elizabeth Gamble accepted the proposal of William Wirt, then thirty years old. Both Elizabeth and William concluded that romantic love outweighed all other factors when making a match. Her parents' preference for another man, Elizabeth later wrote, only "awakened her to a sense of the fervor and immoveable constancy of her sentiments for the only being capable of filling her imagination and her heart." Speaking privately with William in the "middle parlour" of the Gamble mansion, Elizabeth admitted that he had a place "deep in her secret heart" and promised to marry him. The wedding took place September 7, 1802.[9]

Elizabeth and William did not correspond during their courtship. Following their wedding, however, they began a detailed correspondence that would last for the rest of their lives. On October 16, 1802, William wrote his first letter to "Mrs. Wirt." Busy with his new duties as the chancellor of a new court of chancery in Williamsburg, where Elizabeth would not move until the following month, William eagerly read her letters and requited her with lengthy epistles of his own. Dreaming of his bride's long curls, dark eyes, and "her kiss," William hoped that "this drear seperation" [*sic*] would soon end. Responding to Elizabeth's query, he assured her that "I confidently hope that when we meet again we shall part no more on this side of eternity[.]" William's aspiration would not be fulfilled. While Elizabeth remained at the couple's homes in Williamsburg (1802), Norfolk (1803–5), Richmond (1806–16), Washington, D.C. (1817–29), and Baltimore (1830–34), William traveled throughout the upper South.[10]

The Wirts used their early letters to explore each other's thoughts and feelings and to discuss their hopes for the future. During their first decade or so of marriage, Elizabeth and William penned scores of love letters. Couples were largely on their own at this stage. Letter-writing guides, which did not address courtship until the 1830s, seldom moved beyond one or two exchanges of letters or a man's official application for permission to address a woman. While later etiquette handbooks offered strict guidelines for letters exchanged by men and women, couples in the early national period enjoyed relative freedom to invent their own love-letter form. Newlyweds in this era, like courting and engaged couples, used correspondence to move beyond the constrained interaction of formal courtship to the mutual intimacy recommended for a companionate marriage.[11]

Absolute privacy was required for the sincere self-disclosure in love letters. Elizabeth told William either to burn her letters or to keep them carefully concealed. William also anxiously sought to preserve the "sacred" privacy of lovers' correspondence. After filling a page with what he called "the language and thoughts . . . of nature and love," William interrupted himself to remind Elizabeth to "let no one read this letter but yourself. . . . Our communications should be sacred—then we shall be perfectly unreserved[.]"[12]

Elizabeth took William's warning too seriously and burned many of the letters she wrote to him during the first few years of their marriage. Fortunately, William was in the habit of quoting back Elizabeth's own words before responding to them, allowing some insight into her writing despite the gap in documentation. Like other women in the early republic, Elizabeth worried that her letters failed to express her true feelings. They tended to be brief and were more concerned with local news and gossip and worries about her correspondent's health than with the lengthy romantic fantasies that filled William's letters. Elizabeth described her letters as "barren, uninteresting and inelegant" and lamented that "I am a poor letter-writer at best." William, who was skilled at the language of love, assured her that this was not the case: "The simple, artless, style of the heart is certainly the most elegant that can be adopted for the purposes of epistolary intercourse—the pure and correct language, the easy flow of genteel conversation, or the natural language of passion, where passion is excited, this is all that a letter should be," he assured her, "and, in my judgment such are my Betsey's in a superlative degree[.]" As long as Elizabeth's letters came "warm from my Betsey's heart," William assured her, form and style did not matter. Indeed, he maintained that "stiffness is abominable . . . in a letter[.]"[13]

Intimacy, not empty formality, was the purpose of Elizabeth and William's correspondence. After 1830, courtship letters in the South were characterized by careful recopying, fine stationery, and the use of literary conventions rather than open expressions of sentiments. In contrast, the Wirts' letters to each other were blotted and hastily written. Both William and Elizabeth often described their missives to each other as "scrolls." What the letters lacked in style they made up in content; through their letters, this couple effectively moved beyond courtship into intimacy. Elizabeth knew that William would make allowances for the "illegible scroll" of her letters, which she did not bother to read over or copy. "H[ow] illy does any thing that I have written above express the animated & glowing affection of my heart," she remarked years later. "It is overflowing with love, and an ardent desire to be worthy of a reciprocal return: But you will make every allowance for me that I could wish—as you always do."[14]

William had no difficulty finding love in Elizabeth's letters, even the ones she burned. Shortly after their marriage, William described his response to one of Elizabeth's burnt love letters. "Beloved of my soul! dearest, dearest Betsey! you cannot imagine how this letter affects me!" he exclaimed. "My eyes are swimming with tears," wrote William, "this is the delicious tumult which you inspire[.]" William's replies to his bride's letters indicate that, despite her own doubts, Elizabeth was fluent in the language of love. "Ah! my dear," he reassured her in 1803, "regret not any imaginary incapacity, to do justice to the feelings and affections of your heart—You write in a language most intelligible to your Williams heart—Well can he discern in your letters the affections of your warm heart while his own vibrates every delicate & fervid sensation[.]"[15]

The couple's letters suggest that they valued a shared sentimentality more highly than rigid definitions of masculinity and femininity. Occasionally, William's comments hint that he thought some might find his candid expression of deep emotions improper. In the midst of one particularly loving letter to his new bride, he demurred: "Will you not despise me for all this weakness? Ah! no—Let me yield to my feelings on this subject and I Promise you, on others, to be as grave and stately as any three tail'd bashaw in the land[.]" William continued to write effusive letters to his wife, although he sometimes worried about how they would appear to strangers. "I cannot conceive the world," he confided to Elizabeth shortly after their first anniversary, "in which I could be happy without you. Surely this cannot be sinful. . . . If it be a sin, I hope for the pardon of Heaven in my weakness and blindness." Reading over this letter, William appended a postscript. "For heaven's sake, my dear let no one read this letter but yourself," he warned. "I have been reviewing it—and altho' the language and thoughts are those of nature and love, I am sure they would appear ridiculous to any one but ourselves."[16]

William's concern that "the language and thoughts of nature and love" might appear to be a "weakness" or "ridiculous" suggests that he believed that, at least in public, men should be "grave and stately." In an 1804 letter, William directly addressed the boundaries imposed by conventional definitions of masculinity and femininity. Uncomfortable with conflict between his true emotions and public expectations of manly decorum, William warned that "I must not indulge this love & sensibility (as divine as they are) too far. . . . The points at which a man & woman should stop in this luxurious feeling are wide asunder, according to the maxims of the world; and the softness that would grace the woman would disgrace the man[.]" But William's romanticism persisted, and he often used a playful tone that routinely violated "the maxims of the world." "My own nature, I confess," he wrote to Elizabeth, "is a very rebel against this maxim—but 'so the law is written.' "[17]

William's references to "the maxims of the world" usually came in the context of defying such mores. He discouraged his bride from indulging in so-called feminine weaknesses. "From you, my dear Betsey," he commented in 1805, "I do not expect those fears and apprehensions, which, however groundless, a great part of your sex think pretty and interesting." William encouraged Elizabeth to make her own decisions "under the sole guidance of your own masculine judgment uninfluenced by the pretty weaknesses which have been exclusively and (so far as your example has informed me) unjustly imputed to your sex[.]"[18]

In his letters, William rejected in practice, if not in language, such conventional definitions of masculinity and femininity. Elizabeth avoided use of the terms *masculine* and *feminine* entirely. Perhaps her example as well as his own inability to curtail his emotions pushed William to musings that masculinity and femininity were acquired, rather than innate, characteristics, with both offering qualities that men and women could and should selectively adopt.

William was more likely to refer to Elizabeth as masculine than to himself as feminine. However, in 1805, when he asked her to write him a "feminine" letter, he revealed that, at least in his correspondence patterns, he was the more feminine of the two. Defining a feminine letter as "long and circumstancial in detail," William could well have pointed to his own lengthy missive as a model of femininity. William's explicit request for a feminine letter—and his inclusion of a precise definition of the term—also indicated that Elizabeth's letters, despite their female authorship, did not automatically meet the criteria for femininity. Elizabeth herself ruefully acknowledged that she lacked William's facility with the language of love. Her expressions of affection tended to be shorter than his, sandwiched between recommendations on his diet and self-dosing for malaria, news of the children's progress, and reports on household affairs. Even Elizabeth's love letters were sometimes tinged with monetary overtones that defied categorization as feminine. "If increasing admiration and ever glowing love, would be a suitable return," she wrote in 1810, "I can faithfully declare myself not insolvent, but ready boldly to meet you with my heart in my hand, and demand an acknowledgement of value received."[19]

Elizabeth Wirt's brief, businesslike letters expressed her practical nature and reflected her daily preoccupation with childrearing and housework. She hastily concluded one letter, written while the children were napping, with a postscript explaining her brevity in terms of her need to attend to the waking children. "Robert has just awakened from a long sleep, in a very fretful humour—and a fever," she wrote in 1807. "I have just prepared some sulphur & shall give it [to] him, as soon as this letter is dispatched[.]" On another occasion, two years later, Elizabeth apologized for a delay in writing, explaining to her husband, "I was yet personally so engrossed by a multiplicity of occupations as to prevent my writing. I have had the sick to attend to at home and my poor sick Moth[er] to visit whenever I could steal the time: I have gone through all the intricacies of my *lumber room, storeroom,* & closets, &c. &c.— and in fact have never sat down but when detained by company[.]"[20]

While Elizabeth attended to the unending needs of children, slaves, and relatives, William often concluded his days in court to return to an empty room in a boarding house. In such circumstances, it was small wonder that he so often sat with Elizabeth's portrait before him and wrote lengthy epistles brimming with love. "I know that I shall both feel and sleep better for having first written to you: Nothing reconciles me more to my self or gives me more harmony of nerves than writing to my beloved," he mused in 1809. While William found composing love letters to be a form of relaxation, Elizabeth found letter-writing to be an additional duty. Yet, she too made daily missives a part of her evening ritual. "If I . . . had a little more energy, I might at least fill the rest of my paper by giving to you the effusions of affection," she closed an 1811 letter, "but I cannot set up any longer—my rest has been so broken and disturbed by the nursing of sick children—that I must lay aside my pen—and take out the rest in dreaming, as I often tell you to do."[21]

Both the content and the quantity of the Wirts' letters demonstrate that, despite their frequent separations, the couple maintained their persistent belief that mutual love and respect were the desiderata of marriage and that their goal should be permanent togetherness. For William, love letters were reassurance for Elizabeth as well as a balm for his own loneliness. "My dearest girl," he wrote in 1805, "believe this promise— *I never will forget* you—nor shall one conveyance ever be lost by any fault of mine which will enable me to assure my Betsey that she is dear to me above the created earth."[22]

Elizabeth used her letters to remind her husband that it was only in togetherness that they would find true happiness. In 1807, she spent a day in her parents' garden with the children. She recounted her activities in a way she knew would appeal to William's romantic character. "I was perfectly attuned to harmony and love," she told her husband, "my little prattlers too—skipping around me, made me to sigh, and wish, and sigh again—for their Father's approving eye, o'er their frolic's." William's presence was necessary, Elizabeth reminded him, to perfect this scene. "Hasten, my beloved William," she urged, "the time when you may sit happily and undisturb[ed], in the bosom of your family."[23]

The Wirts used their correspondence to share daily responsibilities as well as to dream of future togetherness. Throughout their marriage, Elizabeth and William exchanged lengthy letters in which they discussed not only their feelings for each other, but relayed the details of their daily routines. Particularly during their years in Virginia, the Wirts often wrote to request each other's assistance. Elizabeth asked her husband to make household purchases or to select textbooks for the children's lessons. William's domestic responsibilities were not limited to buying the items his wife requested; he also wrote directly to the children to encourage them in their lessons, often offering tips on how to improve their grammar and their study habits. When he was at home, William took an active role in supervising the Wirts' slaves and servants at fall housecleaning and meat preservation. In return for this help, Elizabeth served as her husband's "dear help-mate" in household economy. In addition to supervising a household staff of five to ten slaves at domestic production and keeping an account book for the family's finances, Elizabeth advised her husband on his legal business, assisted him in keeping his papers in order, and offered her counsel regarding investments. The Wirts recognized that such practical, reciprocal assistance bolstered their ideal of mutuality, even during their separations. As William whimsically noted in 1810, "I cannot help smiling at the thought of the different attractions by which my brother Poets & myself woo our mistresses to see us." While poets lured their loved ones with promises of shaded bowers, he noted, William promised Elizabeth " 'corn'd beef & turnips so nice'—Mine, however, is the most solid invitation," he concluded.[24]

Letters kept the Wirts' ideal of mutual love, respect, and togetherness at the forefront of their recorded thoughts throughout their years in Virginia. As he sat down to write a letter to Elizabeth in 1809, William remarked that correspondence with his wife was "a kind of religious exercise from which I always rise with a consciousness that I am a better man. It calls up all the husband and father in my heart and makes me feel with poignant force all the duties and obligations which arise from those connexions."[25]

The Wirts regarded their correspondence as tangible evidence of the love they shared. In 1811, while Elizabeth was away from home visiting relatives, William discovered a collection of their letters, tied up in bundles and "regularly filed away & indorsed by the sweet hands of my excellent and most dearly beloved wife." "I read one of the letters," William recalled to Elizabeth, "and it seized my curiosity and affections with so much violence that I could not desist untill I had devoured the whole mass." Reading into the wee hours of the morning, William "recalled in succession . . . every incident of any interest" that had taken place during nine years of marriage. He immediately set about the task of dating and labeling the letters, as well as adding several in his own possession. Discovering that Elizabeth had burned many of her own letters out of "dissatisfaction" with her epistolary skills, he begged her not to do so again. The letters, he predicted, would be "a treasure" for "your husband, your children, and yourself." Now, he pointed out, their children would be able to read "the lives & love of their parents in their own original letters." "Beloved of my soul," concluded William, "that I have ever loved you most tenderly and respected you most deeply, no one who reads these letters can ever doubt; for they bear a stamp of love that no human power can counterfeit."[26]

William's discovery that Elizabeth had carefully preserved the couple's correspondence highlighted the importance of the language of love as proof of their devotion to each other and as a testament to their ideal of mutual love and shared lives. Shortly after, however, their letters took on a new quality. The Wirts' relationship underwent a series of important changes soon after their tenth wedding anniversary. William expanded his law practice to include Supreme Court appearances as well as travels to courts throughout Virginia. He also added commercial investments to his business interests. Finally, he displayed a new interest in politics. William served in the Virginia House of Burgesses during the 1808–9 term, took military office during the War of 1812, and finally became U.S. attorney general, a position he held from 1817 to 1829. Meanwhile, Elizabeth's domestic responsibilities increased. Between 1803 and 1818, she bore twelve, possibly thirteen, children, ten of whom survived. By the time the Wirts moved to Washington in 1817, the children ranged in age from infancy to adolescence. Elizabeth also supervised a staff of five to ten slaves and the occasional white servant in household production and maintenance. And, as the attorney general's wife, she was expected to "maintain the Presidential standard" as a hostess. Pulled apart by their different duties, Elizabeth and William also were apart from each other more than ever before. In 1825, they spent only two months together. During these difficult years, the Wirts' letters often took on a quarrelsome tone. Despite their frustration, Elizabeth and William continued their former practice of regular correspondence, honoring in the breach the ideals they had expressed in their earlier letters to each other.[27]

Beginning in the 1810s, the Wirts' former intimacy was threatened by William's new attraction to the male world of work and politics. Over Elizabeth's protests, William accepted the captaincy of an artillery unit during the War of 1812. Although war never came to Richmond, William was away from home for long months drilling the soldiers in his command. In his letters from camp, he curtailed his expressions of affection, remarking that soldiers should subject emotion to the most rigid restrictions. In the fall of 1814, William read a letter from Elizabeth "with a heart too swelling and eyes too over-flowing for a soldier—let us bid adieu to this subject—it is too tender for me." He then diverted his letter to camp news. Again and again, William suppressed his emotions and his expressions of love for his family, writing that "this subject is too tender to dwell on—I am forced perpetually to tear my mind away from it."[28]

Unpleasant camp conditions and the difficulty of maintaining discipline among the enlisted men gradually weakened William's commitment to soldiering, and in October 1814 he returned home. Almost immediately, however, new duties called him to Washington. During the war, William had invested in coal fields in Chesterfield County, Virginia. Together with founder John Clarke and other investors, he also had begun work on an arsenal and foundry for cannon casting. William traveled to Washington in 1814 to secure governmental contracts for the foundry. He was successful, and until the completion of the Bellona Arsenal in 1817, William traveled frequently to the national capital to protect the Wirts' coal interests. Business trips to Washington, like William's involvement in the War of 1812, interfered with the couple's correspondence. William made frequent apologies for his brief letters, asserting that "the pressure of business" prevented him from writing at length about his love for his wife. Despite his obvious pleasure at being a "man of consequence," however, William felt compelled to justify his lapses. In 1816, he defended himself to his wife: "that I have not written to you from this place [Washington] has been owing to my anxiety to be with you. . . . I have twice drawn my chair to the table to write to you, when my friend Clarke has suggested to me that I should please you much more by devoting the rare moments of seclusion, to our business, and thereby hastening our return than by employing it in a love letter which would protract my stay."[29]

William combined his new commercial interests with periodic arguments in the Supreme Court, and in October 1817 his new visibility paid off with an invitation to serve as U.S. attorney general. While William made a prolonged sojourn to Washington to clear away pressing matters in the attorney general's office and make arrangements to purchase a new home for the family, Elizabeth began to express doubt about his commitment to her, suggesting that his affection for those at home was secondary to his interest in business and politics. "I did not suppose you would care to hear from us every day," she commented in November. "I expected you would be so engrossed by your new cares, and novel situation, as not to be often troubled by thoughts of home." In contrast, Elizabeth reminded her absent husband, "here you are so much missed . . . as to make us feel and lament your absence *in every passing moment*."[30]

William responded by renewing the couple's love-letter tradition. He demanded daily letters and responded immediately to all those he received, offering in each a variant on the sentiment "I am quite as anxious to see you . . . as you can be to see me—I do not know when I have felt a seperation [*sic*] more cruelly." Through his letters, William hoped to convince Elizabeth of his continued devotion to her and his enduring commitment to togetherness. "I cannot have any peace of mind 'till I get you, here. I am quite moped and melancholy without you," he confessed.[31]

Elizabeth joined her husband in Washington late in 1817, and the "almost compleat divorcement" that Elizabeth had feared seemed safely in the past. However, William Wirt was not satisfied with the income from his official post, and he traveled frequently to courts in Maryland and Virginia. More than ever, correspondence was needed to bridge the gap between husband and wife. Although the Wirts no longer shared their responsibilities through the exchange of memoranda and advice, their letters remained the most important way for them to maintain their relationship. They continued to write to each other regularly, filling their letters with the details of their different daily activities. Elizabeth and William's experiences diverged sharply from the late 1810s through the 1820s, but their correspondence permitted them a vicarious sharing of their lives.[32]

Although they lacked the warmth of the couple's earlier letters, the letters that Elizabeth and William exchanged during their years in Washington tempered Elizabeth's frustration with her husband's continued travels. "I thank you for your very acceptable letter," she wrote to William in 1818. "And although it gives me a certainty of lengthened absence—*that* is what I had made up my mind to expect, and am therefore the more easily reconciled to it." A few days later, Elizabeth again credited her husband's "sweet favours" for consoling her for his continued absence.[33]

As the Wirts continued to live apart, letters proved to be their only means of affirming their abiding commitment to each other. The burden of responsibility fell most heavily upon William. When he fell behind in his correspondence, Elizabeth responded with recriminations. "How vexatious, and disappointing this prolonged absence," she scolded, "and I *do* want to see you so bad—for all *you* are not half so good as you used to be, in writing to me every day." Repeatedly, William had to defend himself against charges of literary inconstancy. In late 1818, the Wirts's oldest daughter began a letter to her father in which she wrote that "my imagination represents you as so busy as not to be able on account of the pressures of your business to spare time to—" before she broke off. Elizabeth peevishly filled in the incomplete letter: "to *think* of us—I suppose she would have said [.]"[34]

Despite their marital problems, Elizabeth and William remained committed to each other and to their vision of marriage as a shared experience. Divorce was not an option for this couple. Divorce rates lagged in the American South in the early nineteenth century, and the Wirts' home state, Virginia, granted divorces of bed and board (legal separations) only by actions of the state legislature. Such pragmatic considerations obviously discouraged couples from legally severing their union, and the

Wirts never expressed any interest in divorce. However, the couple could have decided to come to an understanding in which role definitions and emotional distance replaced mutual companionship and intimacy. Instead, the Wirts upheld an ideal of shared love. Although they did not reach this ideal during this period, they retained expectations of marriage in which similarity, not difference, defined a good relationship. Once the immediate crisis was over, this shared ideal allowed the Wirts to restore their former intimacy.[35]

During this critical period in the Wirts' relationship, their letters to each other took on extraordinary importance as the symbols of their continuing commitment to a relationship of mutuality and reciprocity. In 1819, although preoccupied with the demands of housekeeping, rumors of a slave revolt, economic recession, and two ill children, Elizabeth wrote daily letters to her husband and expected the same in return. "If *I*, amidst such a multiplicity of avocations—and *never rested fatigue* take the time to write to you *every* day," she informed William, "I have a right to expect *you* would do as much." Similarly, William made correspondence an indispensable part of his daily routine. In letters home, William insisted that he thought of Elizabeth daily, despite his "apparent neglect of your kind attentions." "Think not, blessed dear, that duties, severe as they are, have excluded my own dear fireside from my heart's core," he reassured his wife. Though William's letters were increasingly preoccupied with the difficulties of his ongoing cases and the prospects for fame and fortune, he never omitted to add "all my love to you dearest and best of wives."[36]

Despite their physical separation, the Wirts continued to emphasize full disclosure and a longing for future togetherness in their correspondence. As the years dragged on and conditions did not improve, however, the letters lost their efficacy. "These separations, so long protracted, are vexatious drawbacks to happiness, my dear Husband," wrote Elizabeth in late 1821. "If I knew how to better my self, I would not submit to them, so I wouldent." Correspondence with her mate, Elizabeth indicated, had lost its power to reconcile her to his absences. "I hope this is the last letter you will receive from me," she concluded, "this year at least."[37] It was not Elizabeth's "last letter," but from that point forward Elizabeth began to write less frequently and less fully. Her husband did not wish to hear about her unhappiness, she noted in 1822, so she would suppress her emotions henceforth. "I would spare you every painful emotion," she vowed, "my letter at this time therefore must be short—for if I write more—my feelings may overstep the bounds prescribed to them [.]"[38]

The boundaries that Elizabeth placed on her emotions in the early 1820s, like the rules of manly self-control that William adopted during the War of 1812, were soon abandoned. The Panic of 1819 hit Virginia investors and landholders, including the Wirts, hard. With the election of Democrat Andrew Jackson as president in 1828, William, an ardent Republican, lost his post as U.S. attorney general. Personal tragedy also took its toll. In 1824, the Wirts' oldest son, Robert, died of pneumonia following a lengthy illness that may have included a nervous breakdown. Six years later, in 1830, their youngest daughter, Agnes, also died. These losses made Elizabeth and William feel their own failing health all the more keenly.

Hard times brought the Wirts closer and, in the late 1820s and the early 1830s, their letters regained the essential qualities of the language of love: ardent expressions of love for each other and a firm commitment to mutual love, respect, and togetherness. Both Elizabeth and William consecrated the remainder of their lives to each other, their children, and their preparations for heaven. Thanks in part to his weakened condition, William spent less time away from home. During his absences, he and Elizabeth exchanged letters in which they laid plans for his retirement and the family's retreat to a Florida plantation.

The overwhelming emotions brought on by the deaths of two children provoked the Wirts to restore their former intimacy. When news of Robert's death arrived from France in late 1824, William was away from home. Preoccupied with her own grief, Elizabeth neglected writing to him for most of January. When she resumed her correspondence, however, she demonstrated her renewed desire to share her innermost thoughts and feelings with her husband. "I have not loved you less!" she assured him. "No, my dear husband:—whenever even the idea of happiness is present—my heart reverts to you—and to you alone—with any certainty of happiness:—over all things else there rests a cloud of obscurity, and fearful uncertainty."[39]

As the Wirts' trials increased, their correspondence built on this theme. Following Agnes's death in December 1830, both Elizabeth and William wrote lengthy letters to each other that displayed emotional closeness and a shared commitment to their original goal of togetherness. "I have nothing to care for now," declared William, "but my wife and remaining children . . . this [world] has no longer any allurement for me, out of my own family circle[.]" Elizabeth's letters drew attention both to the Wirts' continued physical separations and to their spiritual reunion. "It is indeed a severe trial to be so seperated [*sic*], at such a time," she wrote. "But our spirits meet and mingle at the throne of grace, often, often[.]"[40]

In the 1830s, the Wirts laid plans to establish a family home in Florida. William had begun to invest in the new territory's lands as soon as they opened to settlement in 1825, buying huge tracts in Jefferson County, near Tallahassee, along with Elizabeth's brothers, Robert and John Gamble. The Wirts' oldest daughter, Laura, moved to Florida in 1827 with her husband, Thomas Randall, and in 1833 her younger sister, Elizabeth, followed with her husband, Louis Malesherbes Goldsborough. In Florida, the Wirts believed, they could achieve both family togetherness and economic security. William was enthusiastic about the plan, which would finally enable the couple to enter the idyllic state they had dreamed of in the first years of their marriage. "I feel as if, with Gods blessing, I am securing a quiet retreat for the evening of our days," he mused in a letter to Elizabeth in 1833. "I feel snug & comfortable in the anticipation," he noted happily. "It seems & feels as if we are *doing* something, instead of *dreaming*, merely, of Castles in the air[.]"[41] But it was not to be. William's poor health, attributed by his physicians and his family to years of overwork, left him susceptible to infection, and on February 18, 1834, he died suddenly.

The power of the language of love survived William's death. After her husband's funeral, Elizabeth made it her mission to acquire "copies of His numerous and widely dispersed letters," which she intended to incorporate into "His Biography." The Wirts' letters would now serve as a memorial to William's life as "one among the most tender, devoted, and enlightened of husbands," as the obituary that Elizabeth clipped and labeled "For dear William" described him. "To be associated with him in this commemmoration [*sic*]," mused Elizabeth, was all that she could ask, now that she was "forever cut off in this world, from . . . intimate communion with him."[42]

For Elizabeth and William Wirt, the language of love offered the opportunity to share an "intimate communion" despite their frequent separations and their different responsibilities. Throughout their marriage, the Wirts relied on correspondence—whether in the form of love letters or lovers' quarrels—to express their ideals, to criticize their failures, and finally to renew their commitment to each other. In a society in which the differences between men's and women's lives often threatened to divide marriage partners, the Wirts found that the language of love had the power to unite and sustain them.

In their correspondence, Elizabeth and William Wirt proposed an important alternative to the dominant models of patriarchy and separate spheres. Where patriarchy emphasized differences between men and women, the language of love celebrated similarities. Where separate spheres recommended different activities for husbands and wives, the language of love idealized blissful union. The tenacity with which the Wirts clung to the ideals they elaborated in the language of love—even during marital difficulties—should encourage scholars to take alternative models of marriage as seriously as this nineteenth-century couple did.

NOTES

1. William Wirt to Elizabeth Wirt, October 16, 1803, William Wirt Papers, Maryland Historical Society (hereafter WWPMHS).

2. See, for example, Peter D. Bardaglio, " 'An Outrage upon Nature': Incest and the Law in the Nineteenth-Century South," in Carol Bleser, ed., *In Joy and in Sorrow: Women, Family, and Marriage in the Victorian South, 1830–1900* (New York: Oxford University Press, 1991), 32–51; Suzanne D. Lebsock, *The Free Women of Petersburg: Status and Culture in a Southern Town, 1784–1860* (New York: W. W. Norton, 1984), Chap. 2; Bertram Wyatt-Brown, *Southern Honor: Ethics and Behavior in the Old South* (New York: Oxford University Press, 1982), chaps. 9 and 10.

3. For an overview of the companionate family, see especially Carl N. Degler, *At Odds: Women and the Family in America from the Revolution to the Present* (New York: Oxford University Press, 1980), 8–9; and Lawrence Stone, "Family History in the 1980s: Past Achievements and Future Trends," *Journal of Interdisciplinary History* 12 (summer 1981): 51–88. Several scholars of the slaveholding states have argued that the South resisted this development, and that the hierarchical assumptions of slave society preserved patriarchy—with its accompanying extended families (including slaves), male honor, and female submissiveness—in the South. A growing number of studies, however, have presented evidence that companionate marriage was a phenomenon shared by North and South. For studies that emphasize the patriarchal nature of Southern family life, see Joan E. Cashin, *A Family Venture: Men and Women on the Southern Frontier* (New York: Oxford University Press, 1991); Catherine Clin-

ton, *The Plantation Mistress: Woman's World in the Old South* (New York: Pantheon, 1982); Anne Firor Scott, *The Southern Lady: From Pedestal to Politics, 1830–1930* (Chicago: University of Chicago Press, 1970); and Wyatt-Brown, *Southern Honor*. On companionate marriage in the South, see Melinda S. Buza, " 'Pledges of Our Love': Friendship, Love, and Marriage among the Virginia Gentry, 1800–1825," in Edward L. Ayers and John C. Willis, eds., *The Edge of the South: Life in Nineteenth-Century Virginia* (Charlottesville: University Press of Virginia, 1991), 9–36; Jane Turner Censer, *North Carolina Planters and Their Children* (Baton Rouge: Louisiana State University Press, 1988); and Jan Lewis, *The Pursuit of Happiness: Family and Values in Jefferson's Virginia* (Cambridge: Cambridge University Press, 1983), chap. 5.

4. Useful studies of Southern couples are Carol K. Bleser, "The Perrys of Greenville: A Nineteenth-Century Marriage," in Walter J. Fraser, Jr., R. Frank Saunders, Jr., and Jon L. Wakelyn, eds., *The Web of Southern Social Relations: Women, Family, and Education* (Athens: University of Georgia Press, 1985), 72–89; Virginia Burr, "A Woman Made to Suffer and Be Strong: Ella Gertrude Clanton Thomas, 1834–1907," in Bleser, ed., *In Joy and in Sorrow*, 215–32; and Steven M. Stowe, "Intimacy in the Planter Class Culture," *Psychohistory Review* 10 (spring-summer 1982): 141–64. See also Drew Gilpin Faust's "Epilogue" to Bleser, ed., *In Joy and in Sorrow*, 254–55. For an introduction to the historiography on "woman's sphere," see Jeanne Boydston, *Home and Work: Housework, Wages, and the Ideology of Labor in the Early Republic* (New York: Oxford University Press, 1990); Nancy F. Cott, *The Bonds of Womanhood: "Woman's Sphere" in New England, 1780–1835* (New Haven: Yale University Press, 1977); Linda K. Kerber, "Separate Spheres, Female Worlds, Woman's Place: The Rhetoric of Women's History," *Journal of American History* 75 (June 1988): 9–39; and Mary P. Ryan, *Cradle of the Middle Class: The Family in Oneida County, New York, 1790–1865* (Cambridge: Cambridge University Press, 1981).

5. [Margaret Bayard Smith], *The First Forty Years of Washington Society, Portrayed by the Family Letters of Mrs. Samuel Harrison Smith (Margaret Bayard)*, ed. Gaillard Hunt (New York, 1906; reprint, New York: F. Ungar, 1965), 244.

6. On the importance of correspondence in the South, see Steven M. Stowe, "Rhetoric of Authority: The Making of Social Values in Planter Family Correspondence," *Journal of Family History* 73 (March 1987): 916–33; and Stowe, "Singleton's Tooth: Thoughts on the Form and Meaning of Antebellum Southern Family Correspondence," *Southern Review* 25 (spring 1989): 323–33. Useful studies on courtship and love letters include Karen Lystra, *Searching the Heart: Women, Men, and Romantic Love in Nineteenth-Century America* (New York: Oxford University Press, 1989); Ellen K. Rothman, *Hands and Hearts: A History of Courtship in America* (New York: Basic Books, 1984); and Steven M. Stowe,

Intimacy and Power in the Old South: Ritual in the Lives of the Planters (Baltimore: Johns Hopkins University Press, 1987). For published examples of love letters, see Edith W. Gregg, ed., *One First Love: The Letters of Ellen Louisa Tucker to Ralph Waldo Emerson* (Cambridge: Harvard University Press, 1962); and Vivian R. Pollak, ed., *A Poet's Parents: The Courtship Letters of Emily Norcross and Edward Dickinson* (Chapel Hill: University of North Carolina Press, 1988).

7. For the "language of love," see, for example, William Wirt to Elizabeth Wirt, October 16, 1803, WWPMHS. For "an almost compleat divorcement," see Elizabeth Wirt to William Wirt, November 23, 1817, WWPMHS.

8. For background on William Wirt, see especially John Pendleton Kennedy, *Memoirs of the Life of William Wirt, Attorney-General of the United States,* 2 vols. (Philadelphia, 1849; rev. ed., Philadelphia: Blanchard and Lea, 1851). On the Gambles, see Lyman Chalkley, *Chronicles of the Scotch-Irish Settlement in Virginia Extracted from the Original Court Records of Augusta County, 1745–1800,* 3 vols. (Baltimore: Genealogical Publishing Company, 1966); Nell McNish Gambill, *The Kith and Kin of Captain James Leeper and Susan Draker, His Wife* (New York: National Historical Society, 1946); and George R. Gilmer, *Sketches of Some of the First Settlers of Upper Georgia, of the Cherokees, and the Author* (Baltimore: Genealogical Publishing Company, 1965). On Elizabeth, see also *The South in the Building of the Nation,* 12 vols. (Richmond: Southern Historical Publication Society, 1909–13), 12: 567; and Sarah P. Stetson, "Mrs. Wirt and the Language of Flowers," *Virginia Magazine of History and Biography* 57 (October 1949): 376–89. For William's remark, see William Wirt to Elizabeth Wirt, November 6, 1805, WWPMHS. For Elizabeth's letter to another suitor, Thomas Bayly, see Elizabeth Wirt Letter, March 11, 1801, Virginia Historical Society. See also Anya Jabour, " 'No Fetters But Such as Love Shall Forge': Elizabeth and William Wirt and Marriage in the Early Republic," *Virginia Magazine of History and Biography* 104 (spring 1996): 211–50.

9. The only description of the betrothal comes from the wrapper of the Wirts' first letters, presumably written by Elizabeth. For quotations, see introduction to engagement letters (first and third quotations); William Wirt to Elizabeth Wirt, May 22, 1805 (second quotation); William Wirt to Elizabeth Wirt, August 31, 1811 (fourth quotation), WWPMHS. See also their marriage bond, filed in the Henrico County Courthouse, noted in Anne Waller Reddy and Andrew Lewis Riffe IV, *Virginia Marriage Bonds: Richmond City* (Staunton, Va.: McClure Company, [1939]), 1:2; and the announcement of their marriage in the *Virginia Gazette,* September 11, 1802.

10. William Wirt to Elizabeth Wirt, October 16, 1802, WWPMHS.

11. On love letters, see Lystra, *Searching the Heart,* Chap. 1. On engagement, see Frances B. Cogan, *All-American Girl: The Ideal of Real Womanhood*

in Mid-Nineteenth-Century America (Athens: University of Georgia Press, 1989), Chap. 5. On letter-writing guides, see Stowe, *Intimacy and Power*, 58–67.

12. William Wirt to Elizabeth Wirt, October 23, 1803 (quotation); May 17, 1806, WWPMHS.

13. William Wirt to Elizabeth Wirt, October 16, 1802; October 28, 1802; October 16, 1803; November 27, 1803, in WWPMHS. According to Rothman, *Hands and Hearts*, 11, it was not uncommon between 1770 and 1840 for women's letters to be short, hasty, or delayed.

14. Elizabeth Wirt to William Wirt, June 15, 1810, WWPMHS. Although this letter was written after eight years of marriage, its sentiments accord with the content suggested by William's replies to earlier letters. On courtship letters in the Old South, see Stowe, *Intimacy and Power*, 90.

15. William Wirt to Elizabeth Wirt, October 26, 1802; December 13, 1803, WWPMHS.

16. William Wirt to Elizabeth Wirt, October 16, 1802; October 23, 1803, WWPMHS.

17. William Wirt to Elizabeth Wirt, July 14, 1804, WWPMHS.

18. William Wirt to Elizabeth Wirt, May 19, 1805; July 21, 1805, WWPMHS.

19. William Wirt to Elizabeth Wirt, April 7, 1805; Elizabeth Wirt to William Wirt, July 18, 1810, WWPMHS.

20. Elizabeth Wirt to William Wirt, April 27, 1807; October 27, 1809, WWPMHS.

21. William Wirt to Elizabeth Wirt, September 11, 1809; Elizabeth Wirt to William Wirt, September 28, 1811, WWPMHS.

22. William Wirt to Elizabeth Wirt, November 6, 1805, WWPMHS.

23. Elizabeth Wirt to William Wirt, April 28, 1807, WWPMHS.

24. William Wirt to Elizabeth Wirt, March 30, 1806 (first quotation); September 9, 1810 (second quotation), WWPMHS. See also Jabour, " 'No Fetters But Such as Love Shall Forge,' " 237–50.

25. William Wirt to Elizabeth Wirt, September 11, 1809, WWPMHS.

26. William Wirt to Elizabeth Wirt, August 31, 1811, WWPMHS.

27. On William's activities, see Joseph Charles Burke, "William Wirt: Attorney General and Constitutional Lawyer" (Ph.D. diss., Indiana University, 1965). For quotation, see William Wirt to Elizabeth Wirt, December 3, 1817, WWPMHS.

28. William Wirt to Elizabeth Wirt, September 24, 1814; September 26, 1814, WWPMHS.

29. William Wirt to Elizabeth Wirt, January 6, 1816; January 1, 1816; December 30, 1816, WWPMHS. On the coal fields and arsenal, see Virginius Dabney, *Richmond: The Story of a City*, rev. ed. (Charlottesville: University Press of Virginia, 1990), 20, 93–94.

30. Elizabeth Wirt to William Wirt, November 23, 1817, WWPMHS.

31. William Wirt to Elizabeth Wirt, November 20, 1817; November 28, 1817, WWPMHS.

32. For quotation, see Elizabeth Wirt to William Wirt, November 23, 1817, WWPMHS. On William's attorney-generalship and other legal work, see Burke, "William Wirt."

33. Elizabeth Wirt to William Wirt, May 8, 1818; May 11, 1818, WWPMHS.

34. Elizabeth Wirt to William Wirt, July 30, 1818; Laura Wirt to William Wirt, November 20, 1818, WWPMHS.

35. On divorce, see Glenda Riley, *Divorce: An American Tradition* (New York: Oxford University Press, 1991), Chap. 2.

36. Elizabeth Wirt to William Wirt, April 17, 1819; William Wirt to Elizabeth Wirt, November 30, 1818; November 25, 1818; December 10, 1818, WWPMHS.

37. Elizabeth Wirt to William Wirt, December 20, 1821, WWPMHS.

38. Elizabeth Wirt to William Wirt, March 29, 1822, WWPMHS.

39. William Wirt to Laura Wirt, January 8, 1825; Elizabeth Wirt to William Wirt, January 16, 1825, WWPMHS.

40. William Wirt to Elizabeth Wirt, February 14, 1831; Elizabeth Wirt to William Wirt, January 27, 1831, WWPMHS.

41. William Wirt to Elizabeth Wirt, February 26, 1833, WWPMHS. On the Florida scheme, see Jerrell H. Shofner, *History of Jefferson County* (Tallahassee, Fla.: Sentry Press, 1976), 88–91 and passim.

42. For quotations, see Elizabeth Wirt to John P. Kennedy, September 18, 1834; Elizabeth Wirt to Samuel L. Southard, April 7, 1834, Elizabeth Wirt Letterbook, Wirt Family Papers, Southern Historical Collection, University of North Carolina, Chapel Hill, N.C.; for the obituary, see *Daily National Intelligencer,* February 19, 1834, in WWPMHS.

Chapter Six

Tippecanoe and the Ladies, Too
White Women and Party Politics in Antebellum Virginia

Elizabeth R. Varon

The nineteenth-century ideology of "separate spheres," which prescribed that men occupy the public sphere of business and politics and women the domestic sphere of home and family, has exercised a powerful hold over historians of the antebellum United States. As a result, the fields of antebellum political history and women's history have used separate sources and focused on separate issues. Political historians—relying on sources such as voting records, newspapers, and the writings of politicians—have described the emergence in the 1840s of what the historian Joel H. Silbey has called a new "American political nation." Gone was the political world of the early republic, with its widespread antiparty sentiment, deferential behavior by voters, and political dominance by social elites. In the new order, political parties, led by professional politicians, demanded disciplined partisanship from the electorate. The "electoral universe" was in constant motion. Men participated in a frenzied cycle of party rallies, processions, committee meetings, conventions, caucuses, and elections. What about women? Since they were neither voters nor politicians, women have received only brief mention in the new political history.[1]

Women's historians, for their part, have shown little interest in the subject of party politics. Drawing primarily on personal papers, on legal records such as wills, and on the organizational records of female associations, they have illuminated women's domestic lives, their moral reform activities, and the emergence of the woman's rights movement. Those few scholars—Paula C. Baker, Mary P. Ryan, and Michael E.

McGerr—who have tried to integrate political history and women's history have not challenged the historiographical impression that the realm of antebellum party politics was a male preserve. While these scholars note that women took part in political campaigns, they stress the theme of female exclusion from male political culture. As McGerr has written, women were let into the political sphere only "to cook, sew, and cheer for men and to symbolize virtue and beauty." They were denied "not only the ballot but also the experience of mass mobilization."[2]

The distance between antebellum political history and women's history is perhaps nowhere so great as in the historiography on the Old South. While northern feminist abolitionists who demanded political enfranchisement have begun to receive their due from historians of northern politics, no such radical vanguard existed in the South to command the attention of political historians. Both the major historians of antebellum southern politics and the major practitioners of southern women's history have neglected the subject of female partisanship. The current historiographical consensus holds that southern women, in keeping with the conservatism of their region, by and large eschewed politics even as northern women were fighting for access to the political sphere.[3]

This essay attempts to close the gap between women's history and political history. Focusing on the Commonwealth of Virginia, it argues that historians have underestimated the extent and significance of women's partisanship in the antebellum period. In the presidential election campaigns of the 1840s, Virginia Whigs made a concerted effort to win the allegiance of the commonwealth's women by inviting them to the party's rallies, speeches, and processions. Though the Whigs never carried the state for their presidential candidates, they repeatedly claimed that the majority of women favored their party over the Democrats. Whig campaign rhetoric, as presented by the party's newspapers, and women's private and public expressions of partisanship articulated a new ideal of feminine civic duty, one that I call Whig womanhood. Whig womanhood embodied the notion that women could—and should—make vital contributions to party politics by serving as both partisans and mediators in the public sphere. According to Whig propaganda, women who turned out at the party's rallies gathered information that allowed them to mold partisan families, reminded men of moral values that transcended partisanship, and conferred moral standing on the party.

The Whigs' claim that there was a "gender gap," to use a modern phrase, between them and the Democrats did not go unanswered. During the 1844 campaign, the Virginia Democrats made sporadic appeals to women. A full-scale public debate over women's partisanship erupted in the months after the presidential election of 1844, when the Whig women of Virginia formed the Virginia Association of Ladies for Erecting a Statue to Henry Clay. The Clay Association believed its work was the perfect expression of female patriotism. The Democrats disagreed, branding the association's activities unladylike and even rebellious. The debate fizzled out in a few months, with the Whigs apparent winners. Gradually, Democrats in Virginia adopted Whig tactics for developing female allegiance to their own party. By the mid-1850s the inclusion of women in the rituals of party politics had become commonplace, and the ideology that justified such inclusion had been assimiliated by Democrats.

In Virginia, the Whig party's "Tippecanoe and Tyler, Too," campaign of 1840 marks a turning point in women's partisanship. Prior to 1840, women, with a few notable exceptions, were marginal to the public discourse and rituals of political parties in Virginia. To be sure, many women felt partisan allegiances. Evidence of such partisanship can be found primarily in the letters of female relatives of politicians. Such women as Judith Rives, wife of United States senator William Cabell Rives, were trusted advisers to their husbands and frequently expressed partisan opinions in their correspondence with family members. Some women, particularly relatives of officeholders and those who lived near Washington, D.C., or Richmond, attended political speeches and legislative deliberations, but political parties made no systematic efforts to encourage or to publicize women's presence in the galleries.[4]

The rhetoric and symbolism of presidential election campaigns in the 1830s were predominantly masculine and martial. For example, the *Staunton Spectator* of October 20, 1836, featured the following exhortation to the voters of Augusta County: "Let every man then gird on his armour for the contest! Let the beacon FIRES be lighted on every hill, to give warning to all that the enemy is at hand! Let the WAR DRUMS beat a loud REVEILLE!"[5]

The only expression of partisanship by a woman found in the Virginia newspapers from the 1830s sample is a poem to William Henry Harrison that appeared in the *Staunton Spectator* of September 1, 1836. A "young lady" from Pennsylvania defended Harrison and chided his critics with the words: "Those who would thus *disgrace their land* / Are found in every age; / Not ev'n our Washington could stand / Untouch'd by *Party rage.*" The *Spectator's* editors said of the poet, "We are glad she is for Harrison—though we understand most of the Ladies are so."[6]

The *Staunton Spectator* editors were ahead of their time in suggesting that an affinity existed between women and the Whig party; so, too, was Lucy Kenney of Fredericksburg, who made a similar claim. A single woman aspiring to be a professional writer, Kenney published a series of pamphlets in the 1830s, including one in which she proclaimed her support for Democratic president Andrew Jackson and his heir apparent, Van Buren. In 1838 Kenney switched allegiances and became a Whig. A fervent supporter of slavery and states' rights, Kenney believed that the passing of the Democratic torch to northerner Van Buren—who had supported the Missouri Compromise and, so southerners charged, had abolitionist supporters—boded ill for the South. But her defection from the Democrats was not purely ideological. When Kenney had called on Van Buren in 1838, asking that he and his party remunerate her for her efforts on their behalf, the president, much to her disgust, had offered her a mere dollar. Some "honorable Whigs," however, had a different notion of Kenney's worth and offered her one thousand dollars for her services.[7]

Kenney took the Whigs up on their offer, and later that year published a scathing pamphlet, *A Letter Addressed to Martin Van Buren,* in which she predicted that the 1840 election would strip Van Buren of the "usurped power" he had gained by "false pretences." Kenney's attack on the president prompted a response, in pamphlet form, from Van Buren supporter Eliza B. Runnells. According to Runnells, Kenney possessed none of the "elevated tone of feeling and celestial goodness, that has distinguished the female character." Kenney had been enlisted and armed for battle by "Whig magicians" and in the process "transfigured from an angel of peace, to a political bully."[8]

The exchange between Kenney and Runnells prefigures later developments. In 1840, as Whig recruitment of women began on a grand scale, Democratic commentators echoed Runnells's doubts about the propriety of women's partisanship. Stung by their loss in the presidential campaign of 1836, the Whigs in 1840 overhauled both their message and their strategy for taking it to the voters. In the South that message was, in the words of historian William W. Freehling, "safety on slavery and reversal of political immorality and economic chaos." Too ideologically divided in 1836 to settle on a single presidential ticket, the Whigs in this election cycle chose two sons of Virginia—Harrison and John Tyler.[9]

The new medium for the message was equally important. The Whigs decided that to win the election, they needed to "agitate the people"— and that the people included women. Leading Whigs around the country called for strong local organization and the use of "every lawful means" to bring men to the polls. Means for influencing the electorate included dinners, barbecues, picnics, and processions, with women as spectators and participants.[10]

Historians generally agree that the Whigs' 1840 campaign marks the first time a political party systematically included women in its public rituals. All around the country, women turned out at Whig rallies; on occasion they even made speeches, conducted political meetings, and wrote pamphlets on behalf of the Whigs. And yet, while many scholarly studies note these developments, none draw out their implications. Historians have relegated women's partisanship to a few pages of description here and there; and they generally present women, not as political actors, but as "audience and symbol." The pioneering treatment of Whig women, Robert Gray Gunderson's *The Log-Cabin Campaign*, characterizes women's role at rallies as "conspicuous, but passive." A recent study by Mary Ryan makes a similar case: women who attended Whig political events in 1840 did so "not in public deliberation but as symbols," as "passive and respectable representatives of femininity."[11]

The Virginia evidence suggests that to characterize women's partisanship as passive is to obscure the transformation in women's civic roles that the election of 1840 set in motion. Newspapers, pamphlets, and speeches, taken together with women's diaries, letters, and reminiscences, chart that transformation. The function of antebellum newspapers, which were the organs of political parties, was to make partisanship seem essential to men's identities.[12] With the campaign of 1840, Whig newspapers took on the additional task of making partisanship seem essential to women's identities.

Whig newspapers in Virginia, in lockstep with the party's national organ, the *Washington National Intelligencer*, featured invitations to women to attend the speeches and rallies of "Tippecanoe and Tyler, Too," clubs and provided glowing reports of such events. The *Staunton Spectator* noted, for example, that the women of Mt. Solon favored its "Tipp and Ty" club with their attendance and "enjoyed very highly the display of eloquence" by the speakers. Whig rhetoric argued that the presence of women at such events bespoke not only their admiration for Harrison but also their opposition to the policies of the Democrats. In an article in the *Washington National Intelligencer*, one Whig correspondent, commenting on the high turnout of women at Whig rallies, declared that women supported the Whigs because the "selfless schemings" of the Van Buren administration had "made themselves felt in the very sanctum sanctum of domestic life."[13]

Anecdotes celebrating women's influence began to circulate in the Whig newspapers of Virginia. One such story, "Another Conversion," told the tale of Miss Bond, "a warm Harrison woman," who refused to marry Mr. Provins, her Democratic suitor. After hearing a particularly convincing Harrison speech, Provins finally came around: "*he* declared for Harrison, and *she* declared for PROVINS on the spot." The very fact that the writer referred to Bond as a "warm Harrison woman" reflects the new political climate. Women who felt partisan identities in the 1820s and 1830s were often referred to as "men": in 1827 James Mc-Dowell wrote to his wife, Susan, that his sister Sopponisha was an "Adams-man"; in 1834 William Cabell Rives referred to his friend Mrs. James Cocke as a "warm *Jackson-man*." In 1840, and in the presidential campaigns that followed, partisan women were commonly described, and described themselves, as "Whig women" and "Democratic women."[14]

According to the Whig press, women could contribute to the campaign not only by listening to speeches and by exerting influence over men but also by making public presentations. On October 1, 1840, the "Whig Ladies of Alexandria" presented a banner with the motto "Gen. Wm. H. Harrison, the Glory and Hope of our Nation" to the local Tippecanoe club; male delegates of the club carried the banner in a Whig procession that took place four days later in Richmond. Whig newspapers also occasionally published Harrison songs and poems by women. One Virginian wrote a song in honor of her party's candidate that ended with the refrain "Down with the Locos/dark hocus-pocus/The Banner of Liberty floats through the sky."[15]

The single most vocal female contributor to the Tippecanoe campaign was Kenney. She published two pamphlets, *A History of the Present Cabinet* and *An Address to the People of the United States,* in support of Harrison's 1840 campaign. He was an honorable statesman who had earned the "blessings of thousands of women and children" in his career as an Indian fighter. In keeping with a favorite Whig theme, Kenney asserted that Harrison's private character was as unassailable as his public record. He was an "honest and upright" and "chivalric" man who would restore the United States to "peace, plenty and prosperity." "Let the present party leaders remember that in November next we will shout the harvest home," she declared, sure of Harrison's triumph.[16]

The personal papers of Virginia women confirm that the 1840 campaign was different from its predecessors. "Fashionable topics seem to turn on politics more than anything else at present," Whig Judith Rives wrote her son in February 1840, from the family plantation in Albemarle County. "I never saw anything like the excitement here," Sarah Pendleton Dandridge of Essex County informed her sister; "we hear of nothing but Gen. Harrison." Girls as well as women were caught up in the campaign hoopla. Sara Pryor, who grew up near Richmond, relates in her reminiscences that she knew many a young girl who enjoyed "singing the campaign songs of the hero of the Log Cabin." Thirteen-year-old Frances Ann Capps of Portsmouth attended a crowded Whig meeting at which she listened to a four-and-a-half-hour speech; she found the occasion "very pleasing."[17]

Private residences and businesses became sites for the consumption and production of partisan material culture. Women not only bought a vast array of Whig paraphernalia (such as stationery, songbooks, plates, buttons, glassware, and quilts bearing Harrison's name) but also made their own. In preparation for a Whig procession, Celestia Shakes of Alexandria made a model log cabin, which she placed in the window of her shop where everyone was sure to see it; "the Cabin pleased the Whigs very much [and] they cheered it," she wrote her sister.[18]

In the age of mass politics, even women's housekeeping could serve partisanship. Party conventions, rallies, and processions might bring thousands of visitors who had to be lodged, fed, and cared for. Naturally, women played a key role in providing these services and so facilitated the political process. One such woman, Mary Steger of Richmond, wrote to a friend in September 1840 about her preparations for the upcoming state convention of the Whig party:

> every Whig house in the city is to be crammed we expect to have 10 or 12 sleep here to say nothing of the stragglers in to dinner &tc you will think perhaps it needs not much preparation but we are all in a bustle. ... it is no easy task in this filthy place to keep a three story house clean. ... there are from 6 to 8 thousand Delegates and members of our Tip-

pecanoe Club here determined to pay all their expenses. . . . Our Log Cabin is open almost every few nights (the regular meetings being once a week) to some speakers from a distance. the Cabin holds 1,500 and it is always full.

In all likelihood, Steger had been to the "Log Cabin" (the Whig campaign headquarters) herself to hear Whig discourses. It was quite impossible to remain aloof from politics, she told her friend: "I never took so much interest in politics in my life. . . . the fact is you have to know something about them for nobody here thinks of any else."[19]

For Whig women in Virginia, the crowning event of the 1840 campaign was Whig luminary Daniel Webster's visit to Richmond during the October convention. Susan Hooper, who achieved some renown as a writer during the Civil War, was at a reception for Webster on his arrival in Richmond and later wrote a detailed description of the event. Her father, a staunch supporter of Webster, "could not permit so golden an opportunity of his child's seeing his political idol to pass unimproved; so, girl, almost baby as I was, he hurried me down to the honorable gentleman's reception . . . that in after years I might boast of having heard Webster, the immortal."[20]

After giving two speeches to huge crowds of enthusiastic Whig men and women, Webster yielded to the "particular request of the ladies of Richmond" and agreed to present a special address on women's political role to them at the Whig campaign headquarters. On October 7, some twelve hundred women turned out for the event. Webster took issue with the popular maxim that "there is one morality for politics and another morality for othe₁ things," and he looked forward to the day when the standards of private life would govern public conduct. It was women's special duty, he suggested, to bring that day about.[21]

Because their moral perceptions were "both quicker and juster than those of the other sex," Webster continued, women could infuse society with the "pure morality" on which sound government depended. Mothers had to teach their children that

> the exercise of the elective franchise is a social duty, of as solemn a nature as man can be called on to perform; that a man may not innocently trifle with his vote; that every free elector is a trustee as well for others as himself, and that every man and every measure he supports has an important bearing on the interests of others as well as on his own.

Webster refrained from analyzing specific political issues, not because he feared the women would not be interested, but because, he said, "You read enough—you hear quite enough on those subjects."[22]

Webster's views were echoed by two of Virginia's leading Whigs, former governor James Barbour and Richmond lawyer James Lyons, who spoke to the crowd after Webster had finished. They made explicit what Webster had implied: women's civic duty was to create Whig families, and their public participation in Whig events empowered them to fulfill that role. Barbour expressed delight at having seen throngs of women attend Whig rallies throughout "the length and breadth of this land" during the year's canvass. Those women were "animated with the one holy purpose of redeeming from destruction those liberties earned for us by our fathers, which are equally dear to woman as to man, and which she, with us, is equally bound to transmit untarnished to our children for ages to come." With all the ladies against the Democratic candidate Van Buren, Barbour asked, how could he possibly win? Lyons proclaimed that the "countenance" of the ladies was both a means and a guarantee of the party's success. With Whig mothers there must be Whig sons and Whig daughters; with Whig daughters there would be Whig sweethearts, he asserted. Guarded by the "shield of female purity," Lyons concluded, the Whigs were sure to conquer.[23]

The *National Intelligencer,* which reprinted the speeches in their entirety, praised Webster for celebrating the "vast influence" of women on the well-being of society. The *Richmond Whig* saw the turnout of women as evidence that the "better part of creation were and are, almost unanimously Whig." Women's support for the party "ought to silence Loco Focoism, and sanctify the inevitable Revolution which is about to occur," the editors proclaimed.[24] The "Revolution" the editors had in mind was the victory of Harrison over Van Buren. But they, along with Webster and his colleagues, were helping to actuate another revolution— one in gender conventions.

Webster and his fellow speakers were in effect articulating a new theory of women's civic duty. That theory, Whig womanhood, attempted to reconcile women's partisanship as Whigs with the ideology of domesticity or "true womanhood." The canon of domesticity, like the revolutionary-era theory of republican motherhood, celebrated woman's power and duty to mold the character of her sons, to instill in them civic virtue and a love for the Republic. At the same time, domestic doctrine held that the "true woman" was nonpartisan. Men embodied the "baser instincts"—selfishness, passion, and ambition—which partisanship expressed. By contrast, women were selfless, disinterested, and virtuous. Men pursued their self-interest in the public sphere; women maintained harmony, morality, and discipline in the domestic one.[25]

What was new about Whig womanhood was its equation of female patriotism with partisanship and its assumption that women had the duty to bring their moral beneficence into the public sphere. Whig rhetoric held that women were partisans, who shared with men an intense interest and stake in electoral contests. No longer was patriotism a matter of teaching sons to love the Republic. A patriotic woman would teach her family to love the Whig party; she, after all, understood that the Whigs alone could ensure the health and safety of the Republic.

That very understanding was forged in public. Rather than affirm a cherished tenet of the ideal of domesticity, that women must avoid the contentious political arena in order to safeguard their virtue, Whig speakers argued that by attending campaign events, women could transform the public sphere, fostering "domestic" virtues such as fairness, harmony, and self-control in a larger setting. Women's "countenance" sanctified the Whig cause; their presence bespoke the party's moral rectitude. Not only did women legitimize partisan behavior, they helped set limits on it—they guarded men with a "shield of purity" and made them understand the moral consequences of their actions. In a sense, Whig womanhood was the ultimate testament of faith in true womanhood. Its expositors held that *even* participation in party politics could not corrupt women or erase the fundamental differences between them and men.

How well did Whig rhetoric about women conform to reality? The Whigs' claim that the "ladies are all Whigs" was, of course, a fanciful fabrication. Even though expressions of partisanship by Whig women outnumber those by Democratic women in extant writings from 1840, it seems unlikely that a majority, let alone the entirety, of Virginia women supported the Whigs. Despite Harrison's vigorous campaign, the Democrats still had the support of a majority of voters in Virginia in 1840; women's private papers simply do not bear out the Whig contention that many of these Democratic voters had Whig wives. Since women did not cast ballots, the Whigs' assertion that there was a gender gap in politics cannot be empirically proven or refuted—therein, no doubt, lay some of its viability as propaganda. But the Whig party clearly did much more than its rival to encourage and celebrate female partisanship, and

Whig women, most likely as a result, outdid their Democratic counterparts in displays of partisan zeal.

Judging by the campaign reports of Democratic newspapers, the Democrats were deeply ambivalent about women's partisanship. Jackson, the grand old hero of the Democratic party, drew admiring crowds of men and women when he toured the South, but such Democratic newspapers as the party's national organ, the *Washington Globe,* did not make a concerted effort to publicize or encourage women's presence at Democratic rallies.[26]

The leading Democrats in Virginia did little to contest the Whig party's assertion that it alone had the blessing of women. Some Democrats openly expressed their contempt for Whig tactics. The *Richmond Crisis,* a Democratic campaign paper, mockingly suggested to the Whigs that they might increase the "swelling pageant" at their state convention if they ran the following advertisement: "A meeting of the Babies of Richmond, with their Nurses, is respectfully requested this evening, at the Log Cabin, in order to form a Tippecanoe Infant Club." After Webster's speech to the Whig women of Richmond, a correspondent to the *Richmond Enquirer* lambasted speaker and audience alike, asking "Are the ladies of Virginia so destitute of religious and moral instruction, that they need a thorough politician to enlighten them on the subject of the training of their children?" At least one Democratic paper took a different tack: when a woman in Charlottesville wrote to the *Warrenton Jeffersonian* with the news that the Democratic convention in her town had "caused some of the Whigs to lose their countenance," the editor of the newspaper held her up as a "good Republican." He responded to the Whig insistence that " 'All the Ladies are Whigs!' " by proclaiming, "We never believed it." But most Democratic editors chose to ignore rather than refute the Whigs' claims about women.[27]

Why was the Whig and not the Democratic party the first to seize the opportunity to make, as one Democrat put it, "politicians of their women"? Answers to the question must be speculative, for neither Whig nor Democratic commentators explicitly accounted for this difference in the political tactics of the two parties. Studies of Whig ideology argue that women were central to the Whigs' world view. Although the Democrats sought to maintain a strict boundary between the private and public spheres and resented attempts to politicize domestic life, the Whigs invested the family—and women in particular—with the distinct political function of forming the "stable American character" on which national well-being depended. While the Democrats acknowledged the reality of social conflict, the Whigs preferred speaking of a society in which harmony prevailed; women's "special moral and spiritual qualities," Whigs maintained, fitted them for the task of promoting such harmony.[28]

Historians Joe L. Kincheloe Jr., Ronald P. Formisano, and Richard J. Carwardine suggest that inclusion of women in partisan rituals was a by-product of the Whig party's efforts to blend religion and politics. Many Whig leaders were steeped in evangelical religion and applied what they had learned in the religious sphere to the political one. They practiced "secular revivalism"—the great rallies of the 1840s were, in essence, secular camp meetings. Using the evangelical idiom, Whig orators told crowds of enthusiastic men, women, and children that a presidential campaign was not simply a contest over political principles but a clash between good and evil.[29]

While some Whig men may have conceived of religious revivals as a model for partisan rituals, it is also likely that the connections of Whig leaders to benevolent reform movements predisposed them to recognize the value of women's aid. Scholars have long identified the Whig party with benevolent reform. The Whigs believed, historians Daniel Howe and Lawrence Kohl have argued, in the malleability of human nature. They championed institutions that could help individuals achieve the "self-mastery" on which social order depended: schools, benevolent societies, reformatories, and asylums. All around the country, Whigs were leaders in reform movements. Henry Clay of Kentucky served as president of the American Colonization Society, and Theodore Frelinghuysen of New Jersey served as president of the American Tract Society and the American Bible Society. In Virginia, too, Whigs championed moral reform. Prominent Whigs such as Governor Barbour supported a variety of reform causes, from a conviction that public education and benevolent societies were a means to create a more harmonious society.[30]

As many recent studies show, by 1840, women had long been active in the sphere of benevolent reform. They had proved that they were effective organizers, skilled at mobilizing public support for their projects. In Virginia, men had enthusiastically enlisted female support in the temperance and African colonization causes, arguing that the participation of "disinterested" and virtuous females would legitimate those causes. In short, when reform-minded Whig leaders such as Barbour encouraged women to join in the party's glorious crusade, they were not inventing or advancing new arguments to justify public activism by women, but rather recasting old ones, adapting the ideology of benevolent femininity to the new realities of mass party politics.[31]

On balance, Whig propaganda about women more closely resembled the rhetoric of disinterested benevolence than that of religious enthusiasm. Women's roles in the two settings, evangelical revivals and partisan rallies, differed in one essential way. Camp meetings were known for their high emotional pitch. Kincheloe asserts that women who attended them "screamed, participated in the 'exercises,' exhorted, sang, and did anything else that men could do." Women's role at political rallies, by contrast, was more to contain passions than to give in to them. Political passion, according to nineteenth-century rhetoric, was a sort of "blindness"; critiques of "blind party spirit" float through the campaign rhetoric of the 1840s.[32] Whig rhetoric implied that women, by virtue of their moral superiority, could resist this blindness. Whig men occasionally praised female enthusiasm, but they more often stressed Whig women's disinterestedness, dignity, and decorum.

In other words, the participation of women helped to relieve men's anxieties about changes in electoral behavior. Even though men likened partisan competition to warfare, they were intensely concerned with constraining the behavior of partisans. This concern, it might be argued, ran especially high among Whigs in 1840, when they began their appeals to women. The Whigs wanted to have it both ways: to steal the Jacksonians' democratic thunder and to claim that the Whigs were a breed apart from the Democrats—and a superior one at that. The Whigs' 1840 campaign was masterminded by a new cadre of professional politicians who sought to beat the Jacksonians at their own game of rousing the common man. They hoped that the din produced by Harrison's Log Cabin campaign of 1840 would drown out the Democratic charge that the Whigs had no platform and no policies. Even as they stressed the humble origins of their candidate and claimed to be more democratic than the Democrats, the Whigs also sought to retain the mantle of patrician dignity. In contrast to the Democrats' excessive partisanship and executive corruption, the Whigs, so they claimed, represented disinterested virtue, a love of the Union, and a reverence for the traditions of the Founding Fathers.[33]

If this message seems dissonant, it was. Men such as Webster, Clay, and John Quincy Adams initially resisted the notion that the Whig campaign of 1840 should focus on "style, song and hysteria." When these "old guard" leaders began to taste victory, however, they came around and played the demagogue to crowds of enthusiastic followers in places such as Richmond, telling them what they wanted to hear. The Democrats naturally asserted that the Whigs' efforts to unleash voter enthusiasm were immoral and destructive to the public peace; particularly disturbing, Democrats charged, was the way the dispensing of hard cider by Harrison campaign workers encouraged intemperance.[34] But the Whigs had the perfect counter-argument—the very presence of women at Whig events insured decorum and sobriety. With women on their side, Whigs could lay claim both to popular democracy and to dignity.

The Whig party's victory in the 1840 presidential contest proved to be short-lived. The death of Harrison within a month after his inauguration exposed the fault lines in the Whigs' fragile coalition. Seeking a consensus candidate in 1844, the Whigs chose Clay, whom their northern and southern wings could agree on. Clay, a southerner, opposed the annexation of Texas unless on terms acceptable to the North. And he championed an "American System" of internal development that would bind the country together through commercial ties.[35]

The years between Harrison's victory in 1840 and Clay's campaign in 1844 afforded women and men alike fewer opportunities to display partisanship than the presidential campaign season had. Women did attend political speeches and debates in nonelection years.[36] But they were not generally included in the year-round succession of meetings, held behind closed doors, in which the state business of the Whig party, such as the selection of delegates to state conventions, was conducted. Women's function in partisan life had clear limits: their role was not to choose Whig candidates but to affirm the choices of Whig men, particularly in high-stakes presidential campaigns; to help maintain party discipline; and to bring new members into the Whig fold.

As soon as the presidential canvass of 1844 got underway, the tide of female partisanship rose again, to new heights. The Whig party in Virginia flooded women with a virtual torrent of invitations to Whig events. As in 1840, Whig men thought that the approval of women legitimized the Whig campaign. "If we doubted before," a correspondent wrote after seeing the large number of women at a Whig rally in Goochland County, "now we know the Whigs must be right and will be more than conquerers." Such outpourings of female partisanship led the *Richmond*

Whig to draw a now familiar conclusion: "It is well known that the Ladies are Whigs, almost universally."[37]

Women's support for the Whigs, Virginia newspapers were at pains to point out, was not restricted to such urban strongholds as Petersburg and Richmond. Women attended Whig events in towns, villages, county courthouses, and rural settings around the state. The presence of 350 women at a Whig rally in Clarksburg, for example, was evidence that "ladies in the remote and retired Mountain districts take the same interest in the success of the Whig cause, which they do everywhere else."[38]

The Whig party's campaign rhetoric conjured up an image of the ideal Whig woman: a chaste, honorable lady who attended political rallies to sanction the party, to dignify its proceedings, to affirm her loyalty, and to gather information that would allow her to transmit Whig culture to her family, friends, and acquaintances. Although often spoken of, Whig women rarely got the chance to "speak" for themselves before partisan audiences in 1844. On at least one occasion, however, a Virginia woman addressed a Whig crowd through a male proxy. On September 3 the *Richmond Whig* featured "AN EXAMPLE TO THE WHIG LADIES OF RICHMOND!," the story of Miss Martha Peake of Charlottesville. Peake presented a "splendid Banner" to the Clay Club of Charlottesville in September 1844, along with a "chaste and beautiful letter" that one of its male members read aloud. When Clay is elected, she cautioned the Whig voters of the town, "forget not that those whom you have vanquished are your brothers, subjects of the same government, struggling as ardently and as honestly, as you, for what they believe, with mistaken judgment, in my poor opinion, to be the true path to national honor, happiness and glory." Only if the victorious Whigs were able to transcend the fierce emotions of party competition would the nation "bask in the sunshine of moral, social and political purity and peace."[39]

Webster and his fellow Whig luminaries undoubtedly would have approved of Peake's message, for she was imposing her superior moral sensibilities on the conduct of politics and admonishing men of the proper limits of partisanship. Apparently the *Richmond Whig* agreed that Peake successfully harmonized partisanship and true womanhood: she was bound to get married soon, the editors allowed, for her Whig credentials made her "pre-eminently qualified to confer domestic happiness" on some fortunate man.[40]

In 1844, the Whig party's claim that it had the support of the commonwealth's women was most certainly intended, as it had been in 1840, to provoke the Democrats. The *Lexington Gazette* printed a letter to the Whigs of Fishersville by Benjamin Johnson Barbour, in which he taunted the Democrats for alienating the female population. Eve had been deceived "by the prince of the Locofocos, and had ever since eschewed both him and his party"; no Democrat would stand a chance to get married until after the November election.[41]

Virginia women's own accounts of the campaign of 1844 echo the party's rhetoric. Virginian Marion Harland, a nationally famous novelist and author of domestic guidebooks for women in the mid-nineteenth century, asserts in her autobiography that even as a child of thirteen, she was a violent Whig partisan and supporter of Clay. In 1844 the Whigs invited the women of her county to a political rally, the first time such an invitation had been extended to ladies, according to Harland; the innovation "set tongues wagging," she remembers, and "practically guaranteed the county for Clay."[42]

Like Harland, Missouri Riddick of Suffolk appreciated the Whig party's hospitality. She wrote to her husband in White Sulphur Springs on August 5, 1844:

> Great preparations are making for the Democratic mass meeting, at Cowling's landings on the 10th. . . . we think, as no doubt you do, that it will be a poor affair . . . the ladies are not invited. I believe all of the ladies will attend the Whig Barbecue, as they are particularly invited, and tables and seats are to be provided for them.

In her husband's absence, Riddick felt it her duty to stand in as the political head of the family: "I shall go [to the rally], as your representative," she told him.[43]

In the early stages of the 1844 campaign, Democrats made few overtures to women to join in partisan activities, but by the fall of 1844, the party was actively appealing to women and trying to counter Whig propaganda with its own claims. Hundreds of women attended a Democratic rally in Fairfax in September; twenty-eight young ladies carried flags bearing the "different mottoes of the states." "About 100 ladies favored Mr. L. [Mr. Leake, the speaker at the rally] with their presence, and their approving smiles," wrote the *Richmond Enquirer* of another Democratic meeting, "demonstrating the falsity of the charge that the 'Ladies are all Whigs.' "[44]

These appeals notwithstanding, some Democrats continued to be critical of female mobilization. At a Loudoun County political debate, a Democratic orator "assail[ed] the ladies for attending political meetings" and "for giving their smiles" to the Whigs. Describing a Whig procession in New York, a Democratic correspondent to the *Washington Globe* declared that while the Whigs' "showy pageant" might "amuse the wives, daughters and sisters of our sovereign lord the people . . . it can neither buy, bribe, nor beat the staunch and sterling democracy of New York, when it comes to the matter of MEN." Such skepticism about the propriety and utility of Whig appeals to women was not confined to men. According to Serena Dandridge, a Democrat from Essex County, the reason the Whigs lost the election of 1844 was that they had "too many women & children in their ranks."[45] Ironically, the strongest articulations of Whig womanhood and the most strident attacks on it came after the election of 1844 had been lost. For it was then that Whig women in Virginia tried to snatch a symbolic victory from the jaws of defeat.

On November 19, 1844, the *Richmond Whig* published a seemingly innocuous letter that would touch off months of debate in the Virginia press. The letter, from Lucy Barbour of Barboursville, Orange County, proposed that the "Whig women of Virginia" give some "token of respect" to Clay, who had just lost his third bid for the presidency of the United States. Barbour was a member of Virginia's social elite. Her husband James, who had died in 1842, had been one of the most prominent Whigs in Virginia. He had served as governor of the commonwealth, United States senator, and the secretary of war under John Quincy Adams. The Barbours counted Clay among their close friends.[46]

Barbour anticipated that her call to action would raise eyebrows. "I know our sex are thought by many unstable as water," her letter continued, "but after crowding the Whig festivals, and manifesting so much enthusiasm, few will be found so hollow-hearted as to refuse a small sum to so good—I had almost said, so holy a cause": the tribute to Clay. The editors of the *Richmond Whig* agreed to adopt Barbour's scheme as their own. The editors of the *Richmond Enquirer* wasted no time in ridiculing the plan to honor Clay: "Has it come to this, that the 'gallant Harry' has been turned over to the tender mercies of the ladies . . . ?" The *Enquirer* also printed a letter from one "Incognita," who thoroughly disapproved of the notion that Whig women should hold a meeting to decide on a strategy for honoring Clay: "a public meeting of political amazons! . . . Was such an event ever recorded, or before heard of, in the annals of time?"[47]

Barbour vigorously defended her project. In a December 4 letter to the *Richmond Whig*, she stated that women deserved "freedom of thought even on political subjects; and the power of performing an act of justice to an injured statesman; when, doing so, we neglect no duty assigned to us by the most rigid." "We are the nursing mothers of heroes, statesmen, and divines," she continued, "and while we perform a task so important, we mean to be counted something in the muster-roll of man."[48]

Inspired by Barbour's appeal, a group of Whig women met on December 9 at the First Presbyterian Church in Richmond and formed the Virginia Association of Ladies for Erecting a Statue to Henry Clay; they elected Barbour as president. The statue was to be funded by membership subscriptions, costing no more than one dollar each. Men could make donations but not become members. Auxiliaries to the association, with women as officers and collectors, were organized all around the state and began the work of soliciting donations to pay for the cost of commissioning the statue.[49]

Thanks to the survival of a subscription book from around 1845–1846 that lists contributors to the Clay Association by county, we can get a sense of the breadth and nature of the organization. The book lists the names of 2,563 subscribers, covering counties from Accomac on the Eastern Shore to Nelson on the Blue Ridge; at least 2,236 of the subscribers were women. The association, which received national publicity in the *National Intelligencer,* also had auxiliaries in Alexandria (204 subscribers) and in Boston (215 subscribers). Additional contributions came from families in Vermont, Mississippi, and Georgia.[50]

The list of subscribers confirms there was a strong connection between Whiggery and female benevolence in Virginia. Seventeen of the thirty-six members of the Female Humane Association of Richmond in 1843—an organization that provided food and shelter to destitute girls—subscribed to the Clay Association in 1845. Lucy Otey of Lynchburg and Ann Clagett of Alexandria, directors of orphan asylums in their respective towns, are two more of the many benevolent women who contributed to the Clay project.[51]

As in the case of Lucy Barbour, the social prominence of the Clay

Association's leaders did not insulate them from criticism. As auxiliaries sprang up around the state, so, too, did debate over the propriety of the association. On December 22, 1844, for example, two days after the Whig women of Lynchburg formed an auxiliary, the editors of the Democratic *Lynchburg Republican* attacked the Clay Association, suggesting with derision that "the name of every lady who mingles in this great work of generosity and patriotism will be handed down to posterity as a *partisan* lady." "Is not this whole movement conceived in a spirit of rebellion?" the editors asked. The Democrats mocked the notion that partisanship was appropriate for women—that partisanship and patriotism were synonymous. The Whiggish *Lynchburg Virginian* defended the Clay Association, commending it for advancing the Whig cause: "we shall not be surprised if the vehemence and universality of this female and most honorable sentiment," its editor mused, "will present Mr. Clay again as a candidate for the Presidency in 1848."[52]

A week later, two more male defenders of the association came forward, urging Whig women to stand their ground. A correspondent with the pen name "Peter Caustic" proclaimed, "There is too much firmness of character, and nobleness of soul about Virginia's daughters to suffer themselves to be intimidated by the denunciations of Locofocoism." The second defender agreed, stating that "the Whig ladies of Virginia consider themselves at least as well qualified to judge of their own acts as the Locofoco editor, who has undertaken to lecture them."[53]

Perhaps the most strident defense of the association came from a correspondent of the *Lexington Gazette*, who jumped into the fray after an auxiliary was formed in that town in January 1845. The Democrats, he claimed, were being disingenuous: "The sneering democratic gentry who ridicule the idea of ladies meddling with politics, would not be so bitterly sarcastic if they could have a little of this meddling on their side of the question." "We are willing to avow our own opinion that woman's proper sphere is HOME," the writer continued. But "there are occasions . . . when her domestic duties themselves demand that she should enter the arena which man has considered his exclusive province."[54]

Whig women themselves came forward on their own and Clay's behalf. In December 1844 a female correspondent to the *Richmond Whig* wrote that women had a duty to honor Clay since he had been "shamefully neglected by his countrymen." She had nothing good to say about

the newly elected president, James K. Polk: "The more insignificant a
man is, the greater are his chances, with the Democracy, for attaining
exalted honors."[55]

Susan Doswell, president of the Hanover auxiliary, asserted in an
address to her colleagues that women "cannot but erect a statue . . . that
our children may early learn well to distinguish the true difference between exalted worth and that cringing sycophancy, which, in a Republic,
too often usurps its highest honors." A pledge by the women of Lunen-
burg County also was a clear testament to Clay's worth: "we hereby
resolve to contribute our humble mite in conferring honor where honor
is due." Sarah French, vice president of the Warrenton auxiliary, wrote
to Clay on February 27, 1845, asking him to visit her town (he gra-
ciously declined). The association's goal, she stressed, was to teach the
young men of Virginia to imitate Clay's "noble deeds."[56]

The women who spoke for the association tapped into two currents
in Whig political culture: the party's social elitism and its emphasis on
"statesmanship." The Whigs considered themselves the party of "property and talents." One prominent Virginia Whig recorded in his memoirs
his belief that the Whigs "represented the culture and the wealth of the
State. . . . It had become an old saw that 'Whigs knew each other by the
instincts of gentlemen.' " Furthermore, as historian Thomas Brown has
pointed out, the Whigs claimed to stand for "statesmanship" over "partisanship." The Whig party carried on the Founding Fathers' tradition
of disinterested statesmanship, transcending partisanship and sectionalism in the interests of national unity.[57]

One of the central issues in the 1844 campaign was Clay's stature as
a gentleman and statesman. The Democrats assailed Clay's character,
charging him with the unchristian practices of dueling, gambling, and
womanizing. The Whigs countered that Clay was the epitome of a southern gentleman, a model of gallantry and social grace. Just as women's
support had helped Harrison establish a virtuous reputation, so, too, did
it help, in Clay's case, to defuse the "character issue." Women around
the country flocked to Clay's speeches and showered him with gifts. "If
nothing else, Clay had the women's vote," Clay biographer Robert V.
Remini asserts, repeating a favorite theme of Whig rhetoric.[58]

According to the Whigs, Clay's public record was as spotless as his
character. The man who had steered the Union through the nullification
crisis, Clay was known as "the Great Pacificator." In 1844, Clay's reputation as a peacemaker had special meaning, in light of Whig fears that

Polk's election would bring a bloody war with Mexico. Clay's antiwar stance, Whigs argued, endeared him to women. An article on the Clay statue that appeared in the *Richmond Whig* in March 1845 suggested that Clay represented the "love of peace which is the sweetest attribute of woman."[59]

The notion that Whig women saw Clay as a guarantor of peace finds support in the correspondence of Ellen Mordecai, a fervent Whig from Richmond. Mordecai believed that Clay's defeat was a horrible omen for the Union. On the subject of Polk's inauguration in March 1845, she wrote: "I don't know that I am feeling too much apprehension for the welfare of my country, yet it appears even to me . . . that dark clouds are gathering, which unless scattered by elements now unseen, will thicken and bursting, overwhelm us in misery."[60]

Even as Mordecai penned her lament, debate over the Clay Association was dying down. Perhaps it had become clear to Whigs and Democrats alike that the Whig women were determined to see their project through. In November 1845, barely a year after Barbour's initial appeal, the association commissioned sculptor Joel Tanner Hart to design and to execute the marble statue; he was to be paid five thousand dollars for the project. Once sufficient money had been raised to pay Hart, the association's only purpose was to encourage him to finish the statue. Finally, in 1859, after a series of delays because of ill health, Hart completed his work.[61]

On April 12, 1860, the eighty-third anniversary of Clay's birth, the Clay statue was inaugurated in Richmond, amid great public celebration. Business in the city had been virtually suspended so that the entire community could participate in the inaugural ceremonies; an estimated twenty thousand spectators witnessed the unveiling. The Clay statue, which stood in an iron pavilion in Capitol Square until 1930, now stands in the Old Hall of the Virginia House of Delegates.[62]

The 1844–1845 debates over the Clay Association, though short-lived, are significant for revealing the tensions inherent in Whig womanhood, a new variation on the timeworn and resilient doctrine of "indirect influence." This doctrine, which eventually emerged as a key argument against woman suffrage, held that women's civic duty lay, not in casting a ballot, but rather in influencing men's opinions and behavior.[63] The Whig innovation was to suggest that in the era of mass party politics, women could not fulfill this mandate properly unless they were integrated into the culture of political parties. For all its homages to female influence, the concept of Whig womanhood still ultimately vested women's power in male proxies. An unanswered question at the heart of Whig womanhood was implicitly posed by Lucy Barbour. What if men, despite the benign efforts of women, simply failed to do the right thing? What if they elected the wrong man? What were women to do then?

In the wake of Clay's 1844 defeat, Barbour and her supporters offered an answer: women had the duty to restore the reputation of their party's rejected hero. Barbour conceived of women as opinion makers. They were not simply to affirm the choices of men, but to advance their own ideas of what constituted political worth in men—before, during, and after campaign season. In attacking the association, Democrats worried out loud about the potentially radical implications of this view and paid backhanded tribute to women's influence. When Whig men rushed to defend Barbour, they reminded Democrats that Whig women's partisanship came with the full approbation of Whig men; the women of the Clay Association were not challenging the authority of all men, only of Democratic ones. Rather than symbolizing female rebelliousness, the Clay Association came to symbolize the efficacy and propriety of political collaboration between men and women.

By the time the Clay statue was inaugurated in 1860, both Clay and the Whig party were long gone. Clay had died in 1852, the same year that the Whig party—its fragile coalition of supporters torn apart by sectionalism—ran its last presidential campaign. But in at least one respect, Whig political culture, like the Clay statue that symbolized it, proved more enduring than the party itself. For even as the Whigs disintegrated, their policy of making "politicians of their women" became standard practice in Virginia politics.

In the presidential campaigns of 1848, 1852, and 1856, each of the parties competing for voters in Virginia actively appealed to women to join its ranks. In 1848 and again in 1852, the Whigs sounded familiar themes with respect to female partisanship. One feature that distinguished the 1852 campaign from earlier ones was the frequency with which women made public presentations of campaign decorations, occasionally accompanied by brief addresses. In September 1852, for example, two Whig women presented a banner and a transparency to the members of the local Whig club in Norfolk; each woman also made a short speech.[64]

In 1856, the American party, picking up where the Whigs left off, encouraged and publicized women's displays of partisanship. For example, a grand rally of the Know-Nothings in Kanawha witnessed the presentation of a large flag by Mrs. Ruffner, with a note attesting that she was "warmly attached to the principles of the American Party, and ardently desirous of their success at the approaching election."[65]

The Democrats finally came around by the campaigns of 1848, 1852, and 1856. Virginia Democrats nearly matched their opponents' zeal for female support and participation. The rhetoric of Democratic women and men reveals how fully they had appropriated Whig ideas about female partisanship. At a Democratic meeting in Norfolk in September 1852, a certain Miss Bain addressed the crowd, urging men to support Democratic presidential candidate Franklin Pierce with the following words:

> Patriotic sons of Patriotic sires! . . . Oppose with all power of rectitude that odious and destructive policy that would plant the seed of discord within our borders. . . . battle with the foes of Pierce and King; use all proper exertions to defeat them. . . . You can inspire others with a love for the pure, uncontaminated tenets of democracy, the only principles which represent the best interests of our beloved Union.[66]

Like Barbour before her, Bain fused partisanship and patriotism, but she associated the Democrats with sectional harmony and the Whigs with "discord."

The Whig argument that women both legitimized and purified partisan activities was now enthusiastically advanced by Democrats. Describing an October rally in Norfolk, a Democratic correspondent wrote: "There was no *fuss*—no disturbance. The ladies—guardian angels that control our natures—were around us with their illuminating smiles to cheer, and their bright countenances to encourage us on to victory."[67]

Perhaps the single greatest testament to Democratic acceptance of female partisanship is the novel *The Life and Death of Sam, In Virginia,* which was published in Richmond in 1856. Authored anonymously by "A Virginian," the novel is a stinging indictment of the Know-Nothing party and ringing endorsement of the Democratic party. The author adapted a favorite Whig allegory—the tale of lovers kept apart by partisanship—to his own ends. The central drama of the novel revolves around the courtship of Fannie Bell (a Catholic and a Democrat) and her suitor, Maurice Meredith (a Know-Nothing).[68]

After a short courtship, Meredith proposes marriage to Bell, and she accepts. But the engagement is based on deception, for Meredith, who knows that Bell comes from a Democratic family, has hidden from her the fact that he is a Know-Nothing. Worried that Bell will renounce him if she learns the truth, Meredith tries to reassure himself with the rhetorical question, "what does a woman know or care about a man's political opinions[?]" But doubt plagues him, and one night he has a disturbing dream. In the dream, he approaches a bridge spanning a rushing river between two jutting mountain crags. The bridge is bedecked in Democratic mottoes, and Bell is the gatekeeper, holding in her hands the scales of justice. Meredith watches as his political enemies, the Democrats, cross the bridge singing victory songs. When his Know-Nothing comrades approach the bridge, they are turned away by Bell and sent tumbling off the rocks into the river. Woman, representing justice, has sanctioned the Democratic party and condemned the American party to failure.[69]

Bell eventually discovers Meredith's political identity and calls off their engagement. "Must I marry the man . . . whose political principles would lead him to no higher aim than the proscription of foreigners and Catholics?" she angrily demands of Meredith in their final confrontation. Meredith, who runs as a Know-Nothing candidate for Congress, is dealt a crippling defeat in the state elections. At the story's end, Meredith is a broken man: "he had lost Fannie; he had lost all prospect of rising politically." Bell meanwhile gets engaged to Mr. Dew, a promising young Democrat.[70]

The Life and Death of Sam, In Virginia reveals much about women's political roles at mid-decade. The author's assumption is that women do—and should—know enough about party politics to serve as men's consciences. Bell is both a partisan herself and an arbiter of partisan behavior by men. Bell is the figurative gatekeeper of political righteousness. Her message is that those who win the moral sanction of woman are right and win political power; those who deceive woman to evade her moral judgment are doomed.

Any scholar engaged in a project such as this—the project of expanding our definition of meaningful political activity—is ultimately confronted with the inevitable question: So what? The partisan women described above do not meet the paradigmatic standards of political participation.

They did not vote, nor did they agitate to win the suffrage. We cannot measure their impact on the outcome of elections or demonstrate, for that matter, whether they had any impact at all. Women were partisans. So what?

I would like to address this question head on. The kind of evidence presented here has far-reaching implications for the fields of political history and women's history. On the one hand, my findings underscore what political historians have been saying for years. Partisanship was indeed a consuming passion and pastime for antebellum Americans. On the other hand, the Virginia evidence calls into question a common assumption in the historiography of antebellum politics: participation in campaign activities was a highly significant form of political expression for men, but not for women. McGerr makes a very convincing case that in the nineteenth century, men "voted twice at an election—once at the polls by casting a ballot, and once in the streets by participating in campaign pageantry." Whig women demonstrated that voters and potential voters were not the only ones caught up in the "process of communal self-revelation" that campaigns represented; their wives, mothers, daughters, and sisters, too, were an integral part of the new American political culture.[71] Women, alongside men, expressed political preferences and assumed public identities by taking part in campaign rituals.

A recognition of the extent of women's involvement in campaigns may hold the key to understanding another issue of great interest to political historians: political socialization. Party loyalty was notoriously strong during the era of the second party system. Scholars have explored the importance of families and kin groups in transmitting partisan loyalties; Whig discourse, along with women's own testimony, shows how women played a key role in the socialization of young voters.[72]

Not only were women integral to party politics; gender was integral to party ideologies. Two recent studies suggest that Whig womanhood had its roots in Federalist and Adamsite gender ideologies. Rosemarie Zagarri has found that Federalists were more inclined than Democratic-Republicans to acknowledge publicly women's civic contributions as republican mothers. Supporters of John Quincy Adams, according to Norma Basch, espoused "proto-Whig" ideas about women and politics. They offered women a "few rays of autonomy" by arguing that household and polity were intimately linked, and that the moral standards that governed the former should govern the latter; Jacksonians by contrast upheld the notion of a sharp demarcation between the public and private spheres.[73]

The Whigs' innovation in the 1840s was both tactical and ideological. The party is noteworthy for the sheer quantity of invitations and publicity it offered to partisan women. Even more important was the meaning the Whigs attached to women's presence. Whig propagandists vigorously made the case that women's support said something crucial about the party—women's allegiance was proof of the Whigs' moral rectitude. Whigs in effect claimed that a "gender gap" separated them from the Democrats.

Over the course of the 1850s, the Democratic party in Virginia went a long way toward closing that gap, although Democrats never developed the Whiggish penchant for making grand claims (such as "the ladies are Democrats"). If we focus our attention on the North and West, however, where the Republican party had significant backing, it appears that the Democrats were not through playing catch-up in the race to mobilize female support. In 1856 the fledgling Republicans, running John Frémont as their first presidential candidate, upped the ante by placing Frémont's wife, Jessie, at the center of their national campaign. Renowned for her political pedigree, beauty, and intelligence; her daring decision to elope with Frémont at the age of seventeen in 1841; and her antislavery convictions, Jessie Benton Frémont was celebrated in campaign songs, stories, and paraphernalia. Democrats around the country greeted this development with indignation and scorn. The Republican practice of according candidates' wives prominence in campaigns carried over into the postbellum period; Democrats generally did not favor such an approach.[74] A growing body of scholarship suggests that a gender gap between political parties—measurable before woman suffrage in appeals and assertions, not in votes—may be an enduring feature of the American political landscape.

If evidence on antebellum women's partisanship serves both to deepen our understanding of party politics and to suggest avenues for further inquiry, so, too, does it shed light on fundamental issues in women's history. Whig womanhood represents a distinct stage in the historical evolution of women's civic role. Linda K. Kerber's pathbreaking study has established that in the early republic, republican motherhood, the notion that women should serve the state by raising civic-minded sons, was the dominant theory of women's civic duty. Numerous studies have shown that in the first three decades of the antebellum period, republican motherhood was transformed into benevolent femininity—the idea that women had the duty to promote virtue not only within their families but also in the surrounding community by supporting benevolent enterprises.[75]

Whig womanhood took the assumption of female moral superiority embedded in these existing concepts of female duty and adapted it to the realities of mass party politics. Women's moral virtue, their influence within the home, and their proven benevolence fitted them, the Whigs held, to play a distinct role in the new political order. They could exert a civilizing influence on partisan competition, even as they fostered partisan loyalties in their families and communities. Whigs wedded the doctrine of indirect influence to the notion of women's incorruptibility—women who assumed a public identity as Whigs did not, so the party asserted, lose their claim to special virtue.

Baker has rightly argued that the "cultural assignment of republican virtues and moral authority to womanhood helped men embrace partisanship" by relieving their anxieties about electoral competition; what she and others have failed to appreciate is the extent to which women themselves embraced partisanship in the antebellum era and were embraced by parties.[76] The testimony of Marion Harland, Lucy Barbour, and others reveals that women understood that their inclusion in mass politics was a profoundly significant development. Through the medium of partisan campaigns, both womanhood as a construct and individual female voices entered the public discourse on politics in a way they had never done before.

The Whigs reconciled female moral superiority and women's partisanship and opened up new opportunities for women in the process. But did Whig womanhood represent a step toward full political enfranchisement for women? Rather than fitting comfortably into a narrative of progress, my findings affirm Suzanne Lebsock's hypothesis that meaningful change can take place for women in an antifeminist atmosphere. Although female partisanship flourished in antebellum Virginia, no woman's rights movement took shape there. The very same Virginia newspapers that encouraged women's partisanship routinely mocked and lambasted the woman's rights movement, likening its supporters to Amazons and "cackling geese."[77]

Lebsock and Anne Firor Scott have effectively challenged the notion that southern women lagged behind northern ones in benevolent activity.

Women's partisanship demonstrates, even more dramatically than their work in benevolent societies, that our dichotomous picture of northern women's political activism and southern women's political marginalization needs to be rethought. Southern women were, indeed, much less inclined to embrace woman suffrage than northern ones. But we should not equate their conservatism with uniformity of opinion or with passivity. Women in antebellum Virginia—like conservative women in the modern era—debated each other fiercely over political issues and actively worked on behalf of political causes.[78]

During the 1840s, the principal political fault line in Virginia was the line dividing Democrats and Whigs. Allegiances to party not only bound like-minded women and men together but also linked them to their political counterparts in other states. At its height, the second party system, by pitting two national parties against each other, united northern and southern partisans and thereby minimized the impact of sectional issues.[79] While northern and southern women may have lived in strikingly different settings, those who followed political events and identified themselves as partisans shared the experience of mass mobilization. The advent of Whig womanhood and the story of the Clay Association reveal that partisanship united women, as well as men, across sectional boundaries.

Even in the heyday of mass politics, however, sectional tensions suffused partisan rhetoric. Southern Whig women shared with northern ones the experience of participating in political rallies, but what southern women heard at those rallies was different—sometimes subtly and sometimes dramatically—from what northern women heard. For the southern Whigs and southern Democrats, in contrast to northern ones, claimed their party and theirs alone could simultaneously protect slavery from northern intervention and preserve the Union. In the 1850s, as slavery became the overriding theme in partisan discourse, political parties increasingly promoted rather than restrained sectionalism.[80] The splintering of the second party system along sectional lines culminated in the election of 1860, the first in which regional rather than national parties squared off against each other in the North and South.

Just as the emergence of the second party system is reflected in political discourse by and about women, so, too, is its demise. During the crucial election campaign of 1860 and throughout the Virginia legislature's famous secession debate of 1861, unionists and secessionists called on women to join their ranks and adapted the Whigs' old battle cry to their own purposes. "The ladies are all for *Union*," declared the unionist *Lynchburg Virginian* in September 1860; six months later, a Petersburg correspondent to the pro-secession *Richmond Dispatch* declared that women "have all abandoned the Union and raised the cry of secession."[81]

As the antebellum period drew to its explosive close, Whig womanhood was transmuted in Virginia into Confederate womanhood. Male and female secessionists argued that women should be Confederate partisans and should play a public role in promoting the cause of southern independence. Sectional identities had come to eclipse partisan affiliations: for example, on April 18, the day after Virginia seceded from the Union, a woman from Louisa County submitted a piece entitled "A Woman's Appeal" to the *Richmond Dispatch*. "Farewell to Whigs and Democrats, Secessionists and Submissionists, and political characters of every variety of here heretofore," she wrote. "Farewell, forever! 'Tis now North or South, Liberty or Slavery, Life or Death. . . . Mothers, wives and daughters, buckle on the armor for the loved ones; bid them, with Roman firmness advance, and never return until victory perches on their banners." This "woman's appeal" can and should be read two ways: as a statement inaugurating a new stage in the sectional conflict in Virginia, and as the product of two decades of political activity and discourse by women. In Virginia, and quite possibly in the South as a whole, the political mobilization of white women that began in 1840 culminated, not in the formation of a woman suffrage movement, but in active support of the Confederacy by most women and active support of the Union by some.[82]

NOTES

1. Women's partisanship occupies two footnotes in a recent synthesis of American political history: Joel H. Silbey, *The American Political Nation, 1838–1893* (Stanford, 1991), 270, 308–9. See also ibid., 46–48. For short discussions of women's partisanship, see Ronald P. Formisano, *The Transformation of Political Culture: Massachusetts Parties, 1790s–1840s* (New York, 1983), 262–67; Harry L. Watson, *Liberty and Power: The Politics of Jacksonian America* (New York, 1990), 221–22; and Lawrence Frederick Kohl, *The Politics of Individualism: Parties and the American Character in the Jacksonian Era* (New York, 1989), 72–74.

2. For a synthesis of recent scholarship on domesticity, moral reform, and

woman's rights in the antebellum period, see Sara M. Evans, *Born for Liberty: A History of Women in America* (New York, 1989), 67–112. On women and antebellum party politics, see Paula C. Baker, "The Domestication of Politics: Women and American Political Society, 1780–1920," *American Historical Review* 89 (June 1984), 627–32; Mary P. Ryan, *Women in Public: Between Banners and Ballots, 1825–1880* (Baltimore, 1990), 135–38; and Michael E. McGerr, "Political Style and Women's Power, 1830–1930," *Journal of American History* 77 (December 1990), 866–67.

3. On Southern politics, see, for example, William J. Cooper Jr., *Liberty and Slavery: Southern Politics to 1860* (New York, 1983); and John McCardell, *The Idea of a Southern Nation: Southern Nationalists and Southern Nationalism, 1830–1860* (New York, 1979). On southern women, see Catherine Clinton, *The Plantation Mistress: Woman's World in the Old South* (New York, 1982), 181–82; Elizabeth Fox-Genovese, *Within the Plantation Household: Black and White Women of the Old South* (Chapel Hill, 1988), 195; and Suzanne Lebsock, *The Free Women of Petersburg: Status and Culture in a Southern Town, 1784–1860* (New York, 1984), 224. The party designations "Whig" and "Democrat" do not even appear in the indexes of these three works.

4. Eugene Genovese, "Toward a Kinder and Gentler America: The Southern Lady in the Greening of the Politics of the Old South," in *In Joy and In Sorrow: Women, Family, and Marriage in the Victorian South, 1830–1900*, ed. Carol Bleser (New York, 1991), 129–33; Judith Rives to William Cabell Rives, Dec. 8, 1838, William Cabell Rives Papers (Manuscript Division, Library of Congress, Washington, D.C.). On women attending political speeches, see, for example, Anne Royall, *Mrs. Royall's Southern Tour; or, Second Series of the Black Book* (Washington, 1830), 34–39.

5. *Staunton Spectator*, October 20, 1836.

6. Ibid., September 1, 1836.

7. Lucy Kenney, *Description of a Visit to Washington* (Washington, 1835), 4–12; Lucy Kenney, *A Pamphlet, Showing How Easily the Wand of a Magician May be Broken, and that if Amos Kendall Can Manage the United States Mail Well, a Female of the United States Can Manage Him Better* (Washington, 1838), 2–5, 15. On southern opposition to Van Buren, see William J. Cooper Jr., *The South and the Politics of Slavery, 1828–1856* (Baton Rouge, 1978), 74–75.

8. Lucy Kenney, *A Letter Addressed to Martin Van Buren, President of the United States, In Answer to the Late Attack Upon the Navy, By the Official Organ of the Government* (Washington, 1838), 6; E. B. Runnells, *A Reply to a Letter Addressed to Mr. Van Buren, President of the United States; Purporting to be Written by Miss Lucy Kenny, The Whig Missionary* (Washington, 1840), 4–6.

9. William W. Freehling, *The Road to Disunion: Secessionists at Bay, 1776–*

1854 (New York, 1990), 295–99, 345, 359–63; Richard Patrick McCormick, *The Second American Party System: Party Formation in the Jacksonian Era* (Chapel Hill, 1966), 186–98.

10. *Staunton Spectator*, Sept. 10, 1840; *Fredericksburg Political Arena*, March 24, Sept. 22, 1840.

11. Ronald P. Formisano, "The New Political History and the Election of 1840," *Journal of Interdisciplinary History*, 23 (Spring 1993), 681; Watson, *Liberty and Power*, 221; Robert Gray Gunderson, *The Log-Cabin Campaign* (Lexington, Ky., 1957), 4, 7–8, 135–39; Ryan, *Women in Public*, 135–38.

12. Silbey, *American Political Nation*, 54.

13. *Staunton Spectator*, September 10, 1840; *Washington National Intelligencer*, September 21, 1840. References to the *National Intelligencer* are to the daily (not the semiweekly) run of the paper.

14. *Richmond Yeoman*, September 10, 1840; James McDowell to Susan McDowell, May 24, 1827, James McDowell Family Papers (Southern Historical Collection, University of North Carolina, Chapel Hill); William Cabell Rives to Judith Rives, September 7, 1834, Rives Papers.

15. *Richmond Yeoman*, October 15, 1840; *Fredericksburg Political Arena*, September 1, 1840.

16. Lucy Kenney, *An Address to the People of the United States* (n.p., [1840]), 1, 6, 11. (There is a copy of *An Address* in the Library of Congress.) Lucy Kenney, *A History of the Present Cabinet* (Washington, D.C., 1840), 6.

17. Judith Rives to Frank Rives, February 29, 1840, Rives Family Papers; Sarah (Pendleton) Dandridge to Martha Taliaferro Hunter, April 18, 1840, Hunter Family Papers (Virginia Historical Society, Richmond); Mrs. Roger A. Pryor, *My Day: Reminiscences of a Long Life* (New York, 1909), 47; Frances Ann Bernard Capps Diary, September 10, 1840 (Virginia Historical Society).

18. Edith P. Mayo, "Campaign Appeals to Women," in *American Material Culture: The Shape of Things around Us,* ed. Edith P. Mayo (Bowling Green, 1984), 128–32, 143; Celestia Shakes, as quoted in T. Michael Miller, " 'If elected . . .'—An Overview of How Alexandrians Voted in Presidential Elections from 1789–1984," *Fireside Sentinel* 10 (October 1988), 100.

19. Mary Pendleton (Cooke) Steger to Sarah Harriet Apphia Hunter, September 13, 1840, Hunter Family Papers.

20. Mary T. Tardy, ed., *The Living Female Writers of the South* (Philadelphia, 1872), 409–10.

21. *Richmond Whig*, October 9, 1840. References to the *Richmond Whig* for the years 1840–1844 are to the semiweekly run of the paper; references to it for 1845–1860 are to the daily run.

22. Ibid.

23. Ibid.; *Washington National Intelligencer*, October 9, 1840.

24. *Washington National Intelligencer,* October 10, 1840; *Richmond Whig,* October 9, 1840.

25. Linda K. Kerber, *Women of the Republic: Intellect and Ideology in Revolutionary America* (Chapel Hill, 1980); Nancy F. Cott. *The Bonds of Womanhood: "Woman's Sphere" in New England, 1780–1835* (New Haven, 1977), 66–70; Baker, "Domestication of Politics," 629–31.

26. *Washington Globe,* October 27, 1840.

27. *Richmond Crisis,* September 16, 1840; *Richmond Enquirer,* October 15, 1840; *Warrenton Jeffersonian,* September 19, 1840.

28. Ryan, *Women in Public,* 136; William R. Taylor, *Cavalier and Yankee: The Old South and American National Character* (Cambridge, Mass., 1957), 115–40; Watson, *Liberty and Power,* 219–21; Kohl, *Politics of Individualism,* 72–73, 108.

29. Joe L. Kincheloe Jr., "Transcending Role Restrictions: Women at Camp Meetings and Political Rallies," *Tennessee Historical Quarterly* 40 (summer 1981), 159; Formisano, *Transformation of Political Culture,* 262–64; Richard J. Carwardine, *Evangelicals and Politics in Antebellum America* (New Haven, 1993), 33–34, 53–55, 65.

30. Daniel Walker Howe, *The Political Culture of the American Whigs* (Chicago, 1979), 36, 158; Kohl, *Politics of Individualism,* 72–74; Robert V. Remini, *Henry Clay: Statesman for the Union* (New York, 1991), 179, 664; Charles D. Lowery, *James Barbour, A Jeffersonian Republican* (University, Ala., 1984), 229.

31. Lori D. Ginzberg, *Women and the Work of Benevolence: Morality, Politics, and Class in the Nineteenth-Century United States* (New Haven, 1990); Lebsock, *Free Women of Petersburg,* 195–236; Elizabeth R. Varon, " 'We Mean to Be Counted': White Women and Politics in Antebellum Virginia" (Ph.D. diss., Yale University, 1993), 53–62, 102–4.

32. Kincheloe, "Transcending Role Restrictions," 165; Baker, "Domestication of Politics," 630–31.

33. Silbey, *American Political Nation,* 112–17; Kohl, *Politics of Individualism,* 89; Sydney Nathans, *Daniel Webster and Jacksonian Democracy* (Baltimore, 1973), 127–31; Freehling, *Road to Disunion,* 361.

34. Gunderson, *Log-Cabin Campaign,* 125, 144, 183; Carwardine, *Evangelicals and Politics,* 61.

35. Freehling, *Road to Disunion,* 411–36.

36. For an example of a woman attending a political debate, see Capps Diary, December 15, 1843.

37. *Richmond Whig,* April 26, May 2, 1844.

38. Ibid., September 6, 1844.

39. Ibid., September 3, 1844.

40. Ibid.

41. *Lexington Gazette,* October 31, 1844.

42. Marion Harland, *Marion Harland's Autobiography* (New York, 1910), 121, 127–29.

43. Missouri Riddick to Nathaniel Riddick, August 5, 1844, Riddick Family Papers (Archives Division, Library of Virginia, Richmond).

44. *Washington Globe,* September 26, 1844; *Richmond Enquirer,* October 7, 1844.

45. *Richmond Whig,* August 13, 1844; *Washington Globe,* November 1, 1844; Serena Catherine (Pendleton) Dandridge to Mary Evelina (Dandridge) Hunter, December 11, [1844], Hunter Family Papers.

46. *Richmond Whig,* November 19, 1844. See Lucy Barbour's obituary, ibid., December 3, 1860. Lowery, *James Barbour,* 9–16, 39–40, 52–53, 178–79, 196.

47. *Richmond Whig,* November 19, 1844; *Richmond Enquirer,* November 29, December 2, 1844.

48. *Richmond Whig,* December 13, 1844.

49. Letters and articles from December 1844, which describe the formation of the Virginia Association of Ladies for Erecting a Statue to Henry Clay, were printed as part of the coverage of the unveiling of the Clay statue in *Richmond Whig,* April 12, 1860.

50. Virginia Association of Ladies for Erecting a Statue to Henry Clay, Subscription List, c. 1845–1846 (Archives Division, Virginia Historical Society). Some subscribers can be identified as men; some signed only their initials. *Washington National Intelligencer,* November 18, 1845; *Staunton Spectator,* February 6, 1845; *Richmond Whig,* March 17, 18, 1845.

51. *Constitution and By-laws of the Female Humane Association of the City of Richmond* (Richmond, 1843), 1; Legislative petitions, Lynchburg, January 2, 1846 (Archives Division, Library of Virginia); *Lynchburg Virginian,* December 22, 1844; Legislative petitions, Alexandria, February 19, 1847 (Archives Division, Library of Virginia).

52. *Lynchburg Republican,* December 22, 1844; *Lynchburg Virginian,* December 26, 1844.

53. *Lynchburg Virginian,* January 2, 1845.

54. *Lexington Gazette,* January 9, 1845.

55. *Richmond Whig,* December 13, 1844.

56. *Ibid.,* February 12, 22, 1845; Sarah S. B. French to Henry Clay, February 27, 1845, in *The Papers of Henry Clay,* vol. 10, ed. Melba Porter Hay (Lexington, Ky., 1991), 203.

57. John Herbert Claiborne, *Seventy-Five Years in Old Virginia* (New York, 1904), 131; Wilfred Binkley, *American Political Parties: Their Natural History* (New York, 1965), 152; Thomas Brown, *Politics and Statesmanship: Essays on the American Whig Party* (New York, 1985), 154–69.

58. Carwardine, *Evangelicals and Politics*, 72–75; Remini, *Henry Clay*, 539, 544, 578, 613, 633–43, 650–58.

59. Howe, *Political Culture of the American Whigs*, 138; *Richmond Whig*, March 15, 1845.

60. Ellen Mordecai to Peter Mordecai, March 3, 1845, Mordecai Family Papers (Southern Historical Collection).

61. *Richmond Whig*, April 12, 1860; W. Harrison Daniel, "Richmond's Memorial to Henry Clay: The Whig Women of Virginia and the Clay Statue," *Richmond Quarterly* 8 (spring 1986), 40; Elizabeth R. Varon, "The Ladies Are Whigs'; Lucy Barbour, Henry Clay, and Nineteenth-Century Virginia Politics," *Virginia Cavalcade* 42 (Autumn 1992), 72–83.

62. The city stretched the celebration out over the next few days, with a banquet honoring Clay at which former president John Tyler spoke. Newspaper reports reprinted the host of letters that famous Americans such as President James Buchanan and Gen. Winfield Scott had sent to the directors of the Clay Association, praising its work. *Richmond Whig*, April 12, 13, 16, 17, 18, 1860.

63. Sarah Hale, Whiggish editor of *Godey's Lady's Book*, summed up the doctrine of indirect influence perfectly when she stated, "This is the way women should vote, namely, by influencing rightly the votes of men." Sarah Hale, "How American Women Should Vote," *Godey's Lady's Book* 44 (April 1852), 293.

64. *Alexandria Gazette*, September 3, 15, 1848; *Norfolk American Beacon*, September 25, 1852.

65. *Richmond Whig*, September 30, 1856. On gender and American party rhetoric, see Janet L. Coryell, *Neither Heroine nor Fool: Anna Ella Carroll of Maryland* (Kent, 1990), 13–29. The Republican party's constituency in Virginia in 1856 was negligible. Richard G. Lowe, "The Republican Party in Antebellum Virginia, 1856–1860," *Virginia Magazine of History and Biography* 81 (July 1973), 259–67.

66. *Norfolk Southern Argus*, September 23, 1852.

67. *Richmond Enquirer*, October 23, 1852.

68. "A Virginian," *The Life and Death of Sam, In Virginia* (Richmond, 1856).

69. Ibid., 211–14.

70. Ibid., 254–60, 307.

71. Michael E. McGerr, *The Decline of Popular Politics: The American North, 1865–1928* (New York, 1986), 37.

72. Formisano, "New Political History and the Election of 1840," 674–75; Jean H. Baker, *Affairs of Party: The Political Culture of Northern Democrats in the Mid-Nineteenth Century* (Ithaca, 1983), 45–52.

73. Rosemarie Zagarri, "Gender and the First Party System," in *Federalists Reconsidered*, ed. Doron Ben-Atar and Barbara Oberg (forthcoming); Norma

Basch, "Marriage, Morals, and Politics in the Election of 1828," *Journal of American History* 80 (December 1993), 914–18.

74. Pamela Herr and Mary Lee Spence, eds., *The Letters of Jessie Benton Frémont* (Urbana, 1993), xxiii; *Richmond Dispatch,* September 23, 1856; Rebecca Edwards, "Gender and American Political Parties, 1880–1900" (Ph.D. diss., University of Virginia, 1995), 18–71.

75. Kerber, *Women of the Republic;* Ginzberg, *Women and the Work of Benevolence.*

76. Baker, "Domestication of Politics," 646.

77. Lebsock, *Free Women of Petersburg,* 243; *Alexandria Gazette,* October 20, 1852; *Richmond Dispatch,* September 16, 1852.

78. Lebsock, *Free Women of Petersburg,* 240–44; Anne Firor Scott, *Natural Allies: Women's Associations in American History* (Urbana, 1991), 19–20, 195.

79. Richard P. McCormick, "Political Development and the Second Party System," in *The American Party Systems: Stages of Political Development,* ed. William Nisbet Chambers and Walter Dean Burnham (New York, 1975), 90–116; Daniel W. Crofts, *Reluctant Confederates: Upper South Unionists in the Secession Crisis* (Chapel Hill, 1989), 49–51.

80. Crofts, *Reluctant Confederates,* 51–54.

81. *Lynchburg Virginian,* September 5, 1860; *Richmond Dispatch,* March 8, 1861.

82. Drew Gilpin Faust, "Altars of Sacrifice: Confederate Women and the Narratives of War," *Journal of American History* 76 (March 1990), 1200–1228; *Richmond Dispatch,* April 18, 1861; Varon, " 'We Mean to Be Counted,' " 446–67; George C. Rable, *Civil Wars: Women and the Crisis of Southern Nationalism* (Urbana, 1989).

Chapter Seven

"Not So Wild a Dream"
The Domestic Fantasies of Literary Men and Women, 1820–1860

Laura McCall

> It is domestic intercourse that softens man, and elevates woman; and of that there can be but little, where the employments and amusements are not in common.[1]

Studies of nineteenth-century gender prescriptions cling to the notion of separate sexual spheres. The standard accounts portray men who lived publicly in an increasingly hostile and competitive environment that was tempered by the "true woman," who created an idealized haven in her domestic province. According to many scholars, the acute dichotomy between home and the world beyond "paralleled the sharp differences between male and female natures."[2]

Traditional explanations of nineteenth-century manhood and womanhood rely heavily on women's fiction and ladies' magazines, but neglect men's writings and thereby fail to compare the productions of literary men and women. Thanks to the groundbreaking efforts of historians of the book, who have discovered that men's and women's reading habits were strikingly similar, scholars now have a legitimate claim to test the power of literature as a didactic stratagem for both sexes.[3]

Putting long-held notions about domesticity to the test, I conducted a content analysis of 104 stories published between 1820 and 1860. Dividing the sample equally between male and female authors helped deter-

mine whether nineteenth-century literary culture promoted a strict segregation of the sexes. It also tested the assumption that middle-class
society viewed the home as exclusively "woman's sphere."[4]

The analysis produced two important discoveries that contradict virtually every investigation of early nineteenth-century gender relations.
First, male and female authors shared similar opinions on a wide variety
of issues ranging from religion and sexuality to feminine submissiveness.
Second, male authors shared with women the love of home, depicted
domestic male characters who sought to physically beautify and morally
uplift their homes, and emphasized the importance of marriage as a
source of joy and fulfillment for *men*. Men who wrote between 1820
and 1860 relished the domestic, recognized their capacities to contribute
to a satisfying home life, acknowledged the centrality of women in their
lives, described domestic arrangements with exacting detail, and analyzed the conditions that made for unhappy as well as happy love relationships. In their writings, neither men nor women authors endorsed a
system of male dominance; rather, they insisted upon partnerships
founded through devotion, companionship, cooperation, and felicity.

Studies of women's fiction concede that love and marriage were key
themes. Thus, it was not surprising when the computer analysis revealed
that, in the novels written by women, 82.7 percent emphasized these
issues. In addition, 32.1 percent of the women characters in these tales
married and 5.3 percent were betrothed by story's end. In 76.9 percent
of the novels written by men, the themes of love and marriage were just
as prominent: 34.7 percent of their women characters married and 5.3
percent were on the threshold of marriage by story's end. Male authors
wrote eloquently about marital relationships, the nature of male-female
interaction, and the sentiment of love. Writers of both sexes agreed that,
in love and marriage, the characters would find their keenest happiness.

Catharine Sedgwick's *Live and Let Live* (1837), for example, twice
suggests that young women fantasize about homes and wedded life.
When the novel's heroine Lucy Lee thinks about the happy home of the
Lovett family, whose son she will marry, Sedgwick interrupts the narrative, declaring that "what girl or woman does not construct a home for
herself, and weave her own golden fabric of domestic joys!" When the
favorably depicted Mrs. Hyde introduces her servant to the mysteries of
cooking, she piques the maid's interest by suggesting that someday she
will be preparing meals for a man. In so doing, "Mrs. Hyde had touched

the right spring. No American girls' [sic] perspective is without a home and a good husband." This novel also infers that romantic love is the most powerful form of earthly affection. In a letter from Lucy to her mother, she confesses her love for Charles Lovett, calling it "a feeling so much stronger than any other." She also knows her mother will understand, "for every woman knows that there is one love that masters all others—God has ordained it, and how can we help it?"[5]

Emphasis on love and marriage in women-authored texts was not a surprising discovery. Society provided most middle-class women with few career options and from press to pulpit reinforced the idea that women's power and authority came from marriage.[6] What emerged in the sources written by men, however, was the unanticipated finding that love and marriage were tantamount for *men*. The heroes of these tales were not grown adults acting out boyhood fantasies in a womanless world, but friends, husbands, and fathers seeking love and happily wedded lives. Men who were gentle, demonstrative, home-oriented, and faithful represented a shared ideal.

In *Guy Rivers* (1834), William Gilmore Simms, the enormously popular Southern novelist and biographer, could find "no influence in the world's circumstances so truly purifying, elevating, and refining" as love.[7] In *The Yemassee* [sic] (1835), a tale of Indian warfare in his native South Carolina, Simms professed "There is no life, if there be no love. Love is the life of nature—all is unnatural without it."[8] In Simms's *The Forayers* (1855), Willie Sinclair must wait and watch over the home of Bertha Travis, all the while knowing he is denied time to spend with the woman he adores. A brave soldier, Willie "was not, it is true, a soft sentimental cavalier; but he was an earnest and very passionate one. Love with him was not a mere sentiment. It was a necessity and a life."[9] Simms chided those who ridiculed the need to be cherished, suggesting that true manhood was defined by the capacity to love. When Mark Forrester declares to Ralph Colleton that he loves Kate Allen, he wonders if " 'it be scarcely a sign of manliness to confess so much, yet I must say to you, 'squire, that I love her so very much that I can not do without her.' " His companion replies:

> I honor your avowal, Forrester, and see nothing unmanly or unbecoming in the sentiment you profess. On the contrary, such a feeling, in my mind, more truly than any other, indicates the presence and possession of those very qualities out of which true manhood is made. The creature who

prides himself chiefly upon his insensibilities, has no more claim to be considered a human being than . . . the rocks over which we travel.[10]

Simms's passage reflects the great emphasis male authors placed upon the elevating and purifying power of love. Emerson Bennett, a prolific and popular romancer of American society, analyzes abiding love in several passages of *The Prairie Flower* (1850), one of which deserves lengthy quotation. When Francis Leighton is about to take leave of Lilian Huntly, the farewell is emotional for both. Francis, who narrates the tale, can hardly speak; and when Lilian rises to him, "her feelings found vent in tears upon my heaving breast."

> Smile, if you will, reader—you who have passed the romantic bounds of a first pure and holy passion, and become identified with the cares and dross of a money-getting, matter-of-fact, dollar-and-cent-life—smile if you will, as your eye chances upon this simple passage; and curl your lip in proud disdain of what you now consider foolish days of love-sick sentimentality; but remember, withal, that, in your long career of painful experience, you can refer to no period when you felt more happiness, more unadulterated joy, than that when the being of your first ambition and love lay trustingly in your arms. It is a point in the life of each and all who have experienced it (and to none other are these words addressed), which can never be erased from the tablet of memory; and though in after years we may affect to deride it as the weakness of youth, it will come upon us in our reflective moments, like a warm sunshine suddenly bursting upon a late cold and gloomy landscape; and insensibly, as it were, our spirits will be borne away, to live over again, though briefly, the happiest moments of our existence. The man who has passed the prime and vigor of manhood without ever having felt this—without this to look back to— I pity; for he has missed the purest enjoyment offered to mortal; and his whole path of life must have been through a sterile desert, without one green blade or flower to relieve its barren waste.[11]

Nathaniel Beverley Tucker's *George Balcombe* (1836) employed nautical metaphors to envision marriage as a man's most trusted source of stability and joy: " 'This is a great thing, this marriage,' " one of Tucker's characters exclaimed: " 'It is the only anchor of affections that will hold us through the storms of life. Without this we drift from our moorings, the sport of every gale of fortune or passion. . . . The harbour of matrimony affords the only safe anchorage, and he who overshoots that may go cruise with the Flying Dutchman.' "[12]

Literary Americans agreed that the best marriages were based upon equality, shared interests, and an even temperament. In *Wyandotté* (1843), a novel set in Revolutionary New York, James Fenimore Cooper characterized a successful marriage as founded upon mutuality and shared social background. The union of Beulah Willoughby and Evert Beekman, the book's protagonists, "was, in truth, one of those rational and wise connections which promise to wear well, there being a perfect fitness, in station, wealth, connections, years, manners, and habits, between the parties. . . . Evert was as worthy as Beulah as she was of him."[13] Simms made precisely the same point in *Guy Rivers* when he described the relationship between Edith Colleton and her cousin Ralph: "They lived together, walked together, rode together—read in the same books, conned the same lessons, studied the same prospects, saw life through the common medium of mutual associations; and lived happily only in the sweet unison of emotions gathered at a common fountain, and equally dear, and equally necessary to them both. And this is love— they loved!"[14]

Simms also asserted that women were not ornaments available simply for man's gratification, but that men must accommodate women. In *The Yemassee*, Bess Matthews, who spurns the romantic overtures of Hugh Grayson, tells him to look closely into his heart " 'and then ask how you loved me? Let me answer—not as a woman—not as a thinking and feeling creature—but as a plaything, whom your inconsiderate passion might practice upon at will.' " Later, Grayson admits that the "firmness of the maiden had taught him her strength as well as his own weakness." He promises to reform, telling Bess, " 'thou shalt hear well of me henceforward.' "[15]

Despite these paeans to companionate unions, the extent to which environments were sexually defined remains uncertain. Although only three sources in this sample of 104 stories contained the phrases "woman's sphere" or "the sphere of women," many of these authors implied that different roles existed for men and women, yet, once again, they agreed in equal numbers. For example, 42.3 percent of the male-authored sources and 48.1 percent of the novels written by women assumed that environments were sexually defined. Thirty-five percent of the men and 40.3 percent of the women felt women should dominate the home. Clearly, these statistics reflect some advocacy of different roles for men and women; but the texts also reveal that constant interaction, mutual growth, and friendship were the true keys to marital happiness. The authors urged their readers to keep the lines of communication open and amicable.

James Kirke Paulding, a prominent political and literary figure of the antebellum period, wrote that the domestic world within could not bear a divided empire and that "the lordly garment . . . should always be hung up at the side of the door." He also stated that "women have a right to know what their husbands have been about during their absence" and that "married men should make a point, when they return home from the daily round of occupation or pleasure, to answer the inquiries of their helpmates frankly and fully." He then entered into a lengthy discussion about "brutes of husbands" who make mysteries out of their absences, which Paulding affirmed "to be treason against the domestic queen." He pointedly told his audience that one of his purposes is to instruct, "and those who don't like it may solace themselves with cheap literature and picture books."[16]

Nevertheless, Paulding also believed couples should not get involved in the extreme petty details of their lives, as this may lead to serious but unnecessary bickering. "Were it possible to penetrate the deep mysteries of wedlock, it would probably be found that in a vast many, perhaps a majority of cases, matrimonial dissensions arise from a difference of opinion on matters of not the least consequence and to which the parties are totally indifferent."[17]

Another source that illustrated the fine line between cooperation and diplomacy is Catharine Sedgwick's *Live and Let Live,* which featured the domestic arrangements of the Hyde family. Mr. Hyde, a wealthy merchant, was happy "in the confidence . . . that his home was regulated in the best manner without his interference or supervision." Mrs. Hyde never bothered him about the minor details of the home such as the "complaints of her servants" or "consultations about her table, her furniture, or her children's dress." Nevertheless, in all "important matters, such as the proper amount of their annual expenses, the destiny of their children in life, their religious, moral, and intellectual education, the father and mother consulted and cooperated."[18]

Despite these recommendations about the extent and degree of male-female reciprocity in the home, women writers were more concerned about a woman's ability to provide domestic comforts and perform domestic duties well. Male authors addressed the domestic skills of only 24.2 percent of their female characters. In the men's writings, moreover, not one woman was regarded as incompetent in the discharge of her

homely toils. However, this also indicates that for 75.8 percent of the
women in the male-authored sample, this issue simply was not addressed. In other words, although literary women were slightly more
concerned with this question, the infrequent mention of domestic abilities suggests that scholars have overemphasized this aspect of the "cult
of true womanhood." Women writers depicted only 35.4 percent of their
female characters as skillful at domestic tasks and 3.9 percent as not
skillful. In most instances (60.7 percent), women's domestic accomplishments were not discussed. (See Tables 7.1 and 7.2)

Women were, nevertheless, more engaged with this issue. When the
content analysis tested whether the home was perceived as a haven from
the evils of the outside world, greater numbers of women writers alluded
to this question, although only one source actually described the home
as "a little haven of repose."[19] In addition, more of the novels written
by women were concerned about the home not being a haven, although
the men's percentages were in proportion. (See Table 7.3) Authors of
both sexes were more interested in analyzing domestic harmony rather
than domestic accomplishments.

When discussions of household arrangements did arise, however, men
and women writers wrote with emphasis and enthusiasm. Given the
nature of present-day scholarship, which emphasizes flinty Victorian
men eschewing the feminine while their wives and daughters ironically

TABLE 7.1. *Women Characters' Skill
Performing Domestic Tasks*

	Male Authors	Female Authors
Yes	24.2%	35.4%
No	00.0%	3.9%
Not addressed	75.8%	60.7%

TABLE 7.2. *Stories' Perceptions of Men's
versus Women's Ability to Care
for the Home*

	Male Authors	Female Authors
Equal	00.0%	00.0%
Superior	36.5%	38.5%
Inferior	00.0%	00.0%
Not addressed	63.5%	61.5%

TABLE 7.3. Is the Home Depicted as a
Haven from the Evils of the Outside World?

	Male Authors	Female Authors
Yes	7.7%	17.3%
No	25.0%	42.3%
Not addressed	67.3%	40.4%

created male sanctuaries in sheltered homes,[20] it was astonishing to discover how often male authors described the home as a vital and necessary place which their male characters preferred above all others. Men embraced a virtually identical domestic fantasy.[21]

This is readily evidenced in male authors' minute attention to homely details. In *The Pathfinder* (1840), Cooper describes how Mabel Dunham "had taken possession of a hut, and with female readiness and skill she made all the simple little domestic arrangements of which the circumstances would admit, not only for her own comfort, but for that of her father." In Cooper's *The Oak Openings* (1848), Benjamin Boden, who lives the solitary life of a bee-hunter, gratefully acknowledges the role that Margery and Dorothy Waring play in setting his shanty, or *chiente*, to rights. Ben playfully accuses Margery of having "spoiled my housekeeping." He sincerely admits, however, that "I really did not know, until you came up here, how much a woman can do in a *chiente*."[22]

Charles Fenno Hoffman specified the positive aspects of woman's presence in his novel *Greyslaer: A Romance of the Mohawk* (1840). During the Revolutionary War, a British officer is sent on a reconnaissance mission to the home of aged Mr. de Roos and his two daughters. Looking into the window of the sitting room, he notes the fowling piece and the trophies of the chase, which indicate the presence of men. "But there were traces also of the presence of woman in this rural household, in the framed needle-work that adorned the walls, the vase of freshly-gathered flowers upon the mantelpiece, and, above all, in the general air of neatness that pervaded its simple arrangements."[23]

Finally, men readily acknowledged the hard work women endured to maintain domestic comfort and order under the most trying conditions. David Belisle's *The American Family Robinson; or, The Adventures of a Family Lost in the Great Desert of the West* (1854) not only discussed this issue several times and in lengthy detail, but also provided a textbook version of the domestic fantasy supposedly articulated only by women.

Belisle's crisp tale of the Duncan-Howe clan, a resourceful band of Missouri farmers, praises women's pivotal role in maintaining family life under harsh frontier conditions. Hearing favorable reports about Oregon, the emigrants join a wagon train to the Far West. When they become separated from the main body and eventually from each other, various family members wander from Kansas to California, where they are joyfully reunited.

Belisle spends an inordinate and, if we are to believe the modern-day analysts, unexpectedly lengthy amount of time chronicling women's ability to recreate a home on their wilderness journey. Five days out of Missouri, the families camp along the Kansas River and enjoy a meal whose description would have been applauded by the veriest sentimentalist: "Delicious steaming beef stakes [sic], wheat cakes, butter, cheese, new milk and tea, spread out on a snow white cloth, on their temporary table . . . made a feast worth travelling a few days into the wilderness to enjoy."[24] When a prairie fire followed by a torrential rainstorm destroys their wagon tent and soaks their precious clothing, the women remain undaunted. They spread the tent in the sunshine, "and everything that had been wet during the night, together with the blackened suits that went through the fiery ordeal the day before, were taken to the brookside by Mrs. Duncan and Jane, and very soon were waving in spotless purity from the bushes where they had been hung to dry, giving the scenery around the encampment a home-like appearance."[25]

Following this bout with the elements, and in order to give their cattle time to fatten in preparation for their long trek, the family establishes a temporary abode "in a lovely valley, on the borders of a clear stream, surrounded by everything that could make the lordly groves enchanting." Mrs. Duncan, who "had ever been noted for a love of orderly household arrangements, set up a tent which bore more the semblance of a large room in a thriving farmer's house, than a temporary camp in the wilderness, so homelike was its appearance." It has so often been alleged that men were uninterested in chronicling domestic arrangements that the rest of this passage deserves quoting at length.

> A cupboard made by standing two boards perpendicular, with cleets [sic] nailed across, in which were laid the shelves, held her crockery and tinware; a temporary table, made in equally as primitive a style, but now covered with a table cloth, stood at one side, while at the left, was a barrel covered also by a white cloth, on which was set a dressing glass, the top wreathed with mountain laurel, and wild flowers, and placed in that post

of honor by little Anne, who was sure to renew it every day. Camp stools stood around the tent, while the whole surface of the ground in the tent was matted with dried buffalo skins, making it free from dampness, and not altogether uncomely in appearance.[26]

In addition, Mrs. Duncan displayed her domestic skills "in the thousand little comforts that she had thoughtfully stowed away; and now that they were needed, added essentially to their comfort and pleasure." Her husband was so gratefully impressed that "he believed she was in possession of Aladin's [sic] lamp."[27]

Not only did male authors vividly express their appreciation and recognition of women's abilities to render any surrounding comfortable, but they, too, shared the domestic dream. To these writers, home was essential to happiness and a place they sorely missed when deprived of its pleasures and loving associations.

In Bennett's *The Prairie Flower*, for example, wayfarers Francis Leighton and Charles Huntly recall their homes: "Home! what a blessed word of a thousand joys! With what pleasing emotions the thought would steal upon our senses!" In Belisle's *The American Family Robinson*, home is not merely a physical place but wherever one's family resides. Four of the travelers are captured by Indians and thus separated from the rest of their party. They escape their captivity, winter in Utah, and, with the coming of the spring thaw, revive hopes of being reunited with their families. "Home—father, mother, brothers, sister; for where they are, there is home." In "The New Moon," James Hall uses religious imagery to emphasize home's importance: "How sacred is the spot which a human being has consecrated by making it his *home*!"[28] Timothy Flint, the erstwhile chronicler of western travel, makes a similar allusion in *George Mason* (1829): "When [the hero] had taken the last look of mother, sister, and brothers, and the humble cabin, which together made that dear and sacred word *home,* a word which means more to a good mind and heart, than almost any other in our language, he turned round . . . and gave the dear spot the benediction, that rose to the Almighty from a pious child, an affectionate brother, and an unpolluted nature."

Later, when George returns after a two-month absence, he requisitions a horse known for its fleetness.

I can see the tears of tenderness rush to his eye; I can see the heaving of his bosom, as he came in view of the clearing. He sprang over the stile, and in the next moment he was in the arms of his mother. My dear young reader, such a meeting is worth more, than all the pleasures of dissipation and vice for an eternity. Besides God, religion, and the hope of indulging friendship and these delightful feelings in eternity, there is nothing worth living for on earth, but the love springing from such relations. All on this earth is a dream but virtuous affection and the charities of home. Riches, power, distinction, are all cold externals.[29]

Simms repeatedly echoes this domestic refrain.[30] In *The Forayers*, Captain Travis undertakes a dangerous mission to save his daughter from marriage to the criminal Richard Inglehardt. Although Travis engaged in questionable business dealings, Simms emphasized that in the home he had been "an indulgent husband and a kind father. His evil aspect had been usually turned away from his household." Travis is visually moved during what will be the last interview he will have with his wife of thirty years. Their marriage, which Simms characterizes as one of gladness and love, succeeded because of mutual felicity and faithfulness. Travis departs, "A fond and lingering look he cast about him over the fair fields and old groves of Holly-Dale. The place never looked so beautiful before. It seemed the very home of peace."[31]

Simms's most poignant statements about the importance of a happy home were registered in *The Cassique of Kiawah* (1859), where he discoursed at length about the sources of marital happiness and discord. The cassique, Edward Berkeley, is not a happy man. Unaware of the reasons why his "family gave him no succor, no companionship," he spends a great deal of time in agony because his domestic fantasy is not being realized. "Those blissful evenings of which he had dreamed, of rural happiness and sweet content in the primitive forest; cheered with the smiles and songs of love; a calm of heaven over the household, and a brooding peace, like a dove in its happy cote, sitting beside his hearth and making it glad with serenest joys—these were dreams which he no longer hoped to realize."[32]

In addition, Simms modified the notion that men, because they are the movers and the doers, can find solace in their beyond-the-home pursuits. In an aside to his readers he states, " 'Well,' you will be apt to say, 'at least this man's nature is satisfied. He is working in his vocation, *con amore*; he is one of those men who can not help but work—who derives his enjoyments from his employments—the greatest mortal secret.' " Simms answers his own query, admitting that "to a certain degree, you will resolve correctly." But he then follows the cassique as he enters his dwelling, the "sudden cloud" passing over his brow, "a gloomy shadow upon that spirit which the intellect does not offer to disperse."[33] The cassique enters the library, where he broods over the shattered ruins of his domestic dream. These excerpts clearly prove that Simms, along with many of his male counterparts, believed that a man without a loving women and a congenial home was an incomplete and tragic character.

Women authors' elaborate discussions of home and their characters' espousals of domestic virtues paralleled those of men. Except for their concern regarding women's skillfulness at performing domestic duties well, neither their rhetoric nor their emphases differed.

In E.D.E.N. Southworth's *India; Or, The Pearl of Pearl River* (1856), Rosalie Sutherland moves from the South to the Rock River country on the eastern shores of the Mississippi. Of Sutherland's first culinary experience the author comments that "I doubt if, in all the elegance and luxury of her Southern home, she was ever gayer, gladder, *happier,* than when preparing, with her own hands, this first little supper in her log cabin."[34] Like Belisle's Mrs. Duncan and Cooper's Mrs. Willoughby, Rosalie Sutherland takes pleasure in her ability to accomplish domestic tasks under less-than-perfect circumstances. All of these women, furthermore, leave Eastern domiciles to join husbands in the wilderness, thus assuring their "American Adams" affection and companionship in distant and isolated abodes.[35]

Like their male counterparts, literary women appropriated religious imagery in their discussions of home. In *Beulah* (1859), Augusta Jane Evans waxes warmly on this issue, also suggesting, as did David Belisle, that a home symbolized more than merely four walls. Evans writes, "Home! if it consists of but a sanded floor, and unplastered walls, what a halo is shed upon its humble hearth! A palatial mansion, or sequestered cottage among the wild forests, were alike sanctified by the name. Home! the heart's home! who shall compute its value?"[36]

Further, women writers' male characters appeared strikingly similar to those described in men's fiction. William Fletcher's homecoming in Catharine Sedgwick's *Hope Leslie* (1827), for example, smartly parallels Captain Travis's leave-taking in Simms's *The Forayers.* Fletcher, returning from Boston with the orphaned heroine, nears "his rustic dwelling in the wilderness." He turned to smile at Hope but "he could not speak; the sight of his home had opened the floodgates of his heart."[37]

Flint also emphasized the sanctity of home, noting that the gains received were greater than those derived from riches or power. William Sullivan, a principal actor in Maria Cummins's *The Lamplighter* (1854), expresses a similar sentiment. In a long conversation with Philip Amory, Sullivan relates his unsatisfying experiences in the fashionable world. With great emphasis he tells Amory that his travels and all the flattery he received from wealthy and beautiful women compare nought with his chief goal, which is to establish " 'something more enduring, more satisfying, than doubtful honors, precarious wealth, or fleeting smiles.' "

> What is there in the wearisome and foolish walks of Fashion, the glitter and show of wealth, the homage of an idle crowd, that could so fill my heart, elevate my spirit, and inspire my exertions, as the thought of a peaceful, happy home, blessed by a presiding spirit so formed for confidence, love and a communion that time can never dissolve, and eternity will but render more secure and unbroken?[38]

The literary men and women of antebellum America shared similar thoughts and feelings about many concerns central to their lives. They were not, however, terribly concerned with many of the issues that twentieth-century scholars have ascribed to them, particularly the segregation wrought by the supposed separate sexual spheres. On the contrary, they resoundingly advocated blissful home environments, committed love relationships, and affectionate partnerships. They studiously interpreted the forces disruptive to domestic harmony and sought to correct them in similar ways.

The male novelists of this period, furthermore, did not describe men acting out their erotic fantasies of mastery in a world devoid of women. Instead, they depicted male characters who eagerly sought marriage and a domesticated life. As Southern novelist James Hall explained, "All, except confirmed bachelors and misanthropes, admit the felicity and blessedness of the holy state of matrimony."[39] Writers of both sexes celebrated romantic love as among the highest, purest, and most elevating emotions to which men and women could aspire.

Love and marriage were central, not peripheral, to the tales penned by men. While their male actors may have engaged in traditional business, agricultural, or military pursuits, the particulars of their courtships and marriages, the designing of homes and gardens, and the chronicling of their love relationships were equally essential to the plots. Male authors assiduously detailed the personal attributes of their female characters and crafted memorable women of substance. Women were not, as one scholar has alleged, merely " 'the prize' in the adventure stories."[40] Even the Daniel Boone and Davy Crockett types, like Daniel Nelson in Simms's "The Two Camps" (1845), returned after searching out fertile farmland "for the one thing most needful to a brave forester in a new country,—a good, brisk, fearless wife, who, like the damsel in Scripture, would go whithersoever went the husband to whom her affections were surrendered."[41]

Both sexes concurred that women's influence was elevating and that their presence in the home provided surer comfort. Tales written by women were not simply chronicles of home and family life, however. Political machinations, warfare, danger, mystery, and work were equally important themes.

Nathaniel Hawthorne, who plumbed the depths of many poignant issues of the nineteenth century, was intensely fascinated by interactions between the sexes and shared with his contemporaries the hope that relationships could become more egalitarian and satisfying. In the closing paragraphs of *The Scarlet Letter* (1850), Hawthorne hearkened to the day when "a new truth would be revealed, in order to establish the whole relation between man and woman on a surer ground of mutual happiness."

Hawthorne's language reflects his culture's belief that marital bliss, domestic harmony, and selfless devotion are among the highest and most gratifying attainments of humankind. Even the aged and deformed Roger Chillingworth, while admitting he wronged Hester Prynne by marrying her because of her youth and beauty, revealed one of his many domestic fantasies when he told her that, prior to their marriage his life had been meaningless. " 'The world had been so cheerless! My heart was a habitation large enough for many guests, but lonely and chill, and without a household fire. I longed to kindle one! It seemed not so wild a dream . . . that the simple bliss, which is scattered far and wide, for all mankind to gather up, might yet be mine.' "[42]

NOTES

1. This statement was made by a "Mrs. Grant." Cited in Margaret Fuller, *Summer on the Lakes, in 1843* (Boston: Charles C. Little and James Brown; New York: Charles S. Frances and Co., 1844; reprint, Urbana: University of Illinois Press, 1991), 110. I wish to thank James Drake, Peter Laipson, Stephen Leonard, Katherine Osburn, and Lisa Wilson for their helpful comments on earlier drafts of this chapter.

2. Barbara J. Harris, *Beyond Her Sphere: Women and the Professions in*

American History (Westport, Conn.: Greenwood Press, 1978), 33. For a discussion of the evolution of the separate spheres debate, consult Laura McCall, " 'The Reign of Brute Force Is Now Over': A Content Analysis of *Godey's Lady's Book, 1830–1860*," *Journal of the Early Republic* 9 (summer 1989), especially pages 217–20. Studies highlighting the negative aspects of the "cult of domesticity" include Barbara Welter, "The Cult of True Womanhood: 1820–1860," *American Quarterly* 18 (summer 1966): 151–74; Gerda Lerner, "The Lady and the Mill Girl: Changes in the Status of Women in the Age of Jackson, 1800–1840," *Midcontinent American Studies Journal* 10 (spring 1969): 5–14 (reprinted in Nancy F. Cott and Elizabeth H. Pleck, eds., *A Heritage of Her Own* [New York: Simon and Schuster, 1979], 182–96); Kathryn Weibel, *Mirror, Mirror: Images of Women Reflected in Popular Culture* (New York: Anchor, 1977); Leslie Fiedler, *Love and Death in the American Novel,* rev. ed. (New York: Stein and Day, 1966); and Ann Gordon et al., "Women in American Society: An Historical Contribution," *Radical America* 5 (July–August 1971): 3–66. For the argument that women used the cult of domesticity to their own ends and advantages, see Keith Melder, *Beginnings of Sisterhood: The American Women's Rights Movement, 1800–1850* (New York: Schocken, 1977); Barbara Berg, *The Remembered Gate: Origins of American Feminism: The Woman and the City, 1800–1860* (New York: Oxford University Press, 1978); Susan Conrad, *Perish the Thought: Intellectual Women in Romantic America, 1830–1860* (New York: Oxford University Press, 1976); and Glenda Riley, "The Subtle Subversion: Changes in the Traditionalist Image of the American Women," *The Historian* 32 (February 1970): 210–37. See also Mary P. Ryan, *Women in Public: Between Banners and Ballots, 1825–1880* (Baltimore: Johns Hopkins University Press, 1990); Nancy A. Hewitt, "Beyond the Search for Sisterhood: American Women's History in the 1980s," *Social History* 10 (October 1985): 299–321; Linda K. Kerber, "Separate Spheres, Female Worlds, Woman's Place: The Rhetoric of Women's History," *Journal of American History* 75 (June 1988), 9–39; Christine Stansell, *City of Women: Sex and Class in New York, 1789–1860* (Urbana: University of Illinois Press, 1982), 90–100, 129, 219; and Suzanne Lebsock, *The Free Women of Petersburg: Status and Culture in a Southern Town, 1784–1860* (New York: Norton, 1984), xv, 143, 232. Studies addressing the power and pervasiveness of prescriptive literature include Barbara Welter, *Diminity Convictions: The American Woman in the Nineteenth Century* (Athens: Ohio University Press, 1976), 82; Herbert Ross Brown, *The Sentimental Novel in America, 1789–1860* (Durham, N.C.: Duke University Press, 1940), 106–8, 281–82, 288; Barbara Leslie Epstein, *The Politics of Domesticity: Women, Evangelism, and Temperance in Nineteenth-Century America* (Middletown, Conn.: Wesleyan University Press, 1981), 81; Nina Baym, *Women's Fiction: A Guide to Novels by and about Women in America* (Ithaca, N.Y.: Cornell University Press, 1978), 26; Annette Kolodny, *The Land before Her: Fantasy and Experience of the American Frontiers, 1630–1860* (Chapel Hill: University of North Carolina Press, 1984), 110–11. Studies that challenge the separate spheres construct are listed above, in notes 2–4 of the Introduction to this volume.

3. Ronald J. Zboray, *A Fictive People: Antebellum Economic Development and the American Reading Public* (New York: Daedalus, 1993), 167. See also Mary P. Ryan, *The Empire of the Mother: American Writing about Domesticity: 1830–1860* (New York: Harrington Park Press, 1985), 14–15.

4. The content analysis was designed to test the novels and characters independently. The "tales" coding sheet included 145 variables, while the "character" coding sheet contained 130 variables. The data were quantified in an Osiris computer file. Both codebooks are published in my dissertation, which also includes a lengthy discussion of my methodology. Consult Laura McCall, "Symmetrical Minds: Literary Men and Women in Antebellum America" (Ph.D. diss., University of Michigan, 1988), 363–424.

The 104 novels and stories published between 1820 and 1860 were written primarily by white, middle-class, Protestant men and women who lived in the Northeast, South, and Old Northwest. Multiple Classification Analysis revealed that neither the story's publication date, sex of the author, nor regional setting were strong predictors of whether domestic issues would be addressed. Of the 304 women characters coded, the overwhelming majority were native-born and white (80 percent male authors; 85 percent female authors) and middle to upper class (41 percent and 40 percent respectively). The portraits fashioned by literary men and women rarely described either the expectations or the reality for the working class, immigrants, or women of color.

In collecting my sample, I sought popular works of fiction. I also wished to test the hypotheses of other scholars. The following studies and bibliographies were consulted: James D. Hart, *The Popular Book: A History of America's Literary Taste* (New York: Oxford University Press, 1950); Frank Luther Mott, *Golden Multitudes: The Story of Best Sellers in the United States* (New York: Macmillan, 1947); Baym, *Women's Fiction;* Annette Kolodny, *The Lay of the Land: Metaphor as Experience and History in American Life and Letters* (Chapel Hill: University of North Carolina Press, 1975); Kolodny, *The Land before Her;* Henry Nash Smith, *Virgin Land: The American West as Symbol and Myth* (Cambridge: Harvard University Press, 1950); Leo Marx, *The Machine in the Garden: Technology and the Pastoral Ideal in America* (New York: Oxford University Press, 1964); Fiedler, *Love and Death in the American Novel;* Ann Douglas, *The Feminization of American Culture* (New York: Avon, 1977).

5. [Catharine Maria Sedgwick], *Live and Let Live; Or, Domestic Service Illustrated* (New York: Harper and Brothers, 1837), 197, 198, 215.

6. Emily Edson Briggs expressed this sentiment quite strongly in her novel

Ellen Parry, or Trials of the Heart, published in 1850. "A married woman," she wrote, "is, unless under very unfortunate circumstances, more favorably situated for the development of her character than if unmarried. She has more and weightier responsibilities; she has more to call forth and nourish her affections; she is removed from dependence into power; no longer an orb borrowing its domestic sunshine from a superior source, she becomes herself the sun from which attendant planets must derive the moral light and warmth which makes the genial and healthful atmosphere of home." Cited in Baym, *Women's Fiction,* 237. Both sides of this issue are aired in Nicole Tonkovich, *Domesticity with a Difference: The Nonfiction of Catharine Beecher, Sarah J. Hale, Fanny Fern, and Margaret Fuller* (Jackson: University Press of Mississippi, 1997), 168, 172, 194.

7. [William Gilmore Simms], *Guy Rivers: A Tale of Georgia* (New York: Harper and Brothers, 1834), 231.

8. [William Gilmore Simms], *The Yemassee: A Romance of Carolina* (New York: Harper and Brothers, 1835; reprint, New York: American Book Company, 1937), 205. This is a fictional account of the Yamassee Wars of 1715–16.

9. William Gilmore Simms, *The Forayers; or, The Raid of the Dog-Days* (New York: Redfield, 1855), 273.

10. Simms, *Guy Rivers,* 211.

11. Emerson Bennett, *The Prairie Flower; or, Adventures in the Far West* (Cincinnati: Stratton and Barnard, 1850), 269.

12. [Nathaniel Beverley Tucker], *George Balcombe: A Novel* (New York: Harper and Brothers, 1836), 70.

13. [James Fenimore Cooper], *Wyandotté; or, The Hutted Knoll* (Philadelphia: Lea and Blanchard, 1843; reprint, *The Complete Works of J. Fenimore Cooper,* Volume 21 [New York: Putnam's, n.d.], 157).

14. Simms, *Guy Rivers,* 41.

15. Simms, *The Yemassee,* 303, 305.

16. James Kirke Paulding, *The Puritan and His Daughter,* 2 vols. (New York: Baker and Scribner, 1849), 2: 68, 72–73.

17. Ibid., 1: 105.

18. Sedgwick, *Live and Let Live,* 181.

19. E.D.E.N. Southworth, *The Discarded Daughter; or, The Children of the Isle: A Tale of the Chesapeake* (Philadelphia: A. Hart, 1852; reprint, New York: Grosset and Dunlap, Publishers, n.d.), 95.

20. Catherine Clinton, *The Other Civil War: American Women in the Nineteenth Century* (New York: Hill and Wang, 1984), 148; Mary Ryan, *Womanhood in America from Colonial Times to the Present,* 2d ed. (New York and London: New Viewpoints, 1979), 98; John D'Emilio and Estelle B. Freedman, *Intimate Matters. A History of Sexuality in America* (New York: Harper and Row, 1988), 70.

21. Laura McCall, " 'With All the Wild, Trembling, Rapturous Feelings of a Lover': Men, Women, and Sexuality in American Literature, 1820–1860," *Journal of the Early Republic* 14 (spring 1994): 71–89.

22. [James Fenimore Cooper], *The Pathfinder; or, The Inland Sea,* 2 vols. (Philadelphia: Lea and Blanchard, 1840; reprint, *The Works of J. Fenimore Cooper* [New York: P. F. Collier, 1892], 45); [James Fenimore Cooper], *The Oak Openings; or, The Bee Hunter,* 2 vols. (New York: Burgess, Stringer and Co., 1848; reprint: New York: Putnam's n.d.), 327.

23. Charles Fenno Hoffman, *Greyslaer: A Romance of the Mohawk,* 2 vols. (New York: Harper and Brothers, 1840), 1:78.

24. David W. Belisle, *The American Family Robinson; or, The Adventures of a Family Lost in the Great Desert of the West* (Philadelphia: W. P. Hazard, 1854; reprint, Philadelphia: Porter and Coates, 1869), 17.

25. Ibid., 64–65.

26. Ibid., 66–67.

27. Ibid., 67.

28. Bennett, *The Prairie Flower,* 217; Belisle, *American Family Robinson,* 214; James Hall, "The New Moon," in *The Wilderness and the Warpath* (New York: Wiley and Putnam, 1846; reprint, New York: Garrett Press, 1969), 45.

29. [Timothy Flint], *George Mason, the Young Backwoodsman; or, "Don't Give Up the Ship": A Story of the Mississippi* (Boston: Hillard, Gray, Little, and Wilkins, 1829), 119–20, 125–26.

30. David Reynolds has mistakenly dubbed William Gilmore Simms as a "man's author" who wrote in the "dark adventure mode." In reality, Simms clearly aligned with the culture of sentiment. See *Beneath the American Renaissance: The Subversive Imagination in the Age of Emerson and Melville* (Cambridge: Harvard University Press, 1988), 188–93.

31. Simms, *The Forayers,* 388–89.

32. William Gilmore Simms, *The Cassique of Kiawah* (New York: Redfield, 1859), 236–37.

33. Ibid., 209.

34. Emma D.E.N. Southworth, *India; or, The Pearl of Pearl River* (Philadelphia: T. B. Peterson, 1856), 295.

35. Annette Kolodny argues that only women writers fashioned men who shared a "principled involvement in the community around them and demonstrated commitment to home and family life." A central problem plaguing the domestic fictionists, asserts Kolodny, was their inability to counter " 'the most significant, emotionally compelling myth-hero' of American culture, the isolate American Adam." Kolodny, *The Land before Her,* 224–26.

36. Augusta Jane Evans Wilson, *Beulah* (New York: Derby and Jackson, 1859; reprint, New York: Carleton Publishers, 1866), 476.

37. [Catharine Maria Sedgwick], *Hope Leslie; or, Early Times in the Massa-*

chusetts, 2 vols. (New York: Whate, Gallaher, and White, 1827; reprint, New York: Harper and Brothers, 1842), 1:100.

38. Maria Susanna Cummins, *The Lamplighter* (Cleveland: Jewett, Proctor, and Worthington, 1854; reprint, New York: Odyssey Press, 1968), 492, 502.

39. James Hall, "The Red Sky of the Morning," in *The Wilderness and the Warpath* (New York: Wiley and Putnam, 1846; reprint, New York: Garrett Press, 1969), 90.

40. Weibel, *Mirror, Mirror,* 41.

41. [William Gilmore Simms], "The Two Camps. A Legend of the Old North State," in *The Wigwam and The Cabin,* 1st series (New York: Wiley and Putnam, 1845; reprint, New York: W. J. Widdleton, 1856), 40.

42. Nathaniel Hawthorne, *The Scarlet Letter: A Romance* (Boston: Ticknor, Reed, and Fields, 1850; reprint, Danbury, Conn.: Grolier Enterprises Corporation, n.d.), 74, 296, 304–5.

Chapter Eight

"Surpassing the Love of Women"
Victorian Manhood and the Language of Fraternal Love

Donald Yacovone

Thy love to me was wonderful, passing the love of women.

—2 Samuel 1:26

Greater love hath no man than this, that a man lay down his life for his friends.

—1 John 4:12

From the age of Cicero to the beginning of the twentieth century, men formed intimate friendships with other men free from homophobia, anxiety, and suspicion. Only with the "modernization of sex" at the turn of the century did men lose the innocence and freedom they had prized throughout the history of Western civilization. Freud and late nineteenth-century sexologists like Havelock Ellis sought to liberate human passion and transform our understanding of sexuality. But the revolution they began, combined with other fundamental social and economic changes in Western society, especially in Great Britain and the United States, destroyed forever an epoch of human sexuality. The price paid for our current understanding of sex and gender has not been fully accounted. Whether intentional or not, the modernization of sexuality and gender roles produced vehement homophobia.[1]

Western definitions of masculinity, including classical traditions of love and friendship and Christian rituals of agape, varied over time and place, but always allowed for close affectionate relationships among men.[2] Verbal and physical expressions of affection, rather than calling one's "manhood" into question, affirmed good character and, for Christians, provided tangible evidence of saving grace. Since antiquity, friendship and love were inseparable notions. "Both terms after all," Cicero reminds us, "are derived from the verb 'to love' (amos, amicitia, amare), and 'to love' means nothing but to cherish the person for whom one feels affection, without any special need and without any thought of advantage."[3] Although scholars remain divided over the extent and role of homosexual acts in ancient Greek society, clearly Plato's *Symposium* first defined the bonds of fraternal love. Serving as a model for centuries to come, the *Symposium* described how the intimate ties of society's "best men" became the foundation for Greek culture. Society, Plato held, rested on the spiritual, intellectual, and physical bonds of men, which surpassed ties found in heterosexual marriage. Male friends became "married by a far nearer tie and have a closer friendship than those who beget mortal children." The Romans, through the writings of Cicero, perpetuated ideas of fraternal love, conceiving of it as a spiritual bond based on moral virtue, and finding expression in passionate intellectual exchanges as well as in homoeroticism.[4]

The tradition of fraternal love blossomed under Christianity. Agape, or divine love, sustained the early Christians and, more than any other single factor, gave shape to male friendship for a millennium. "We love him, because he first loved us" (1 John 4:19) and "If we love one another, God dwelleth in us, and his love is perfected in us" (1 John 4:12) were cited tirelessly by men to express their friendships and to describe their bonds. The biblical story of Jonathan and David became the most important text that men read to understand true friendship. A spiritual union untainted by carnal desire, the idea of fraternal love helped define personal identity and Christian character. In early nineteenth-century New England, Thomas B. Wait, the fiery Federalist enemy of "greasy fisted Democracy," explained to his close friend, Congressman George Thacher, that *"Love to God"* was the origin of their friendship. "That the love of his parents, of his friends, his neighbors, and of his own love for them, are but emanations from this inexhaustible source of love. . . . Do you love me, my friend?" Wait inquired. "Or, do I love you?—It is because God first loved us both. *Our* love is a portion, however minute, of *his* love."[5]

A remarkably constant language of fraternal love appears in the rhetoric and writings of Americans from the Puritan settlement until the second decade of the twentieth century. Regardless of age, race, class, geographic location, or occupation, American men possessed the freedom to form affectionate relations.[6] This language of fraternal love, no mere passing phase of youth, represented a pervasive cultural ideal. More common than expressions of "traditional manly virtues" of independence, force, will, and power, fraternal love was, in the nineteenth century, the true measure of a man. The nineteenth century created a sentimentalized ideal of manhood, enshrined in both private and public correspondence and by lithographers and photographers, that employs virtues we commonly associate with women and is completely at odds with our understanding of what constitutes a man.[7]

Our modern, simplistic notions of gender have little or no bearing on the history of sexuality and gender before the era of Freud. Terms such as "homosexuality" and "heterosexuality" have no context in the premodern age. For many people today, the absence of rigid guideposts such as male/female or black/white, would be unsettling. Nevertheless, attempts to impose modern categories and labels on a world gone by perpetuates misunderstanding, if not complete mystification. The premodern world was not keenly divided between maleness and femaleness; those terms had different meanings and contexts from the same words as used today. Before the early twentieth century, ascertainable qualities and actions, not labels and categories, determined desirable gender roles.[8]

For New England Puritans, separated from friends, relations, and familiar surroundings, the language of fraternal love provided the emotional support that made the transition to America more tolerable. All were members of a "godly communion" and "faythfull friends." On the eve of John Winthrop's departure from England, he considered the impact of separation on the fraternal bonds he had forged and uttered sentiments that reverberated in the correspondence of New Englanders for the next two hundred years. "I embrace you and rest in your love, and delight to solace my first thoughts in these sweet affections of so deare a friende. The apprehension of your love and worth togither hath over come my heart. . . . I must needs tell you, my soule is knitt to you, as the soule of Jonathan to David."[9]

Separation always evoked passionate expressions, and regardless of the century the sentiments were identical. William Smith Shaw, later librarian of the Boston Athenæum, wrote his friend Arthur Maynard Walter in 1803, then on the grand tour of Europe. Shaw expressed concern for Walter's safety and expressed how much he missed him. "I have frequently thought of you by day and dreampt about you by night," he confessed. When tuberculosis claimed Walter four years later, the shock proved almost unbearable for his circle of friends. Joseph Stevens Buckminister, Unitarian clergyman and Transcendentalist progenitor, was devastated. "They tell me that Walter is dead!—O, dear, dear fellow! have I lost you forever?" Buckminister, who also suffered from "consumption," took solace in the fact that his separation from Walter was but temporary and "only a little lengthened. The voyage of my life will not be very long, and we shall embrace again."[10]

We are accustomed to thinking of eighteenth-century life in relatively impersonal, rationalistic terms and to associate warm male friendships with the romanticism of the next century. But romanticism only gave fraternalism greater intensity and immediacy; it did not create it. The language in surviving eighteenth-century letters could be as inspired as the Puritans' or as fervent as the romantics'. In 1764, Ellis Gray in Charleston, South Carolina, assured his Massachusetts friend Benjamin Dolbeare that although he did not know when he would see Dolbeare again, he hoped "it will not be long—this however you will do me the Justice to believe that no Distance of Time, no Change of Place or of Circumstances can ever erase the memory of my Friend from my Breast." In 1763, Joseph Hooper wrote Dolbeare, who attracted a wide circle of devoted male friends, to remind him of their gloriously youthful days in college and of "the overflowing of Friendship that Noble Passion without which there is no pleasure in Society, or Enjoyment of those Blessings with which we are favored in this Life."[11] Hooper loved Dolbeare earnestly; when some unspecified tragedy struck his friend, he did his best to ease Dolbeare's worried mind. His 1763 letter is worth quoting at length.

> No time nor distance shall ever pas[s] his image from my memory; the sun never rose & set upon me since I parted from you but he brought to my longing Imagination the idea of my Bosom Friend; my faithful memory daily represents him in all the endearing form, that in his presence ever rose in my mind. My fancy Paints him in the most beautiful Colours, & my soul is absorbed in contemplating the past wishing for a reiteration,

and longing to pour forth, the expressions of friendship & receiving those that would Calm the gloom, soften the Horrors, & Wholly extirpate the distractions that your absence creates.[12]

Such expression continued unabated and with the same magnitude in the early years of the nineteenth century. Federalists Thomas B. Wait and George Thacher enjoyed as devoted a union as any at mid-century. Wait and Thacher spent most of their years apart and used letters to sustain their love. "I have, my friend, but this pen and this paper," Wait lamented, "vile *interpreters* of the language of one's heart—I would give nine pounds ten shilling for an half hour's personal interview." Wait, a publisher, depended on Thacher for the latest political news from Congress, but this correspondence meant much more to "*my own heart and soul.*" No matter how physically weakened his heart might become, Wait guaranteed to Thacher, "its last pulsations shall *vibrate* for you." Their friendship endured for over thirty years, "all which time you have not only written but spoken poetry." To Wait, Thacher was simply "the man I love next to myself."[13]

The language of fraternal love established bonds that mimicked family ties and served to extend the domestic circle beyond blood relations. Mothers could play an important role in establishing these bonds. Mary Saltonstall, wife of the conservative Massachusetts Whig congressman Leverett Saltonstall, encouraged Leverett, Jr., to form strong friendships. She expressed her disappointment when one of her son's friends did not display keen interest in a relationship. "I am sorry," she confessed to her husband, that "he does not care more to be with Leverett. It would be more for the happiness & advantage of both to cultivate an affection for each other." But Leverett, Jr.'s relationship with another boy, Frank Lee, pleased her. "L. appears to have many friends who are very kind to him," Mary Saltonstall wrote, "but he has a particular partiality for Frank Lee, whose friendship it will be well to cultivate, as he is a young man of refined tastes & habits, as far as I can judge, & excellent family, in whose society he may be improved."[14] Judged by the accompanying daguerreotype (Fig. 8.1), Leverett, Jr., did not disappoint his mother's hopes and formed ardent male bonds with men of his ilk for the rest of his life.

Throughout the nineteenth century, some men formed their most important and enduring relationships while in college. These men of letters freely expressed their devotion and attachment to one another.[15]

8.1 Leverett Saltonstall, Jr. *(on far right)*, Fred Sheldon, and Chester. Daguerre-otype, courtesy of the Massachusetts Historical Society.

Such bonds proved critical to young men making the transition from school to work and from youth to adulthood. As strong as blood ties, in a sense they achieved greater value because they were deliberate choices rather than accidents of birth. Harvard graduates at the beginning of the nineteenth century left detailed evidence of their bonds and the central role these played in finding jobs, searching for a wife, or overcoming disappointments. "[I]t is to our friends only," Samuel Lowder, Jr., confessed to his fellow Harvard graduate, William J. Whipple, in 1809, "that we open with sincerity our sorrows; for, to us a sentiment as old as Cicero and as true mental gold as ever fell from his lips, there runs a conductor between the hearts of friend & friend which by communicating our joys & our sorrows, heightens the one & alleviates the other."[16]

Other adolescent males used their correspondence to discuss their latest sexual conquests. Virgil Maxy and William Blanding, sexually charged Brown University students (classes of 1801 and 1804, respectively), discussed "a pretty little girl's bare legs. Chum how goes it?" inquired Maxy. "Do you kick up any dust there or is the ground frozen too hard?" Maxy met one gal in Woonsocket, Rhode Island, whom he "squeezed as much as I pleased" and felt "her pretty little legs last night." Maxy also missed Blanding and joked with him that he had slept with a stranger the previous evening who told him that "I hugged him all night. I woke up several times and found both my arms tight around him." He confessed that sleeping alone was joyless and that "I get to hug the pillow instead of you." Betraying his erotic drive, Maxy joked that "Sometimes I think I have got hold of your doodle when in reality I have hold of the bed post." The habit of sharing beds by members of the same sex, though now unfamiliar, was accepted behavior among all classes stretching back hundreds of years. Especially for those away from family, such as travelers or craft apprentices, the desire to share a bed was deep. Those who sought solitude were the ones who raised suspicions.[17]

African-American men, largely denied college educations, formed their own schools and learned societies, such as Philadelphia's Banneker Institute, founded in 1854. The bonds formed in these organizations, like those at white institutions, were long-lasting and proved crucial to the pursuit of successful careers. For African Americans, however, such bonds also helped resist racial oppression. "Give my love to every body," the black abolitionist Parker T. Smith wrote to fellow Banneker Institute member Jacob C. White, Jr., "and consider yourself as entitled to the largest share."[18] Smith, traveling in Canada in 1862, expressed his longing for White. "I want to see you so bad that I would almost live upon one meal a day if by that means I could accomplish an end so desirable." White, Smith confessed, "is to me a friend, and I shall love him as long as I live."[19]

Although comparatively rare, fraternalism across the color line extended beyond the well-known relationship between the abolitionist leader William Lloyd Garrison and Boston blacks.[20] Frederick Douglass expressed his "never failing love" for the New York abolitionist Gerrit Smith. Beriah Green, founder of the Oneida Institute, praised Amos G. Beman, a future black abolitionist leader, as having "won the confidence, secured the love, & raised the hopes of his affectionate instructors."[21] During the Civil War, African-American soldiers freely expressed their love and appreciation to white leaders who helped them in their struggle for equal pay. James Monroe Trotter, a black noncommissioned officer in the Fifty-fifth Massachusetts Regiment, assured Edward W. Kinsley, a military advisor to Governor John A. Andrew, that the men of the regiment "all send their love to you." In the famed Fifty-fourth Massachusetts Regiment, remembered for its heroism at Battery Wagner, South Carolina, in 1863, it was not unusual for an enlisted man to present his white officer with "a bouquet of flowers."[22] Richard Henry Dana, during his famous voyages along the California coast, established bonds with several Hawaiian sailors that were "such as I never felt before but for a near relative." Dana grew especially attached to one Hawaiian named Hope. "During the four months that I lived upon the beach, we were continually together, both in work, and in our excursions in the woods, and upon the water." Dana confessed "a strong affection for him, and preferred him to any of my own countrymen."[23]

The nineteenth century accepted not one, but several styles or phases of masculinity. Victorian sex roles "proliferated, not narrowed."[24] For every example of hypermasculinity, many countervailing ones of gushing sentimentality can be found. If anything, the nineteenth-century masculine ideal was far more likely to be the "civilized" sentient man than the warrior. In a democratic society bereft of class distinctions and preoccupied with English cultural standards, sensitivity and sentiment distinguished the crude and uncultured from the noble and worthy. Since the eighteenth century, American high society valued, if not demanded, refinement and elegance—gentility—in both men and women.[25]

The nineteenth century idealized a form of androgyny and cherished a style of masculinity that combined the defining traits variously assigned to men and women. A cart de visite (Fig. 8.2), printed in the wake of Abraham Lincoln's assassination, richly illustrates the revered position fraternalism had achieved in American society. Printed inexpensively and in a format that permitted framing or allowed the object to be carried throughout the day, the image is as much an icon of fraternalism as of hero worship. Lincoln ascends to heaven and the throne of greatness and is met by George Washington. The figures blur family, gender, and generational lines to forge a permanent voluntary union, untainted by common desires, and evocative of the love Christ has for his children.

Young boys or fully grown adults were judged for their strength of character *and* their ability to be affectionate.[26] Nineteenth-century correspondence overflows with intimacies detailing the centrality of family members and friends in a person's life. Fortunately, for the Victorian era we have compelling literary and visual evidence to illustrate these sentiments. Samuel Joseph May, the early Garrisonian abolitionist, feminist, and Unitarian clergyman, met his lifelong intimate, the naturalist and

8.2 George Washington and Abraham Lincoln. Carte de Visite. Courtesy of the
Massachusetts Historical Society.

8.3 Samuel Joseph May and George B. Emerson. Carte de Visite. Courtesy of the Massachusetts Historical Society.

educator George B. Emerson, while a student at Harvard. When the two discovered they had been born on the same day, their bonds grew even stronger.[27] In one photograph of at least two taken at the same sitting, May and Emerson display their attachment with an engrossing gaze. In this one (Fig. 8.3), the two men display their bonds through physical contact.

Expressions of love and devotion among men were not exclusively the province of reformers or New Englanders. Regardless of class or region, American men formed intimate bonds with other men and the culture glorified those unions in private letters and in mass-consumption art. A mid-nineteenth-century Kelloggs and Comstock lithograph (Fig. 8.4) challenges our assumptions about urban fire fighters. Historians usually have characterized these men as little more than members of working-class gangs, a kind of quasi-official thuggery who preferred beating

PROTECTOR ENGINE Nº 2.

8.4 Kelloggs and Comstock Lithograph. Courtesy of the Connecticut Historical Society.

blacks far more than fighting fires. But as recent research and this image illustrate, most, perhaps the overwhelming number, of firemen were models of respectability who came from all classes.[28] Their firehouses were appointed with all the domesticity of a Victorian home, complete with hearth. White fire companies from Philadelphia and Baltimore even engaged the black commercial artist David Bustil Bowser (1820–1900) to paint flags, banners, signs, and insignias. At the end of the eighteenth and beginning of the nineteenth century in Boston, the city's elite served as firewards. The elite, it stands to reason, would take a personal interest in the preservation of their own property.

The Kelloggs and Comstock lithograph, designed for display in the middle-class homes that would have been protected by such fire companies, captures the nineteenth century's fusion of masculinity, domesticity, and bourgeois comfort. Both the machine and the men are "protectors," representing an "orthodox" vision of masculinity. Yet, the male images depicted are hardly flinty Daniel Boones. They are soft, graceful, and in the case of the two gentlemen on the right, loving. In this striking image, the fraternal love shared by men is put to practical use in the protection of property. The warmth and affection depicted in this popular print assured property owners that they would benefit from the love and honor that underpinned male relations in the nineteenth century.

Examples of fraternalism from working-class contexts are comparatively rare, but the diary of Edward Jenner Carpenter, a Massachusetts apprentice cabinetmaker, is revealing. Carpenter's diary, kept during the 1840s, lacks intimate language but records the intimate behavior that gave depth to friendships among the working classes. In his twenties, Carpenter maintained a wide network of friends—some in college— who remained in touch, despite divergent career paths, and helped form his world. Carpenter shared a bed with his fellow apprentice Dexter P. Hosley and became dejected whenever Hosley was away. "Dexter has gone down to Lyons to sleep with his brother therefore I shall have to sleep alone tonight," Carpenter lamented. In Hosley's absence, he searched for another bedmate. Occasionally, when another chum paid a visit, all three would climb into the same bed. In several poignant passages, Hosley was bedridden and Carpenter remained by his side throughout the night until Hosley recovered.[29]

Among politicians and the manly bulwarks of the South's code of honor, one also can find the most effusive fraternal relations. North Carolina's business and political leaders Calvin H. Wiley and John W.

Cunningham became college chums during the antebellum years and remained intimates. Their correspondence, conducted throughout the century, is replete with expressions of love and devotion. "We have been friends ever since we first met," Cunningham wrote in 1879, "& I love you to-day better than any man on earth." A few weeks later Cunningham again contacted Wiley, assuring him that "I think of you every *day* of my life—particularly at night."[30] Writing to his estranged friend, Alfred Cumming, in 1851, E. D. Stockton professed "my love for you" and declared that Cumming's letter of apology had so touched him that accepting it would be "a poor return for the pleasure of having you still the same noble friend." The Virginia politicians George Booker, Robert M. T. Hunter, and Thomas H. Bayly maintained intimate relations, sometimes punctuated by bouts of jealousy. Future president James Buchanan and William R. D. King of Alabama were well known in Washington as the "Siamese twins" or "he and she" by their critics.[31] Lincoln's rival Stephen A. Douglas accrued the devotion of Urban Linder, who maintained that he loved Douglas "with the love that Jonathan had for David." Reflecting the culture's ready acceptance of male intimacy, Linder declared that for Douglas, he maintained a "love that passeth the love of woman."[32]

Massachusetts congressman Leverett Saltonstall expressed what most nineteenth-century Americans valued in a man. While to modern eyes the description embodies contradictory ideals, it precisely expressed what Victorian culture valued most. "I was extremely pleased with him," Saltonstall said of the Whig vice-presidential candidate Theodore Frelinghuysen. "He is very gentle—manly & interesting."[33] Similarly, Emerson characterized his friend Charles Newcomb as possessing the face of a girl and the aplomb of a general, and considered Henry James, Sr., as representing a fusion of womanly qualities and "heroic manners."[34] In these descriptions, Americans expressed the high value they placed upon an ideal of social androgyny.

One Union commander during the Civil War who took on the unpleasant duty of informing a mother of her son's death, chose to employ the language of social androgyny. He described the fallen soldier as "brave, resolute, and energetic, and at the same time as tender-hearted a man as I ever knew."[35] Charles William Dabney of the Forty-fourth Massachusetts Regiment was remembered for his "toughness of moral fibre as for [his] delicacy." Dabney, according to one Harvard classmate, possessed that "rare combination of the finer and manlier qualities" and impressed his friends "by the exquisite and almost feminine gentleness of his bearing."[36] Even tears, so often associated with "unmanliness," could be, as one Civil War soldier noted, a distinguishing mark of "the kind of man who feels the most."[37] The shedding of tears took on special significance, becoming a kind of exalted masculinity. If "Jesus wept at the tomb of Lazarus," Josiah Quincy once remarked, then men "surely may weep."[38]

Ralph Waldo Emerson, usually viewed as the epitome of cold, bloodless intellectualism, formed heartfelt attachments and worshiped friendship as a spiritual union. He saw in such friendships the opportunity to share in the divine. For him, "a good man" was the "best revelation of God that can be." Henry David Thoreau's praise for the Concord sage was meant to be singular and approach the divine. "In his world," Thoreau wrote, "every man would be a poet—love would reign— Beauty would take place—Man & nature would harmonize."[39] Drawing on Plato and Swedenborg, Emerson equated friendship with marriage. He conceived of friendship as a higher bond, unsullied by physical consummation, where "conversation" became a conscious substitute for sex. "The perceptions of a soul, its wondrous progeny," Emerson held, "are born by the conversation, the marriage of souls."[40]

The work of British poet Alfred Tennyson, revered in England and America, embodied the androgynous and fraternal ideals. *In Memoriam,* as one critic reminds us, is "one of the greatest series of love poems in the English language." We rarely recall that Tennyson's work was by a man about another man. Equally important, *In Memoriam,* a work cherished by Queen Victoria second only to the Bible, became one of the most popular works of poetry in Britain and the United States. It cannot be understood unless placed within the context of the nineteenth-century fraternal—not homosexual—tradition and recognized as a masculine expression utterly at odds with our received views of Victorian gender roles.[41]

Tennyson duplicated language found in countless letters prior to the early twentieth century. He referred to his friend Arthur Hallam as "My Arthur," "Dearest," "My Love," the "man I held as half divine," and "Mine, mine, for ever mine." The domestic imagery he evoked by depicting their friendship as a marriage reflected common expressions of male bonds found in American literature ranging from Herman Melville and Walt Whitman to Mark Twain.

> Two partners of a married life—
> I looked on there and thought of thee
> In vastness and in mystery,
> And of my Spirit as of a wife.[42]

The tradition of agape imbedded in Tennyson's verse expressed the ties that bound male companions together. When he wrote "My love involves the love before," he affirmed the divine origin of human love and the love that bound God to his creation.

> My love is vaster passion now;
> Tho' mix'd with God and Nature thou,
> I seem to love thee more and more.[43]

Tennyson saw in Hallam a fusion of manhood and female grace, "the man-woman in him." Elsewhere, Tennyson wrote: "While man and woman still are incomplete, / I prize that soul where man and woman meet."

In the Anglo-American world, the most esteemed style of manhood combined elements commonly assigned separately to each gender. Articulating the same fusion of gender ideals found in Tennyson, the Transcendentalist Amos Bronson Alcott professed his dislike of men who did not remind him "of the graces proper to women." The "Hermaphrodite," Emerson proclaimed with finality, "is then the symbol of the finished soul."[44]

During the Civil War, Union troops at Brandy Station, Virginia, organized a grand ball. Spurning "Secesh" women, the Yankees manufactured their own females by dressing up fresh-faced troopers, particularly drummer boys, as women. "I'll bet you could not tell them from the girls if you did not know them," one soldier wrote. Some "looked almost good enough to lay with and I guess some of them did get layed with," the soldier noted. "I know I slept with mine," he informed his wife.[45] This incident reveals the vast chasm separating the nineteenth century's vision of manhood from our own. Not an overt play for sex, the incident carries with it familiar Victorian innocence concerning such matters. Sharing a bed, in this case, was made necessary by loneliness and wartime circumstances, if not for warmth.

The Civil War, as with virtually any war, is usually interpreted as an exercise in hypermasculinity. But the war did not alter antebellum views of manhood; if anything, it heightened them.[46] A photograph of officers

8.5 Officers of Forty-fourth Massachusetts Regiment. Courtesy of the Massachusetts Historical Society.

from a Massachusetts regiment (Fig. 8.5), replicated countless times by men in blue and gray, captured the camaraderie, spirit, ease, and spontaneity that men felt before the camera.

"How this war is knitting the hearts of men together," one Union officer informed his wife, "those who stand shoulder to shoulder in the shock of battle and keep step together many & many a weary mile in long marches, drink from the same cup & lie under the same blanket will in after years count themselves as brothers."[47] Veterans who had seen enough killing for ten lifetimes commonly employed the language of fraternal love, made more vital because of the likelihood of death or injury. Those who failed to keep up correspondence, even under difficult circumstances, might provoke concern or jealousy. "I hope you have not inferred from my silence that I do not love you," one soldier in the Army of the Potomac wrote to his friend back home.[48]

Soldiers formed bonds on the battlefield and risked injury or death just to visit with a fellow soldier. Colonel James E. Mallon of the Forty-second New York Regiment was repeatedly warned not to visit a comrade in the nearby Twentieth Massachusetts. A fellow officer begged Mallon to remain under cover and to forget his friend. "No, I cannot stand the suspense," he replied. As soon as Mallon rose to hail his companion, a Rebel bullet struck him down. His friend, Henry Livermore Abbott, was brokenhearted over Mallon's death. "I loved him almost as a brother, & while his eyes were glazing & he could no longer see me," Abbott wrote, "he told me of his friendship."[49]

Perhaps no other Civil War soldier better embodied the nineteenth century's fraternal ideal than Colonel Robert Gould Shaw of the Fifty-fourth Massachusetts Regiment. While still a member of the Second Massachusetts, he learned that his good friend Henry Sturgis Russell lay in a Richmond prison. Shaw missed Russell so much that he considered giving himself up just to be with him. "I never knew till now, how much his society had been to me this last year, nor how much I loved him." When Shaw stumbled upon the body of another friend at Cedar Mountain, his first response was to "stoop down & kiss him."[50] When Shaw served in the Seventh New York at the beginning of the war, the regiment marched down Broadway before leaving for Washington. Shaw "was seized and kissed by man after man" during the parade.[51] When he led the Fifty-fourth through Boston before its departure south, one of Shaw's uncles broke from the crowd and reached up for his nephew on his horse. Shaw leaned over "& kissed him before the crowd as naturally as he would have done at home."[52]

"He was like a day in June," Henry Lee Higginson remembered, "sweet, wholesome, vigorous, breezy."[53] John Chipman Gray, Jr., who cared nothing for Shaw's abolitionism, nevertheless lamented his death at Battery Wagner. He considered Shaw "a very loveable man and will be a great loss."[54] Shaw's field commander, General George Crockett Strong, who later died of wounds sustained at Wagner, wrote Shaw's parents in a letter widely reprinted in the Northern press concerning the death of their son. "I had but little opportunity to be with him," Strong confessed, "but I already loved him. No man ever went more gallantly into battle. None knew him but to love him."[55]

Women accepted and promoted this style of masculinity. The black diarist Charlotte Forten praised Shaw's androgynous quality. "What purity, what nobleness of soul, what exquisite gentleness in that beautiful face!" she gushed. "As I look at it I think 'the bravest are the tenderest.' "[56] After his death leading the Fifty-fourth Massachusetts Regiment, friends and family honored his martyred saintliness. Lydia Maria Child remembered him: "So good, so conscientious, so gentle and refined, and withal so brave!"[57]

Despite vast social change after the Civil War, the language of fraternal love persisted and played a significant role in the process of national
reconciliation. Philanthropists like the Boston blueblood Robert C. Winthrop, president of the Peabody Education Fund's board of trustees,
labored tirelessly to bring the idea of free, universal, public education to
blacks and whites in the South. He worked intimately with the board's
Southern members. The Peabody Fund's second general agent, J. L. M.
Curry, a former Confederate legislator and cavalryman, formed an affectionate relationship with Winthrop, a seventh-generation descendent of
Massachusetts Bay's Governor John Winthrop. Their union symbolized
the reunion of the Yankee and the Cavalier under the revitalized banner
of American nationalism.

Curry, also a university president and professor long committed to
the cause of public education, saw his work with the Peabody Fund as
the most effective way to heal the wounds of the war and help transform
the South. The two men wrote to each other every Fourth of July,
consciously continuing an antebellum letter series that Winthrop had
maintained with the Virginia aristocrat, Hugh Blair Grigsby. Both men
believed that their correspondence would help Massachusetts and Virginia "hold in fresh rememberance the time when these two states were
laboring in fraternal concord, with common hopes and sacrifices, for
independence and liberty." Winthrop came to rely on Curry and considered him his most trusted friend. When Winthrop noted that the two
men often wrote to one another on the very same day, he interpreted
this as evidence of a deeper bond. "Why may not friendship & sympathy
be magnetic & find their way from heart to heart without any wires or
other machinery."[58]

When Grover Cleveland offered Curry the ambassadorship to Spain,
he felt torn between his loyalty to Winthrop and the fund, and a compelling opportunity for himself and for the South to prove its devotion
to the Union. Agonizing over what to do, Curry turned to Winthrop. "I
value as the most prized and pleasant of all earth's gifts, wife and
children excepted, your friendship and labor with you. Pardon me for
the utterance," Curry wrote, "but I love you as I have never loved any
man, outside of my father's family & can consent to do nothing to
which you object—Help me in the dilemma." The prospect of losing
Curry to Spain overwhelmed Winthrop. He had "looked forward to
being lovingly associated with you in the cause of Southern Education
for the little remnant [remaining] of my own life." Although Curry went

to Madrid against Winthrop's wishes, the two continued their warm friendship unbroken and Curry later resumed his position with the fund.[59]

When writing his history of the Peabody Education Fund in the 1890s, Curry read all the surviving correspondence of his predecessor, Barnas Sears, with Winthrop. In 1893, he confessed to the eighty-four-year-old Winthrop that he had "learned to love and admire, if possible, him and yourself more and more. His indebtedness to you, his reliance upon your wisdom, his warm expressions of gratitude for your confidence and aid, remind me so constantly and forcibly of our relations, that once or twice I have been unable to keep back the tears."[60]

The philanthropists and former politicians of the 1880s and 1890s who promoted black industrial education also perpetuated romantic fraternalism. Helping to forge group solidarity among members of the Slater Fund, Rutherford B. Hayes professed his love to fellow managers. Curry, who simultaneously held the general agencies of the Peabody and Slater Funds, proclaimed to Hayes that his visits "drew me to you 'with hooks of steel.' " Hayes, Curry, Daniel Coit Gilman, and Atticus G. Haygood, all Slater Fund trustees, maintained attachments that promoted black education, national reconciliation, and, as they professed, exceeded the bonds they felt for their wives.[61]

Civil War veterans, reformers, and intellectuals like those in Henry Adams's "Five of Hearts" club continued pre–Civil War patterns of manhood into the late nineteenth century.[62] Five of Hearts letters, especially between the normally dour Adams and the poet-diplomat John Hay, still employed the language of fraternal love. "Dear Sonny," "My Dear Heart," and "Dearly beloved" suffused Adams's correspondence.[63] Hay returned the intensity, referring to Adams as "My beloved," "My Angelical Doctor," and "My Onliest."[64]

But the letters of men like Adams and Hay represented the values of another, more "feminine" age. The the last two decades of the century saw vast change in the social construction of gender across the United States and in Europe. Men began to turn away from the fraternal, androgynous ideal. Intellectuals like Harvard's Charles Eliot Norton grew increasingly misogynist and sought to recast their literary legacies by publishing heavily expurgated editions of their letters shorn of fraternal sentiment. Hardly themselves examples of brawny manhood, George Santayana and Henry James helped lead the cultural attack on this genteel tradition and the "feminine . . . nervous, hysterical, challenging, canting age, an age of hollow phrases and false delicacy and exaggerated solicitudes and coddled sensibilities."[65]

Succeeding generations of American men, symbolized by Theodore Roosevelt, grew up in the shadow of the Civil War. Every day, their fathers' heroism and sacrifices found expression in the many monuments that graced the landscape or in the empty sleeves and crutches constantly seen on the streets.[66] Roosevelt's generation venerated the men who fought in the war, ignored their romantic masculinity, and transformed their fathers into marble men, symbols of what the later generation thought it must become. Men of Roosevelt's time repeatedly compared themselves to those who had fought in the Civil War; they found their debt enormous and their own manhood wanting. "Our fathers," Roosevelt explained in his famous work *The Strenuous Life,* were men with "iron in their blood" who saved the nation from ruin. Their fathers had done so much, Roosevelt believed, his generation could not do less. "Let us, the children of the men who proved themselves equal to the mighty days, let us, the children of the men who carried the great Civil War to a triumphant conclusion, praise the God of our fathers that the ignoble counsels of peace were rejected . . . and the years of strife endured."[67]

The rising men of the 1880s and 1890s felt compelled to achieve the same level of heroism as the Civil War generation, though they understood that nothing they did could ever equal the magnitude of their fathers' achievement. Speaking of Robert Gould Shaw in 1897, William James reminded Americans that "no future problem can be like that problem. No task laid on our children can compare in difficulty with the task with which their fathers have to deal." The memory of the war, though, spurred American men "so that we," Roosevelt declared, "may not fall below the level reached by our fathers." The ugly colonial venture of the Spanish-American War was, if anything, intended as evidence that the sons could be as brave as the fathers. Those who opposed the war shrunk from its demands, Roosevelt thought, and were "weaklings unfit to invoke the memories of the stalwart men who fought to a finish the great Civil War."[68]

Roosevelt's emphasis on will, determination, fierce physical activity, and military honor, helped create a form of Darwinian hypermasculinity that put the notion of struggle at the heart of a man's existence. There was honor gained in honest, hard effort. "Far better it is to dare mighty things, to win glorious triumphs, even though checkered by failure," Roosevelt proclaimed, "than to take rank with those poor spirits who neither enjoy much nor suffer much, because they live in the gray twilight that knows not victory nor defeat." By the beginning of the twentieth century, the definition and very texture of manhood had unalterably changed.[69]

The rise of a "muscular Christianity" that emphasized the virility, not the sentimentality, of Jesus, Roosevelt's "strenuous life," and the imperial adventures of the 1890s heralded an end to the androgynous ideal. Simultaneously, Freud and the European sexologists transformed the transatlantic understanding of sexuality. No simple coincidence determined that the language of fraternal love disappeared as knowledge of homosexuality as a human trait increased. The growth of homosexual communities within urban areas, ironically, fueled public suspicion, rather than public understanding. As the oft-quoted Michel Foucault declared, "the sodomite had been a temporary aberration, the homosexual was now a species."[70]

Throughout the nineteenth century, romantic manhood, grounded in classical and Christian traditions, served as an emblem of middle-class respectability. At the century's end, however, intimate male relationships brought a man's masculinity and character into question and transformed proponents of the language of fraternal love into the "gelded men of the Gilded Age."[71]

NOTES

1. Paul Robinson, *The Modernization of Sex: Havelock Ellis, Alfred Kinsey, William Masters and Virginia Johnson* (Ithaca: Cornell University Press, 1989); Lawrence Birken, *Consuming Desire: Sexual Science and the Emergence of a Culture of Abundance, 1871–1914* (Ithaca: Cornell University Press, 1988).

2. This chapter develops my previous work on nineteenth-century manhood. See *Samuel Joseph May and the Dilemmas of the Liberal Persuasion, 1797–1871* (Philadelphia: Temple University Press, 1991); and "Abolitionists and the Language of Fraternal Love," in Mark C. Carnes and Clyde Griffen, eds., *Meanings for Manhood: Constructions of Masculinity in Victorian America* (Chicago: University of Chicago Press, 1990), 85–95.

3. Cicero, "On Friendship," in Eudora Welty and Ronald A. Sharp, eds., *The Norton Book of Friendship* (New York: W. W. Norton, 1991), 79.

4. Kenneth J. Dover, *Greek Homosexuality* (Cambridge: Harvard University Press, 1978); Eva Cantarella, *Bisexuality in the Ancient World* (New Haven: Yale University Press, 1992). The disagreement over the status of "homosexu-

ality" in the ancient world was played out in the 1993 Colorado trial *Romer v. Evans,* usually referred to as the Colorado Amendment 2 Case or the Colorado Gay Rights Case. See Daniel Mendelshon, "The Stand," *Lingua Franca* 6 (September–October 1996): 34–46; Plato, *Symposium,* in Irwin Edman, ed., *The Works of Plato* (New York: Modern Library, 1956), 376.

5. Jeffrey Richards, " 'Passing the Love of Women': Manly Love and Victorian Society," in J. A. Mangan and James Walvin, eds., *Manliness and Morality* (New York: St. Martin's Press, 1987), 92–93, 96–97; Thomas B. Wait to George Thacher, 25, January 1811, 29 July 1814, Thomas B. Wait Papers, Massachusetts Historical Society (hereafter MHS).

6. Karen V. Hansen, " 'Our Eyes Behold Each Other': Masculinity and Intimate Friendship in Antebellum New England," in Peter Nardi, ed., *Men's Friendships* (Newbury Park, Calif.: Sage, 1992), offers some rare evidence for working-class fraternalism. Other rare photographic evidence of such relationships exists in the hands of a private, Boston-area collector who owns strikingly intimate daguerreotypes of working-class men.

7. Rotundo's characterization of this behavior as "largely a product of a distinct phase in the life cycle—youth" is contradicted by overwhelming contrary evidence. E. Anthony Rotundo, *American Manhood: Transformations in Masculinity from the Revolution to the Modern Era* (New York: Basic Books, 1993), 75–91.

8. George Chauncey, *Gay New York: Gender, Urban Culture, and the Making of the Gay World, 1890–1940* (New York: Basic Books, 1994), 120. Chauncey completely misapprehended my previous work. Nowhere did I ever label any nineteenth-century men "heterosexual." Key to understanding nineteenth-century gender is the recognition of how little it resembles modern constructions.

9. Quoted in Francis J. Bremer, *Congregational Communion: Clerical Friendship in the Anglo-American Puritan Community, 1610–1692* (Boston: Northeastern University Press, 1994), 6–7.

10. William Smith Shaw to Arthur Maynard Walter, 4 February 1803, Boston Athenæum Archives, Boston Athenæum; Josiah Quincy, *The History of the Boston Athenæum* (Cambridge: Metcalf and Co., 1851), 18. See also John Hull to James Richards, 6 July 1654, in Malcolm Frieberg et al., eds., *The Winthrop Papers, 1650–1654,* 6 vols. to date (Boston: Massachusetts Historical Society, 1929–1992), 6:400–401.

11. Jeremiah Dummer to Edmund Quincy, 25 May 1727, Quincy, Wendell, Holmes, Upham microfilm, reel 21, MHS. I wish to thank Phyllis Hunter for this reference. Ellis Gray to Benjamin Dolbeare, 16 April 1764: Joseph Hooper to Benjamin Dolbeare, 8 August 1763, Dolbeare family papers, MHS. See also the hundreds of letters exchanged between Jeremy Belknap and Ebenezer Hazard from 1779 to 1792 in "The Belknap Papers," *Collections of the Massachusetts*

Historical Society, 5th ser. (Boston: Massachusetts Historical Society, 1877), vols. 2–3.

12. Joseph Hooper to Benjamin Dolbeare, 4 September 1763; see also Peter Oliver to Benjamin Dolbeare, 20 February 1763, Dolbeare family papers, MHS.

13. Thomas B. Wait to George Thacher, 14 March 1789, 15 April 1789, 17 June 1811, 29 January 1813, Thomas B. Wait papers, MHS. Also see the correspondence of William Wirt and Dabney Carr, 16 October 1802, 13 February 1803, 6 June 1803, 16 January 1804, 8 June 1804, in the John Pendleton Kennedy papers, Maryland Historical Society. I want to thank Anya Jabour for the Wirt-Carr reference.

14. Mary E. Saltonstall to Leverett Saltonstall, 27 December 1842, *The Papers of Leverett Saltonstall, 1816–1845,* 5 vols. (Boston: Massachusetts Historical Society, 1978–1992), 4:320–321.

15. See also Timothy Patrick Duffy, "The Gender of Letters: The Man of Letters and Intellectual Authority in Nineteenth-Century Boston" (Ph.D. diss., University of Virginia, 1993).

16. Samuel Lowder, Jr., to William J. Whipple, 22 August 1806, 22 September 1809, John Langdon Sibley papers, MHS. The MHS's Sibley collection is an especially rich source for examining student bonds. See also Rotundo, *American Manhood,* 62–63; Ellen K. Rothman, *Hands and Hearts: A History of Courtship in America* (New York: Basic Books, 1984), 106–7.

17. Virgil Maxy to William Blanding, 1 January 1800, 28 January 1800, Blanding family papers, MHS. I wish to thank Donna Curtin, Brown University, for this reference. On bed-sharing, see Yacovone, "Abolitionists and the Language of Fraternal Love," 94, and Christopher Clark, ed., "The Diary of an Apprentice Cabinetmaker: Edward Jenner Carpenter's Journal, 1844–45," *Proceedings of the American Antiquarian Society* 89 (1988): 302–94. I thank Guthrie Sayen for the E. J. Carpenter reference.

18. Parker T. Smith to Jacob C. White, Jr., 2 September 1861, [?] November 1861, Jacob C. White, Jr., papers, Moreland-Spingarn Center, Howard University.

19. Parker T. Smith to Jacob C. White, Jr., 5 April 1862, Jacob C. White, Jr., papers, Moreland-Spingarn Center, Howard University.

20. For examples, see William C. Nell to Wendell Phillips, 31 August 1840, Blagden family papers, Houghton Library, Harvard University; *Liberator,* 13 April 1833, 28 August 1840, 11 September 1840, 6 January 1854.

21. Frederick Douglass to Gerrit Smith, 14 April 1863, Norcross collection, MHS; Clara Merritt DeBoer, *Be Jubilant My Feet: African American Abolitionists in the American Missionary Association, 1839–1861* (New York: Garland Publishing, 1994), 51.

22. James Monroe Trotter to Edward W. Kinsley, 18 July 1864, Edward W.

Kinsley papers, Duke University; Appleton papers, 23 June 1864, cited in 54th Massachusetts Regiment papers, vol. 2, MHS.

23. Richard Henry Dana, *Two Years before the Mast* (New York, 1840; reprint, New York: P. F. Collier and Son, 1909), 253–54, 283.

24. Clyde Griffen, "Reconstructing Masculinity from the Evangelical Revival to the Waning of Progressivism: A Speculative Synthesis," in Carnes and Griffen, eds., *Meanings for Manhood,* 183; David S. Reynolds, review of T. Walter Herbert, *Dearest Beloved: The Hawthornes and the Making of the Middle-Class Family, New York Times,* 7 February 1993.

25. Richard L. Bushman, *The Refinement of America* (New York: Knopf, 1992).

26. John Pierce, "Memoirs," 1788–1849, 18 vols., 1:321, ms., MHS; Leverett Saltonstall to Anna E. Saltonstall, 28 February 1843, Leverett Saltonstall Papers, MHS.

27. Yacovone, *Samuel Joseph May,* 101.

28. Amy Sophia Greenberg, "The Manly Fireman: Reevaulating Class and Masculinity in the Nineteenth-Century American City," paper presented at the 1996 Society for Historians of the Early American Republic conference, Vanderbilt University, Nashville. A similar revision applies to military officers; see Samuel J. Watson, "Flexible Gender Roles during the Market Revolution: Family, Friendship, Marriage, and Masculinity among U.S. Army Officers, 1815–1846," *Journal of Social History* 29 (fall 1995): 81–106.

29. Clark, ed., "The Diary of an Apprentice Cabinetmaker," 336, 345, 386, 388–89.

30. Thomas E. Jeffrey, " 'Our Remarkable Friendship': The Secret Collaboration of Calvin and John W. Cunningham," *North Carolina Historical Review* 67 (January 1990): 28–58.

31. Steven M. Stowe, *Intimacy and Power: Ritual in the Lives of the Planters* (Baltimore: Johns Hopkins University Press, 1987), 28; Robert Wiebe, "Lincoln's Fraternal Democracy," in John L. Thomas, ed., *Abraham Lincoln and the American Political Tradition* (Amherst: University of Massachusetts Press, 1986), 20–21.

32. Wiebe, "Lincoln's Fraternal Democracy," 20.

33. Leverett Saltonstall to Mary Saltonstall, 8 May 1844, Saltonstall Papers, MHS.

34. David Leverence, *Manhood and the American Renaissance* (Ithaca: Cornell University Press, 1989), 13; Erik Ingvar Thurin, *Emerson as Priest of Pan: A Study in the Metaphysics of Sex* (Lawrence: Regents Press of Kansas, 1981), 196.

35. Robert Garth Scott, ed., *Fallen Leaves: The Civil War Letters of Major Henry Livermore Abbott* (Kent, Ohio: Kent State University Press, 1991), 150.

36. Edward Wheelwright, *The Class of 1844, Harvard College, Fifty Years after Graduation* (Cambridge: John Wilson and Son, 1896), 68.

37. Scott, ed., *Fallen Leaves,* 74.

38. Quincy, *History of the Boston Athenæum,* 18.

39. Jonathan Katz, *Gay American History* (New York: Thomas Y. Crowell, 1976), 459; Emerson quoted in Karen Kalinevitch, "Emerson on Friendship: An Unpublished Manuscript," *Studies in the American Renaissance* (1985): 55; Robert Sattelmyer, " 'When He Became My Enemy': Emerson and Thoreau, 1848–49," *New England Quarterly* 62 (June 1989): 191–92.

40. Thurin, *Emerson as Priest of Pan,* 170–72.

41. Joanne P. Zuckerman, "Tennyson's 'In Memoriam' as Love Poetry," *Dalhousie Review* 51 (Summer 1971): 202. Richard Dellamora, though he admits that Tennyson was no homosexual, nevertheless attempts to force him into the "Greek pederastic tradition." Dellamora, *Masculine Desire: The Sexual Politics of Victorian Aestheticism* (Chapel Hill: University of North Carolina Press, 1990), 16–41, especially 17.

42. Zuckerman, "Tennyson's 'In Memoriam,' " 207, 213.

43. Alfred Tennyson, *In Memoriam,* ed. Robert H. Ross (New York: W. W. Norton, 1973), 85. The same theme is evident in Henry David Thoreau's writing:

> I think a while of love, and while I think,
> Love is to me a word,
> Sole meat and sweetest drink,
> And close connecting link
> 'Tween heaven and earth

Quoted in Katz, *Gay American History,* 481.

44. Thurin, *Emerson as Priest of Pan,* 187.

45. Cited in Reid Mitchell, *The Vacant Chair: The Northern Soldier Leaves Home* (New York: Oxford University Press, 1993), 71–72. For another similar incident, see Edward J. Bartlett to Martha, 25 January 1863, Bartlett papers, MHS.

46. Clyde Griffen provides a differing view of the impact of the war on the social construction of masculinity; see Carnes and Griffen, eds., *Meanings for Manhood,* 191.

47. Richard Henry Lee Jewett to Eliza Nutting Jewett, 30 October 1864, Jewett papers, Boston Athenæum.

48. Francis C. Barlow to Charles Dalton, 2 June 1863, in *Proceedings of the Massachusetts Historical Society* 56 (1922–1923): 453–54.

49. Scott, *Fallen Leaves,* 223–24.

50. Russell Duncan, ed., *Blue-Eyed Child of Fortune: The Civil War Letters of Colonel Robert Gould Shaw* (Athens: University of Georgia Press, 1992), 230, 233.

51. Henry Lee Higginson, *Four Addresses* (Boston: Merrymount Press, 1902), 84.

52. Henry I. Bowditch, "Recollections," Bowditch Memorial, MHS.

53. Higginson, *Four Addresses,* 95.

54. John Chipman Gray and John Codman Ropes, *War Letters, 1862–1865* (Boston and New York: Houghton Mifflin, 1927), 154.

55. *Boston Post,* 29 July 1863.

56. Brenda Stevenson, ed., *The Journals of Charlotte Forten Grimké* (New York: Oxford University Press, 1988), 493.

57. Lydia Maria Child to Beloved Friends, 28 July 1863, Robie-Sewall papers, MHS.

58. J. L. M. Curry, "Christopher Columbus and American Independence," unidentified clipping, series 1, vol. 5; Robert C. Winthrop to J. L. M. Curry, 7 February 1887, series 1, vol. 6, J. L. M. Curry papers, Library of Congress.

59. J. L. M. Curry to Robert C. Winthrop, 14 and 16 September 1885, 6 December 1892, J. L. M. Curry papers, series 1, vols. 5, 10, Library of Congress.

60. J. L. M. Curry to Robert C. Winthrop, 1 February 1893, J. L. M. Curry papers, series 1, vol. 10, Library of Congress.

61. Roy E. Finkenbine, " 'Our Little Circle': Benevolent Reformers, the Slater Fund, and the Argument for Black Industrial Education, 1882–1908," *Hayes Historical Journal* 6 (fall 1986): 76, 82; and Finkenbine, "A Little Circle: White Philanthropists and Black Industrial Education in the Postbellum South" (Ph.D. diss., Bowling Green State University, 1982), 75–86.

62. Curiously, Patricia O'Toole's study of the Adams circle ignored nearly all of the effusive language that Adams, Hay, and other friends in the group used to cement their relationship. O'Toole, *The Five of Hearts: An Intimate Portrait of Henry Adams and His Friends, 1880–1918* (New York: Clarkson Potter, 1990). See also Finkenbine, " 'Our Little Circle,' " 76, 82; and Finkenbine, "A Little Circle," 75–86.

63. For example, Henry Adams to John Hay, 30 April 1882, 29 May 1882, 7 January 1883, 9 August 1884, in J. C. Levenson, Earnest Samuels, Charles Vandersee, and Viola Winner, eds., *The Letters of Henry Adams,* 6 vols. (Cambridge: Harvard University Press, 1982–1988), 2:455–56, 458–59, 487–88, 548.

64. William Roscoe Thayer, *The Life and Letters of John Hay,* 2 vols. (Boston and New York: Houghton Mifflin, 1915), 2:85, 102, 107, 113.

65. Henry James, *The Bostonians* (New York: Modern Library, 1956), 343.

66. Nina Silber, *The Romance of Reunion: Northerners and the South, 1865–1900* (Chapel Hill: University of North Carolina Press, 1993), 13–21, 58.

67. Theodore Roosevelt, *The Strenuous Life: Essays and Addresses* (New York: Century Co., 1901), 5.

68. William James address in James Atkinson, ed., *The Monument to Robert*

Gould Shaw: Its Inception, Completion and Unveiling, 1865–1897 (Boston: City of Boston, 1897), 86; Roosevelt, *The Strenuous Life,* 211, 223–24.

69. Roosevelt, *The Strenuous Life,* 4.

70. Rotundo, *American Manhood,* 84, 222–24, 278; John D'Emilio and Estelle B. Freedman, *Intimate Matters: A History of Sexuality in America* (New York: Harper and Row, 1988), 121–22; Dellamora, *Masculine Desire,* 1 (quoted).

71. Geoffrey Blodgett, "Reform Thought and the Genteel Tradition," in H. Wayne Morgan, ed., *The Gilded Age,* rev. ed. (Syracuse: Syracuse University Press, 1970), 56.

Chapter Nine

A Northwest Passage
Gender, Race, and the Family in the Early Nineteenth Century

Joan E. Cashin

One of the most memorable incidents in American literature depicts a slave woman's daring escape to the Old Northwest. In Harriet Beecher Stowe's *Uncle Tom's Cabin,* Eliza Harris leaps across the Ohio River clutching her infant son, jumping from one teetering ice floe to another until she reaches freedom's shore. The fictional Eliza Harris's dash over the Ohio has a timeless appeal for its dramatic portrayal of maternal love, but her further adventures are almost as gripping. She is soon reunited with her husband, George Harris, who ran away because slavery threatened to destroy his family as well as his self-respect as a man. Mrs. Harris then endures a pell-mell carriage ride through Ohio and a gunfight with slave-catchers, cuts her hair, disguises herself as a man, dresses her son as a girl, and sails with her family across Lake Erie. The Harrises settle in Montreal, where they live in happy domesticity, much like the white Northern middle class that Stowe celebrated in her writing.[1]

The Harris family had many historical counterparts in the Old Northwest, defined as the territories and states of Ohio, Indiana, Illinois, Michigan, and Wisconsin. Many black women demonstrated courage and wit in their efforts to escape bondage, and many black men fled slavery to preserve their families and their sense of masculinity. But unlike the Harrises, most African Americans ended their flight in the Old Northwest, and there most of them had to contend with legal discrimination, bigotry, poverty, and the ever-present threat of recapture. They had to grapple with dangers that other families in the Northwest did not have to face, perils that forced them to depart from white, middle-class gender conventions in ways that Stowe may not have appreciated. At the same time, their residence in the free states permitted them to resist mistreatment as slaves could not. Their experiences remind us how malleable gender roles can be and how dramatically they may change over time and geographic space. This chapter treats black families in the Old Northwest from the dawn of the nineteenth century through the 1850s and is based on legal records, census returns, registers for free blacks, memoirs, and postbellum interviews with reformers and fugitive slaves.

The region's racial history is filled with paradox, for deep inequities coexisted with the freedom established in the Northwest Ordinance of 1787. The Ordinance's sixth article outlawed the introduction of slavery in the territory, but it had no enforcement provisions, and it permitted whites who already owned slaves to hold them in bondage. Nor did white settlers accept the article's finality, for they tried periodically to overturn or suspend it throughout the early national period. Into the 1840s, some slaves lived in every one of the five states carved from the territory, even though the constitutions in each of those states banned slavery; a few whites even engaged in illegal slave trading. To compound the paradox, the region attracted both black and white Southerners who came for the temperate climate, excellent river system, and immense reaches of "almost unbroken forest," according to one black pioneer. After the various Indian nations were subdued or evicted, black and white settlers poured into Ohio, Illinois, and Indiana in the 1810s and 1820s, and into Michigan and Wisconsin in the 1830s and 1840s. Their political motives diverged, however, because most blacks came in search of liberty. A small number of whites came to escape the noxious influence of slavery, but the majority desired either to extend slavery, maintain the subordinate status of free blacks, or avoid contact with people of color altogether.[2]

The Northwestern states did not provide full legal equality for their black settlers, and those rights they did extend to African Americans they gave grudgingly. Both Illinois and Indiana periodically barred free blacks from entering their borders, and the Hoosier state once appropriated funds to expel its black residents, although it never actually deported any of them. In Ohio, Indiana, and the Michigan territory, black settlers had to register with local authorities, prove their free status, and give bond for good behavior, which slave states already required of free black residents. Only a handful of blacks in the Old Northwest could vote in school elections, and black children could not attend public schools in Indiana, Michigan, or Wisconsin. In 1849 Ohio's legislature finally allowed black students to enter public schools, but in 1850 and again in 1859 the state courts overruled the statehouse. Segregation in other public facilities, such as hospitals and orphanages, was almost universal, even though all the Northwestern states taxed black residents to support those facilities.[3]

Social custom could be just as hostile, for many whites gave a chilly reception to black settlers. Not all whites shared the racial prejudices of the age, and some become the friends and allies of their black neighbors. A few even became abolitionists. Yet the racial prejudice that Alexis de Tocqueville observed in the free states was all too visible in the Old Northwest. Many whites believed themselves to be superior to all people of color. In 1827, the Ohio governor sneered that blacks constituted a "degraded race"; the state's legislators once pronounced them a "serious political and moral evil." Like white Americans elsewhere, some Northwesterners periodically used violence to intimidate blacks. Mobs stormed through black neighborhoods in Cincinnati, Portsmouth, and other Ohio towns, and a crowd once shut down a private school for black children in Zanesville. A gang of whites in Jeffersonville, Indiana, publicly flogged two black men who allegedly had intimate relationships with white women. Whites sometimes attacked black abolitionists with special fury, beating Frederick Douglass after an appearance in Pendleton, Indiana, in 1843, and stoning Martin Delany in Marseilles, Ohio, in 1848. With exquisite understatement, one white Quaker remarked that Indiana was a "hard state for a colored man to live in." The same could be said for the entire Northwest, for black women and men.[4]

African Americans in the Northwestern territory numbered in the hundreds as the nineteenth century opened, but the population grew rapidly after 1830 and reached approximately forty-five thousand in 1850 (although whites greatly outnumbered blacks throughout the Northwest). Over half of the region's black population, some twenty-five thousand people, resided in the state of Ohio. Some of the region's blacks had migrated to the Northwest from other free states, some were slaves who purchased their freedom or were emancipated by their owners, but most came as fugitives from slavery in the Upper South. They settled together in towns or clustered in farms along the river valleys. It was a small population—Baltimore in 1850 had as many free blacks as all of Ohio—scattered across a huge geographic area.[5]

Fugitive slaves in the Northwest brought with them a complex legacy of gender conventions. Their experiences as slaves ran counter to prevailing assumptions about gender in the early republic, namely that the sexes were profoundly different (men being physically strong, rational, brave, and women being physically weak, emotional, and timid), that men and women must play distinct roles in the family, and that the family was the foundation of society. In the antebellum South, slave men and women both did hard labor from childhood on, and they did similar kinds of work. They also had to contend with repeated threats to the family's integrity, as their relatives were sold, mistreated, and sexually abused.[6]

Most scholars agree that these conditions made gender relations among slaves different from those of whites, but they disagree on exactly how different. Historians have concentrated on slave marriage, which scholars have described variously as egalitarian, reciprocal, or inequitable. Slaves had also been exposed to an array of other gender conventions among free blacks, elite whites, yeomen whites, and poor whites; scholars have also described these unions as more or less inequitable, and some believe that these examples heavily influenced slaves. But it seems more likely that slaves' own experiences determined their views on what was appropriate behavior for the sexes, regardless of how free blacks or whites lived, for only the slave family faced the constant threat of sale, physical assaults, and sexual abuse.

Perhaps our discussion of gender roles could benefit from more attention to the requirements of survival in daily life. Because the slave family's integrity was often at risk, men and women had to engage in behaviors that transgressed ordinary gender conventions. At the very least, the slave experience required adaptability from both sexes; the chief gender convention for men and women in these circumstances was flexibility. J. W. Loguen captured this existential necessity in descriptions of his mother, who had to be both "feminine" and "masculine," a devoted caretaker who also fought tenaciously to protect herself from an abusive master. Daniel Shaw recalled that his mother taught him to cook and sew in case he had to run a household by himself one day. According to Shaw's biographer, his mother wanted to prepare him for whatever a slave might "have to do."[7]

The runaway experience only confirmed the need for flexibility, for a successful escape from the South to the Old Northwest required stamina, guile, and bravery from fugitives regardless of gender. The literature on runaways is filled with the remarkable feats that black men and women performed in their quest for freedom, but women diverged from traditional gender roles more than men when they demonstrated these qualities. A woman known only as Rachel escaped from Kentucky to Indiana while dragging a ball and chain on her leg. Some women absconded with male or female companions but then had to go on alone, as parties of runaways broke up in midflight to elude their pursuers. Others took up arms en route when necessary. All three females in a group of eight runaways carried weapons, and one was injured in a shootout with slave-catchers on the way to Ohio.[8]

During their journey, both male and female runaways sometimes cross-dressed to camouflage themselves, one of the most effective ways to elude capture. Like the Harrises in *Uncle Tom's Cabin,* adults, teenagers, and children used this tactic throughout the early national era, sometimes changing gender identities several times to evade slave-catchers. Some slaves put outfits together as they made plans to escape; others decided to change genders on the run, on their own initiative or at the suggestion of black and white conductors on the Underground Railroad. A few bold disguises transgressed the ordinary categories of gender and race: one black man cross-dressed and powdered his face to pass successfully as a white woman. Such creativity and adaptability would continue to be required of both sexes in their new homes.[9]

When they crossed the Ohio River, most fugitive slaves confronted, probably for the first time, the gender conventions of the white, Northern middle class. A few bondsmen may have glimpsed these roles as they accompanied their owners during trips outside the South, but for the great majority this was their initial encounter with the distinctive roles that emerged as the North underwent commercialization, industrialization, and urbanization in the early decades of the century. These new roles had considerable influence among whites in the urban Northeast, where they originated, and many whites strove to conform to them. (Whether they succeeded in living up to the model is another question.) What Barbara Welter deemed the "cult of true womanhood" required women to cultivate piety, purity, domesticity, and submissiveness; white, middle-class men had to support the family in comfort, make all of the key decisions for its welfare, and show restraint and self-control in all of their relationships.[10]

Black natives of the Northwest, as opposed to fugitives from the South, may have already had a nodding acquaintance with these new roles. If they worked for whites as domestic servants, they may have witnessed these transformations in the home itself. But most black Northwesterners had little social contact with whites and few opportunities to absorb the ideas promulgated via white schools, white churches, and the white press.[11] Many blacks, both native Northwesterners and fugitives, already followed some of these conventions, not because they were copying whites but because these behaviors were commonplace among devout Protestants who loved each other. Certainly many black women were pious, and many were faithful to their husbands when freed from harassment by white men; many black men worked to support their families. Most of all, black couples wanted to be let alone to live in peace.

But the material, geographic, and legal circumstances of their lives prevented most blacks from adhering to the white, middle-class conventions of the urban North. To begin with, most of them were poor. A sample of one hundred black households from twelve Northwestern counties in the federal census of 1850 (fifty headed by natives and fifty by Southerners) reveals that their average wealth holdings fell far below national figures. Men headed eighty-eight out of one hundred households; their average age was thirty-seven, and the average household size was five persons.[12] Almost two-thirds of these men worked as farmers or laborers, and in a region with virtually universal white literacy, only one-third could read or write. Only 28 percent of these black households owned any real estate and they were by no means affluent. Holdings ranged from fifty to fourteen hundred dollars, while the average for the one hundred households came to three hundred and fifty dollars. By contrast, the national average in 1850 for all free men in their thirties was eight hundred thirty-five dollars; white Northwesterners in 1860 were even more prosperous, holding on average two thousand dollars' worth of real estate. Even free blacks in the Upper South owned more property than black Northwesterners; their average holdings in 1850 tallied four hundred and seventy-seven dollars.[13]

Furthermore, all black families in the Northwest remained susceptible to the long reach of slavery. The empire of bondage sprawled just over the Ohio River, and its menace was probably never far from the minds of black residents, for throughout the era masters, overseers, and professional slave-catchers searched the region, scouring town and countryside for runaways. Slaveowners' legal power was secured in the Constitution (article four, section two), and the Fugitive Slave Law of 1793 and the

Northwest Ordinance's sixth clause permitted the apprehension of fugitives in the region. Personal liberty laws and other due-process legislation in practice shielded few runaways. Nor were free-born blacks safe, for slave-catchers sometimes kidnapped them by mistake or, rather than go south empty-handed, by design. The legal records show that slave-hunters divided many spouses, appearing like an incubus to destroy marriages, sometimes many years after runaways escaped bondage. One white man discovered a fugitive nineteen years after his escape and hauled him back to the South, leaving the wife behind. In these situations, couples sometimes had to make an agonizing Hobson's choice. When another former slave was captured, his free-born wife had to choose between her spouse and her liberty, and finally, reluctantly, chose her freedom. The black family's vulnerability is perhaps best symbolized by the many assaults upon the home itself. When a slave-owner spied fugitives living in a house in Hamilton County, Indiana, he tore down the chimney and then yanked the door off the hinges.[14]

Children were especially vulnerable in this environment, both those whose parents came as fugitives and those whose parents were free-born. Once again, slave-hunters sometimes resurfaced long after bondsmen made their escape. Seven years after a mother and son arrived in the Northwest, their master discovered them in Cincinnati, sued for possession of the child, and won the case. It was cheaper to bypass the courts, however, and many slave-catchers stalked their victims, quietly observing a household's routines and then springing upon children or luring them away. Several whites, for instance, tried to capture two boys as they left home one day to work on a neighbor's farm. An especially crafty slave-hunter tempted a boy away from his parents with a game of marbles. Most captured children were then lost forever, for their physical weakness made them easy to subdue. One girl was kidnapped from her home in Ohio and carried away in a wagon full of stolen children, all of them sobbing with terror. Slave-traders then sold her into bondage in Tennessee, and she never saw her family again.[15]

The apprenticeship system in the Northwest also separated many black children from their parents. Some whites abused the system to perpetuate servitude for blacks, much as white Southerners used it to ensnare free blacks below the Mason-Dixon line. The legal codes in territorial Indiana permitted long-term indentures of blacks and mulattoes, and terms of ten, twenty, and forty years were common; one sixteen-year-old named Jacob was indentured for ninety years. In other parts of the Northwest, some children were apprenticed to pay for the unfulfilled indentures of their parents, while others were forced into apprenticeships by migrating slaveholders who wanted to continue to profit from their labor. Sometimes desperately poor black parents felt compelled to indenture their children. Sally Mathes of Highland County, Ohio, apprenticed her infant son to a white farmer because she was "unable to support her said child." A few blacks made these arrangements willingly, such as the man who placed his sons with a white abolitionist while he arranged to move his family to Liberia. Other parents indentured their boys to a trustworthy white craftsman to learn a trade. But the apprenticeship system functioned too often as a coercive instrument to pry black children away from their parents.[16]

Black families in the Northwest, then, were too poor to live in comfort and too close to slavery to live without fear. Yet, as residents of the free states, they had the opportunity to respond to various threats to the family as most slaves did not. This combination of circumstances, danger juxtaposed with opportunity, had a powerful effect on gender roles. Some conventions, such as female domesticity, took on a fresh meaning utterly different from white, Northern middle-class standards, and other conventions, such as masculine restraint, had to be put aside. At the same time, entirely new gender conventions developed for men and women, because surviving as free people in this region required exceptional skills from both. Therefore parallel roles emerged for the sexes, revolving around family duty, political activism, and physical combat against slave-catchers. Not all black Northwesterners conformed to these roles, but the spectrum of acceptable conduct among African-American men and women expanded to include actions that both departed from white, Northern, middle-class standards and also transcended what had been possible under slavery.[17]

First, let us turn to African-American men. A runaway from Kentucky stated flatly that slaves felt "no security whatever for their family ties," and by all accounts black men felt outraged that slavery prevented them from exercising the rights and responsibilities of parenthood. Contrary to pro-slavery propaganda, which depicted them as uncaring husbands and fathers, most black men believed that family duty was the foundation of masculinity and therefore the most important gender convention. The themes of disrupted family and outraged masculinity figure in slave narratives throughout the period. One runaway declared that slavery prevented a man from "being a man," which he defined as being able to plan for his childrens' future; another vowed that he would raise his offspring in a free state. Charles Ball, who wanted to "safeguard" his family still enslaved in Maryland, tried several times to rescue his wife and children and felt "tormented" by the separation.[18]

These struggles continued when black men reached the Old Northwest and set up their own households. They sometimes went to considerable lengths to secure opportunities for their dependents, only to be rebuffed by their white neighbors. One father placed his daughter in an academy at Massillon, Ohio, despite objections from local whites. When the principal expelled all the black pupils, he moved his family to Canada. Many black men opened their homes to children other than their own, for a quarter of the eighty-eight two-parent households in 1850 contained children with surnames different from that of the man of the house. (Because all of these households were poor, it is extremely unlikely that the children worked as domestic servants.) Most public orphanages would not admit blacks, and many of these men probably understood how easily children could lose their parents to slave-catchers. They also went to great lengths to recover their own children when possible. For example, slave-hunters snatched Lewis Williamson's children from his Ohio farm, probably with the collusion of his white neighbors, and sold them down the Mississippi River. Six years later Williamson found his children on a Louisiana plantation, proved their free status, and brought them triumphantly home.[19]

Another gender convention developed for black men in the Northwest, one that had no precedent under slavery: political activism. Although individual men emerged as quasi-political figures in many plantation communities, only in the free states could men strive openly for the rights of citizenship. The Northwest was home to such prominent activists as John Mercer Langston, William Howard Day, John Sella Martin, and Henry Bibb. As the abolitionist movement emerged in the 1830s, black men had more opportunities to act in concert. They organized reform societies and fraternal orders across the region to obtain the rights of citizenship, using petitions, referenda, court challenges, and protest meetings. These rights they perceived in gendered terms. In his history of black Americans, Martin Delany called on men of color to reclaim the "manhood" that slavery threatened to rob from them. Other men described their wish for political equality in similar language. One nine-year resident of Indiana complained bitterly that whites did not treat him like "a man" and a citizen. Another migrated from Indiana, where he could not take the oath of citizenship, to Canada so he could enjoy "every right that every man has."[20]

Not all black men had the time or resources to become political activists, but many Northwesterners had to defend themselves against slave-hunters. The traffic in recaptured slaves may have increased after the 1830s, but it was a feature of African-American life throughout the era. From the day they arrived in the Northwest, black men had to keep an eye out for slave-hunters. In this environment, it was unwise to adhere to white, middle-class gender roles of self-control, especially containing anger; vigilance and explosions of rage were more appropriate. Although pro-slavery theorists depicted all African-American men as abject cowards, most black men fought ferociously to avoid going back to bondage. When Sam, a fugitive in Indiana, believed that his master had found him, he grabbed a butcher knife and braced himself for a hard fight, preparing to "sell his life or liberty as dearly as possible." When Horatio Washington and two nephews realized that a man had turned them in to the Ohio authorities, they ambushed him, gave him a furious thrashing, and escaped. As John Parker went about his daily business in Ripley, Ohio, he found it prudent to carry a pistol, knife, and blackjack on his person, and he had to use these weapons more than once to assist runaways and defend himself from attack. Sometimes men took action in groups, apparently indifferent to the ongoing debate among abolitionists about the morality of using physical force. In 1833, a black crowd in Detroit surrounded the sheriff and prevented him from returning a fugitive to Kentucky, and in 1849, several hundred armed men from Michigan swept into South Bend, Indiana, to liberate a party of recaptured slaves. William P. Newman of Cleveland made the link to masculinity explicit when he urged blacks to take up arms, resist the detested Fugitive Slave Law of 1850, and "show yourself a MAN." Again, this outlook on masculinity was specific to black men in the Northwest. White men rarely, if ever, had to defend themselves or their families from kidnappers, and slave men who engaged in open combat risked vicious punishment from whites.[21]

When the United States went to war a second time against Great Britain, black Northwesterners had the chance to fight in uniform. They seized the opportunity eagerly, for the American army had routinely excluded blacks from service since the Revolution, and federal law closed militia duty to them in the 1790s. Furthermore, many whites had either forgotten black contributions to the Revolutionary struggle or believed that African Americans would not fight if given the opportunity. During the War of 1812, however, some blacks served in combat or in support units. On Lake Erie approximately one hundred black men served with Oliver Perry; two regiments fought with Andrew Jackson at the Battle of New Orleans; and a black company defended Detroit from attack. (Because Commodore Perry accepted black men into his forces, many black couples named their sons after him.)[22]

The War of 1812 also had a symbolic significance for black men that it did not for white men. It was a beacon, a metaphor, and sometimes literally an avenue for deliverance from bondage. According to John Parker, the war spread the news through the slave community of the very existence of the free states, establishing a goal in the minds of countless men and women. When John Malvin was a teenaged slave in northern Virginia, he trailed some soldiers to the Ohio River, where he attempted to board one of their boats. Josiah Henson escaped by following a road that had been cut through the Ohio wilderness to transport troops, while Frank McWhorter made so much money running a saltpeter works in Kentucky that he purchased his wife's freedom and his own and migrated to Illinois. The War of 1812 kindled in the collective black memory for decades in a way that the Mexican War, perceived as an underhanded scheme to extend slavery into the West, did not. In 1861 some black men resolved at a public meeting in Cleveland that they would fight for the Union just as they had served in the War of 1812.[23]

A parallel set of gender conventions took shape for black women, and the central role for them, as for men, was family duty. Women, too, had to show heroism to unite their families and hold them together. Although slavery's apologists declared that slave mothers did not really love their children, these women took their obligations to their children with the utmost seriousness. Throughout the early republican era, they lamented what one woman called the "savage" and "relentless" separation of family members, and like some men, they ran away to save their offspring from mistreatment of various kinds. Many women successfully guided their children to freedom against the odds, hiding in wagons, stowing away on steamboats, concealing themselves in barns, or traveling for hours under cover of night.[24]

Once they arrived in the Northwest, black women faced challenges that distinguished them from most American mothers. Those who managed their own households could not abide by white, middle-class norms, of course, for domesticity and submissiveness required a husband in the house. Twelve female-headed households appear in the 1850 sample of one hundred households, all of them very poor. Only one of the twelve women, Hannah Butler of Lenawee County, Michigan, owned any real estate, and that was a mere fifty dollars' worth. All of them probably worked at the typical low-paying jobs of domestic servant, laundress, seamstress, or laborer, and five could not read or write. Their average age was thirty-eight years, and the average household size of three (typically a mother and two children) was even smaller than that of male-headed households, which contained five persons. Some of these mothers may have had to leave children behind in slavery, but the tiny household size probably also reflects the use of birth control or the loss of children through kidnapping, apprenticeship, early death, teenagers leaving home, or some combination of these factors.[25]

The extant sources do not explain why these dozen women remained single, but it was probably not due to a shortage of eligible black men in the Northwest. (Interracial marriages in the Northwest, as elsewhere in the country, were rare.) Census returns for selected Northwestern counties in 1850 show a slight male majority, 101 males for every 100 females, which is probably due to the fact that more successful fugitives were men. Nor does it seem likely that these women chose to remain single, because in this environment marriage offered not only the usual attractions of love and companionship, but also a second wage-earner and an ally in fighting off slave-catchers. Nor does it seem plausible that the African heritage of these women explains their single status. Naming practices, one way to trace the persistence of African culture in the New World, show that only one child among the twenty-four offspring of these twelve mothers had an African name: Phillis High, daughter of a Virginia native, Agnes High. (Naming practices among married couples were similar, for among the 214 children in the 1850 sample, only one, July Weaver, son of North Carolinians Jesse and Cela Weaver, had an African name.) Parents instead chose Biblical names, no doubt because of their devout Protestant faith and the long-term influence of the Second Great Awakening.[26]

Most black women resided in male-headed households, but for these women parenthood also had a distinctive meaning, for they nurtured a small number of children. Married women in the sample of 1850 had an average of only three children per household, well below the average of seven children for slave families or the national average of five for all

American households. The figures in these black households are comparable to the averages of three or four children for white households in the Old Northwest—although it seems likely that white and black households achieved these low averages for different reasons. White women probably used some form of birth control for economic reasons, as did white women across the North, while black women may have practiced birth control because their offspring could be kidnapped by slave-catchers or forced into apprenticeships with whites. Furthermore, some of these black mothers may also have been forced to leave children behind in slavery. Whatever the cause, the small numbers of children in black families made them all the more precious to their mothers and made both parents all the more determined to protect their offspring.[27]

Domesticity also took on another meaning for these married black women, for most had to work for pay, either outside or within the home. Even though the federal census did not list women's occupations until 1860, there is every indication that most black women worked as domestic servants, laundresses, or seamstresses, or did piece-work at home. They had few opportunities to obtain better-paying jobs, for only half of the adult women in the census sample from 1850 were literate. The apprenticeship system heightened the pressures on black women to work, for the indigent might have to surrender their children, as Sally Mathes lost hers. It also helps explain why some mothers returned to work almost immediately after childbirth, such as Jane Washington, a cook in Chillicothe, Ohio, who took her nursing baby to work in a white family's kitchen every day. Other women labored tirelessly to reunite their families—mothers to purchase children in slavery, wives to buy their husbands, and daughters to liberate their mothers. Louise Picquet, for instance, traveled alone through the small towns of Ohio raising money to buy her slave mother's freedom. In a striking reversal of white, middle-class norms, "good" women worked for a wage to bring their loved ones together.[28]

Like their male counterparts, some black women in the Northwest strove to participate in the public sphere. Although women too emerged as informal leaders in slave communities, the role of political activist was feasible only in the states north of the Ohio River. Again, personal circumstances allowed only some women to become reformers, but their efforts merit discussion. It was a black woman, Maria Stewart of Boston, who first called publicly for female suffrage, and renowned activists of the Northwest, such as Sojourner Truth, Mary Shadd Cary, and Mary

Bibb, created their own organizations to advance their legal rights and aid the black community, especially after the birth of the abolitionist movement in the 1830s. Many women explicitly tied their political activism to family concerns. To quote Frances Watkins Harper, who once lived in the region, their goal was to advance the race and address "the wants of their children." It should be noted that this was not a resurgent, African-American version of "republican motherhood," for these women did not allude to the Revolution or their patriotic duty to raise up good citizens for the republic.[29]

Black women wanted to participate as equal partners in reform organizations, even though some black male journalists scolded them for their activities. Other black men, preeminently Frederick Douglass, became the most outspoken supporters of the nascent woman's rights movement. It may well be, as Rosalyn Terborg-Penn suggests, that many black men accepted black women as reformers more readily than white men, who typically barely tolerated female activists of any color. Certainly many black men in the Northwest witnessed the dangers that these women faced, and they could recognize that white, middle-class passivity in these circumstances was inappropriate, even irresponsible.[30]

Like black men, women often had to fight to safeguard themselves and their relatives from harm. Court cases from the Jeffersonian and Jacksonian eras reveal that many women defended themselves with physical force when slave-catchers tracked them down. One Michigan woman ran into a cornfield after her master suddenly appeared, wheeled to face him, and gave him a "terrible pounding." Women also protected their relatives from kidnapping. When a group of white men attempted to capture several girls in Randolph County, Indiana, the girls' grandmother held the men off with a sickle until relatives arrived to assist her. Other elderly folk displayed courage when the occasion demanded it, such as the "old lady" who drove some bounty-hunters into a corn crib and held them at knife point while two fugitives escaped. Adult women and teenaged girls in the Northwest also assisted runaways of both sexes in their quest for freedom. Although there is no evidence that women formed paramilitary companies as men did, they occasionally took action in groups. In one notable incident in 1848, black women wielding shovels and washboards accosted slave-hunters in a Cincinnati neighborhood and prevented them from capturing some runaways.[31]

All of these experiences, as parents, as activists, and as occasional warriors, distinguished black women from other free women. They had to be more resourceful, more political, and more courageous than most white women from the North or South in order to protect themselves and their families from harm. These were not the "superwomen" of modern stereotype, but ordinary people called upon to do extraordinary things because they wanted to enjoy what many white Americans took for granted, a tranquil family life. Moreover, these roles were peculiar to the Northwest, for unlike slave women or free black Southerners these women had the opportunity to resist openly without the certainty of swift, deadly retaliation. The Northwest offered its black residents full measures of danger and opportunity in bittersweet combination.

So how did black women and men feel about these transformations? Most men and women in the Northwest seem to have accepted these changes as necessary, recounting their experiences in a matter-of-fact tone, with no apology and little embarrassment about their supposedly unconventional behavior. The question arises, did blacks even find white, Northern, middle-class gender roles desirable? A handful of women commented on these roles, and Sojourner Truth, probably the most famous of the region's female activists, attacked them outright. In her speech at Akron in 1851, she apparently did not utter the much-quoted phrase "Ar'n't I a Woman," but she did denounce the hypocrisy of conventional gender roles and insisted that black women's hard labor be respected. Sophia Snowden, a young woman from a small town in Ohio, felt more ambivalent about these gender conventions, if we may judge by a scrapbook she kept of newspaper stories, poems, and song lyrics. Some of her clippings lauded white, middle-class femininity while others questioned or subtly criticized it.[32]

Neither Truth nor Snowden ever married as free women, so their attitudes tell us little about how couples experienced these transformations. Almost all private exchanges between the sexes went unrecorded, but an interview from the 1850s suggests that one black couple may have adopted some white, middle-class norms selectively as the circumstances of their lives permitted. When Mr. and Mrs. John Little fled Tennessee for Ohio in the 1840s, he was in his mid-twenties and she was in her late teens. John Little left because he could not endure his owner's mistreatment ("I was as much a man as my master" and "I was a man as well as himself") or the abuse inflicted on his wife. Probably because they belonged to different masters, they did not yet know each other well, which may explain why they told contradictory versions of their three-month odyssey to freedom. Furthermore, by his own account, John Little had rather traditional ideas about gender at this point in his life. During the journey northward, he described himself as the path-finder who helped his faltering wife when she fell asleep or could not run fast enough. They hurried through the Northwest and pushed on to Ontario, Canada, where they settled down to run a farm.

There, the couple worked closely together for the first time, construct-ing a house, chopping wood, and hunting for game. As they labored side by side, John Little's respect for his wife grew exponentially. He came to realize that his wife was a hard worker by nature, not simply because her former master made her work, and he began to appreciate her courage fully. When he was interviewed in the mid-1850s, he stated, "now I see that she was a brave woman." Her true self, concealed during slavery, emerged, and he admired her so-called unfeminine qualities.

Mrs. Little (the interviewer did not supply her first name) already perceived herself as her husband's partner, however, when they ran away from slavery. As she related the tale of their escape, she took her turn standing watch, warned her spouse when they were in danger, and in general "got to be quite hardy" on the road. In Canada, she felt "proud" to be able to clear land, build a house, and work on their farm. Her comments thus far suggest an indifference to, if not rejection of, stan-dards of white, Northern middle-class domesticity. But as the couple prospered, doing well enough to buy a carriage, the commercial econ-omy and its attendant gender roles began to exert some appeal. When Mrs. Little shopped in a nearby town, she was glad that clerks in the finest stores treated her "politely" and gave her "much attention as though I were a white woman." The couple's survival was no longer at issue, making it possible for her to observe the etiquette of a quintessen-tial middle-class activity, shopping.[33]

The Fugitive Slave Act of 1850 initiated a new, more repressive era for black residents of the Northwest. Enacted as part of the Compromise of 1850, it stipulated that runaways living in free states had no legal protections, such as jury trials, and it rewarded federal marshals who sent fugitives back into slavery. As many as twenty thousand African Americans migrated from the Northwest to Canada over the next ten years, and some of the blacks who continued to live in the region took more extreme measures to reunite their families, surpassing the dramatic renditions of any novelist. Dangerfield Newby of Ohio joined John

Brown's raid at Harpers Ferry, Virginia, in 1859 not only to incite a slave rebellion but also to rescue his own family still in bondage. He died during the attack, his lonely wife's letters on his body.

The Union victory in the Civil War launched yet another phase in the lives of black Northwesterners, releasing them from the slave-hunter's grasp. At long last they could raise their children in peace, perhaps designing new gender roles for a new generation.[34]

NOTES

1. Harriet Beecher Stowe, *Uncle Tom's Cabin; or, Life among the Lowly* (New York: Literary Classics of the United States, 1982), passim; Joan D. Hedrick, *Harriet Beecher Stowe: A Life* (New York: Oxford University Press, 1994), 202–17.

2. Paul Finkelman, "Slavery and the Northwest Ordinance: A Study in Ambiguity," *Journal of the Early Republic* 6 (winter 1986): 343–70; Peter S. Onuf, *Statehood and Union: A History of the Northwest Ordinance* (Bloomington: Indiana University Press, 1987), 109–32; R. Carlyle Buley, *The Old Northwest: Pioneer Period,* 2 vols. (Indianapolis: Indiana University Press, 1950), 1:20–50, 2:80–99, 121–46; Merrily Pierce, "Luke Decker and Slavery: His Cases with Bob and Anthony, 1817–1822," *Indiana Magazine of History* 85 (March 1989): 31–49; *Speak Out in Thunder Tones: Letters and Other Writings by Black Northerners, 1787–1865,* ed. Dorothy Sterling (Garden City, N.Y.: Doubleday, 1973), 206; Thomas C. Cochran, ed., *The New American State Papers: Labor and Slavery,* vol. 4; *Slavery in Territories* (Wilmington, Del.: Scholarly Resources, 1973), 17–19, 32, 36–37, 39–41; Leon F. Litwack, *North of Slavery: The Negro in the Free States, 1790–1860* (Chicago: University of Chicago Press, 1961), 3; David M. Katzman, *Before the Ghetto: Black Detroit in the Nineteenth Century* (Urbana: University of Illinois Press, 1973), 5.

3. Litwack, *North of Slavery,* 70, 74, 97, 123, 151; Darlene Clark Hine, *When the Truth Is Told: A History of Black Women's Culture and Community in Indiana, 1875–1950* (Indianapolis: National Council of Negro Women, 1981), 10; Edgar F. Love, "Documents: Registration of Free Blacks in Ohio: The Slaves of George C. Mendenhall," *Journal of Negro History* 69 (winter 1984): 39; Katzman, *Black Detroit,* 6–7, 22–23; Ira Berlin, *Slaves without Masters: The Free Negro in the Antebellum South* (New York: Oxford University Press, 1974), 92–94, 317; Emma Lou Thornbrough, *The Negro in Indiana: A Study of a Minority* (Indianapolis: Indiana Historical Press, 1957), 36, 120–23, 166–67; W. Sherman Savage, *Blacks in the West* (Westport, Conn.: Greenwood Press, 1976), 26, 177; David A. Gerber, *Black Ohio and the Color Line 1860–1915* (Urbana: University of Illinois Press, 1976), 4–6.

4. Alexis de Tocqueville, *Democracy in America,* ed. J. P. Mayer and Max Lerner, trans. George Lawrence (New York: Harper and Row, 1966), 315–16; John W. Quist, " 'The Great Majority of Our Subscribers Are Farmers': The Michigan Abolitionist Constituency of the 1840s," *Journal of the Early Republic* 14 (fall 1994): 325–58; John Mack Faragher, *Sugar Creek: Life on the Illinois Prairie* (New Haven: Yale University Press, 1986), 48–49; Francis P. Weisenburger, *The Passing of the Frontier, 1825–1850* (Columbus: Ohio State Archaeological and Historical Society, 1941), 3:43; Litwack, *North of Slavery,* 122; Carter G. Woodson, *A Century of Negro Migration* (1918; reprint, New York: Russell and Russell, 1969), 57; Thornbrough, *Indiana,* 130; William S. McFeely, *Frederick Douglass* (New York: W. W. Norton, 1991), 108–12; Sterling, ed., *Speak Out,* 134–36; Caroline Newton to Wilbur Siebert, 13 July 1896, Box 78, Siebert Collection (Ohio Historical Society).

5. *Historical Statistics of the United States, Colonial Times to 1970: Part I* (Washington, D.C.: U.S. Department of Commerce, 1975), 27, 29, 33, 37; John Hope Franklin, *The Free Negro in North Carolina 1790–1860* (1943; reprint, New York: Russell and Russell, 1969), 200; Jane H. Pease and William H. Pease, *They Who Would Be Free: Blacks' Search for Freedom, 1830–1861* (New York: Atheneum, 1974), 27; William T. Utter, *The Frontier State, 1803–1825* (Columbus, 1942), 2:397; Thornbrough, *Indiana,* 31; Barbara Jeanne Fields, *Slavery and Freedom on the Middle Ground: Maryland during the Nineteenth Century* (New Haven: Yale University Press, 1985), 62.

6. Deborah Gray White, *Ar'n't I a Woman? Female Slaves in the Plantation South* (New York: W. W. Norton, 1985); Lawrence W. Levine, *Black Culture and Black Consciousness: Afro-American Folk Thought from Slavery to Freedom* (New York: Oxford University Press, 1977); Herbert G. Gutman, *The Black Family in Slavery and Freedom, 1750–1925* (New York: Pantheon, 1976); Eugene D. Genovese, *Roll, Jordan, Roll: The World the Slaves Made* (New York: Random House, 1974).

7. *The Reverend J. W. Loguen, As a Slave and as a Freeman: A Narrative of Real Life* (Syracuse, N.Y., 1859; reprint, New York: Negro Universities Press, 1968), 18; William H. Rogers, *Senator John P. Green and Sketches of Prominent Men of Ohio* (Washington, D.C.: Arena Publishing Co., 1893), 38.

8. Levi Coffin, *Reminiscences of Levi Coffin, the Reputed President of the Underground Railroad* (Cincinnati, 1876; reprint, New York: Arno Press, 1968), 163–68, 170, 178–85; William M. Cockrum, *History of the Underground Railroad, As It Was Conducted by the Anti-Slavery League* (Oakland City, Ind., 1915; reprint, New York: Negro Universities Press, 1969), 70–71.

9. Coffin, *Reminiscences,* 174, 176, 315, 347, 535, 341–42, 457–58, 535, 551–53; Interview with Jacob Cummings, n.d. [September 1894], Box 77, Siebert Collection; Benjamin Drew, *A North-side View of Slavery: The Refugee or the Narratives of Fugitive Slaves in Canada* (Boston, 1856; reprint, New York:

Negro Universities Press, 1969), 43; Alexander Milton Ross, *Recollections and Experiences of an Abolitionist: From 1855 to 1865,* new foreword by Donald Franklin Joyce (Northbrook, Ill.: Metro Books, 1972), 18; Robin W. Winks, *The Blacks in Canada: A History* (Montreal: Harvest House, 1971), 169; Interview with R. S. Miller, 4 April 1892, Box 102, Siebert Collection; Laura S. Haviland, *A Woman's Life Work* (Chicago: C. V. Waite, 1887), 103; H. C. Harvey to Wilbur Siebert, 16 January 1893, Box 109, Siebert Collection; C. D. Booth, "Astabula as a Station on the Underground Railroad," Box 101, Siebert Collection; P. N. Wickerham to Wilbur Siebert, 9 August 1894, Box 101, Siebert Collection; Robert Samuel Fletcher, *A History of Oberlin College from Its Foundation through the Civil War,* 2 vols. (Oberlin, Ohio: Oberlin College, 1943), 1:397.

10. Barbara Welter, "The Cult of True Womanhood, 1820–1860," *American Quarterly* 18 (summer 1966): 151–74; E. Anthony Rotundo, *American Manhood: Transformations in Masculinity from the Revolution to the Modern Era* (New York: Basic Books, 1993); Linda K. Kerber, "Separate Spheres, Female Worlds, Woman's Place: The Rhetoric of Women's History," *Journal of American History* 75 (June 1988): 9–39.

11. Most scholars of the urban Northeast or the trans-Mississippi portray white, middle-class conventions as attractive to blacks; see James Oliver Horton and Lois Horton, *Black Bostonians: Family Life and Community Life in the Antebellum North* (New York: Holmes and Meier, 1979), 98–120; Shirley J. Yee, *Black Women Abolitionists: A Study in Activism, 1828–1860* (Knoxville: University of Tennessee Press, 1992), 4, 58; Bert James Loewenberg and Ruth Bogin, eds., *Black Women in Nineteenth-Century American Life: Their Words, Their Thoughts, Their Feelings* (University Park: Pennsylvania State University Press, 1976), 35–36; Glenda Riley, "American Daughters: Black Women in the West," *Montana: The Magazine of Western History* 38 (spring 1988): 21. The poverty of black Northwesterners, the frontier environment in which many of them lived, and their physical distance from the cultural hotbeds of the urban Northeast may explain their apparent differences with black Northeasterners.

12. The federal census of 1850 is the first to give detailed information on households. I chose twelve counties according to the maps in Wilbur Zelinsky's article: Crawford and Grant Counties, Wisconsin; Cass and Lenawee Counties, Michigan; Gallatin and Monroe Counties, Illinois; Posey and Randolph Counties, Indiana; and Brown, Lawrence, Shelby, and Miami Counties, Ohio. See Zelinsky, "The Population Geography of the Free Negro in Antebellum America," *Population Studies* 3 (1949–1950): 390–92.

13. Lee Soltow, *Men and Wealth in the United States, 1850–1870* (New Haven: Yale University Press, 1975), 70; Jeremy Atack and Fred Bateman, "Yankee Farming and Settlement in the Old Northwest: A Comparative Analysis," in *Essays on the Economy of the Old Northwest,* ed. David C. Klingaman and

Richard K. Vedder (Athens: Ohio University Press, 1987), 81; Loren Schwen-inger, *Black Property Owners in the South, 1790–1915* (Urbana: University of Illinois Press, 1990), 75.

14. Savage, *Blacks in the West,* 22–23; Thomas D. Morris, *Free Men All: The Personal Liberty Laws of the North, 1780–1861* (Baltimore: Johns Hopkins University Press, 1974); Thornbrough, *Indiana,* 107; Helen Tunnicliff Catterall, ed., *Judicial Cases concerning American Slavery and the Negro* (Washington, D.C.: Carnegie Institution, 1926–1937), *Indiana,* 33, 35.

15. Stephen Middleton, "The Fugitive Slave Issue in Southwestern Ohio: Un-reported Cases," *Old Northwest* 14 (winter 1988–1989): 289–92; Cockrum, *History of the Underground Railroad,* 242–244; Catterall, *Ohio,* 10; Loguen, *As a Slave and As a Freeman,* 12–13.

16. T. O. Madden, Jr., with Ann L. Miller, *We Were Always Free: The Mad-dens of Culpeper County, Virginia, A 200-Year Family History* (New York: W. W. Norton, 1993), 21–23; Thornbrough, *Indiana,* 10–11; Catterall, *Illinois,* 51; Black Register, Ross County, Ohio, p. 127, 25 July 1837 (Ohio Historical Society); George P. Rawick, ed., *The American Slave: A Composite Autobiog-raphy: Alabama and Indiana* (Westport, Conn.: Greenwood Press, 1972), 6:37–39; N. Dwight Harris, *The History of Negro Servitude in Illinois and of the Slavery Agitation in That State, 1719–1864* (Chicago, 1904; reprint, New York: Negro Universities Press, 1969), 12; Black Register, Highland County, Ohio, p. 5, 16 July 1825; Black Register, Highland County, Ohio, p. 12, 18 October 1826; Cockrum, *History of the Underground Railroad,* 242–44; Black Register, Highland County, Ohio, 1, 16 February 1825, 2, 13 November 1824.

17. On other cultural adaptations among blacks in a new environment, see William D. Piersen, *Black Yankees: The Development of an Afro-American Sub-culture in Eighteenth-Century New England* (Amherst: University of Massachu-setts Press, 1988).

18. Charles L. Blockson, *The Underground Railroad* (New York: Prentice-Hall, 1987), 89; Drew, *North-side View of Slavery,* 248; William Loren Katz, *The Black West* (Garden City, N.Y.: Anchor Press, 1973), 45–46; Charles Ball, *Slavery in the United States* (New York: John S. Taylor, 1837), 466.

19. Federal census of 1850; Drew, *North-side View of Slavery,* 307; Sterling, ed., *Speak Out,* 145–47. Twenty-two out of eighty-eight male-headed house-holds contained children with surnames different from the household head's. Fourteen of these households owned no real estate at all, and the average real estate holding for the other eight was one hundred twenty-eight dollars.

20. Benjamin Quarles, *Black Abolitionists* (New York: Oxford University Press, 1969), 29–30, 36, 101, 175; R. J. M. Blackett, *Beating against the Bar-riers: Biographical Essays in Nineteenth-Century Afro-American History* (Baton Rouge: Louisiana State University Press, 1986), 187–386; Katzman, *Black De-troit,* 22, 33, 38, 39, 41; Thornbrough, *Indiana,* 147; Katz, *Black West,* 59;

Martin Robinson Delany, *The Condition, Elevation, Emigration, and Destiny of the Colored People of the United States* (Philadelphia, 1852; reprint, New York: Arno Press, 1968), 86–98; Drew, *North-side View of Slavery*, 254, 272–73.

21. Coffin, *Reminiscences*, 154–55; Interview with Horatio Washington, 2 August 1895, Box 102, Siebert Collection; "John Parker Story," n.p., Rankin-Parker Papers, William R. Perkins Library, Manuscript Division, Duke University; Merton L. Dillon, *Slavery Attacked: Southern Slaves and Their Allies: 1619–1865* (Baton Rouge: Louisiana State University Press, 1990), 206–7; Katzman, *Black Detroit*, 9–10; Catterall, *Indiana*, 35–37; C. Peter Ripley et al., eds., *The Black Abolitionist Papers*, vol. 4, *The United States, 1847–1858* (Chapel Hill: University of North Carolina Press, 1991), 4:65.

22. Lorenzo J. Greene, "The Negro in the War of 1812 and the Civil War," *Negro History Bulletin* 14 (March 1951): 133–34; William C. Nell, *Services of Colored Americans in the Wars of 1776 and 1812* (Boston: Prentiss and Sawyer, 1851); Charles H. Wesley, *Ohio Negroes in the Civil War* (Columbus: Ohio State University Press for the Ohio Historical Society, 1962), 15; Bernard C. Nalty, *Strength for the Fight: A History of Black Americans in the Military* (New York: Free Press, 1986), 21–25; Katzman, *Black Detroit*, 6 n. 4; Joseph T. Wilson, *The Black Phalanx: A History of the Negro Soldiers of the United States in the Wars of 1775–1812, 1861–1865* (Hartford, Conn.: American Publishing Company, 1890), 79; Federal census of 1850, Miami County, Ohio, p. 81; Drew, *North-side View of Slavery*, 239; Black Register, Ross County, Ohio, 28 November 1812.

23. "John Parker Story," n.p., Rankin-Parker Papers; *North into Freedom: The Autobiography of John Malvin, Free Negro, 1795–1880*, ed. and with an introduction by Allan Peskin (Cleveland: Western Reserve University, 1966), 30–32; Josiah Henson, *Truth Stranger than Fiction: Father Henson's Story of His Own Life*, with an Introduction by Mrs. H. B. Stowe (1849; reprint, Northbrook, Ill.: Metro Books, 1972), 115; Juliet E. K. Walker, *Free Frank: A Black Pioneer on the Antebellum Frontier* (Lexington: University Press of Kentucky, 1983), 34–46; Kenneth L. Kusmer, *A Ghetto Takes Shape: Black Cleveland, 1870–1930* (Urbana: University of Illinois Press, 1976), 25–26.

24. Loewenberg and Bogin, eds., *Black Women*, 15; Coffin, *Reminiscences*, 170–71; Haviland, *Woman's Life Work*, 102; Catterall, *Indiana*, 34; Russell H. Davis, *Black Americans in Cleveland from George Peake to Carl B. Stokes, 1796–1969* (Washington, D.C.: Associated Publishers, 1972), 27.

25. Federal census of 1850.

26. Federal census of 1850, Shelby County, Ohio, 166; Randolph County, Indiana, 6; Peter H. Wood, *Black Majority: Negroes in Colonial South Carolina from 1670 through the Stono Rebellion* (New York: W. W. Norton, 1974), 182; Gutman, *Black Family*, 186–87; Federal census returns for Crawford County,

Wisconsin, Cass County, Michigan, Gallatin County, Illinois, Randolph County, Indiana, and Lawrence County, Ohio. The most common name for male children was John, while the most common female name was Mary.

27. Federal census of 1850; Donald R. Wright, *African Americans in the Early Republic, 1789–1831* (Arlington Heights, Ill.: Harlan Davidson, 1993), 68; Robert V. Wells, *Revolutions in American's Lives: A Demographic Perspective on the History of Americans, Their Families, and Their Society* (Westport, Conn.: Greenwood Press, 1982), 151–52; Don Harrison Doyle, *The Social Order of a Frontier Community: Jacksonville, Illinois, 1825–70* (Urbana: University of Illinois Press, 1978), 113.

28. Federal census of 1850; Black Register, Greene County, Ohio, 32, 15 October 1838; Gilbert H. Barnes and Dwight L. Dumond, eds., *Letters of Theodore Dwight Weld, Angelina Grimké Weld, and Sarah Grimké, 1822–1844* (New York: Appleton-Century-Crofts, 1934), 1:135, Weld to Lewis Tappan, 18 March 1834; H. Mattison, "Louise Picquet," in *Collected Black Women's Narratives,* with an introduction by Anthony G. Barthelemy (New York: Oxford University Press, 1988), 40.

29. Maria W. Stewart: *American's First Black Woman Political Writer,* ed. Marilyn Richardson (Bloomington: Indiana University Press, 1987), 28–74; James Oliver Horton and Stacy Flaherty, "Black Leadership in Antebellum Cincinnati," in Taylor, ed., *Race and the City,* 73, 79–80; Yee, *Black Women Abolitionists,* 55–56, 60 (Harper quote), 61–85; Linda K. Kerber, *Women of the Republic: Intellect and Ideology in Revolutionary America* (Chapel Hill: University of North Carolina Press, 1980).

30. Rosalyn Terborg-Penn, "Black Male Perspectives on the Nineteenth-Century Woman," in Sharon Harley and Rosalyn Terborg-Penn, eds., *The Afro-American Woman: Struggles and Images* (Port Washington, N.Y.: Kennikat Press, 1978), 28–29, 33; Quarles, *Black Abolitionists,* 178.

31. "Slavery Days Recalled: Death of William Casey," *Detroit Free Press,* 24 January 1893, Box 91, Siebert Collection; Coffin, *Reminiscences,* 172–74; Interview with Jacob Cummings, n.d. [September 1894], Box 77, Siebert Collection; Interview with Horatio Washington, 2 August 1895, Box 102, Siebert Collection; Hallie Q. Brown, *Homespun Heroines and Other Women of Distinction,* with an introduction by Randall K. Burkett (New York: Oxford University Press, 1988), 73; Thornbrough, *Indiana,* 44; Sterling, ed., *Speak Out,* 154–55.

32. Ripley et al., eds., *Black Abolitionist Papers,* 4:81–82; Carlton Mabee with Susan Mabee Newhouse, *Sojourner Truth: Slave, Prophet, Legend* (New York: Oxford University Press, 1993), 67–82; Howard L. Sacks and Judith Rose Sacks, *Way up North in Dixie: A Black Family's Claim to the Confederate Anthem* (Washington, D.C.: Smithsonian Institute Press, 1993), 101–23. The couple had one infant daughter.

33. Drew, *North-side View of Slavery,* 198–233.

34. Vincent Harding, *There Is a River: The Black Struggle for Freedom in America* (New York: Harcourt Brace Jovanovich, 1981), 172–94; Litwack, *North of Slavery,* 248–49; Benjamin Quarles, *Allies for Freedom: Blacks and John Brown* (New York: Oxford University Press, 1974), 86–87, 95; Stanley W. Campbell, *The Slave Catchers: Enforcement of the Fugitive Slave Law, 1850–1860* (Chapel Hill: University of North Carolina Press, 1968), 110–86.

Chapter Ten

"I Am Going to Write to You"

Nurturing Fathers and the Office of Indian Affairs on the Southern Ute Reservation, 1895–1934

Katherine M. B. Osburn

In pre-reservation times, when a child was born to the Ute Indians of Southwestern Colorado, the baby's father and mother lay in separate shallow troughs filled with warm ashes covered in cedar bark and green brush. The mother remained on this "hot bed" for thirty days, abstaining from eating meat and fish lest she spoil her husband's abilities to hunt and fish. The father had a four-day lying-in. At the end of this period, the newborn's grandparents (or older relatives acting as grandparents) cooked meat for the father and, as they ate, admonished him to provide for the child, blessing him to increase his prowess as a hunter. After the meal, the father went on a mock hunt lasting several days. During this ritual he ran frantically through the surrounding countryside in the exaggerated motions of a skillful hunter. This ceremony ensured that he would have the speed and endurance to be a successful provider. Ute rituals surrounding the mother and child also focused on their important productive roles and were crucial to the family's survival. These ceremonies continued for a time after the Ute people were confined to a reservation, indicating that the father's role as provider remained critical to tribal survival.[1] Yet, by the late nineteenth and early twentieth centuries, men had lost their role as hunters and struggled to provide for their families by farming, stock raising, and wage labor.

In studying how Indians adjusted to reservations, historians and anthropologists have analyzed the public roles of Indian men. The emphasis has been on men's political behavior as they coped with the government's assimilationist programs and the degrees to which they cooperated with or resisted the government agenda for their tribes. Native American men, however, also interacted with reservation officials for more personal reasons. Among the Southern Utes, Native American men attempted to enlist the help of agents and boarding school superintendents to protect their children's health and safety in government schools. In so doing, they created a public caretaking role for themselves. Deprived of their traditional activities and identities as hunters and warriors, Ute men nonetheless created a means to continue their traditional role of family protector and provider by using new skills such as literacy. Ute men took up the pen to maintain their traditional roles of monitoring their children's progress and their health.

Historical Background

Before confinement to a reservation, the Ute Indians moved throughout the present states of Colorado, New Mexico, and Utah in seasonal migrations, hunting, fishing, and gathering berries and roots in the mountains from early spring until late summer and then moving to lower elevations for the winter. Hunting and foraging groups, consisting of small groupings of bilateral extended families, tended to stay in the same areas and were thus identified as territorial bands. The entire tribe numbered about eight thousand at the time of contact with Europeans. There were seven Ute bands; the southernmost bands—the Capote, Mouache, and Weminuche—were known as the Southern Utes. The Utes acquired horses sometime in the mid-seventeenth century. Several bands then began hunting buffalo, which provided tipis, clothing, blankets, and horn implements.[2]

Gender relations in pre-reservation Ute culture were egalitarian. Men and women participated equally in all important decisions concerning both the family and the band. Individual families acted as the primary unit of social control, settling all interpersonal disputes and violations of Ute social and moral codes. Within their families, Utes recognized a gendered division of labor, but valued the contributions of men and women equally. Men hunted, fished, butchered meat, cleared campsites, gathered tipi poles, conducted raids and defensive warfare, and made all implements for their tasks. Women gathered and processed wild plants, tanned hides, made tipis and camp household equipment, and cared for children. They also sometimes accompanied men on raids to scalp and gather loot. Although men usually directed military and communal subsistence activities, women could participate in public decision-making. Male leadership depended upon the consent of the entire group. If anyone disapproved of a collective decision, he or she was free to leave the group. Ultimately, authority within the band was based on age rather than gender, and no one had the power to coerce behavior from another. Egalitarian gender roles held even after contact with Europeans.[3]

The United States took control of Ute territory in 1848 after the Mexican War. Beginning in 1849, the U.S. government signed a series of treaties with the Utes, creating and—as conflict occurred between Utes and settlers—continually redefining a reservation for them. In 1868, the Great Ute Treaty outlined a reservation containing about one-fourth of the Colorado Territory. In 1873, under the Brunot Agreement, the Utes surrendered six thousand square miles of their land (about one-quarter of the reservation) to the United States in return for a perpetual $25,000 annual payment. Finally, in 1880, Congress created the current Southern Ute reservation, a narrow strip of land in the extreme southwestern corner of Colorado. There, the Office of Indian Affairs (OIA) carried out a program of forced assimilation.[4]

From 1887 to 1934, the federal government, through the OIA, used legislation known as the Dawes Act to compel Native Americans to adopt Euro-American culture. The OIA hoped to transform Native Americans into yeoman farmers and farm wives through the assignment of individual land holdings known as allotments. The Dawes Act outlawed Native American culture and established a code of Indian offenses regulating individual behavior according to Euro-American norms of conduct. Violations of the code were tried in a Court of Indian Offenses on each reservation. The plan also included funds to instruct Native Americans in Euro-American patterns of thought and behavior through Indian Service schools. The government implemented the Dawes Act on a tribe-by-tribe basis; in 1895, Congress passed the Hunter Act, administering Dawes among the Southern Ute.[5]

An important objective of the Dawes program was to restructure Native American gender roles. The *Rulebook for the Court of Indian Offenses,* published in 1883, outlined the OIA's agenda for male gender roles. The new code of conduct prohibited feasts and dances that celebrated warrior culture because they taught children to value the warrior role. Because policymakers viewed Indian men as lazy and irresponsible, the OIA established policies to force Indian husbands and fathers to provide for their families and act as the heads of their households. Any man who failed "without proper cause to support his wife and children" lost his rations until he could prove to the Court of Indian Offenses that he would "provide for his family to the best of his ability." The OIA compelled able-bodied men to support their families through their own efforts at farming, forbidding them from leasing their lands. Procedures for establishing annuities rolls further defined the husband-father as the head of his household. "The father and head of the family will be allowed to receive and receipt for the shares of himself, his wife, and minor children." A wife could accept payment only if, "due to sickness or very old age," the husband and father could not be present to receive the family's payment, or if "the husband and father is known to be improvident, a drunkard, a gambler, a spendthrift, or for any other reason an unfit person to handle the money of his wife and children." (The OIA also allowed women to be household heads if they were single, widowed, or divorced.)[6]

The OIA expected Indian men, as heads of their households, to place their children in schools. Education was compulsory for Indian children and agents made schooling arrangements with "influential men" (men the agents dealt with as leaders). Office circulars issued in 1892–93 empowered reservation superintendents to withhold rations from parents whose children were not enrolled in a school. As late as 1920, the OIA reaffirmed these regulations. Yet, OIA personnel also attempted to coax cooperation from Indian parents, especially fathers. On the Ute reservation, men who enrolled their children were rewarded with farming implements and jobs on the reservation police force. On the Cheyenne-Arapaho reservation in Oklahoma, the agent appointed three Indian men to inspect the reservation school and inform the agent of parental complaints. In return, the committee was to advocate tribal cooperation with the school's program. The OIA also allowed Indian parents, mostly in delegations of "headmen," to visit schools. Finally, parental consent was necessary to remove any child from the state to attend school.[7]

Educational facilities available to the Ute included day and boarding schools. The OIA conducted a "boarding camp" school on the reservation from 1885 to 1890. Two Presbyterian mission schools also opened on the reservation around the turn of the century. While mission schools claimed some pupils, reservation personnel pressured Ute men to send their children to OIA institutions; in the late nineteenth and early twentieth centuries, this generally meant boarding schools. The OIA opened several schools near the reservation: the Fort Lewis Boarding School in 1892; the Southern Ute Boarding School in 1902 (which closed in 1920); the Allen Day School in 1909; and the Ute Mountain Boarding School in 1915. Because these schools did not offer instruction beyond the third grade, many Ute children attended schools out of state. One of these institutions was the Santa Fe Indian Boarding School.[8]

The Santa Fe School: Parents and Administrators

The Office of Indian Affairs opened the Santa Fe Indian Boarding School in Santa Fe, New Mexico, in 1890. Between 1910 and 1934, twenty-seven boys and thirty-two girls from the Southern Ute reservation attended the school. Student folders housed in the National Archives from these years contain extraordinary letters from Ute parents and children to other family members and to Santa Fe and Ute Agency superintendents.[9] The letters of Ute men to reservation and boarding school officials in the early twentieth century reveal a poignant inner world of men struggling to create a tolerable life for their children under extremely difficult conditions.

Eight Ute fathers contacted Santa Fe superintendents during this period, either by writing directly or requesting that the Ute agent write. One of these, John Taylor, was a former slave who had married into the tribe. John was illiterate and asked agent Edward E. McKean to write for him. Another father, Charlie Adams, had been raised by an Hispanic family near the reservation, who probably saw to it that he was educated. Of the remaining six, Robert Burch, Cyrus Grove, and Joe Price were too old to have gone to reservation schools. Burch had McKean write for him, but Grove and Price either wrote their own letters or had family members write them. Jacob Box and Julian Baker had attended the Santa Fe school and could read and write. Information on Sam Williams's education is not available.[10]

Several themes appear in these letters. Fathers communicated their desire to participate in decisions concerning their children and resonated hopes for their children's futures. They expressed sadness over their separation and continually inquired when and under what conditions the children would be sent home. Children who wrote letters either to their families or the reservation agent expressed profound homesickness.

The most frequently mentioned concern of Ute fathers, however, was their children's health. Utes had lost children to disease in government schools from their establishment in the nineteenth century. Of the twenty-five Ute students sent to boarding school in Albuquerque in 1883, twelve died. When the Utes grudgingly sent sixteen children to the Fort Lewis Boarding School in 1894, three of them died and three returned home blind. This pattern continued in the early years of the twentieth century, as nine girls sent to Santa Fe between 1919 and 1925 died of either influenza or tuberculosis.[11] Most parents who wrote to the Santa Fe superintendents, Frederick Snyder (1910–18), John D. DeHuff (1919–28), and Burton L. Smith (1928–30), had lost some member of their extended families to diseases contracted in boarding schools. Consequently, these men had great anxiety about the health of their children. When fathers heard rumors of their children's illness, they immediately attempted to have them sent home.[12]

School and reservation administrators, however, were more likely to deny these requests than to honor them. Unless a child's illness was clearly life-threatening, superintendents generally refused to allow children to leave, despite fathers' pleas. The frequently tentative phrasing of the fathers' letters and the administrators' often terse replies in part reflect the power dynamics between the OIA and its "wards." Once parents signed papers admitting their children to Indian Service schools, the school superintendent assumed the primary authority over the child. With the advice of their school physicians, superintendents decided what sickness warranted a child's leaving. In serious cases, such as tuberculosis, they often sent the children to sanatoriums rather than grant permission for them to return home. Although administrators followed this procedure in hopes of aiding the students' recovery, the decision sometimes cost a child its life. For example, in 1919, Santa Fe superintendent John D. DeHuff sent Euturpe Bancroft to the tuberculosis sanatorium in Dulce, New Mexico, where she subsequently died. In 1921, he sent Alice and Nudza Clark there; Alice recovered, but Nudza died. Parents' heartbreak at not being able to see their children before they died is a frequent theme in agents' correspondence on this topic.[13]

School officials, somewhat sympathetic to this consideration, assured parents that they would be notified immediately should their offspring become ill. In 1920, when Southern Ute agent Edward McKean inquired after Ute pupil John Frances Taylor (at the request of his father, John Taylor), Superintendent DeHuff replied that the boy only had a cold.

"You may assure this boy's father," he wrote, "that it is our invariable rule at this school that whenever any child is sick enough to warrant any feeling of anxiety or alarm upon the part of anybody, the parents or the home superintendent will be duly notified from this office." Despite these assurances, Ute parents sometimes suspected the worst if their children failed to write. Sam Williams, father of John (who entered in 1920), Andrew (in 1921), and Joe (in 1923), wrote in July 1921:

Mr. John DeHuff[,]
Well[,] I like to know how my little boys [are] getting along there be[sic] this time. I hope fine [.] . . . If they get sick write to me J. D. Dehuff [sic] so I know about Ind[ians.] [T]ell John Williams to write to me[.] I never hear from him for [a] long time. So let me hear from him soon. Well[,] can you let Ind[ians] come home for Christmas. So ans[wer] soon.

Although Sam's letter expresses concern and requests information about his sons, the tone of his writing lacks any real parental authority. De-Huff's brief reply, noting that "the boys are fine," suggests that he feels Sam's inquiry does not require much of a response. In 1923, Charles Adams, worried that he had not heard from his son Albert "since he left for your school," beseeched DeHuff on behalf of his son: "It would certainly please me if you would write me concerning his conduct, health, and happiness. Especially write me concerning his throat, he's had quite a bit of trouble with it in the past." Again, DeHuff's response appears imperative. He ignored Adams's request for detailed information, writing only: "I will make sure your son writes you. His physical condition is just fine."[14]

Superintendents sometimes disregarded fathers' concerns because they viewed the students' complaints of illness as excuses to get out of work. In 1917, for example, agent McKean informed Santa Fe superintendent Frederick Snyder: "Robert Burch wishes me to write you regarding Sam. He heard that he was sick or troubled with rheumatism. The old man says he is very anxious for the boy as he lost two girls in South Dakota and seems very anxious about this boy." Robert wanted his son sent home if he was sick. Snyder replied that Sam did indeed have rheumatism, but that he could not leave until school was out. At the end of the term, Sam did not return home and McKean, writing with the authority of an agent, telegraphed Snyder: "Send Sam Burch home." Snyder informed McKean that Sam now could go home because he "has signed an agreement that he will make no excuses when the time comes to return on September 8. Too often they [the students] make excuses to stay gone."[15]

When September came, Sam did not return and Snyder telegraphed McKean inquiring of his whereabouts. McKean replied: "Sam desires to attend [Sherman Institutein] Riverside, [California] three years. His people are very much opposed to his return to Santa Fe. [I] [b]elieve under the circumstances it would be best to allow him to go to Riverside. Will you o.k. his transfer?" Snyder refused McKean's appeal on the grounds that it was against OIA policy to allow students to switch schools once they had agreed to attend one. He demanded that "Sam is doing well and I want him back." McKean replied that he knew his request contradicted policy, but he felt compelled to ask for Sam's transfer because of "the earnest requests of his father to do so." Honoring policy over the father's feelings, and bowing to the authority of the school superintendent, McKean persuaded Sam to go back to Santa Fe. In October, Sam wrote McKean saying: "Well[,] I am doing fine in school. [I] have improved in every way. Also[,] I'm glad to be receiving an education at this place."[16]

By November, however, his rheumatism returned and he again wrote McKean:

I am going to drop you a few lines telling you that I am very sorry to say that I'm not going to be able to continue my school term any longer. I hope I can go where the climate is suitable for me. I am in pain. Sometimes I can hardly walk. Will you please tell my father about this and ask him what he thinks about it. If he wants me to go back home. I can leave here soon because there is not any use for me to stay around here and suffer. This is all I can say.

At the bottom of this letter McKean wrote:"Sam is up to his old complaint but I can take no action in this matter." It is not clear from the records why McKean's assessment of Sam's illness suddenly turned cynical. Snyder concurred with McKean and told Sam that he could not go home. The Santa Fe school physician, on the other hand, diagnosed Sam as seriously ill and recommended that he be permitted to leave. Faced with this appraisal, Snyder sent Sam home. Reversing his earlier assessment of Sam's progress, Snyder concluded that Sam's transfer was for the best, since "Sam has always acted like a small child ever since he has been in our school." Robert's worries for Sam, then, proved legitimate. Sam was ill; he was not, as Snyder and (later) McKean had assumed, simply lazy. Sam apparently did desire to continue his education, for he enrolled in the Sherman Institute in Riverside, California. In 1918, McKean told Snyder that Sam was "getting along nicely" at Riverside. Snyder did not reply.[17]

A similar case further illustrates the struggle between agents and fathers over who was sick and who was "just lazy." In February 1923, Burton B. Price wrote to his father Joe Price:

> Today I am going to ask you if you can get to see McKean for me so tell him to sen[d] for me as soon as he can. I am also sick if you [had] k[n]own. I also get sick easy so I don't like this just because I am sick all the time. Say father[,] I am sick in the hosp[ital] on my hands and feet also [.] [S]o get McKean to sent for me soon and tell him as soon as you get this letter[,] father. How are you getting along[,] [I] hope fine and dandy and having good time with your friends. So please tell McKean to write to J. D. Huff so he can let me going home and [send] some money also. [B]e sure and tell McKean about it and [that I am] sick and write to me what he said about it [, for] I don't like to stay here. From your son, Burton Price.[18]

McKean asked DeHuff to investigate. DeHuff replied:

> [Burton] has a running sore on one of his legs. It may be a tuberculosis sore and it may not. He is not in a dangerous condition. I should just as leave the boy were taken home. He has never been able to do any good in his school work . . . he is hopeless. Very much like his two sisters Laura and Anna, who were here formerly.[19]

After McKean's inquiry, DeHuff took Burton to the doctor, who confirmed that the sore was not tubercular. DeHuff notified McKean, but apparently McKean did not bother to forward the information to Burton's father, for within several days Price wrote DeHuff himself.

> Dear Friend:
> I am going to write to you and ask you how is Burton Price getting along there. I hear that boy is very sick. [P]lease tell me how is that boy getting along [,] if that boy is getting better and [should be] sent home. If he has money there.
> Your[s] truly, Joe Price.[20]

On March 15, DeHuff answered that Burton had "an abscessed leg and [was] unable to work or study but he will be all right if left alone." He did not answer the question about Burton's funds and told Price to take up Burton's homecoming with McKean.[21]

Price responded to this information immediately, for the next day McKean authorized Burton's return and sent money to cover transportation costs. DeHuff did not reply, however, and on April 9 McKean telegraphed both DeHuff and the school physician requesting Burton's return. The school doctor replied that Burton was too ill to walk and would have to be returned on a stretcher. DeHuff wrote that Burton was "just now getting able to travel. In fact, it is not without misgivings that I am sending him off for home tomorrow." DeHuff felt the psychological effects of returning home would help Burton to "get through the trip without breaking down." He also asked McKean never to return him to Santa Fe. On one hand, DeHuff was glad to be rid of students he considered lazy; on the other, he seemed determined to force them to stay and work.[22]

Whether or not Sam or Burton used their illness to escape boarding school, their parents appeared sincere in their desire to see their children educated. In this respect, they were typical of the men who wrote these letters. This sentiment sometimes surfaced over the issue of running away. Sam Williams, writing for his boys Andrew, John, and Joe, asked DeHuff to please "tell Ind[ians] to not run away from the school and tell them to be good boys [.]" When Antonio Buck ran away from Santa Fe in 1918, McKean told DeHuff that the child's father, Buckskin Charley, was "anxious that he remain in school." Likewise, when Alice Washington and Edna Gunn ran away in September 1920, McKean again told DeHuff that "their folks want them to stay in school."[23] The clearest spokesman for education, however, was Jacob Box, a tribal elder respected by both the Utes and the Euro-Americans.

Jacob Box wrote letters for his children and for the children of friends. Four of his eight children attended the Santa Fe school during this period: Marjorie, who entered school in 1917; Florence, in 1918; Ellen, in 1924; and Fritz, in 1927. A former pupil of the school, Box believed in education. In 1919 he wrote superintendent De Huff: "We must make an honest living[.] [T]here is no choice in such a matter[,] for it is one of the common necessities and obligations of nature." Box believed this "obligation of nature" extended to girls as well as boys, saying, "I like to see my girls got [sic] graduates." In another letter he wrote: "The girls [will] soon be over there again. I send [Marjorie's] sister [Florence] to you this fall. [Would] [y]ou like more girls[?]" When Marjorie graduated in 1923, Box sent her to Haskell Junior College in Kansas.[24] He proudly advised DeHuff of her progress.

I am going to write to you[.] Marjorie B. Box [is] getting along alright at Haskell Inst[titute]. . . . I like to see my tribe['s] boys and girls try like Marjorie B. Box. I like to see so big [a] school [for] some girls [of] my tribe. I think Marjorie [will] stay [at] Haskell till [she] finish[es] over there. I am glad [to] see my daughter working [for the] Indian service.[25]

Box also recommended the school to other Ute children and inquired after those he had persuaded to go. DeHuff praised his diligence and asked him to please "use your good influence to get more Ute pupils."[26]

Enthusiastic for education, Box was nevertheless cautious for his children's well-being. His letters reflect his role as family protector and the assertiveness of his writing suggests confidence in dealing with OIA personnel. Almost immediately after Marjorie's admittance, Box wrote Superintendent Snyder: "If my little girl [gets] sick bad[,] send [her] home if you please[.] I forgot to tell you all about it[.] I [will] be over there some time in the Christmas day."[27] Snyder did not reply. Box frequently asked if his children needed anything or directed the superintendents to purchase clothing. He sent money every year so that they could come home for the summer: "I am going to write to you. How is [*sic*] all my daughters getting along with her study [*sic*] [?] When school [is] out[,] you send the girls home. [N]ow you let me know when school [is] out [at] Santa Fe. You send these girls because her [*sic*] mother[']s not well[.] [H]er mother like to see the girls."[28] Box always assured the superintendents that he would "send them back again when school opens" and, true to his word, he did, accompanying the children on several occasions. "I [let] you know we be over there in Sept. 22. Five girls and one boy [will come]. I like to see you about the girls['] matters. I am glad to see you again."[29]

Both DeHuff and McKean seemed to respect Box, probably because of his cooperation in procuring children for OIA schools. Box's decisive letters exemplified this relationship: he knew his inquiries would be taken seriously. When Florence fell ill in March 1921, McKean advised DeHuff: "Her parents are anxious for her to return and I believe, under the circumstances, that the best interests of your school and the future cooperation of these Indians will thus be served." DeHuff suggested that Florence instead be sent to the Jicarilla Tuberculosis Sanatorium, but she insisted on going home. Unlike some other cases, DeHuff allowed Florence to go home immediately. Within one month, a telegram from McKean arrived at Santa Fe: "Florence Box very sick, the father requests you send Margaret home to leave in the morning [on] Saturday." Margaret left for home without delay, but Florence died before she got there.[30]

Despite Florence's death, Box returned his daughters to Santa Fe, but he did not take any further chances with them. In May 1923, Marjorie took sick and Box went to Santa Fe and brought her home. Marjorie recovered and entered Haskell Junior College in the fall.[31] In March of the following year, Ellen came down with a skin disease and Box informed DeHuff:

I am going to write to you. To want to know about my daughter Ellen Bent Box. [H]ow [is] she getting along[?] [S]he [is] not sick[,] if she sick send her home. Mary Graves died yesterday afternoon. If Ellen [is] alright at school I am glad. One boy died from over there at Ute Mountain, Towaoc, Colo. I [would] like to hear from you soon.[32]

DeHuff replied respectfully, asking Box "to convey an expression of my deepest sympathy" to Mary's parents, and assuring him that Ellen's condition was not serious. He informed Box that he would personally "keep close watch on Ellen's case and, if she fails to make proper progress toward recovery, I shall not keep her here." In May, Mable Spencer, a Ute student at Santa Fe, returned to the reservation due to tuberculosis and told Box that Ellen was still sick. Box advised DeHuff: "If she sick yet we [would] like to have her here at home to tak[e] care of her. Maybe she [will] get well now." DeHuff again reassured Box: "If at any time Ellen's case should take a serious turn, I will let you or Mr. McKean know promptly and endeavor to send the child home."[33] In June, Box's anxiety over Ellen spilled over in poignant prose.

I am thinking about my daughter Ellen[.] She never write to me for a long time[,] about three months now. [I]f she [is] sick don't . . . give her too long. I['ll] take care of her. Because [if you] send children too late home, [they] can['t] get well. Mabel got bad again. [N]ow I want to know [to] be sure how she was now and get bad and well. God knows. Light of the world.[34]

Although he again assured Box that "your daughter Ellen is not suffering from any dangerous skin disease," DeHuff nonetheless sent Ellen home. Apparently the intensity of Box's pleas, with their heartfelt references to Christian scripture, moved him. Ellen recovered after her return but, for undocumented reasons, never went back to Santa Fe. She instead attended the Albuquerque Indian School until her father's death in 1928.[35]

The problem of student illnesses grew worse in the spring and summer of 1925, when five female students at Santa Fe became gravely ill. Mable Spencer (who had apprised Box about his daughter), Jane Thompson,

Annie Snow, Alice Brown, and Mary Grove all died after they were sent home, Mabel with tuberculosis and the others with the flu. In the fall, Cyrus Grove, Mary's father, wrote DeHuff, frantic about his other daughter, Margaret. These letters, born of a father's grief, declared Grove's disquiet most assertively: "I am asking you if it[']s time that Margaret Grove is sick. I want to know right away if she [is] sick or not. I don't want her to get too sick or we don't want to lose her like we did Mary. [I] [w]ould like to hear from you soon." DeHuff replied that Margaret was indeed ill and he was sending her home. He telegraphed McKean to meet her train. Margaret died nonetheless, confirming her father's worry and disproving the superintendents' oft-repeated claims that they "immediately" notified the parents of any child who was seriously sick.[36]

In the immediate aftermath of the Santa Fe epidemic, Superintendent DeHuff showed more caution. When Edith Shoshone wrote McKean in February 1926 that she was very sick and wanted to return home, McKean notified DeHuff. DeHuff initially rejected the idea, but changed his mind about one month later. Although school physician Dr. Massie could find nothing wrong with Edith, DeHuff decided she should probably go home. Edith was run down, frightened, and had lost weight. DeHuff decided that a second opinion by the agency doctor at Southern Ute would either confirm her illness or ease her apprehension and allow her to return and finish her work. This decision is especially puzzling because Edith was only three months from graduation. As much as he wanted her to complete her studies, DeHuff concluded that he "did not want to chance it" if Edith proved seriously ill. Perhaps DeHuff had discovered that Edith's sister Nancy had died of the flu after returning home from Santa Fe in 1919. Although Nancy probably did not contract the disease at Santa Fe (she worked as a maid for a Santa Fe family for several months before she went home) perhaps DeHuff decided that losing one sibling was enough for the Shoshone family. He may also have felt pity for Edith because she was an orphan.[37]

Nonetheless, other students did not receive the same treatment. When B. L. Smith took over at the Santa Fe school in 1926, the level of cooperation between the school and Ute fathers declined. Student deaths in 1925 had frightened the pupils, who conveyed alarming letters home. Rose Thompson (sister of Jane, who had died in the flu epidemic) wrote a plaintive letter to McKean in September 1926.

Dear sir[,]
I am going to write to you and let you know how I am down here at school[.]
[Y]ou know[,] Mr. McKean[,] I am going to let you know I am very lonesome
and I always think of home and I want to go home[.] [Y]ou know how lonesome
this school is and I want to go home and when the girls get sick here and get
[sore] when they go home and die[.] I am not going to do that and die[.] [P]lease
Mr. McKean[,] send for me[.] I know [the students] always get blind when the
children that [*sic*] get sick and die when they go home[;] and I want to go
home[.] I must close here[.]

[F]rom[,] Rose Thompson

McKean requested information but Superintendent Smith answered dis-
missively, "Rose is homesick. She has a very pronounced case of the itch
and has been regularly treated in the hospital every since this was discovered." Smith saw no reason to allow Rose to return home. Four years
later, Smith notified McKean that "Rosa Thompson, daughter of Jim
Thompson is sick w/ pneumonia; there was an epidemic here; will keep
you posted." McKean replied that "the parents are very anxious about
her. Will you please notify me every day for a few days and let me know
how she is. If you think she is dangerous wire me or call me up on the
telephone that I may notify these parents so they can go and see her."
Smith's reply was noncommittal, suggesting that Rose's temperature was
down a little and hoping she would come through all right. He promised
to keep McKean informed about her condition. Unlike many other students, Rose recovered and went home.[38]

Similarly, Mary Baker's request to return to the reservation was dismissed as mere homesickness. Julian Baker, a tribal leader, began asking
for his daughter's return in September 1928 when she advised him of
her illness. He had the Southern Ute agent, W. F. Dickens, inquire after
Mary's health. Dickens assured Smith that this was not an idle request.
Baker, he noted, "is a very good Indian and anxious for her to go on
with her studies." Smith replied that there was "not a word of truth in
[Mary's] statement that she is not well" and said that she was "just
homesick." This answer did not satisfy Baker, however, and he sent
Smith a letter on October 3. Like Jacob Box, Baker wrote forcefully,
explaining to Superintendent Smith exactly what he wanted him to do:
"Am dropping you this letter to let you know that I want my daughter
Mary to come home." He included a check to cover Mary's travel
expenses and instructions concerning what hotel to use on the journey.
Smith answered that there was "no reason whatever for Mary to go

home. She is just homesick and will get over it—hundreds of students do." Dickens urged Mary to stay, as did Mellie Daniels, matron at the Southern Ute Boarding School at Ignacio, Colorado. Daniels sent Mary a cheerful letter asking her to "try to feel good about it all if you can." All the OIA personnel seemed united to keep Mary at Santa Fe.[39]

Baker, however, was tenacious. He wrote twice in late October and both times Smith again replied that Mary was "doing quite well." He asked Baker to please write her letters encouraging her to stay. Annoyed, Baker wrote again on November 14.

I am going to write to you again for the third time to ask you again to send my girl Mary back to home. . . . I have been to Mr. Dickens so many times and I don't want to bother him so much and one thing that I don't want to do is write to you so many times. Because you might say what is the matter with me. I am very sorry for her even that it was I who sent her to there. I am not feeling very good. So I am trying to get her back again through all you peoples so you will know that I am asking with my own mind. I made up my mind to let her be send [*sic*] back to home. So I am going to look for her this week and I want you to let her come home and start from there on Saturday.[40]

Baker's letter of November 14 was his longest and most emotional communication. He acknowledged both his willingness to go through the proper channels and his frustration at the OIA's unwillingness to heed his requests. Through self-disclosure, and by taking responsibility for his child's unhappiness, Baker attempted to disarm Smith and thus persuade him to return Mary. The letter clearly expresses Baker's individuality and refutes stereotypical notions of the "slothful Indian."

On December 6 Mary was still in Santa Fe, and Baker's next letter became pleading:

Please send Mary to home. I hear she is very sick and I am very anxious and so I wish that you let her come home please do that please let her get on the train Saturday so that she get[s] home on Sunday. And [she will] go [to] school here on Monday.[41]

He reaffirmed his commitment to his daughter's education. Again, the message is explicit—he based his request for Mary's return on his emotional distress and on his previous cooperation with the OIA. On December 26, Smith finally conceded that Mary had contracted the flu. Although her illness was "not serious," they were sending her home as soon as they deemed it safe for her to travel. On January 3, 1929, Baker expressed his irritation with the OIA. "I am sorry to hear that my girl is

260 KATHERINE M. B. OSBURN

sick and that is why I always try to get her back home before she gets worse. Because she was not very strong. I will wait for her on Saturday." The very next day Baker, feeling empowered, sent another letter declaring his intention to get Mary himself, fearing that she was not strong enough to travel alone. "And I hope I will find my girl in good condition," he warned, and "I don't want to wait long for her. I want to see her as soon as I can." Baker retrieved his daughter, who eventually recovered and never returned to Santa Fe.[42]

Mary's illness apparently frightened the family of Laura Price. In 1929, Laura's parents requested that Dickens determine the condition of their daughter's health.

The family of Laura Price wish to know the state of her health. They have heard she is very sick and are uneasy. They also add that if there is any danger of her not recovering well and speedily from the flu that they would wish her to come home while she is alive, and not just come home to die.[43]

Smith answered that Laura was healthy. In a grudging nod to the legitimacy of Laura's parents' fears, he concluded: "Doubtless her parents became alarmed when Mary Baker was returned home."[44]

Agents sometimes exhibited contradictory attitudes about family worries over their loved ones' health. When Ute pupil Dick Tom's uncle, Jim Bush, expressed consternation over his nephew's well-being in September 1928, Ute reservation superintendent Dickens initially responded sympathetically, writing to Santa Fe:

A report has come to his relatives that he is quite sick. Will you kindly give me full information concerning his condition? I wish to be able to tell them and, I trust, calm their fears on this account. His older brother having just died, a report of Dick's being sick naturally worries them.[45]

One month later, however, Dickens was disgusted when Dick Tom wrote his uncle, Jim Bush:

Dear Friend[,]
Well[,] I am going write to you this morning[.] [A]nd so how are you getting along . . . at home and [I will] tell you I am still sick now and I was get real hot all over my body yesterday afternoon[.] We was very sick yesterday in my heart and stomach and head always and we don't like school anymore now. I did study hard every day [to] please you[.] Tell father and Mr. Dickens and we don't like to [be in] school any more. . . . We [would] like to go back at home and we don't like to stay here[.] I will stop here[.] Write to me again[.]
From your friend[,] Dick Tom[46]

"Letters of this character keep the Indians stirred up all the time," Dickens retorted, "I don't know how it is to be overcome but send it on to you for your information."[47] Perhaps Smith had told Dickens that Tom was healthy, leading him to view Tom's letter as an example of indolence. Nevertheless, given the reality of the Tom family's losses, Dickens might have maintained his earlier empathy.

While their children attended the Santa Fe Boarding School, Ute fathers monitored their children's lives and attempted to look out for their best interests. Responding to their children's letters or to reports about their offspring, these men made their wishes known to the school superintendents. In encouraging education, they sought to provide for their children's futures. In requesting their return upon hearing rumors of illness, they also sought to protect their children from epidemic diseases. While their behavior might be expected from a concerned parent in any culture, it may also be viewed as a continuation of their traditional roles as protectors and providers. Reflecting the complicated nature of acculturation, however, Ute fathers combined traditional parenting roles with government farming programs.[48] Any analysis of their behavior and their ability to fulfill their parental goals thus requires sorting out several complex variables. What does the interaction of Ute men and school officials disclose about the process of assimilation and the ability of administered peoples to retain a measure of autonomy over their families?

The eight Ute fathers in this sample represent some of the more "assimilated" Indian men at Southern Ute reservation. All were farmers, cultivating anywhere from 10 to 160 acres. Jacob Box, Robert Burch, and Joe Price were on the 1909 "honor roll," giving them the right to lease their property without agency supervision. Julian Baker was such a successful farmer that in 1932 agent Edward Peacore chose him to testify on Indian farming for a Senate subcommittee on Indian affairs. Moreover, they were stable husbands and fathers. Although this stability in itself is not an indicator of assimilation, it happened to correspond with the OIA agenda. Of the eight, only one, the former slave John Taylor, was separated (and that was due to his wife's actions); six remained married to the same women for the entire Dawes period, and one was widowed and remarried. Several of them were educated and all were anxious for their children to attend school. They were, to the best of their abilities, meeting the government's expectations of them as heads of their households and as fathers. They did not fit the OIA stereotype of lazy, irresponsible parents. Their letters to superintendents are further evidence of their attempts to care for their families.

The language in their correspondence also reveals several important things about these men. The emotional quality of these letters debunks the stereotype of the stoic, passive Indian that has been one of the most ubiquitous images of Native Americans since early contact.[49] Moreover, the relative levels of assertiveness in the letters may provide insights into the assimilationist process. With the exception of Cyrus Grove, Jacob Box, and Julian Baker, most Ute fathers did not express themselves in terms that exerted parental authority. Although the more reserved letters suggest the writers, as subject people, felt a lack of power, they may also reflect traditional patterns of communication in which requests are phrased politely rather than forcefully.[50] Conversely, the more authoritative missives could denote a greater degree of assimilation or more experience and confidence in dealings with OIA personnel. That Box and Baker were political leaders who worked closely with the agents lends credence to this hypothesis. Finally, the forcefulness of Grove's letter may also indicate that a child's recent death impelled Ute fathers to decisive communication. Regardless of the phrasing, each letter represented a father seeking to assert his parental rights.

The role of father on the reservation, then, was a potential middle ground where agents and Indians could meet. Both the OIA and the Utes viewed fathers as protectors and providers. Yet, in the larger context of the reservation, fathers' power to help their children was circumscribed by the government. For all the OIA rhetoric about training Indian men to assert leadership and assume responsibility for their families, agents and boarding school superintendents controlled these children's lives. On some level, naming Indian men as "heads of their households" represented a formality that sanctioned their colonization—it was a method of bringing them into the dominant culture without giving them substantive power and responsibility.[51] Additionally, while some anxious fathers received reassurances when their children became ill, other men's concerns were dismissed. Even when agents attended to the men's worries, they rarely respected the fathers' wishes. Ute fathers, therefore, were up against powerful political forces far beyond their control. A closer examination of Indian policy during this period reveals the conditions that limited Ute men's ability to parent effectively.

For all of their cooperation with the assimilationist agenda, Ute fathers' success in supervising their children's lives seems largely to have been contingent on the personality of school superintendents. While it would seem logical for administrators to pay more attention to the wishes of the wealthier Ute men, this was not always the case. Of the three men who ran the Santa Fe school during this period, Superintendent DeHuff appears to have been the most helpful. Jacob Box, who farmed 150 acres and advocated education, received a great deal of consideration, but DeHuff also maintained reassuring relationships with men who worked smaller farms. Charlie Adams and Sam Williams, each with thirty-acre farms, and John Taylor, cultivating forty acres, received letters affirming their children's well-being. Still, even DeHuff could be insensitive to parental concerns. He did not notify Cyrus Grove (who farmed forty acres) that his daughter Margaret was ill. Only when Grove's inquiries prompted him did DeHuff admit Margaret's illness and send her home to die. Moreover, he kept Burton Price at school until his leg was so abscessed that he could not walk and had to be returned home on a stretcher. His remark to McKean that Burton "has never been able to do any good in his school work [because] he [is] hopeless," suggests that school superintendents' personal biases may sometimes have played a part in their responses to Ute fathers. With school superintendents holding the ultimate power to direct these children's lives, Ute fathers' parenting role was severely restricted.

Superintendents Smith and Snyder appear even less cooperative. While Smith replied somewhat sympathetically to Joe Price (who cultivated ten acres with his brother Andrew and was on the 1909 honor roll), Julian Baker (who farmed 160 acres) had a terrible time getting his sick daughter Mary sent home. Smith also "stonewalled" Rose Thompson's father Jim, who farmed twenty-three acres, and his response to Dick Tom's uncle, Jim Bush (with a thirty-acre farm), was also noncommittal. Frederick Snyder was equally uncooperative with Robert Burch (who farmed forty acres), insisting that Sam's rheumatism was merely laziness despite the school doctor's diagnosis of serious illness. In nearly every case, Smith and Snyder frustrated Ute fathers' attempts to shield their children from harm.

Career considerations may also have figured in superintendents' reluctance to honor Ute fathers' requests. Boarding school superintendents were under pressure to fill their schools, and competition for the best students was fierce. Administrators spent a great deal of time recruiting students and trying to induce reservation agents to help them secure

parental consent for off-reservation schooling. To prevent superintendents from "stealing" students and to force Indian parents to keep their
children in school, the OIA required parents to sign contracts committing their children to one institution for three years.[52] Ironically, the fact
that these Ute fathers were fairly assimilated may have worked against
them. The children of "progressive" Indians were undoubtedly valued as
students. Realizing that career advancement was tied to operating a full
school, administrators may have been reluctant to concede to fathers'
concerns. Ute fathers who cooperated with government educational programs still found themselves entangled in the OIA bureaucracy.

Finally, policy changes on the national level may have acted to encourage administrators' heavy-handedness. Commissioners of Indian Affairs during the Progressive era—William A. Jones (1879–1905), Francis
E. Leupp (1905–9), Robert G. Valentine (1909–13), and Cato Sells
(1913–21)—disdained off-reservation boarding schools. They regarded
them as ineffective at assimilation and concluded that they "coddled"
Indians into continued dependence on the federal government. Further,
while the OIA never officially abandoned the goal of assimilation, commissioners scaled back their most ambitious assimilationist rhetoric during this period. They began to assert that perhaps Indians could never
be fully assimilated American citizens. Perhaps the best the OIA could
do was to give Indians menial vocational skills. Thus, policymakers at
this time viewed the off-reservation school, with its lofty goals of removing Indian children from the "barbaric" influences of their homes to
"civilize" them, as a waste of funds. Desiring a more effective and less
costly educational system, they sought Indian education at the reservations or at public schools near reservations. Charles Burke, commissioner from 1921 to 1929, continued these policies. Additionally, the
Burke administration came under assault by a new group of reformers
who harshly criticized the OIA's assimilationist vision. The new reformers called for cultural pluralism, rather than forced assimilation, and the
off-reservation boarding school became a focal point of their attack.[53]
All the Santa Fe superintendents, therefore, were fighting a rear-guard
battle for their schools and, consequently, their careers. In this defensive
atmosphere, the concerns of Indian fathers, and thus their ability to be
effective parents, went unheeded.

Although the men's correspondence was usually ineffective, it provides a fascinating glimpse into the activities of Ute fathers in the early
reservation years. The letters reveal Ute men to be thoughtful, caring,

concerned parents who were active in their children's lives. In this, they continued their traditional domestic roles as protector and provider, and refuted the OIA's characterization of Indian men as lazy, irresponsible, and unconcerned fathers. Additionally, each of these men made a decision to help his family adjust to the changes brought about by confinement to a reservation. He accepted the new role of farmer and recognized the necessity of education for his children. Thus, each embraced assimilation as a means of continuing his traditional parental role.

Nonetheless, the voices of Indian fathers seeking to protect and provide for their offspring were often lost in the cacophony of conflicting policies set forth by the Indian Service. On the one hand, the OIA attempted to force Indian men into a Euro-American patriarchal role, designating them as heads of their households. On the other, they constrained Ute fathers' effectiveness by reserving nearly absolute power over Indian families for OIA administrators. For all their rhetoric about inculcating Indian men with a sense of familial responsibility, the paternalism of Indian policy meant that there was really only room for one father on the reservation: the Great Father in Washington.

NOTES

1. Marvin K. Opler, "The Southern Ute of Colorado," in *Acculturation in Seven American Indian Tribes,* ed. Ralph Linton (New York: Harper and Row, 1940), 137–39. I would like to thank John Finger, Rita Barnes, Matt Silvey, Donald Yacovone, and Laura McCall for critical readings of this chapter.

2. S. Lyman Tyler, "The Yuta Indians before 1680," *Western Humanities Review* 5 (spring 1951): 157; S. Lyman Tyler, "The Spaniard and the Ute," *Utah Historical Quarterly* 22 (October 1954): 344; Donald Callaway, Joel Janetski, and Omer C. Stewart, "Ute," in *Handbook of North American Indians (HBNAI),* vol. 11, *Great Basin,* Warren L. d'Azevedo, vol. ed. (Washington, D.C.: Smithsonian Institution, 1986), 336; James Jefferson, Robert W. Delaney, and Gregory C. Thompson, *The Southern Ute: A Tribal History* (Ignacio, Colo.: Southern Ute Tribe, 1972), vii; Robert W. Delaney, *The Ute Mountain Utes* (Albuquerque: University of New Mexico Press, 1989), 5; Jan Pettit, *Utes: The Mountain People,* rev. ed. (Boulder, Colo.: Johnson Books, 1990), 5; J. Donald Hughes, *American Indians in Colorado,* rev. ed. (Boulder, Colo.: Pruett Publishing Co. 1987), 20. For discussions of the prehistory of the Ute, see Opler, "The Southern Ute of Colorado," 124–25 and 128–29; Carling Malouf and John M. Findlay, "Euro-American Impact before 1870," in *HBNAI,* 11:500. Opler estimated the population of the Southern bands at one thousand, but the

estimate has been revised upwards by Joseph Jorgensen in *Sun Dance Religion* (Chicago: University of Chicago Press, 1972), 37–38.

3. Opler, "The Southern Ute of Colorado," 124, 128–29, 131–40, 146–53, 163–66. Although the Utes preferred matrilocality, a couple would live with the husband's family if their need for labor was greater. Also see Callaway, Janetski, and Stewart, "Ute," 340–54. The data from Southern Ute supports the hypothesis that societies in which women make a significant contribution to the economic survival of the group are generally more egalitarian concerning gender roles. See Peggy R. Sanday, "Female Status in the Public Domain," in *Women, Culture, and Society,* ed. Michelle Zimbalist Rosaldo and Louise Lamphere (Stanford, Calif.: Stanford University Press, 1974), 189–205. For women's gender roles under the Dawes Act, see Katherine M. B. Osburn, *Southern Ute Women: Autonomy and Assimilation on the Reservation 1887–1934* (Albuquerque: University of New Mexico Press, 1998).

4. Wilson Rockwell, *The Utes: A Forgotten People* (Denver, Colo.: Sage Books, 1956), 64–70; P. David Small, *Ouray, Chief of the Utes* (Ouray, Colo.: Wayfinders Press, 1986), 39; Jefferson, Delaney, and Thompson, *The Southern Ute,* 16–23; Gregory Coyne Thompson, *Southern Ute Lands, 1848–1899: The Creation of a Reservation,* Occasional Papers of the Center for Southwest Studies, no. 1 (Durango, Colo.: Fort Lewis College, 1972), 3–6; Richard O. Clemmer and Omer C. Stewart, "Treaties, Reservations and Claims," in *HBNAI,* 11:534. The 1880 Agreement followed the Meeker Massacre in which a band of Northern Utes rose up and killed their agent, Nathan Meeker. Hughes, *American Indians,* 66–70; Thompson, *Southern Ute Lands,* 19–22; Rockwell, *The Utes,* 164–73.

5. Frederick E. Hoxie, *A Final Promise: The Campaign to Assimilate the Indians, 1880–1920* (Lincoln: University of Nebraska Press, 1984), 249; Thompson, *Southern Ute Lands,* 50–51; Francis E. Leupp, "The Southern Ute," Report to the Board of Indian Commissioners (BIC), in *Annual Report of the Board of Indian Commissioners (ARBIC),* 1895, 1001–2; "Act of February 20, 1895" (The Hunter Act), in Charles J. Kappler, *Indian Affairs: Laws and Treaties,* vol. 1 (Washington, D.C.: Government Printing Office, 1904), 556–57.

6. In the early reservation years the OIA issued rations to tribes while they established their new economic bases. Annuities are payments given individual Indians according to the terms of treaties, land claims settlements, and oil, gas, and timber leases. *Rulebook Governing the Court of Indian Offenses* (Washington, D.C.: Department of the Interior, 1883), 1–3, in Records of the Consolidated Ute Agency (RCUA), Box 7, National Archives and Records Administration (NARA), Rocky Mountain Region, Denver, Colorado (hereafter cited as *Rulebook*); "Amended Rules and Regulations to Be Observed in the Execution of Leases of Indian Allotments," RCUA, Box 11; *Regulations of the Indian Department* (Washington, D.C.: Government Printing Office, 1904), 59–60. For

a discussion of the importance of the provider role to Euro-American gender roles, see E. Anthony Rotundo, *American Manhood: Transformations in Masculinity from the Revolution to the Modern Era* (New York: Basic Books, 1993), 26–30 and chap. 8.

7. Laurence F. Schmeckebier, *The Office of Indian Affairs: Its History, Activities, and Organization* (Baltimore: Johns Hopkins Press, 1927), 223; Henry M. Teller, Secretary of the Interior, to Warren Patten, Southern Ute Agent (SUA), 23 March 1883, Letters Received by the Office of Indian Affairs (LROIA), 1883: 5510; William B. Clark, SUA, to Commissioner of Indian Affairs (CIA), 21 November 1884; Charles A. Bartholomew to Louis Morgan, Superintendent, Fort Lewis School, 22 October 1892; Bartholomew to CIA, 21 November 1892; H. B. Freeman, SUA, to CIA, 27 July 1893; David A. Day, SUA, to CIA, 29 November 1894, RCUA, 44010: General and Statistical, Outgoing Correspondence, Bound Letterbooks; William Peterson, Superintendent, Fort Lewis School, to Mrs. Virginia McClurg, Colorado Springs, Colorado, 3 October 1904, RCUA, 44012: General and Statistical, Outgoing Correspondence, Bound Letterbooks; David Wallace Adams, *Education for Extinction: American Indians and the Boarding School Experience, 1875–1928* (Lawrence: University of Kansas Press, 1995), 245–55.

8. Milton Hoyt, "The Development of Education among the Southern Utes" (Ph.D. diss., University of Colorado, Boulder, 1967), 335–48; Hughes, *American Indians,* 85–89; "Rev. Antonio Jose Anastacio Rodriguez," typescript biography in the files of the Presbyterian Historical Society, Philadelphia, Pennsylvania, no date, 109; Belle M. Brain, *The Redemption of the Red Man* (New York: Board of Home Missions of the Presbyterian Church in the U.S.A., 1904), 100; D. M. Browning, CIA, to David A. Day, 23 March 1897, RCUA, 44105: Education, Industries, Box 162, Folder: "Religious Education 1884–1928"; Annual Report to the Commissioner of Indian Affairs (ARCIA), 1900, p. 214; William Peterson, Superintendent, Fort Lewis School, to CIA, 31 January 1906, RCUA, 44011: Outgoing Correspondence in Bound Letterbooks.

9. For a general history of Indian education, see Margaret Connell Szasz, *Education and the American Indian: The Road to Self Determination, 1928–1973* (Albuquerque: University of New Mexico Press, 1973); Sally Hyer, *One House, One Voice, One Heart: Native American Education at the Santa Fe Indian School* (Albuquerque: Museum of New Mexico Press, 1990), x; Records of the Santa Fe Indian School (RSFIS), Entry 47, "Student School Folders, 1910–1934," NARA, Denver, Colorado (hereafter cited as RSFIS, with student file name). These files are not to be confused with the "Alphabetical Status File of Indians, 1879–1939," found in RCUA, NARA, Denver, Colorado.

10. Census of the Southern Ute Tribe for 1900, 1912, 1923, in the Omer Stewart Papers, Western History Collection, Norlin Library, University of Colorado, Boulder; Folder of Charles Adams, "Alphabetical Status File of Indians,

1879–1939," RCUA, Box 8; "Student School Folders, 1910–1934"; "Annual School Reports of the Southern Ute Reservation, 1886–1910," RCUA, Box 8.

11. ARCIA, 1887, p. 15; Christian Stollsteimer, SUA, to CIA, 28 December 1887, LROIA, 1887:566; ARCIA, 1886, p. 49; Stollsteimer to CIA, 28 December 1887, LROIA, 1887:566; ARCIA, 1902, p. 180; RSFIS, Boxes 13–16.

12. Hyer, *One House, One Voice, One Heart*, 15, picture of Smith with dates. Other terms of service for Santa Fe superintendents are dated from their correspondence.

13. See Files of Euturpe Bancroft and Nudza and Alice Clark, RSFIS.

14. Edward E. McKean, SUA, to John D. DeHuff, Santa Fe Superintendent, 2 December 1920; DeHuff to McKean, 4 December 1920, File of John Taylor; Sam Williams to DeHuff, 19 July 1921; DeHuff to Williams, 28 July 1921, File of Andrew Williams; Charles Adams to DeHuff, 2 January 1923, DeHuff to Adams, 5 January 1923, File of Albert Adams, RSFIS.

15. Osburn, *Southern Ute Women*, chap. 5; McKean to Frederick Snyder, Santa Fe Superintendent, 15 June 1917; Snyder to McKean, 18 June 1918; Snyder to McKean, 16 July 1917, File of Sam Burch, RSFIS.

16. Snyder to McKean, 11 September 1917; McKean to Snyder, 12 September 1917; Snyder to McKean, 20 September 1917; McKean to Snyder, 25 September 1917; Sam Burch to McKean, 24 October 1917, Burch Family File, "Alphabetical Status File of Indians, 1879–1939," RCUA, Box 4.

17. Sam Burch to McKean, 10 November 1917, File of Sam Burch, RSFIS; Snyder to McKean, 1 December 1917, File of Nathan Bird, RSFIS; McKean to Snyder, 4 February 1918, File of Sam Burch, RSFIS.

18. Burton Price to Joe Price, 1 February 1923, File of Burton Price, RSFIS.

19. McKean to DeHuff, 6 February 1923; DeHuff to McKean, 9 February 1923, File of Burton Price, RSFIS.

20. Joe Price to DeHuff, 13 March 1923, File of Burton Price, RSFIS.

21. DeHuff to Price, 15 March 1923, File of Burton Price, RSFIS.

22. McKean to DeHuff and to F. Becker, School Physician, 9 April 1923; DeHuff to McKean, 9 April 1923, File of Burton Price, RSFIS.

23. Sam Williams to DeHuff, 19 July 1921, File of Andrew Williams, RSFIS; McKean to DeHuff, 9 October 1918, File of Antonio Buck, RSFIS; McKean to DeHuff, 9 September 1920, File of Alice Washington, RSFIS.

24. Jacob Box to DeHuff, 16 September 1919; Box to DeHuff, 15 August 1918, 12 May 1923, File of Marjorie Box, RSFIS.

25. Jacob Box to DeHuff, 28 March 1924, File of Marjorie Box, RSFIS.

26. Jacob Box to DeHuff, 19 July 1920, File of Marjorie Box, RSFIS; Box to DeHuff, 29 May 1920, File of Florence Box, RSFIS; Box to DeHuff, 25 December 1919, RSFIS, File of Frank Richards; DeHuff to Box, 2 April 1924, File of Marjorie Box, RSFIS.

27. Box to United States Indians [sic] School Superintendent, 9 October 1917, File of Marjorie Box, RSFIS.

28. Box to DeHuff, 10 May 1920, RSFIS, File of Marjorie Box, RSFIS.

29. Box to DeHuff, 19 July 1920, 16 September 1919, File of Marjorie Box, RSFIS.

30. McKean to DeHuff, 22 March 1921; DeHuff to McKean, 23 March 1921, 26 March 1921; Sara Jefferies, School Matron, to DeHuff, 26 March 1921; McKean to DeHuff 29 April 1921, File of Florence Box, RSFIS.

31. DeHuff to Box, 14 May 1923, 28 March 1924, File of Margorie Box, RSFIS.

32. Box to DeHuff, 6 March 1925, File of Ellen Box, RSFIS.

33. DeHuff to Box, 7 March 1925; Box to DeHuff, 5 May 1925; DeHuff to Box, 8 May 1925, File of Ellen Box, RSFIS.

34. Box to DeHuff, 4 June 1925, File of Ellen Box, RSFIS.

35. DeHuff to Box, 6 June 1925; R. Perry, Superintendent, U.S. Indian School, Albuquerque, New Mexico, 5 March, 1928, File of Ellen Box, RSFIS.

36. For records on the five returned students who died, see RSFIS, files of Mable Spencer, Jane Thompson, Annie Snow, Alice Brown, and Mary Grove. Cyrus Grove to DeHuff, 23 October 1925; DeHuff to Grove, 27 October 1925; DeHuff to McKean, 27 October 1925, File of Margaret Grove, RSFIS.

37. McKean to DeHuff, 13 February 1926; DeHuff to McKean, 15 February 1926; DeHuff to McKean, 13 March 1926, File of Edith Shoshone, RSFIS. Also see RSFIS, Files of Nancy and Flora Shoshone.

38. Rosa Thompson to McKean, 13 September 1926; McKean to B. L. Smith, Santa Fe Superintendent, 1 October 1926; Smith to McKean, 4 October 1926; Smith to Peacore, 4 April 1930; Peacore to Smith, 7 April 1930; Smith to Peacore, 7 April, 9 April 1930, File of Rosa Thompson, RSFIS.

39. W. L. Dickens, SUA, to B. L. Smith, 20 September 1928; Smith to Dickens, 24 September 1928; Julian Baker to Smith, 3 October 1928; Smith to Baker, 8 October 1928; Mellie Daniels, School Matron, Southern Ute Boarding School, to Mary Baker, 5 October 1928, File of Mary Baker, RSFIS.

40. Baker to Smith, 14 November, 6 1928, File of Mary Baker, RSFIS.

41. Baker to Smith, 6 December 1928, File of Mary Baker, RSFIS.

42. Smith to Baker, 26 December 1928; Baker to Smith, 3 January 1929; Baker to Smith, 4 January 1929, File of Mary Baker, RSFIS.

43. Edward Peacore, SUA, to B. L. Smith, 12 January 1929, File of Laura Price, RSFIS.

44. Smith to Peacore, 14 January 1929, File of Laura Price, RSFIS.

45. Dickens to Smith, 24 September 1928, File of Fritz Box, RSFIS.

46. Dick Tom to Jim Bush, 29 October 1928, File of Fritz Box, RSFIS.

47. Dickens to B. L. Smith, 9 November 1928, File of Dick Tom, RSFIS; Dickens to Smith, 24 September 1928, RSFIS, File of Fritz Box, RSFIS.

48. For an excellent discussion of the problem of identifying assimilated Native Americans, see David Rich Lewis, "Reservation Leadership and the Progressive-Traditional Dichotomy: William Wash and the Northern Utes, 1865–1928," in *Major Problems in American Indian History*, ed. Albert Hurtado and Peter Iverson (Lexington, Mass.: D. C. Heath and Company, 1994), 420–34.

49. Robert F. Berkhofer, Jr., *The White Man's Indian* (New York: Vintage Books, 1978), 28–29. Film scholar John A. Price quotes Indian actor Jay Silverheels on film images of Indians "as being stoic, undemonstrative, incapable of showing emotion, and entirely lacking in a sense of humor" (86). John A. Price, "The Stereotyping of North American Indians in Motion Pictures," in *The Pretend Indians: Images of Native Americans in the Movies,* ed. Gretchen M. Bataille and Charles L. P. Silet (Ames: Iowa State University Press, 1980; UMI Books on Demand xerographic reprint), 75–90.

50. See Richard O. Clemmer, "Differential Leadership Patterns in Early Twentieth-Century Great Basin Indian Societies," *Journal of California and Great Basin Anthropology* 11 (1989): 35–49.

51. I am grateful to my colleague Rita Barnes of the Department of English, Tennessee Technological University, for this insight.

52. Robert A. Trennert, Jr., *The Phoenix Indian School: Forced Assimilation in Arizona, 1891–1935* (Norman: University of Oklahoma Press, 1988), 59–68.

53. Hoxie, *A Final Promise;* Francis Paul Prucha, *The Great Father: The United States Government and the American Indians,* vols. 1 and 2, unabridged (Lincoln: University of Nebraska Press, 1995), 814–40; Trennert, *Phoenix,* 57–70, 96–97, 169–81; Clyde Ellis, *To Change Them Forever: Education at the Rainy Mountain Boarding School, 1893–1920* (Norman: University of Oklahoma Press, 1996), 131–52, Adams, *Education for Extinction, 307–33.*

Part III

Toward the Modern Age

Chapter Eleven

Socrates in the Slums
Homoerotics, Gender, and Settlement House Reform

Kevin P. Murphy

The settlement house movement of the late nineteenth century occupies a central place in the history of American women. The two most prominent and influential American settlement houses, Chicago's Hull House led by Jane Addams and New York's Henry Street Settlement led by Lillian Wald, functioned as sites where educated and committed middle-class women could live and work together for the social good. Situated in urban immigrant neighborhoods, settlement houses provided material assistance and educational and cultural programs primarily targeted at poor women and children. Recent scholarship has shown that, through the settlement house movement, American women built the political skills and networks that not only launched the careers of famous female reformers and politicians, but also established the blueprint for twentieth-century American welfare policies.[1]

The settlement house movement also occupies a central place in the history of American women's sexuality. Scholars have long noted that the majority of American settlement women remained unmarried and formed their primary relationships with one another.[2] The prominence of these relationships, or "romantic friendships," has raised a number of interesting questions: Were they sexual? Are such "romantic friendships" appropriate subjects for lesbian history? What connections, if any, exist between these romantic attachments among women and the political ideologies and practices of the settlement house movement?[3] Although vigorously debated in the 1970s and 1980s, these questions have retreated to the background in more recent examinations of settlement houses.[4]

An examination of men's involvement in the movement yields new perspectives on the connections between same-sex eroticism and settlement house politics. Although women quickly came to dominate, many men lived and worked in urban settlement houses. Indeed, the early American effort began as a collaboration between middle-class men and women influenced by European reform efforts. Two of the most prominent builders of American settlement house reform were Charles B. Stover, head of the University Settlement on New York's Lower East Side, founded in 1887 as the earliest American settlement, and John Lovejoy Elliott of the Hudson Guild on Manhattan's West Side. Stover and Elliott shared much in common with their more famous female counterparts. All took their inspiration from the world's first settlement "experiment," London's Toynbee Hall; drew to a remarkable extent on the same intellectual traditions; and embraced the social democratic notion of cross-class "human brotherhood" rooted in humanist ethical theory. Moreover, all became active participants in national politics.[5]

Elliot and Stover shared two other important similarities with settlement women. First, they embedded a critique of middle-class sexuality and gender roles within their ideal of human brotherhood. Addams, in particular, wrote a great deal about the limitations of the "family claim"—the constraints imposed by marriage and family—on young members of the middle class. Like Addams, Elliott and Stover argued that the family was not sufficient; that other forms of social family, linked to what Addams called "the universal claim," were necessary to achieve social democracy.[6] Second, Elliott and Stover lived their lives in a way that reflected and supported this dissatisfaction with a limited conception of family. Like many settlement women, they forged their primary emotional and erotic attachments to members of the same sex. For Stover and Elliott, as well as for many reform-minded women, settlement houses represented experiments in creating an alternative family in which sexuality was not linked to reproductive ends. In so doing, they developed a politics of same-sex eroticism that stood in contrast to emerging medical models of homosexual pathology and heterosexual normativity.

Like the more famous female leaders of American settlement houses, Stover and Elliott came from comfortable, middle-class families that stressed education and social involvement. Elliott, born in 1868, grew up in Princeton, Illinois. His father was a Civil War colonel and his mother was an abolitionist.[7] Stover, born in 1861, was raised in a prominent and religious Presbyterian family in eastern Pennsylvania. Both men attended college, Elliott at Cornell University, where he was president of his senior class and a member of the football team, and Stover at Lafayette College and the Union Theological Seminary. Both had rejected mainstream Protestantism. Elliott, whose family belonged to no religious organizations, had adopted at a young age the religious convictions of the famous agnostic orator Robert Ingersoll, a close family friend. Stover, who underwent a painful "crisis of faith" as a young man, renounced his Christianity and abandoned plans for the ministry.[8]

Rejection of organized Christianity left both men adrift and in search of organizing spiritual or moral principles. Elliott remembered feeling aimless at Cornell, even though he was a popular and active participant in the college's social life.[9] Stover, who traveled to the American West and Europe after leaving the seminary, suffered from a "phalanx of terrible doubt" about the "genuineness of [his] divine calling," which "like a thunder-clash in the clear heavens" led to an assault upon his faith that "after years of agony, led to its total eclipse."[10]

Both men soon found direction in the form of the secular Society of Ethical Culture. Elliott first encountered the society when Felix Adler, its leader, came to speak at Cornell. Adler's declaration that "it is possible to live without a formal creed" and his call to social commitment through "right action" and ethical living inspired Elliott. Stover was first introduced to ethical culture by Stanton Coit, a prominent follower of Adler who had founded the Neighborhood Guild. Coit convinced Stover that, although he had lost faith in the Christian doctrine, he could carry out the kind of "Christ-like life" he believed in at the settlement.[11] Through Adler and Coit, Stover and Elliott had found powerful secular principles that could replace the Christianity each had abandoned.

The Society for Ethical Culture, a well-funded organization with branches in the United States and Europe, also provided a powerful institutional base from which Stover and Elliott could develop and disseminate their philosophical beliefs and enact reform programs. After meeting Adler, Elliott immediately affiliated himself with the organization and, at Adler's insistence, attended the University of Halle in Germany to study for a doctorate in philosophy in preparation for a position as Adler's assistant. Stover, on the other hand, became a resident at the

University Settlement in 1887 and took charge of that organization when Coit left to lead the Ethical Culture Society in Great Britain. In 1894, Stover took brief leave from the Guild to take a second trip abroad, in part to learn about European reform movements.

Stover and Elliott took advantage of their travels by immersing themselves in secularized European discourses on ethical philosophy and reform. They studied the works of Thomas Carlyle, John Ruskin, and Matthew Arnold and visited Toynbee Hall, the famous London settlement house. Exposed to unfamiliar intellectual traditions, and separated from the constraints of American moral conventions, these men further questioned the foundations upon which they had constructed their identities. As a result of their European travels, they reimagined themselves and their gendered social roles. For both men, this self-reconstitution involved developing identities around the formation of primary bonds with other men.

For Stover, this process of self-reinvention was filled with considerable anguish and persistent religious doubt. Throughout his life, he suffered from spells of severe depression. In the few instances when he communicated to friends the origins of his psychic anguish, he linked his problems to issues of procreation and marriage. Moreover, despite his renunciation of the Christian faith, he continued to employ a rhetoric of Christian sin and divine will when discussing his depression. When he suffered from one of these depressive spells during his second trip to Europe, for example, he wrote to friends about his suicidal thoughts and spoke bitterly of the "greatest crime of which a man can be guilty"—the perpetuation of the human species. Stover also referred to an unspecified problem "outside of himself" which had caused his loss of faith.[12]

Only in later years did Stover begin to resolve his anxieties. At the University Settlement, he separated himself from family life and eschewed potential romantic interactions with women. In 1899, a "Miss Greene" of the neighboring College Settlement accused Stover of a "sad short-coming," which she referred to as a "blind bias" and "indiscriminate hostility" that characterized his dealings with women. Stover responded that he felt "unqualified by disposition" to visit socially with the women at the College Settlement. He added that, although Miss Greene "may have good authority for some outward facts" regarding his interaction with women, "the fault lies in the interpretation. I confess to frequent sinning against conventionalities. No, not sinning, for I would have it otherwise." Stover went on to argue that the fault lay not with himself, but with some outside "power . . . with whom I have not yet arrived at a satisfactory understanding. This I hope yet to accomplish." Many years later, in 1916, he indicated that he had come closer to such an understanding. In apologizing for not attending dinner at the home of a woman friend, he wrote that "The Almighty . . . wills that I have no participation in home pleasures."[13]

Stover had, in the words of his settlement colleague James Kirke Paulding, a "following on the East Side [that] was a preponderantly masculine one."[14] Yet, not all of Stover's female colleagues in the settlement reform movement interpreted his attention to boys and men in the manner of Miss Greene. In fact, Stover maintained friendly relationships with such leading settlement workers as Lillian Wald, Jane Addams, and Mary Kingsbury Simkhovitch. Some of these women had sympathetic insight into Stover's "peculiarities" and "occasional erratic movements," including his periods of depression and occasional and sudden disappearances. Simkhovitch, for example, thought that for all his gregariousness, "there was something withdrawn about him, as if he cared only to disclose his activities, while holding shyly and inviolate some core of his personality which was simply his love for all his fellow men."[15] Wald spoke of "a probable deeper struggle within" Stover.[16]

All of these expressions pointed toward a common element, linking Stover's vexed relationships to women, his alienation from the traditional family, and his primary interest in relationships with males. Although tentative and coded, these expressions invoked a model of gender and sexuality, first espoused in the late nineteenth century by sexologists as "homosexuality": an innate quality, a sexual inversion that constituted one's personality. Such a model did not inherently stigmatize "the homosexual," although many reformers and politicians deployed it to that end. In fact, as developed by British intellectuals John Addington Symonds and Edward Carpenter—whose work was well-known and highly regarded by many settlement reformers—this new model provided a unique social role and even an inherent superiority to "homosexual" people.[17] Wald, in particular, utilized this positive model in her memorial to Stover. She fondly remembered her first visit to the book-lined quarters that Stover shared with fellow settlement resident Edward King, recalling the "frank and instructive" advice that this "unconventional pair" showed her. She credited this experience with inspiring her to take up residence in the nearby college settlement with her companion, Mary Brewster. That Wald moved from an account of Stover and King's domestic scene to a reference to her own relationship with Brewster—themselves an "unconventional pair"—suggests that she saw some basis for comparison between male and female same-sex relationships. Carpenter drew similar comparisons in his theorizing on the politics of what he called "homogenic" love, suggesting that male same-sex relationships should be modeled after the relationships of "New Women."[18]

Elliott appeared to be less troubled by his bachelorhood. Like Stover, at a young age he structured his life around primary relationships with other men. But he did not interpret these relationships as especially problematic or sinful. In 1892 and 1893, during his years of graduate study in Germany, Elliott enthusiastically wrote home about the men he met there and about his experiences with German fraternal organizations. In his letters, Elliott juxtaposed expressions of delight in this fellowship with those of disinterest in forging romantic relationships with women. "I've met some nice fellows here," he wrote in one letter, "some . . . professors whom I like very well, much better than the girls. I'll tell you when my heart is in danger, but so far it has never even been exposed."[19] Later, when he returned to the United States, he responded to his mother's complaints about his unmarried status by writing that he had nothing against marriage, "in principle."[20] Elliott expressed a disenchantment with the limitations of reproductive family life that echoed Stover's. He did not denounce the institution of the family, but espoused other models of familial association linked to broader forms of social organization. As teacher of ethics at the Hudson Guild and at the school of the Ethical Culture Society, Elliott spread his new gospel that such alternative associations would promote social "brotherhood."

Like the great settlement reformer Jane Addams, Elliott and Stover embedded their dissatisfaction with circumscribed sexuality and traditional family life within an idealistic vision of a society organized by a cross-class "brotherhood." They called on Platonic models of a society dedicated to a common good and invoked the figure of Socrates to argue for their social vision. Yet Stover and Elliott also had access to two nineteenth-century traditions that linked male homoeroticism to particular social ideologies and practices: the "social mobility" tradition, best exemplified by writer and philanthropist Horatio Alger, and the "democratic comradeship" tradition heralded by the poet Walt Whitman. Although seemingly at odds with one another, these two traditions inter-sected in significant ways in the careers of Stover and Elliott.

The "social mobility" model of male homoerotic ideology and prac-tice has been brilliantly explicated by literary scholar Michael Moon. Moon has shown that American reform narratives—whether produced as nonfiction, as in the case of Children's Aid Society founder Charles Loring Brace, or as fiction, most famously in Alger's stories of male social ascent—eroticized fraternal relationships among working-class boys and men. Alger, whose Harvard education concentrated on a study of Hellenic culture, wrote popular novels about relationships between middle-class "saviors" and poor youths, framing the act of "saving" as one of seduction. In Alger's stories these narratives of "rescue" involve crossing "seemingly intractable class lines" and terminate, happily, with a romanticized portrait of masculine domesticity.[21]

Writings by Brace and Alger combined overlapping trajectories of "descent" (movement into the working-class slums by middle-class re-formers and benefactors) and "ascent" (the social and economic rise of poor working-class youths), creating an eroticized portrait of masculine class amicability during a time of considerable labor unrest and violent class conflict in urban America. In this sense, these narratives shared certain characteristics with the literary work of Walt Whitman, espe-cially his *Leaves of Grass,* which includes the highly homoerotic "Cala-mus" poems. In fact, one of Whitman's early literary efforts, the 1841 short story "The Child's Champion," forecast the plot line of the popu-lar "rags to respectability" stories of Horatio Alger.[22]

Whitman quickly abandoned this format in favor of work that pos-ited a more leveling model of male homoerotic attachment. *Leaves of Grass,* published in 1855, created a politicized utopian narrative of masculine comradeship and "adhesiveness" that would bind American men together in democratic society. In the "Calamus" poems, Whitman explicitly sexualized these bonds, presenting himself to modern eyes as both "the poet of homosexual love and the bard of democracy."[23] Whit-man himself commented on the political significance of the "Calamus" poems:

> Important as they are in my purpose as emotional expressions for hu-manity, the special meaning of the Calamus cluster of Leaves of Grass . . . mainly resides in its Political significance. In my opinion it is by a fervent, accepted development of Comradeship, the beautiful and sane affection of

man for man, latent in all the young fellows, North and South, East and West—it is by this, I say . . . that the United States of the future, (I cannot too often repeat), are to be most effectually welded together, intercalated, anneal'd into a Living Union.[24]

For Whitman, as for Brace and Alger, "personal" desire and the "public" politics of class relationships were intricately interlinked.

This inextricable link between homoerotic desire and homosocial class relations is illustrated not only in the literary productions of Whitman and Alger, but also in their life stories. In a sense, both of these writers lived these narratives by forging personal eroticized relationships with young working-class men. While Alger was writing his famous stories, he also worked as a social reformer in the Newsboy's Lodging House founded by Brace's Children's Aid Society. Alger also "adopted" several young working-class men, who lived with him and assisted him in his work.[25] Alger, who had previously been dismissed from a ministerial position for "the abominable and revolting crime of unnatural familiarity" with a young male parishioner, embedded his erotic interests within his social roles as philanthropist and author.[26]

Whitman also formed primary relationships with young working-class men who lived with and worked for him. Yet Whitman constructed his social performance in a way that both reflected and influenced the theme of a leveling, manly democracy that characterized his work. Rather than assuming the role of philanthropist, Whitman presented himself as a physically virile man who shared the habits, attire, and pastimes of the "rough" working-class men whose company he kept. Reflecting popular notions of the manly virtue of the American yeoman, Whitman situated this communion between men in an idyllic Arcadian setting, thereby naturalizing a "community of desire sharing a sexual, social, and psychological condition."[27] The idealized expression of manly comradeship and desire that Whitman conveyed in his work, and lived with his body, provided a compelling discourse for late-nineteenth-century men—including Stover and Elliott—who resisted the growing stigmatization and pathologizing models of male same-sex attachments. Whitman served as a major influence for intellectual leftists on both sides of the Atlantic who sought to incorporate homoerotics within their political vision.[28]

Among those inspired by Whitman's "manly comradeship" were the famous British theoreticians of "homogenic" love, John Addington Symonds and Edward Carpenter.[29] Whitman's influence on these British thinkers reflected a broad cross-Atlantic collaboration in the discourses of homoeroticism and class relations. Symonds and Carpenter drew on Whitman's model of manly comradeship and on the models of pederasty and pedagogy of ancient Greece to construct an explicitly political argument that presented homosexual relations as morally valid and socially useful and challenged the repression of homosexuality by the state. Carpenter, in his 1894 essay "Homogenic Love," expanded on arguments previously made by Symonds that, if freed from repression by the state, homosexuality could effect a major social transformation. He contended that homosexual relations could draw "members of the different classes together" by forming "an advance guard of that great movement that will one day transform the common life by substituting the bond of personal affection and compassion for the monetary, legal and other external forces which now control and confine society."[30]

The political theories of homogenic love espoused by Symonds and Carpenter circulated in socialist intellectual circles in Great Britain, especially at Oxford and Cambridge, and found an institutional setting in London's settlement houses. At the end of the nineteenth century, young Carpenter enthusiasts, including C. R. Ashbee and Frank Llewellyn-Smith, took up residence in London's Toynbee Hall, in order to re-create the familiar all-male world of the university and form relationships with "rough" working-class boys. These privileged reformers boxed and roughhoused with young East Endmen, recording the sights and smells of these experiences in their journals, and took them on trips to the countryside that, according to Ashbee, bonded reformers and youths in "eternal love." Historian Seth Koven argues that these young reformers, who used the same sexualized and class-based rhetoric of the "rough lad" developed in London's gay subcultures, sought to "create nation and community through vertical bonds of comradeship across class lines."[31]

A similar combination of homoerotic desire and social reform characterized the careers of Stover and Elliott. Stover exulted in the companionship of young working-class men at the University Settlement, developing a following that others referred to as "Stover's boys."[32] Stover, who fashioned himself as a "rough" Whitmanesque figure, was especially close to a "belligerent and excitable" group of young men who belonged to the "Chadwick Juniors" club. Their ringleader was Jacob Epstein, who would later become a renowned sculptor. Stover and his associate James Kirke Paulding were extremely "permissive" with this crowd, and when other residents felt that the youths' mischievous antics had gotten out of hand, Stover "sided with their belligerence" and invited them to meet in his private quarters.[33]

Like his British counterparts, Stover embedded his desire for comradeship with young working-class men in a decidedly Arcadian vision. He believed that natural settings provided the ideal location for forging social bonds. Not surprisingly, he was influential in establishing a settlement camp in upstate New York. He maintained quarters at the camp, and was happiest spending time there with youths from the settlement whom he taught natural history. Stover carried this belief in the transformative power of nature—especially for working-class boys—to his other reform activities, especially in his capacity as New York City Parks Commissioner between 1910 and 1914. In fact, his commitment to making parks accessible for the recreation of working-class men contributed to his losing that position. He advocated "popularizing" the parks, including Central Park, by providing playing fields. Wealthy New Yorkers, appalled at a policy that they thought would mar the parks' landscapes and fearful that the parks would attract "gangs of hoodlums," lobbied for Stover's removal.[34]

Like Stover, Elliott found himself drawn to the "rough" masculine culture of New York's working-class neighborhoods. According to Algernon Black, Elliott's colleague in the Society of Ethical Culture, when Elliott first heard about the "rough and tough" Manhattan neighborhood Hell's Kitchen, he responded with great enthusiasm. Black reported that Elliott began to frequent the neighborhood, where he "walked through the streets and along the docks" and "watched the men working on the docks unloading the ships, the truck drivers taking the cargo away to factories and markets."[35] Elliott rented an apartment in the neighborhood and soon attracted a gang of boys called the "Hurly Burlies," with whom he boxed and shot craps. Elliott reported that the visits of this gang to his apartment would sometimes end in a brawl, with the lights turned off and objects broken. One neighborhood minister, according to Elliott, reported that the boys who visited his apartment were "a menace to neighborhood morality" and disturbed the peace.[36]

In reminiscing about his experiences with the Hurly Burlies, which led to his subsequent establishment of the Hudson Guild, Elliott recalled being immediately taken with one "blond haired boy" who was "the first to box." This "handsome and strong boy with a wonderful Irish brogue" was Mark McCloskey, with whom Elliott formed the closest relationship of his life.[37] Elliott took a special interest in McCloskey, whom he referred to in his letters as "Marksie" and "Beloved."[38] He financed McCloskey's education at Princeton University, and thereafter named him as his successor as director of the Hudson Guild. McCloskey went on to play a leading role in several federal programs during the New Deal and World War II. In later years, Elliott established similar relationships with youths from the neighborhood.[39]

Elliott also constructed his persona in the Whitmanesque mold. He eschewed coat and tie in favor of shabby casual clothing and often walked through the streets of the West Side followed by a gang of youths referred to as "Elliott's boys."[40] Those who met Elliott inevitably commented on his large stature, handsome face, booming voice, and "manly" personality. His associates often queried why a man so "handsome and affectionate and loving" never expressed any interest in marrying. Elliott's unmarried status, in fact, proved to be a source of troubled speculation for his associates, especially in the years after his death. Those who addressed this topic frequently invoked a gendered model of the homosexual male as "effeminate" by contrasting Elliott's virile, charismatic personality with his unmarried status. One explanation that circulated among Elliott's acquaintances was that he lived his life "like a priest"; that his overwhelming social commitment would have been diluted if he gave his attention to a wife and family. Algernon Black, in a chapter of an unpublished biography of Elliott, suggestively titled *The Gay Life,* discussed this and other possible explanations for Elliott's bachelorhood before concluding, "No matter how much people asked and guessed, no one was ever able to find out the real truth about why John never married. All they could do was guess and wonder."[41]

Elliott did not interpret his homosocial and homoerotic desires only as matters of personal preference. Lesson plans from the ethics classes that Elliott taught in the early years of the twentieth century indicate that his conceptions of male homoeroticism and comradeship bore a striking resemblance to the political models espoused by Carpenter and Symonds. For example, Elliott shared the penchant of those two writers for making political arguments about class relationships by telling eroticized stories about two sets of famous comrades: Damien and Pithias of Greek mythology and the biblical pair of David and Jonathan. In one lesson, Elliott set up the telling of these stories through a voyeuristic account of the body of the young shepherd, David:

> You will see a shepherd boy, about fifteen or sixteen years old, playing and singing. . . . If you look at the boy's arms you would see the great large muscles and large bones, and his wrists are strong. He is a strong young fellow. His back was straight, and his chest is large and his legs are long and muscular, and he was swift of foot. He was a splendid young chap if there ever was one. . . . He is a mighty nice kind of a youth. So big and brave and skillful. He touched the harp with skillful fingers and such beautiful deep music like religious music, and then just love music, and then nature music, or of the eagle flying in the sky.[42]

Elliott continued this story with a description of David's battle with Goliath and his subsequent "beautiful friendship" with Jonathan. Elliott related this story as a class-infused morality tale by claiming that David was "a poor boy" to whom Jonathan "gave his best things."[43]

In similar fashion, Elliott framed the story of Damien and Pithias as one of "the love of brothers . . . too rare to be destroyed." He contrasted the "beauty" of their relationship to the tyranny of the king who was ready to execute Damien. "The meaning of the story is that the tyrant king cannot learn or know friendship." In one telling of this story, he defined those who "cannot join in this friendship" as the wealthy industrialists, "Rockefeller, Whitney, and Ryan. . . . Money cannot cure Rockefeller's indigestion." Elliott also linked these stories to an argument that validated one's decision to remain unmarried. After giving examples of "unmarried brothers who lived their whole life together," he stated, "This was a very lovely life. . . . When they marry they separate. That is a very beautiful relation and there are other beautiful examples."[44]

Similar stories of loving brotherhood appear in the context of the University Settlement. Although there are no extant records of the pedagogical strategies employed there, the artistic production of members of boys' clubs led by Stover and Paulding suggest that they taught lessons similar to those of Elliott. One example of such production in visual form are the homoerotic Calamus paintings by Jacob Epstein. Produced by Epstein at the very beginning of his career, these drawings of intertwined, naked young men were inspired by his encounter with Whitman's writing in a University Settlement Boys' Club led by Stover and his colleague Paulding.[45] Other examples are found in literary magazines, which include numerous poems and stories on the beauty of comradely love that were published by the young members of the clubs. One such story, "A Tale of Two Souls," tells of the love between "the flower-like

Elmer" and his friend Enoch, who had eyes as "blue as the calmest summer-sky" and hair "like gold—beautiful gold." One typical passage reads:

> They were very great friends. Sometimes, out of the busy striving and struggling world, two souls reach out, recognize in each other the inmost desires of their hearts and cling to each other forever. The friendship of Enoch and Elmer was such a fellowship of souls. There was not a joy for the one, but that it was born from the other's gladness and not a tear, but shed because of the other's grief.[46]

Similar themes were sounded throughout the pages of these journals, often in explicitly class-based political contexts. For example, David Colin, a member of the Emerson Club, celebrated the ability of the poet to "Proclaim on high, True Friendship and Fraternity" and thereby "awake the weary slave of toil" and "destroy the chains that bind him tight."[47]

This ideal of loving bonds between male friends was not restricted to artistic expressions. In fact, members of turn-of-the-century University Settlement clubs—with names like the Comrade Club, the Spartan Athletic Club, Athenians, and the Young Citizens—considered this ideal the basis of their very existence and of their social mission. The constitution of the Promethean Club, for example, states that because "conditions exist which are contrary to the ideals of truth, justice and brotherhood . . . we youths do hereby band together to preserve and foster by education of word and deed, and by stimulating friendship, the lofty idealism of youth, to create a sensitive consciousness to conditions about it . . . so that youth, when it matures, shall become the strength of the nation to the end that idealism shall govern conduct." The young men in the Promethean Club and other clubs enacted this call to social improvement and nation strengthening by involving themselves in various movements, including labor unionization and tenement house reform.[48]

In one sense, the expressions of youth club members suggest that ideals of male "friendship" and "fraternity" were embedded in a utopian vision of a democratic and classless society developed in opposition to the materialism, "selfishness and cynicism" of an industrialized urban society.[49] Yet these clubs were constrained by the very class-based society they criticized in that they were located in social settlements supervised by middle-and upper-class reformers and dependent on philanthropic funding. Within the clubs, liberal-capitalist tenets of improvement and social uplift through education often stood in tension with the more leveling ideals of democratic brotherhood. This tension is inherent within the youth club rhetoric, which speaks of "brotherhood" in the privileged language of Western male intellectuals. Although this ideal may have intersected patterns of working-class male camaraderie and solidarity performed in the streets and taverns of New York's tenement house districts, its goal was to transform and "uplift" the men who inhabited this milieu through the privileged realm of literary culture. Moreover, the life trajectories of these young men, many of whom went on to play prominent social roles as businessmen, scholars, and political reformers, suggest that their introduction to "culture" in the settlements served primarily to help them achieve individual social advancement.[50]

This tension between vertical and horizontal forms of male relationships was also evident in the careers of Elliott and Stover. Their movement "down" into the immigrant neighborhoods of New York conformed in many ways to the similar erotic and political male "descents" enacted elsewhere in turn-of-the-century New York. Men like Brace and Alger who fashioned themselves as social reformers coupled their own "descent" with the "uplift" of men they encountered in the "slums." Similar stories were reenacted and renarrated in Stover's and Elliott's own time by other prominent New Yorkers, including Charles Parkhurst, Jacob Riis, and Theodore Roosevelt, who gave sensational accounts of their reform escapades.[51] During the same period, middle-class men in search of sexual pleasure and freedom from the constraints of "respectable" culture frequented the bars and streets of immigrant neighborhoods.[52] Although many sought sex with working-class women, others participated in a burgeoning "fairy culture" based on gender inversion, and still others pursued sexual relations with "rough" working-class men whose appearance and masculine style they eroticized. Many of these men, like Stover and Elliott, heralded Whitman "as a prophetic spokesman" and identified with his notion of "the manly love of comrades."[53]

The careers of Elliott and Stover point to the area where erotic and reform models of "descent" overlapped and illustrate the tense coexistence of vertical and horizontal models of class relations that inhered in these narratives. The trajectories these reformers enacted and the stories that were told about them had a more horizontal structure than those of typical "slummers." After their initial "descent," both men remained throughout their lives in immigrant neighborhoods and formed long-lasting relationships with men who lived there. Like other reformers, they recounted their experiences to middle-class audiences through reform publications, but they also built constituencies within the neighborhoods in which they lived. Their moves to costume themselves as "simple" men, for example, registered not only with middle-class audiences, but also with those living in the tenement districts, many of whom interpreted the absence of "dress suit" and "high hat," along with their desire to form close relationships with "even the humblest laborer," as signs of humility and solidarity.[54] Moreover, each developed a politics which, in its advocacy of benefits for working-class people, was interpreted as radical by other reformers. Stover, for example, was criticized not only for his attempts to build playing fields in Central Park, but for the campaign he led to open museums to working people on Sundays. Likewise, Elliott's efforts to help convicted criminals from his Chelsea neighborhood and to assist neighborhood youths to resist the draft in World War I were met with great suspicion by many of his counterparts.[55]

The tense interplay between vertical and horizontal models of class-based and eroticized male relationships is perhaps best illustrated by the "Socratic role" performed by Elliott and Stover, a role with significant explanatory and legitimating power for both men. Like Whitman, Socrates functioned as a historical figure through which these men located themselves in relation to the young immigrant men with whom they worked and lived. The influence of Socrates was not lost on those who surrounded these men. Coit, for example, claimed that "Stover was different—and in the same way—from every other mortal whom I have ever known as was Socrates from all the other Athenians of his day."[56]

Elliott's colleagues and students likewise referred to Socrates as his "revered hero" and spoke of "the kind of Socratic probing [Elliott] liked to practice."[57] Indeed, Elliott performed the Socratic role with great enthusiasm. His ethics classes, organized as Socratic dialogues, frequently revolved around accounts of Greek devotion to the beauty of the male body and the role of pedagogy in the development of this beauty. After asking his students to recite the Athenian oath, Elliott narrated stories about "those Greek boys . . . each one with his teacher or pedagogue," who

would start out in the morning about day light and they stayed there until sundown. They would go through the streets in a kind of procession until they came to a place set aside for gymnastic exercises and there, from sunrise until noon, they would exercise and play games in the open air. Think of the tremendous skill and strength they would get—twisting and turning and rolling over in the dirt by the hour. It would really make them strong and skillful. Then they had what they called dancing. They wanted to make their boys wonderfully strong, skillful and beautiful.

In other lessons, Elliott theorized about the kinds of male friendships forged in the Greek gymnasia. "Finer, stronger, and more powerful . . . than the individual friendship between two men," this "social friendship" would bring about a renewed "social feeling" in society, transcending the interest in the individual. The creation of this "social friendship," he argued, was the responsibility of the social worker.[58]

The links Elliott made between a democratic form of "social friendship" and an eroticized Socratic pedagogy did not go unnoticed or unchallenged by all of his colleagues or students. Lucy Mitchell, who taught with Elliott at the Fieldston School, remembered complaining to Felix Adler that Elliott's entire pedagogy was based on "the study of the life and conditions that man . . . The Greek . . . the one who took hemlock." She felt that Elliott's preoccupation with Socrates "had become a joke among the pupils." Mitchell also raised the specter of the "unspeakable" when discussing Elliott's relationships with his students. When asked to give an anecdote about Elliott, she responded: "Oh dear me, not anything I'd want to tell. . . . It was more what the children said and what the children thought and that isn't anything to be repeated." Others who recounted their memories of Elliott after his death expressed unease when asked to talk about his relationship with his charges. One woman, when asked about McCloskey's relationship with Elliott, characterized it as "a very different kind of relationship . . . a very close one" and told her interviewer, "if you and I were simply talking as people I might tell you things that I haven't today but I can't neglect the purpose of your inquiry."[59]

The troubled response to Elliott's interactions with his students reflects the uneasy relationship between Socratic pedagogy and pederasty, a relationship inherent in a pedagogical model that eroticizes youthful male bodies within a vision of society built around bonds between men. The role of the Socratic pedagogue—the older man who instills this ideal of male friendship in young men—proved especially troubling because it resonated with contemporary fears about the sexual corruption of youth. Such fears circulated widely in late-Victorian America and became the subject of numerous reform crusades. When these fears dealt with sexual relations between men they became much more troublesome and more difficult to address. Indeed, the emergence of a Socratic form of pedagogy at British universities earlier in the nineteenth century had caused similar "problems." Troubled by the role of Socrates as a "corrupter of youth" and the simultaneous recovery of "Greek Love," colleagues accused British classicists like Benjamin Jowett of corrupting youth and promoting "boy love." Such connections between pederasty and Socratic pedagogy brought about an uneasy, though hesitant, critique of Elliott as well.[60]

Because Elliott and Stover drew so heavily on male traditions of cross-class homoeroticism and on privileged male access to public space, their careers differed in significant ways from those of their more prominent female counterparts. Most important, settlement women formed their primary relationships, not with working-class clients, but with one another. Yet the belief that a reimagined sexuality was essential for bridging the chasm between social classes was not exclusive to male settlement reformers. Indeed, a class-based analysis of sexuality was central to the concept of "human brotherhood" espoused by Jane Addams, the movement's most prominent social thinker. "Tak[ing] a page from the Greeks," Addams argued that the "fundamental sex susceptibility . . . suffused the world with its deepest meaning and beauty."[61] She felt, however, that sexuality had become misdirected in industrial society, manifesting itself in "vice and enervation." She located "vice" primarily in the commercialized street life of working-class neighborhoods, and "enervation" within the confines of the middle-class family, which thwarted the desire of young people to participate in the cultivation of democratic civic life.[62] Drawing on Plato's dialogue between Socrates and Diotima, Addams argued that the sexual impulse must be freed both from limited family reproduction and from mere sensual pleasure. Redirected to "the affairs of imagination" by people of all classes, the sexual impulse would bring renewed life to the city.[63]

These connections between Addams's writing on sexuality and the careers of Elliott and Stover carry two implications for our understanding of the settlement movement. First, a re-formation of American sexuality stood at the center of settlement house ideology. Male and female leaders of the settlement movement alike believed that a refashioning of sexual desire was crucial to the project of overcoming class difference. Although they shared a broad middle-class perception that working-class neighborhoods were highly sexualized spaces, they also saw the sexuality of working-class neighborhoods as a source of great possibility for the formation of new types of social organization. Such a reorganization never came to be, but these men and women established sexual identities and practices that conformed neither to the middle-class norms of their day, nor to current binary notions of heterosexuality and homosexuality.

Second, the settlement movement was not organized solely along lines of gendered identity. The settlement movement promoted collaboration among men and women who did not subscribe to dominant gender and sexual roles. This collaboration remained fruitful and held out the possibility for a transcendence of strict gender categories well into the twentieth century. Indeed, Elliott and Stover maintained close friendships with Addams and Wald throughout their lives. The friendship between Elliott and Wald grew especially close: Wald even requested that "her dear friend John Elliott" speak at her funeral and serve as executor of her will.[64] Correspondence between the two aging reformers in the twentieth century suggests that an understanding of each other's sexuality comprised a primary bond of their friendship. In one 1933 letter, for example, Elliott wrote to Wald raving about the controversial film *Maedchen in Uniform,* which depicted lesbian relationships in a German boarding school.[65] That same year, Wald wrote to Elliott about her "very, very nice" new companion with language of playful gender inversion: "I call her 'Everyman'," she wrote, "and she is very pleasing."[66] These exchanges point to the intriguing possibility that in addition to the gendered networks of the "female dominion," settlement reformers also developed networks of sexual subjectivity that crossed gender lines.

NOTES

I thank Thomas Bender, Lisa Duggan, Mark Elliot, Martha Hodes, Seth Koven, Regina Kunzel, and Rebecca Welch for their helpful comments on earlier drafts of this chapter. Special thanks to Terence Kissack for helping me think through the arguments presented here.

1. This argument is treated extensively in Robin Muncy, *Creating a Female Dominion in American Reform, 1890–1935* (New York: Oxford University Press, 1991). Among others, prominent women who worked in settlements include Florence Kelley, Eleanor Roosevelt, and Frances Perkins. On the settlement movement in general, see Minna Carson, *Settlement Folk: Social Thought and*

the American Settlement Movement, 1885–1930 (Chicago: University of Chicago Press, 1990); Allen Davis, *Spearheads for Reform: The Social Settlements and the Progressive Movement, 1890–1914* (New York: Oxford University Press, 1967); and Michael B. Katz, *Under the Shadow of the Poorhouse: A History of Social Welfare in America* (New York: Basic Books, 1986), 158–63. On Hull House, see Muncy, *Creating a Female Dominion;* and Katherine Kish Sklar, "Hull House in the 1890s: A Community of Women Reformers," *Signs* 10 (summer 1985): 658–77. On Florence Kelley, see Katherine Kish Sklar, *Florence Kelley and the Nation's Work: The Rise of Women's Political Culture, 1830–1900* (New Haven: Yale University Press, 1995). On Eleanor Roosevelt at New York's College Settlement, see Blanche Wiesen Cook, *Eleanor Roosevelt,* vol. 1, *1884–1933* (New York: Viking, 1992), 135–38.

2. See, for example, Davis, *Spearheads for Reform;* and Sklar, "Hull House in the 1890s."

3. Much scholarship on "romantic friendships" among nineteenth-century women has dealt with settlement women, especially Jane Addams and Lillian Wald. Blanche Wiesen Cook, in "Female Support Networks and Political Activism: Lillian Wald, Crystal Eastman, Emma Goldman," *Chrysalis* 3 (1977): 43–61, argued that Wald and Addams, along with many other political women of the period, could be categorized as lesbians in that they formed their primary attachments to other women. This argument was expanded by Adrienne Rich in her much debated 1980 essay, "Compulsory Heterosexuality and Lesbian Existence," *Signs* 5 (summer 1980): 631–60. A number of feminist scholars argued that labeling these women "lesbian" was ahistorical but at the same time expressed concerns about the implications of disassociating romantic friendships from lesbian history. On this issue, see Carroll Smith-Rosenberg, *Disorderly Conduct: Visions of Gender in Victorian America* (New York: Oxford University Press, 1985); Esther Newton, "The Mythic Mannish Lesbian: Radclyffe Hall and the New Woman," *Signs* 9 (summer 1984): 557–75; and Martha Vicinus, " 'They Wonder to Which Sex I Belong': The Historical Roots of the Modern Lesbian Identity," in Henry Abelove et al., eds., *The Lesbian and Gay Studies Reader* (New York: Routledge, 1993).

4. In many recent works, same-sex relationships among settlement women have been treated in cursory and unsatisfactory fashion. Robin Muncy asserts that Jane Addams's companion Mary Rozette Smith played the role of "a Victorian wife" (*Creating a Female Dominion,* 16). Mina Carson writes briefly on Lillian Wald's "crushes" on female residents at Henry Street (*Settlement Folk,* 93). Linda Gordon, in her influential *Pitied but Not Entitled: Single Mothers and the History of Welfare* (Cambridge: Harvard University Press, 1994), asserts that settlement women and other female reformers involved with other women shared a "nuns' sensibility" and dismisses their "sexual activity" as irrelevant (79).

5. On settlement ideology, see Carson, *Settlement Folk;* and Christopher Lasch, ed., *The Social Thought of Jane Addams* (New York: Irvington Publishers, 1982). On Elliott's career, see Tay Hohoff, *A Ministry to Man: The Life of John Lovejoy Elliott* (New York: Harper and Brothers, 1959); and Howard B. Radest, *Toward Common Ground: The Story of the Ethical Societies in the United States* (New York: Frederick Ungar, 1969), 109–21. On Stover, see J. K. Paulding, *Charles B. Stover: His Life and Personality* (New York: International Press, 1938); and Jeffrey Scheuer, *Legacy of Light: University Settlement's First Century* (New York: University Settlement, 1985). On Addams's life, see Jane Addams, *Twenty Years at Hull House* (New York: Macmillan, 1910); and Allen Davis, *American Heroine: The Life and Legend of Jane Addams* (New York: Oxford University Press, 1973). On Wald, see Lillian Wald, *The House on Henry Street* (New York: Henry Holt, 1915); and Beatrice Siegel, *Lillian Wald of Henry Street* (New York: Macmillan, 1983).

6. Addams made her critique of the "family claim" in two essays, "The Subjective Necessity for Social Settlements" (1892) and "The College Woman and the Family Claim" (1898), both reprinted in Ellen Condliffe Lagemann, ed., *Jane Addams on Education* (New York: Teachers College Press, 1985). The first essay was originally delivered at a meeting of the Ethical Culture Society, to which both Elliott and Stover belonged. For more on Jane Addams' thought, see Daniel Levine, *Jane Addams and the Liberal Tradition* (Madison: State Historical Society of Wisconsin, 1971); and Lasch, ed., *The Social Thought of Jane Addams.*

7. John Lovejoy Elliott's parents were Isaac and Elizabeth Lovejoy Elliott. His maternal grandfather was antislavery congressman Owen Lovejoy. For biographical information on Elliott, see Hohoff, *A Ministry to Man;* and Radest, *Toward Common Ground;* 109–21.

8. For biographical information on Stover, see Paulding, *Charles B. Stover;* and Scheuer, *Legacy of Light.*

9. Radest, *Toward Common Ground,* 110.

10. Quoted in Paulding, *Charles B. Stover,* 15–16.

11. Ibid., 18.

12. Letters to Henry J. Rode, quoted in Paulding, *Charles B. Stover,* 35–38.

13. Paulding, *Charles B. Stover,* 112–13.

14. Ibid., 112.

15. Mary K. Simkhovitch, "Recollections and Reflections," in Paulding, *Charles B. Stover,* 136–38.

16. Lillian D. Wald, "Recollections and Reflections," in Paulding, *Charles B. Stover,* 131–35.

17. See, for example, Linda Dowling, *Hellinism and Homosexuality in Victorian Oxford* (Ithaca, N.Y.: Cornell University Press, 1993), 104–54; and Byrne R. S. Fone, *A Road to Stonewall: Male Homosexuality and Homophobia in*

English and American Literature, 1750–1969 (New York: Twayne Publishers, 1986), 129–56.

18. Edward Carpenter, "Homogenic Love" (1894), in Brian Reade, ed., *Sexual Heretics: Male Homosexuality in English Literature from 1850 to 1900: An Anthology* (New York: Coward-McCann, 1970), 324–47. See also Elaine Showalter, *Sexual Anarchy: Gender and Culture at the Fin de Siècle* (New York: Penguin Books, 1990), 47.

19. John Lovejoy Elliott to family, January 29, 1893, copy at Ethical Culture Society Archives (ECSA), chronological card file, 1893.

20. Quoted in Hohoff, *Ministry to Man,* 57.

21. Michael Moon, " 'The Gentle Boy from the Dangerous Classes': Pederasty, Domesticity, and Capitalism in Horatio Alger," *Representations* 19 (summer 1987): 87–110.

22. See Michael Moon, "Disseminating Whitman," in Ronald R. Butters et al., eds., *Displacing Homophobia: Gay Male Perspectives in Literature and Culture* (Durham, N.C.: Duke University Press, 1989), 235–54. "The Child's Champion" was published in the mass-circulation periodical *The New World.*

23. Betsey Erkkila, *Whitman the Political Poet* (New York: Oxford University Press, 1989), 183.

24. Quoted in Ibid., 180.

25. For information on Alger's reform activities and his relationships with working-class youths, see Carol Nackenoff, *The Fictional Republic: Horatio Alger and American Political Discourse* (New York: Oxford University Press, 1994).

26. Moon, "The Gentle Boy of the Dangerous Classes," 91.

27. Fone, *A Road to Stonewall,* 57–74.

28. Terence Kissack refers to these intellectuals as "the Whitmanite Left." See Kissack, "Free Comrades: The Politics of Homoeroticism in the Life and Work of John William Lloyd," unpublished manuscript, 1995.

29. See, for example, Fone, *A Road to Stonewall,* 75–84; Dowling, *Hellenism and Homosexuality in Victorian Oxford,* 130; and David S. Reynolds, *Walt Whitman's America: A Cultural Biography* (New York: Alfred A. Knopf, 1995), 578–79.

30. Carpenter, "Homogenic Love."

31. This account of Toynbee Hall is drawn from Seth Kaven's excellent "From Rough Lads to Hooligans: Boy Life, National Culture and Social Reform," in Andrew Parker et al., eds., *Nationalisms and Sexualities* (New York: Routledge, 1992), 365–91.

32. See Heymann Fliegel, "Memorial Address," in Paulding, *Charles B. Stover,* 179–82.

33. One of Stover's colleagues, for example, reported that Stover would take a young man as his roommate at the camp and would take him on nature walks.

The Papers of the University Settlement Society of New York City (USSNYC), microfilmed by the State Historical Society of Wisconsin, A. J. Kennedy Notes, "SEI-1894, History and Comment," Reel 15.

34. Gregory F. Gilmartin, *Shaping the City: New York and the Municipal Art Society* (New York: Clarkson Potter, 1995), 241–51.

35. ECSA, Papers of Algernon Black, Box: "John Lovejoy Elliott."

36. Quoted in *From One Small Room,* pamphlet (Hudson Guild, 1945), ECSA, John Lovejoy Elliott Papers, Box: "Elliott, pre-1933." For other accounts of the Hurly Burlies and the founding of the Hudson Guild, see Hohoff, *A Ministry to Man,* 41–42, 51–55; Radest, *Toward Common Ground,* 114–20.

37. ECSA, Algernon D. Black Papers, draft manuscript of "Biography of John Lovejoy Elliott," 43. See also *From One Small Room.*

38. Reports of the closeness between McCloskey and Elliott abound in Hudson Guild documents and were affirmed in the early 1960s by Frieda Moss in interviews with, among others, Jerome Nathanson, Algernon Black, and Helen Reichenbach, ECSA, Box: Oral History Project. A small amount of correspondence exists at the ECSA in a folder entitled "McCloskey, Mark" in the John Lovejoy Elliott Papers. See, for example, letter of 9 February 1942 from McCloskey to JLE, and letter of 9 January 1942 from McCloskey to Elliott.

39. Interview with Bresci Thompson, 20 November 1995.

40. On "Elliott's boys," see, for example, Horace L. Freiss, "John Lovejoy Elliott: A Living Legacy of Ethical Humanism," ECSA, Algernon Black Papers, Box: "John Lovejoy Elliott, 1"; and "Interview of Helen Reichenbach by Frieda Moss," undated, 18, ECSA, Box: Oral History Project. On Elliott's appearance, see Hohoff, *A Ministry to Man,* 5; and "Interview of Jerome Nathanson by Frieda Moss," 1964, 24, ECSA, Box: "Oral History Project."

41. Algernon D. Black, draft manuscript, "Biography of John Lovejoy Elliott," 82–83, ECSA.

42. "Ethics Lesson Plan, Class V, Elliott, 1906," ECSA, Box: "Ethics Classes, J. L. Elliott."

43. The story of David and Jonathan appears several times in Elliott's lesson plans. This quote comes from a plan dated 5 January 1906, ECSA, Box: "Ethics Classes, J. L. Elliott."

44. Elliott told the Damien and Pithias story in the following lesson plans: "Class V, Ethics, Lesson, January 5, 1906," "Lesson 18, Ethics, February 23, 1906," "Beta A, Lesson, December 8th, 1905."

45. Epstein was the ring leader of a boys' group under the supervision of Stover and Paulding. In addition to Whitman, the boys read Ruskin, Carlyle, and Emerson. Other members of the circle who later achieved renown include Henry Moskowitz and Meyer Bloomfield. USSNYC, Reel 15, Series 7, Box 1, "Clubs." For Epstein's account of his experiences on the Lower East Side, see Jacob Epstein, *Epstein: An Autobiography* (New York: E. P. Dutton, 1955), 1–

11. Epstein's Calamus drawings caught the attention of both George Bernard Shaw and Robert Ross, Oscar Wilde's literary executor. Ross later awarded Epstein the much sought after commission to create Wilde's tomb. See Frank Felsenstein, "Epstein as Book Illustrator," in Evely Silber, et al., eds., *Jacob Epstein: Sculpture and Drawings* (London: W. S. Maney and Son, 1989), 197–98.

46. Bernard Hirshberg, "A Tale of Two Souls," *The Emersonian,* March 1911, 8–9, USSNYC, "Clubs-E," Reel 16.

47. David Colin, "Arise, O Bard," *The Emersonian,* March 1911, USSNYC, "Clubs-E," Reel 16.

48. "Preamble of the Promethean Constitution," USSNYC, Reel 15, Series 7, Box 1, "Clubs."

49. Ibid.

50. Many of the boys who were members of the Chadwick Civic Jr. Club and the S.E.I. (Social Educational Improvement) Club achieved great success. These included Epstein, Bloomfield, Moskowitz, Albert A. Yolk, and the paleontologist Elias Lowe.

51. On Parkhurst, see Charles Gardner, *The Doctor and the Devil, or Midnight Adventures of Dr. Parkhurst* (New York: Macmillian, 1890).

52. George Chauncey, *Gay New York: Gender, Urban Culture, and the Making of the Gay Male World* (New York: Basic Books, 1994), 36–37.

53. Ibid, 104–5.

54. Reminiscence by NYC Parks Department Laborer, Charles B. Stover Papers, University Settlement Society Papers (USSP) Reel 15. Another Park Department laborer, Emil T. Delaney, remarked that Stover talked "humbly even with the men of the plainest and most illiterate type." Similar testimonials by Parks Department employees were collected by Stanley Bero and are recorded in "Recollections and Appreciations," in Paulding, *Stover,* 158–63.

55. Elliott's correspondence with prison inmates from the Hudson Guild neighborhood are extensive. ECSA, Elliott Box, "Prison Correspondence." Elliott was a frequent visitor to Sing Sing, and he often took in recently released prisoners as "housekeepers"—a subject of great concern to his family and friends. Hohoff, *A Ministry to Man,* 56.

56. Other colleagues who eulogized Stover also referred to Socrates. Remembrances are reprinted in Paulding, *Charles B. Stover,* 129–91. Coit adds that "whoever gained access to [Stover's] mind found within, as Plato says of Socrates, divine and golden images of surpassing beauty," 129.

57. Horace L. Freiss, "John Lovejoy Elliott: A Living Legacy of Ethical Humanism," 6, ECSA, Algernon D. Black Papers, Box: "John Lovejoy Elliott, 1."

58. ECSA, Box: "Elliott—Ethical Lessons," File: "Class V."

59. ECSA, Box: "Oral Interviews," "Miss Lucy Mitchell's Oral Interview" by Frieda Moss, 9 January 1964.

60. Dowling, *Hellenism and Homosexuality*, 67–103.

61. Jane Addams, *The Spirit of Youth in the City Streets* (New York: Macmillan, 1909), 16–17.

62. On vice, see Ibid., 25–30. On enervation, see "The Subjective Necessity for Social Settlements" (1892) and "The College Woman and the Family Claim" (1898), reprinted in Lagemann, ed., *Jane Addams on Education.*

63. Addams, *The Spirit of Youth,* 16–17.

64. Hohoff, *A Ministry to Man,* 67–104.

65. Letter of 4 February 1933 from J. L. E. to Lillian Wald, ECSA, Box: "Hudson Guild—Elliott," File: "Wald."

66. Letter of 8 November 1933 from Lillian Wald to J. L. E., ECSA, Box: "Hudson Guild—Elliott," File: "Wald."

Chapter Twelve

Chivalrous Men and Voting Women
The Role of Men and the Language of Masculinity in the 1911 California Woman Suffrage Campaign

Eric Dwyce Taylor

I believe [the woman suffrage amendment] will carry, and the greatest argument I can find that points conclusively to that fact is in the number of men who favor the movement.
> —Mrs. R. L. Craig, California suffragette[1]

How will you vote, my man-child; strong son of my joy and youth; Will you, my son, my treasure, stand a big man among men; Will you, my son, be noble and grant me the thing I need, Or have I bred a monster, clutched in the grip of greed?
> —Charles Farwell Edson,
> California poet and suffragist[2]

It is our duty, as men, to give protection to the women, who prefer their houses to the burden of government.
> —Mr. Flint, California resident and anti-suffragist[3]

When the "Female Suffrage Bill" came up for a vote in the California Assembly on March 24, 1880, the *Sacramento Bee* reported, the "Sergeant-at-Arms and his deputies sprang to the doors and locked them in the face of spectators and members alike. Then ensued some of the wildest confusion. Members sprang to their feet all over the House, shouting incoherent motions and swinging their arms wildly in mid air." Although this bill would have guaranteed women "limited" suffrage—they would only be allowed to vote in school board elections—it nonetheless evoked considerable emotions from both supporters and opponents. However, "[a]fter a long and laborious fight," noted a reporter, "the promoters of woman's suffrage were defeated."[4]

A few days prior to the House vote, assemblymen had already debated the bill with equal fervor. The *Daily Alta California* reported that among the spectators in the House were "hundreds of ladies of all ages and types and beauties. This fact," the paper observed, "was enough to inspire oratory into the manly breasts of our Assemblymen." Matthew Lane led the fight against the bill. "Supposing this bill passed," pronounced the Assemblyman, "when I returned home, tired and hungry, on election day, I'd find my wife at the polls. Who's to light the fires, get me my grub, and wash the dishes?" After "read[ing] some poems attacking women," reported the *Alta*, "he sat down and was immediately surrounded by members, tendering their congratulations."[5] Yet while they may have been tendering congratulations, they were also more than likely exchanging reassurances. For the reporter also noted a "roar of laughter" following Lane's remarks. This suggests that women's decreasing domestic confinement was a source of anxiety for those disquieted by the changing status of women during the late nineteenth century. Although the opponents of woman suffrage successfully defeated the 1880 bill, they apparently sensed their own vulnerability.

During the debate, Assemblyman G. W. Tyler took the floor to champion the cause of woman suffrage and to challenge his disapproving male colleagues. "Have you any fear," he asked, "that the wife of your bosom, the mother of your children, the comfort of your manhood shall not walk side by side with you to the polls, and cast her vote with you?" "The man who would not allow a woman to enjoy any privilege he enjoys himself," he chided, "is not a fit type of American manhood." Tyler concluded his appeal in dramatic fashion: "I hope in this day of civilization, in this nineteenth century, in this day of advancement, and on the Western-coast of the Pacific, we will be the last as legislators—as men—to refuse to her the same rights that we enjoy ourselves."[6]

Tyler's was not the only pro-suffrage voice in the Assembly. Assemblyman George Anthony went so far as to argue that "women are not a class separate from men," and—though somewhat patronizingly—to concede that he "always thought my wife was the better man of the two, in goodness; that her judgment in matters of business was superior in some respects to my own."[7] Although sentimentalized, Anthony's and Tyler's comments suggest that nineteenth-century men and women shared a lived experience that belies the rigid rhetoric of separate and hierarchical gender roles that twentieth-century historians have ascribed to them.

Tyler's and Anthony's challenges were not the only, nor the first, public declarations of male support for woman suffrage in California.[8] Both drew upon the rhetoric of other nineteenth-century California men. For example, an impressive display of male support for woman suffrage occurred in 1870. That year, 1,308 California women signed and submitted a petition to the state legislature demanding "immediate action for an amendment of Section First, Article Second, of the Constitution of this State, as shall secure to the women of this commonwealth the right of suffrage." Current historical interpretations of the suffrage struggle as a contest solely between men and women might leave the researcher unprepared for what else was on that document: alongside the names of those female petitioners were the signatures of 2,026 men, almost double the number of women.[9]

One woman suffrage supporter, Sacramento department store founder David Lubin, used women's increasing involvement in the marketplace to justify their voting rights. He argued that the women who frequented his store were judicious and discriminating shoppers, and thus deserving of suffrage. "The wife is entitled to as much credit for intelligently expending, as is the husband in earning wages by labor," he reasoned. "The recognition of this will place the wife in the position of an equal, a partner."[10] However, as Lubin's comments about male producers and female consumers reveal, many pro-suffrage men wrestled with the contradiction between gender equality and the belief that men were natural providers. In the economic and the political realm, men struggled to adjust their assumptions about gender to a rapidly changing society. While some men fought the changes in gender relations during the late nineteenth century, others sought to shape those changes.

Despite their confusion and contradictory language, however, many nineteenth-century male supporters of female suffrage recognized that men's position at the center of public life would not hold. In an 1884 "Special Committee Report to the California Legislature," the three-man committee reported, with remarkable candor, "Yes, the times have indeed changed. In dominating the affairs of the Republic, those old notions of sex superiority are daily becoming less potential."[11] Even male anti-suffragists begrudgingly acknowledged the adamant spirit of the woman's suffrage movement. "[Woman] suffrage is like the poor," groaned one anti-suffragist senator, "it is with us always."[12]

In addition to their sometimes muddled statements, the pro-suffrage men of Assemblyman Tyler's generation shared another characteristic: they were a minority voice. They were unable to persuade enough nineteenth-century men that women had a legal place in the political arena.[13] Until 1911, the majority of California's voting men opposed woman suffrage when they had the opportunity to express themselves at the polls. In 1911, however, the efforts of both men and women convinced enough male voters that supporting woman suffrage was in keeping with the assumptions of "fit manhood."

This study of male supporters and opponents of the 1911 California woman suffrage campaign attempts to connect the scholarship of masculinity with that of the woman suffrage movement. It argues that the woman suffrage campaign created a climate in which men on both sides of the debate found it necessary to express their ideals of masculinity. Although much of the suffrage debate obviously focused on the qualities and characteristics of women, ideas about masculinity also shaped both the debate and its outcome. A change in the status and role of women engendered a revealing debate about the role of men.

Public life at the turn of the twentieth century "seemed to be filling with women. After 1890 women push[ed] ahead to perfect the politics of influence, to build organizations of working women, and to bring together the republican claim of female citizenship."[14] The "New Woman" of the late nineteenth and early twentieth centuries challenged the middle-class convention of separate spheres. According to this ideology, which supposedly took shape in the early nineteenth century with the emergence of industrial market economies and an ascendant middle class, men controlled the competitive and hostile public sphere, while women assumed the duties of domesticity—a private sphere of morality and motherhood. Middle-class ideology operated, in part, on the belief that these worlds could be kept separate.[15]

By the turn of the century, however, increasing numbers of women were assuming a more prominent place in public life. Colleges, corporations, arts and literature, and urban reform movements offered women opportunities to challenge male monopoly of the public arena. Scholars of middle-class masculinity have argued that men responded to these changes by attempting to escape or counteract its effects. They have identified the years 1880–1920 as a period of "crisis" for American men. "American women succeeded all too well to suit many American men, who by the late nineteenth century were becoming increasingly fearful of female moral, social, and cultural pre-eminence, to say nothing of growing female interest in politics."[16] According to this interpretation, men registered their discontent with the emergence of feminine cultural values by engaging in strenuous physical pursuits.

By another account, the "self-made man" of the nineteenth century gave way to the ideal of "passionate manhood" at the outset of the twentieth century. While the self-made man had been free to pursue his individual interests, he had exhibited "reason" and "governed" his passion. He had also manifested tenderness and intimacy, often forming close, emotional relationships with other males. As women entered the public realm, and as work became increasingly bureaucratized— thus emasculating men who equated masculinity with economic independence—men developed a new model of manhood. "Ambition," "combativeness" and a cult of toughness emerged as core values of masculinity.[17]

An exploration of the California woman suffrage movement of the late nineteenth and early twentieth centuries reveals a more varied scenario than the "feminization versus remasculization" dualism outlined by some historians of gender.[18] California men both *reacted to* and *participated in* the movement of women into the public sphere. The behavior of many men during this period contradicts the assertion that men simply "reacted with vehemence" to woman suffrage, and that "[f]ew middle-class men were eager to share their power and prerogatives with the opposite sex." Not all men "strenuously opposed woman suffrage," nor were they most concerned with "revitalizing manhood by opposing excessive femininity."

Many men were indeed opposed to woman suffrage. Yet in believing that all men fiercely opposed women's suffrage, scholars have failed to appreciate the intense debate among men that helped shape the woman suffrage movement and, ultimately, victory itself.[19] Without denying the extraordinary agency of women, the role men played in the suffrage campaign is critical to a full portrait of the interplay of gender during the late nineteenth and early twentieth centuries.

Because the suffrage campaign was so highly charged, it provides insight into the way many men defined masculinity during the Progressive Era. An intriguing and conspicuous theme emerged in their discussions of masculinity: *chivalry*. Associated with the antebellum South, chivalric language nonetheless appeared frequently and proved surprisingly useful to many twentieth-century California men confronting changing gender roles. Chivalry's utility and prominence were in part attributable to its elasticity. Pro-and anti-suffrage men employed the codes of chivalry, including courage, honor, and a duty to protect women, in their efforts either to help or to hinder the cause of woman suffrage. For example, whereas anti-suffrage men argued that it was men's duty to protect women from the "burdens" of the political sphere, pro-suffrage men contended that true chivalric men acted out of honor and obligation to extend women the vote.

Yet this estimate of masculine duty and honor was at cross-purposes with women's full political participation. Although pro-suffrage men contributed significantly to the victory of the campaign, those who adhered to a sense of chivalry undermined the idea of true political equality between men and women. Many pro-suffrage men cracked the chivalric armor of anti-suffrage men in 1911, but they never completely abandoned their own sense of knighthood. The comments of one pro-suffrage male a month before the 1911 campaign suggests the irony and constraints the concept of chivalry imposed upon men's ability to envision a public arena of political equality. "This is as it should be," he declared. "It is the work of the men to give you women the ballot. You have no right to be compelled to go about begging for this thing. I am glad that I shall never have to see you women of California going through the streets carrying a banner."[20]

A third group of men also engaged in this critical debate. These men attempted to break away from the inequalities inherent in chivalric discourse and attacked the foundations upon which the chivalric code rested. They challenged the assumption that men were or should be the protectors of women. In an age often characterized as a "crusade for masculinity,"[21] these men questioned the value of physical strength as a signifier of masculinity and as the pillar of social order. These vocal, "less gallant" men, although a minority, compellingly suggest the difficulty in generalizing about masculinity during the early twentieth century.

In 1911, the legal status of California's women voters was resolved when suffrage was approved. During the nine-month campaign preceding the vote, both sides of the suffrage debate reached new heights in organizing and exploiting the press. Because California voting men were so evenly divided, both sides waged a fierce campaign. As a result, although woman suffrage was only one of twenty-three issues for voters to decide in the October special election, it dominated the press, particularly during the summer and early fall of 1911.

A Victory So Narrow

In 1896, after more than a quarter century of organized pressure, pro-suffrage forces successfully persuaded California legislators to put the question of woman suffrage before the voters. Pro-suffrage women and men cooperated in their efforts to galvanize public support. Although some men may have acted independently, it appears that most contributed to the cause under the direction of female suffrage leaders. Campaign literature from 1896 reveals the various ways in which men served the needs of woman suffrage. Leaflets and posters announced the names of male speakers at suffrage rallies and women's conventions. Other men devoted time and energy canvassing districts. One booklet thanked various male county surveyors and registrars and encouraged women to seek out men "who take an active interest in politics [and] will help you out."[22] Working for the San Francisco Equal Suffrage League, "Mr. L. E. Blackman placed copies of Mill's 'Subjection of Women' on reading tables at summer resorts all over the state."[23]

A pamphlet published by the Joint Amendment Campaign Committee, an early women's association, included "Twenty Opinions on Woman Suffrage by Prominent Californians." These "Prominent Californians," all male, argued in favor of woman suffrage. One optimistic man stated that he "hope[d] that the Constitutional Amendment will be carried by so large a majority as to convince our sister states that the people of the young and vigorous West are as just as they are energetic." Businessman Taylor Rogers declared that "the ballot has only two essential elements—morality and intellect. Equally with men, women have both of these."[24] A poster used during the 1896 campaign similarly highlighted male support by listing the names of thirty pro-suffrage California men and challenged other voting men: "All of these men will vote for woman suffrage. Will you?"[25]

Anti-suffrage sentiment in 1896 was strong, though unorganized, and included both men and women. The decision of whether or not to grant women the vote was, of course, ultimately left to male voters. Although the highly organized suffrage associations conducted a determined campaign, the proposition lost by more than 10 percent (or 29,000 votes).[26] The majority of California's voting males apparently were not yet ready to concede their monopoly over voting rights.

After the 1896 defeat, pro-suffrage forces were unable to secure another proposition measure until 1911. In 1907, Assemblyman Grove L. Johnson of Sacramento authored a woman's suffrage bill that "squeaked through the Assembly on the second ballot but failed in the Senate by two votes."[27] If 1907 represented one more defeat for California's woman suffrage supporters, it also held promise: that year, the state's first Progressive organization, the Lincoln-Roosevelt League, was founded. In 1910, Progressive Republicans took control of the legislature and Hiram Johnson was elected governor on a platform that included a commitment to a public referendum on a state constitutional amendment guaranteeing woman suffrage. In her memoir of the 1911 suffrage campaign, activist Selina Solomons recalled that at the "1910 California Republican Convention we had the men whom we had worked with as a mighty bulwark for the support of our suffrage resolution."[28] Despite the allegiance of these men, woman suffrage proponents had reason to doubt whether 1911 would bring success. Nationwide, between 1870 and 1910, "four hundred and eighty campaigns produced only seventeen referenda and only two of those resulted in a victory for woman suffrage."[29]

On January 26, 1911, a state senator introduced a bill to amend the constitution to include the rights of women voters. The bill passed thirty-five to five. It then faced considerable opposition in the Assembly. Although Republicans had included woman suffrage as a plank in their 1910 party platform, many legislators balked at the concept of women's political equality. Attempting to maintain Republican credibility, according to aide E. A. Dickson, "Governor Johnson asked the recalcitrant legislators to meet in his office. He then read the suffrage platform plank on which every one of them had been elected. Bringing his hand down firmly on his desk, the Governor said, 'Gentlemen, you pledged yourself to that plank and you cannot repudiate it now.' That ended the opposition."[30]

Assemblyman James Rogers was apparently still unconvinced. During floor debate, he asked Speaker of the Assembly Oscar Hewitt, "Does it take 54 votes to pass this measure?" "It does," replied Hewitt. "Then tell me," responded Rogers, "are there 54 men in this Assembly weak enough to be led around by the nose by women?" "I don't know if there are 54," retorted Hewitt, "but I know there is one." By the end of the debate there were sixty-four more; the measure passed sixty-five to five.[31] The legislature once again agreed to let California's men decide whether women should become voters. Part of a cluster of twenty-three amendments, the woman's suffrage amendment—"Amendment Eight"—was presented to the male electorate in a special election on October 10, 1911.

Although Governor Johnson's fist-pounding might have convinced many Republican legislators to support Amendment Eight, many Californians remained unconvinced. Fueled by intense organizing and mobilizing on both sides, debate over Amendment Eight dominated the press during the summer and fall of 1911. Women's suffrage organizations had grown from twenty during the 1896 campaign to more than fifty by 1911.[32] Again, men performed a variety of roles within these organizations, including participating in woman suffrage pageants, delivering speeches, and introducing female speakers. In San Francisco, the College Equal Suffrage League employed boys to walk the streets and pass out campaign literature.[33] Men also headed auxiliaries of women's groups, such as the Men's Auxiliary of the San Francisco Equal Suffrage League, and formed independent pro-suffrage organizations, including the Men's Equal Suffrage Campaign League, the Business Men's Equal Suffrage League, and the Political Equality League of Los Angeles.[34]

Men and women also organized the first anti-suffrage organizations in the state. In early September, in Los Angeles, male business and professional leaders formed the anti-suffrage Committee of Fifty. Women formed the Northern California Association Opposed to Woman Suffrage, which had an executive committee with more than thirty members. These women distributed literature "for the purpose of conducting a purely educational campaign [to] respectfully protest against the proposed Amendment." Suffrage, claimed one of their leaflets, "IS THE DEMAND OF A MINORITY OF WOMEN, AND THE MAJORITY OF WOMEN PROTEST AGAINST IT." Another pamphlet stated:

> We are content that [men] represent US in the corn-field, on the battle-field, and at the ballot-box, and we THEM in the school-room, at the fireside, and at the cradle, believing our representation even at the ballot-box to be thus more full and impartial than it would be were the views of the few who wish suffrage adopted, contrary to the judgment of the many.[35]

Whether or not a majority of women actually opposed Amendment Eight—and that is difficult to measure—on October 10, 1911, a majority of California's male voters finally granted women the right to vote. *The Nation* proclaimed the achievement as

> the most momentous decision yet given in this country in favor of woman suffrage. So long as women could vote only in four Rocky Mountain States, of comparatively small population, the movement to enlarge the political rights of their sex might be dismissed as almost negligible. . . . This means nearly doubling at one stroke the number of women in the United States with the legal right to vote.[36]

Although it was a significant victory, the margin was so narrow that the following morning much of the press reported the *failure* of Amendment Eight. Front-page headlines in the *Los Angeles Times, San Francisco Chronicle, Sacramento Bee,* and *San Diego Tribune* all announced its defeat. By October 13, however, it became clear that the amendment had passed, 125,037 to 121,450. The slim margin of victory suggests a bitter division among male voters in 1911.

Chivalrous Men

Many men simply did not view the woman suffrage challenge as a struggle between women and men. Whereas women demonstrated extraordinary resolve in forging and advancing this movement toward their own political liberation, few men on either side of the debate found very appealing the possibility of a political contest between men and women. Numerous men on both sides perceived the woman suffrage issue as a struggle among *men*, which *men* would resolve. "The decision," stated one pro-suffrage man, "rests with the men, and it is among men that the work must be done to get active results."[37] One consequence of this assumption was that many men viewed women's new political participation not only in terms of separate gender roles, but hierarchically as well. Legally, of course, only men could *bestow* upon women the right to vote; hence, chivalry figured prominently as men deliberated whether to grant that right. Understanding the ways in which many men manipulated the rhetoric of chivalry helps explain how anti-suffrage men tried to deny women all political opportunities, and how pro-suffrage men attempted to reconcile their liberal sentiments with their persisting desire to maintain gender hierarchy in the political arena.

Anti-suffrage men believed that woman suffrage threatened the hierarchy of male and female roles. "I am opposing woman suffrage because I do not want to see women made masculine, or men becoming effeminate," stated Maurice Newmark. "I oppose anything which would change the relationship," he added.[38] An alarmed John Irish predicted that "the ultimate drift of the women's suffrage movement in this state [will] be an attack upon the husband as the legal head of the family."[39] One not-very-subtle anti-suffrage advertisement seemed to capture what many men believed to be at stake:

> MEN! In the quiet of the election booth remember the
> *Quiet* Woman At Home
> and VOTE *NO* on Amendment No. 8[40]

Anti-suffrage men found chivalric ideology particularly useful to combat their fears about a feminized public sphere and a masculinized cadre of women. According to the tenets of chivalry, man's first duty is to protect women. Thus, anti-suffrage men portrayed public politics as a competitive and dangerous arena in which only men were fit to participate. Chivalry allowed these men to defend the increasingly untenable position of separate gender spheres. Anti-suffragists argued that it was man's duty to protect women from the "dirty pool of politics" and the "burdens of government." Anti-suffragist Anthony Cummins, for example, argued that men "in good conscience can not force women to fight the battles of men." Cummins stated that only men were "equipped [to] wage political warfare."[41] Likewise, Mr. James C. Woods from northern California wrote to the *Lake County Bee* an "appeal to men as fathers, husbands, brothers and sons to protect and keep them in their womanly ways and graces."[42] And Mr. Flint of Los Angeles defended his membership in the anti-suffrage organization Committee of Fifty as his "duty to give protection to the women, who prefer their homes to the burden of government."[43]

In a letter to Secretary of State Frank Jordan, California Senator J. B. Sanford used similar reasoning to protest against the proposed Amendment Eight. In his letter, which he prefaced with the assurance that "everything said here is true and I have the data," Sanford claimed that "[t]he men are able to run the government and take care of the women." "The courageous, chivalrous, and manly men," he asserted, "and the womanly women, the real mothers and home builders of the country, are opposed to this innovation in American political life." Although

Sanford's language implied a faith in an essential "maleness" and "femaleness," he was more persuaded by "historical experience" than biology. Like many male anti-suffragists who employed the codes of chivalry, Sanford believed that men were "battle-tested" and had earned the privilege of suffrage. (Anti-suffragists agreed that only men were "fit" to vote, but they were divided over whether this was a God-given *right* or a *privilege* that was won from physical struggle.) "Do women have to vote in order to receive the protection of man?" asked Sanford. "Why, men have gone to war, endured every privation and death itself in defense of woman. There is no extreme to which he would not go for his mother or sister."[44]

An active and prolific anti-suffragist, future World War II general George S. Patton often found himself embroiled in debates over the role and meaning of masculinity in politics, and he, too, relied upon chivalric discourse to support his cause. Patton argued that since "the great majority of the women of California do not want the ballot," it was men's "duty and purpose to protect them."[45]

In a September 1911 article entitled "Why Women Should Not Be Given the Vote," Patton articulated his view of the foundation upon which political power rested, as well as the function of chivalry. "I submit that the electoral franchise is by its origin, by its evolution, a duty and an obligation, and not a privilege. . . . Politics is in its final analysis, a struggle, a contest, a combat; [it] is, in fact, merely modified war." Therefore, Patton argued, only males could claim the right of suffrage. Man possessed "courage, fortitude, and endurance"; he was a "fighting creature." Patton believed that men were "naturally" courageous fighters, and that only fighters could vote. "It is force and force only, fighting, physical brute force, if you will, that stands behind and gives efficacy to the verdict of the majority cast at the polls." Patton found it historically inaccurate—if not absurd—that women ever demonstrated, or could demonstrate, this capacity. "You cannot have an army of women," he declared. "You cannot have the city of Los Angeles policed by women."[46]

Patton responded with equal hostility to the argument that enfranchised women would ensure a virtuous, middle-class public sphere. According to Progressive proponents of woman suffrage, women "could help stamp out the liquor traffic, help pass pure-food laws, abolish child labor, and contribute to other reforms." Men "needed allies . . . who could be brought over to their cause by precisely those arguments."[47]

But if Patton, a Republican attorney, favored these types of reform, the gender barrier prevented him from welcoming female allies. "Women are prone to compare themselves with men of much inferior education and ability," complained Patton. "They Say: 'My coachman or chauffeur whom I pay can vote. . . . But this is not the true consideration. . . . [T]he same chauffeur and the same day laborer can bear arms and may be called upon to bear arms in defense of the laws which they have made."[48]

Pro-suffrage men appealed to chivalric principles as well. These men, however, drew upon the chivalric duties of honor, courage, and a willingness to *assist,* rather than an obligation simply to *protect* women. They were to be the stewards of women's entry into public political life. Sometimes this "guidance" was demonstrably condescending, as in the case of one pro-suffrage male's feeling of heavy responsibility: "The baby doesn't want to be dressed; the child doesn't want to obey, and some women don't want the ballot. But these things are good for them."[49] More often, however, this patronizing attitude was couched in the rhetoric of obligation and honor. Thomas Stevens, for example, believed that he "owe[d] women this favor" and challenged other men to "stand up and fight for her."[50]

The comments of Alva Adams, governor of Colorado, vividly illustrate that men had some sense of the dual uses of chivalry. On the one hand, he praised the California pro-suffrage men who "pride themselves upon their chivalry. Their vote upon the equal suffrage amendment will prove whether that boast is genuine or bogus." Thus he affirmed the (pro-suffrage) function of chivalry, adding that women would be safe at the polls because "every manly instinct protects her." Adams also recognized the harmful (anti-suffrage) potential of chivalry, questioning the chivalry of his opponents. " 'Save women from the dirty pool of politics,' is a frequent battle cry," he asserted. "These Chivalrous (?) men in their hearts fear that the women will clean the dirty pools." He termed such anti-suffrage men "political Don Quixotes."[51]

Other pro-suffrage men talked about woman suffrage as a "challenge" to masculinity. But unlike the anti-suffragists, and in contrast to the way many scholars have interpreted early twentieth-century masculinity, these men challenged others to prove their masculinity not by displays of bravado and physical prowess, but by supporting woman suffrage. "To take a stand against woman suffrage," declared Mr. C. C. Pierce, "is illogical, unconstitutional and silly—and, worst of all, it is unmanly!"[52] Such men viewed support for woman suffrage as a badge of honor and courage. On election eve, for example, one man appealed to the chivalry of other men by reminding them that man "has it within his power to help her, or to push her back. Shall he go ahead alone; or shall he extend her a hand; Shall he be a brute; or shall he be a MAN?"[53] For this writer, courage and honor constituted core values of masculinity, and men could demonstrate those characteristics by granting women the right to vote. Similarly, in his poem "To the Women of California with the Love of a Native Son," suffrage supporter Charles Edson adopted an imploring female persona in an appeal to men as fathers, brothers, husbands, and sons to "be noble and grant" women the vote:

> How will you vote, my father, on the thing that affects my life?
> How will you vote, my brother, in this mighty need of ours? How
>   will you vote my husband, dear half of the mighty soul[?]
> How will you vote, my man-child; strong son of my joy and
>   youth[?]
> To skulk like beaten coward! Oh! it were better he died.
> And I wait in lonely silence to hear what he has to say;
> To see if my boy deny me! God! what a bitter day![54]

Edson's language poignantly illustrates the perception among many pro-suffrage men that women were at the mercy of chivalric men. Edson's poem goes on to portray women as "maidens" and "loving breeders" who fear "strife," expressing the difficulty many pro-suffrage men had envisioning political equality between men and women. This romantic view of the vulnerability of women undergirded chivalry and undermined male pro-suffrage support. Another California pro-suffrage poet, Marcus A. Stewart, likewise suggested that woman suffrage would ensure "a purer mode of life and better laws."[55]

Although female suffragists also had used the argument of social expediency (that women's virtue would benefit society),[56] the arguments of many pro-suffrage men appeared to leave little room for women to engage in meaningful political struggles. The comments of woman suffrage supporter Robert Burdette provide an excellent example of the way some pro-suffrage men placed women upon political pedestals. A female anti-suffragist had publicly challenged Burdette to a debate. He responded to her in print: "My Dear Mrs. Scott: I must decline acceptance of your challenge. I am not, and have never been a 'woman fighter.' I fight for her, and do my best to help her secure the privileges to which I think she is entitled. But I have never taken the field against her."

However, Burdette made a counteroffer more fitting to his sense of chivalry: "Select any on of your 'Committee of Fifty' and I will meet him gladly. In a righteous cause it is a joy to grapple with a man.

But I don't know how to fight a woman. I have never tried."[57] Although Burdette never made clear what political role he believed women should have, he clearly shared an assumption with his male anti-suffrage counterparts that women were not fit for public political combat.

A battle more appropriate to Burdette's chivalric sensibilities took place between anti-suffragist John Irish and pro-suffragist Charles Aked. The much-anticipated debate between these two men almost did not happen. The *San Francisco Call* announced, "Irish Dodges Suffrage Duel with Dr. Aked." Apparently, Irish, "the forensic gladiator and champion of the anti-suffrage cause," had "violated the code duello and repudiated the terms arranged for debate [by each] man's seconds." Once the difficulties were resolved, however, the "duel" proceeded. The *Call* reported that the large audience "followed every thrust and parry with about the same inhibition of enthusiasm as is found at a heavyweight ringside." In the end, the reporter judged the contest a draw and was pleased that both men had adhered to the "code of honor."[58]

Occasionally, women also acknowledged the centrality of chivalry among pro-suffrage males, and sometimes even reinforced the very chivalric rhetoric that militated against their own political equality. Selina Solomons, for example, recalled the role of chivalrous men during the 1911 campaign. "We heard a great deal during the suffrage campaign about the 'dirty pool of politics,' " she remembered. "We California women know nothing of such a place. Our California men with real chivalry cleaned up our state. We would never have had the ballot otherwise."[59] Bridelle Washburn concluded her speech to a meeting of businessmen by demanding, "Men of California, do not be afraid to do your duty to your women folk October 10."[60]

In contrast, one anti-suffragist female recognized the role of chivalry among male supporters, but critiqued its usage. "I feel confident that you gentlemen here," Mary Martin told an audience of pro-suffrage men, "wearing votes-for-women buttons which have been pinned upon you preforce [*sic*] and which are allowed to remain only by the sufferance of chivalry, will vote according to the dictates of your intelligence and not of your suffragettes."[61] Martin acknowledged the importance of chivalry for pro-suffrage men, but suggested that women were manipulating these men. This challenged the chivalric idea of male stewardship.

Unsurprisingly, her comments provoked a reaction. Mr. L. N. Whealton wrote to the newspaper that published Martin's comments, condemning her "insult to those men advocating the cause by saying they were sissy and were cowards for attempting to shift the burden of the government on women." Whealton defended the "duty of courageous men" to "extend to women" the right of suffrage.[62]

Extending the right to vote did not necessarily signal that pro-suffrage men had committed themselves to women's full political equality. In fact, many pro-suffrage men manifested an exceedingly literal interpretation of Amendment Eight: women should be permitted to vote. But many also found it difficult to move beyond this limited measure of political emancipation.

An Innocuous Vision

"Are the Men of California about to admit the Women of California to full partnership in the affairs of government?" asked woman-suffrage supporter Arthur Pillsbury. "That is the issue put to us in this proposed amendment in striking out the word 'male' wherever it occurs." His own answer suggests the contradictions inherent in the support of many male supporters. "It is perhaps true enough that a woman cannot always reason much straighter than she can throw a stone," he stated, but the social benefits that would result from her "more sensitive instincts" persuaded Pillsbury to support "full political partnership with the men of California." Yet his condescension betrays his lack of sincerity. "Therefore we must accept woman at the polls," he continued, "if we are to grant her the right of suffrage, as we accept her at the marriage altar, for better or for worse, because we love her and [she deserves] every advantage in so far as she is physically capable of participation in the free life of a free people." Pillsbury concluded with an appeal to the chivalry of his fellow male pro-suffragists: "Let us therefore bravely take the hazard [and] adopt Constitutional Amendment Eight."[63]

Many pro-suffrage men tried to negotiate the entry of women into public political life by denying the potential consequences woman suffrage presented. Even before the victory of 1911, many pro-suffrage men were already attempting to fit female voters into an increasingly obsolete ideological box. These men continued to maintain an allegiance to a male-dominated political sphere and failed to realize—or perhaps realized all too well—the contradiction in granting women political rights while trying to keep them in the home. Many men strained to keep control of these profound political changes. "Women should have the vote," wrote Mr. S. A. Crary from Palo Alto.

> I quite agree that home is distinctly the woman's sphere, and when she leaves it, even temporarily, to enter politics, she lowers herself. . . . [B]ut there is no necessity for woman doing more than to vote. Give women the vote and only a few will abuse it by descending to the level of man and neglecting their homes for the sake of politics.[64]

The desire that women not "descend" to the level of men was consistent with the codes of chivalry. By presenting gender hierarchy in which women were presumably (morally?) at the top, men such as Crary hoped to maintain control of the battlefield on which men waged political struggle. Arming women to engage as equals with men in that arena would, in actuality, have represented an "ascent" for many women in terms of political power and influence.

Suffrage supporter Chas Bell expressed the way many pro-suffrage men hoped that women would utilize the franchise.

> She is the happiest among women who is blessed with a home and a family. If women vote it will not destroy the home. It only means a short time once or twice a year to go to the polls and deposit a marked piece of paper, and during these few minutes she wields a power that is doing more to protect her home and all other homes than any other possible influence, and she need not neglect her household nor her children in order to do it.[65]

This innocuous and constraining vision of women voters contradicted the expectations of many suffragists. Bell envisioned little change in the responsibilities of (and opportunities for) women. But many suffragists viewed woman suffrage as another way, along with women's experiences in settlement houses and other reform groups, to exploit the rhetoric of motherhood and family to enlarge the social role of women.[66] As one California woman stated, "what this country of ours needs and needs badly is some mother-made laws."[67] To those who thought that woman suffrage would lead to an enlarged sphere of influence and activity for women, Bell responded: "On the contrary, she will stick closer to her home after having reached the goal of her ambition."[68]

Although not a Californian, Adolphus Knopf, in an article for the Progressive magazine the *California Outlook,* addressed the fears of anti-suffragists (and many pro-suffragists) that woman suffrage would destroy the home. "I ask, why in the name of common sense, should a woman's love for home, husband, and children be lessened because she absents herself three or four times a year for either local, state, or federal elections?"[69] Like many pro-suffrage men, Knopf did not acknowledge the potential of woman suffrage, beyond periodical ventures from the home to quickly cast a ballot.

Mr. H. G. Redwine's views similarly demonstrate the contradictory notions held by many men about women's domestic responsibilities and political opportunities. Redwine declared that "it is fitting and proper that the independent, manly and free-thinking west should be the first part of the Union which places its women upon a real equality with man." He then reassured himself and others that while "[i]t is perhaps unfortunate that using the ballot will take woman away from her work[,] probably a little rest of an hour or so for one or two days in the year will do her little harm and the family can afford it."[70] Suffrage supporter Mattison B. Jones candidly admitted his fears concerning the "effect of woman suffrage on the home." "That phase of the question has given me more study and fear than all others combined," he admitted. "I bow with all respect to the many men of California who have never entertained a fear that the ballot in the hands of our women would tend to dethrone the queen of the home."[71]

Although men who disagreed over woman suffrage often agreed over a hierarchical view of gender and politics, the 1911 campaign also witnessed a third group of men who rejected the codes of chivalry and even some who questioned the logic of separate gender spheres. These pro-suffrage males, more than any other middle-class men in California, expressed—and appeared to accept—the idea of political equality between men and women.[72] They refuted the arguments and assumptions that the strength and courage of men obligated them to protect women.

The Attack against Chivalry

Chivalry was also an important element in the arguments of this third group of men in the woman suffrage debate. However, these pro-suffrage men used chivalry as a way not to reject or limit women's political participation, but to define what they believed were antiquated theories of masculinity and politics. Indeed, they began to question the long-held association of masculinity with politics. Some even began to acknowledge the "domestication of politics." As the state began to assume many of the functions formerly associated with women and the family, women claimed a right to help shape those state policies. Consequently, "sharp separations between men's and women's participation abated."[73] Some pro-suffrage men supported and contributed to this transformation.

San Francisco resident Frederick Baker forcefully articulated the logic of the new order. "If woman's sphere was restricted to the home, as in the old days," he wrote,

> then the argument that there is no necessity for her to share the burden of government would have weight. But, in the face of the economic conditions which have forced her from the home into the arena of the business world, in factory, store, workshop, and the thousand avenues of toil, for man to say he shall have the exclusive right to prescribe the conditions under which she shall labor is to place his co-partner in life's battle in the category of the dumb brute."[74]

Arguing in support of woman suffrage and addressing a popular fear of anti-suffragists, a male editorial writer stated that "Barbarous man did not become unsexed when he occasionally left his spear in the hut and worked with his mate in the field. Woman will not become unsexed when she lays down her distaff and joins her mate in the field of politics." This author, as well as other pro-suffrage men, recognized and rejected the patriarchal and historically constructed idea of separate gender roles. As Charles Borger, secretary of the Citizens' Suffrage League, explained, "it would be funny if it were not so serious, to listen to the arguments [of anti-suffragists] that 'woman should keep the places and attend the duties God intended her for.'"[75]

Many pro-suffrage men countered the arguments of the anti-suffragists by attacking the idea that physical force buttressed the public political arena. "Government in this day," wrote a Mr. Parker to the *Santa Monica Daily Outlook,* "is not founded upon sheer force." J. S. B. likewise expressed his dismay with the attitude that men must "retain the manly power of lawgiving."[76] Rufus Steele took a slightly different approach, arguing that women were also battle-tested. The argument is made, he said, "that women should not be allowed to vote because women can not carry arms. This blank cartridge is fired repeatedly quite as though Jeanne d'Arc had never led her army to the relief of Orleans, as though Moll Pitcher had never been made a sergeant by Washington, as though it were never a commonplace for the soft voiced ladies of Plymouth to pot an Indian between hymns."[77]

In an article in the *West Coast Magazine,* pro-suffragist Clifford Howard wrote,

> Politics, declares [the anti-suffragist,] is merely modified war; it rests ultimately upon brute force, and therefore belongs exclusively to the masculine, combative element of society. But it is not true that that condition still inheres in modern politics, and is the underlying directing force of our government. . . . It no longer avails to declare that the man can represent the woman, and that he can act for her in politics. Politics is no longer a one-sex function. It has become involuntarily bisexual.[78]

In his attack against anti-suffragist John Irish, suffragist Clinton White challenged the idea that physical ideals of masculinity guaranteed men suffrage rights over women:

> The papers state that John P. Irish and others are advancing the argument that women should not be permitted the right of suffrage because men are called upon to do police duty and serve in the army. My observation is that there is only about one man in fifty physically fit to be a policeman and perhaps not more than one in twenty when age and bodily health are considered, who would be accepted as a soldier. No doubt Irish thinks himself entitled to the right of suffrage, but if he bases it upon the proposition that he is also fit to be a policeman or a soldier, it would seem to his friends and acquaintances perfectly evident that his vote would have to be rejected.[79]

Charles Willard "confessed" that "fifteen years ago [1896] I voted against woman's suffrage in California, and up to a few years ago wrote and argued against it. But that was before I was converted and born again." Willard explained that he finally found hollow the argument that men alone endured the burdens of society. Pointing to the Civil War, he noted that "we hear a lot about the fighting spirit of the Southern men"; but, he asked, "does history show anything more magnificent than the courage and the patience and the strength of the Southern Women in that terrible conflict?" In using this example, Willard appears to attack the idea of chivalry at the site of what is perhaps its American birthplace. "The definition of a vote as a burden rather than a right is nothing but word play," he argued. "When we elect a mayor and council we never measure their bicep muscles."[80]

These pro-suffrage men attempted to expose the inequality inherent in the rhetoric of chivalry. "Of course it is very gallant on the part of us men," chided T. J. Brenan, "to assume the whole responsibility of government; and to flatter ourselves that we do it in order to spare the 'weaker sex' the strain and stress incidental to political life."[81] Clifford Howard also wasted few words in his attack on chivalry, stating that "the assertion that the women without the ballot are readily able at all times to secure through petition whatever reasonable laws they may desire, springs wholly from the chivalric instinct of the gentleman." "Always the woman has been handicapped," he concluded, "by the chivalrous man, who, thinking to shield and to help her, has acted as a constant deterrent to her development."[82] Howard and other pro-suffrage men realized that chivalry was their strongest opponent in the fight for women's full political participation.

Although the codes of chivalry may seem to hold little meaning for us today, they resonated deeply with the men and women involved in California's political turmoil in the early twentieth century. During the 1911 California woman suffrage campaign, men positioned themselves around the concept of chivalry—whether employing it or attacking it. Understanding its function in the struggle over woman's suffrage deepens our perception of mens' experience during the early twentieth century and demonstrates the significance of the language of masculinity in the woman suffrage movement. The contradictions and irony found in the positions taken by the three groups of men outlined in this study illuminates, rather than obstructs, our understanding of gender during the early part of this century.

Choosing winners and losers from the 1911 woman suffrage campaign is more complicated than simply counting votes. The women of California won the right to cast ballots alongside men. Despite their victory and their stronger political voice, women's full political participation remained elusive even after 1911. Anti-suffragist men (and women) lost their cause. But, along with some pro-suffrage men, they continued to work to limit equality. The pro-suffrage men who attempted to defeat the resilient codes of chivalry appear to have achieved some success. By exposing the incompatibility of chivalry and democracy, they pulled the props out from underneath gender hierarchy. "The hands of the clock never go backward," stated one pro-suffrage male, who perceptively added, "The question may not be settled right on

October 10, but the world moves and women are coming into their own."[83]

Nearly one year after the woman suffrage victory, a California magazine published a retrospective article about the campaign, reminding its readers that chivalry had been a central theme of the woman suffrage struggle. For many Californians, already adapting to fundamental changes in gender roles, the verses of a suffrage poem sounded quaint and increasingly strange.

> The spirit of chivalry—ages at rest—
> Has sprung like a phoenix to life in the west.
> That women should vote, says a group of gallants,
> Is wrong and oppressive—unless they wear pants
> We're chivalrous men and we won't have a fuss
> The women be damned; why, the government's US.[84]

NOTES

1. "Men Will Help Our Fight," *Los Angeles Herald,* September 1, 1911, p. 5.

2. "To the Women of California with the Love of a Native," in Charles Edson Biographical Letter File, California State Library, Sacramento.

3. "Men's Association to Fight Equal Suffrage," *Los Angeles Times,* September 8, 1911, sec. 2, p. 1.

4. *Sacramento Bee,* March 25, 1880, p. 3.

5. *The Daily Alta California,* March 21, 1880, p. 2.

6. "Assembly Report," *Sacramento Daily Record-Union,* March 27, 1880, p. 1.

7. Ibid., 3.

8. In 1878, U.S. Senator Aaron A. Sargent of California introduced an (unsuccessful) amendment to the U.S. Constitution favoring woman's suffrage. Wyoming and Utah men legislated woman suffrage in 1869 and 1870, respectively.

9. "Petition for Woman's Suffrage. In Senate, March 2, 1870," in California Woman Suffrage Archive, Bancroft Library, University of California, Berkeley (hereafter UCB). An organized woman's suffrage movement in California began in 1870. Associations such as the California Woman Suffrage Association and, during the next two decades, the College Equal Rights League, the San Francisco Equal Suffrage League, the Political Equality Club of Alameda County, and the Young Woman's Suffrage Club, mobilized the support of women and men. Although it is clear that women overwhelmingly supplied the creative and energetic

force of these organizations, it is also evident from the memoirs of these pioneering women and the campaign literature itself that men participated in these movements in various ways, including speaking, canvassing, and consulting. By 1911, men had formed auxiliary groups within many of the women's suffrage organizations, in addition to forming independent associations such as the several chapters of the Men's Equal Suffrage Campaign League. As the campaign literature illustrates, female suffragists also frequently drafted male speakers. *California Women: A Guide to Their Politics* (San Francisco, n.p., [1967]).

10. David Lubin, "Are the Scales Evenly Balanced?" p. 12, in California Woman Suffrage Archive, Bancroft Library, UCB.

11. "Special Committee Report to the California Legislature," p. 5, in California Woman Suffrage Archive, Bancroft Library, UCB.

12. Quoted in Lillian Harris Coffin, "The Woman Suffrage Amendment," *California Weekly,* December 30, 1910, p. 75.

13. I say "legal" because, as scholars have noted, women participated in politics through reform movements and even political parades. See Mary P. Ryan, *Women in Public: Between Banners and Ballots, 1825–1880* (Baltimore: Johns Hopkins University Press, 1990).

14. Sara Evans, *Born for Liberty: A History of Women in America* (New York: Free Press, 1989), 142–43.

15. See, for example, Mary Ryan, *Cradle of the Middle Class: The Family in Oneida County, New York, 1790–1865* (New York: Cambridge University Press, 1981), 155. See also Stuart M. Blumin, *The Emergence of the Middle Class: Social Experience in the American City, 1760–1900* (New York: Cambridge University Press, 1989); Nancy Cott, *The Bonds of Womanhood: "Woman's Sphere" in New England, 1780–1835* (New Haven: Yale University Press, 1977); Karen Halttunen, *Confidence Men and Painted Women: A Study of Middle-Class Culture in America, 1830–1870* (New Haven: Yale University Press, 1982).

16. Joe L. Dubbert, "Progressivism and the Masculinity Crisis," in Elizabeth H. Pleck and Joseph H. Pleck, eds., *The American Man* (Englewood Cliffs, N.J.: Prentice-Hall, 1980), 307.

17. E. Anthony Rotundo, *American Manhood: Transformations in Masculinity from the Revolution to the Modern Era* (New York: Basic Books, 1993), 5–6, 227–32.

18. Other scholars are involved in efforts to challenge and refine the broad brush strokes of the pioneering work by historians of masculinity. For a representative example, see Mark C. Carnes and Clyde Griffen, eds., *Meanings for Manhood: Constructions of Masculinity in Victorian America* (Chicago: University of Chicago Press, 1990).

19. Rotundo, *American Manhood,* 220.

20. Quoted in Coffin, "Woman Suffrage Amendment," 75.

21. This phrase is Ann Douglas's in *The Feminization of American Culture,* rev. ed. (New York: Anchor Press, 1988), 327.

22. "Instructions to Chairmen of Assembly Districts," in California Woman Suffrage Archive, Bancroft Library, UCB.

23. Woman suffrage leaflet, November 1896, in California Woman Suffrage Archive, Bancroft Library, UCB.

24. "Twenty Opinions on Woman Suffrage," Joint Amendment Campaign Committee, San Francisco, November 3, 1896, in California Woman Suffrage Archive, Bancroft Library, UCB.

25. California Equal Suffrage Association poster, in California Woman Suffrage Archive, Bancroft Library, UCB.

26. Susan B. Anthony and Ida Husted Harper, eds., *The History of Woman Suffrage,* vol. 4 (New York: National American Woman Suffrage Association, 1922), 478–93.

27. Susan Englander, *Class Conflict and Coalition in the California Woman Suffrage Movement, 1907–1912* (Queenston, Ont.: Edwin Mellen Press, 1992), 78.

28. Selina Solomons, *How We Won the Vote in California: A True Story of the Campaign of 1911* (San Francisco: New Woman Publishing Co., n.d.).

29. Evans, *Born for Liberty,* 153.

30. Quoted in Royce D. Delmatier et. al., *The Rumble of California Politics, 1848–1970* (New York: John Wiley and Sons, 1970), 168.

31. Quoted in College Equal Suffrage League of Northern California, *Winning Equal Suffrage in California: Reports of the Committees of the College Equal Suffrage League of Northern California in the Campaign of 1911* (San Francisco: National College Equal Suffrage League, 1913), 27.

32. Englander, *Class Conflict and Coalition,* 76.

33. College Equal Suffrage League, *Winning Equal Suffrage,* 29, 42.

34. Solomons, *How We Won the Vote,* 10–16.

35. "Some Reasons Why We Oppose Votes for Women," Northern California Association Opposed to Woman Suffrage pamphlet, in California Woman Suffrage Archive, Bancroft Library, UCB.

36. *The Nation,* October 19, 1911, p. 17.

37. C. D. Willard, "The Women's Campaign," *California Outlook,* August 26, 1911, p. 3.

38. "Men's Association to Fight Equal Suffrage," *Los Angeles Times,* September 8, 1911, sec. 2, p. 1.

39. John Irish, *Sacramento Bee,* October 6, 1911, p. 2.

40. *Fullerton News,* October 4, 1911, p. 4.

41. "Suffrage Opponents Organize," *San Diego Sun,* June 26, 1911, p. 4.

42. James C. Woods, letters to the editor, *Lake County Bee,* October 5, 1911, p. 1.

43. "Men's Association to Fight," *Los Angeles Times,* September 8, 1911, p. 7.

44. J. B. Sanford, letter to Secretary of State Frank Jordan, June 24, 1911, in "1911 Special Election—Arguments for and against Constitutional Amendments" file, California State Archives, Sacramento.

45. "Men's Association to Fight," 1, 7. Most anti-suffragists argued that a majority of women did not want the vote because men already protected them. In a strange twist of this logic of chivalric duty and guidance, one male anti-suffragist stated that if Amendment Eight passed he would "insist on his wife's exercising it [the vote], if he had to march her to the polls with a shot-gun." Quoted in Solomons, *How We Won the Vote,* 16.

46. George S. Patton, "Why Women Should Not Be Given the Vote," *West Coast Magazine,* September, 1911, 689–90.

47. Aileen Kraditor, *The Ideas of the Woman Suffrage, 1890–1920* (New York: W. W. Norton, 1981), 73–74.

48. Patton, "Why Women Should Not Be Given the Vote," 698.

49. "Has His Hopes: Woman's Right to the Ballot," *Los Angeles Times,* September 4, 1911, sec. 2, p. 3.

50. *San Diego Sun,* August 7, 1911, p. 3.

51. "Alva Adams Tells Truth about Suffrage," *Pasadena Star,* October 9, 1911, p. 3.

52. "700 Men Cheer Argument for Ballot for Women," *Los Angeles Herald,* September 23, 1911, p. 3.

53. "Not One Convincing Argument against Woman Suffrage," *Sacramento Bee,* October 9, 1911, sec. 1, p. 3.

54. Edson Biographical Letter File, California State Library, Sacramento.

55. "Votes-for-Women Invasion Inspires Sacramento Poet," *San Francisco Bulletin,* September 1, 1911, p. 3.

56. See, for example, Kraditor, *The Ideas of Woman Suffrage;* Anne Firor Scott, *Natural Allies: Women's Associations in American History* (Urbana: University of Illinois Press, 1991).

57. *Santa Ana Register,* September 27, 1911, p. 4.

58. *San Francisco Call,* October 5, 1911, p. 19; October 6, 1911, p. 16.

59. Solomons, *How We Won the Vote,* 4–5.

60. "Votes for Women Is the Slogan of the Fair Sex," *Salinas Daily Index,* August 16, 1911, p. 1.

61. "Realty Board Enjoys Animated Discussion of Woman's Suffrage," *Long Beach Press,* October 4, 1911, p. 10.

62. Letter to the editor, *Long Beach Press,* October 6, 1911, p. 2.

63. "Senate Constitutional Amendment Number 8," *California Outlook,* July 22, 1911, p. 3.

64. Letter to the editor, *Palo Alto Times,* October 9, 1911, p. 5.

65. Chas Bell, letter to Secretary of State Frank Jordan, June 8, 1911, in "1911 Special Election—Arguments for and against Constitutional Amendments" file, p. 4, California State Archives, Sacramento.

66. Mary P. Ryan, *Womanhood in America: From Colonial Times to the Present* (New York: New Viewpoints Publishers, 1975), 137–39.

67. Mrs. Chauncey H. Dunn, "Let's Have Mother-Made Laws, Too," *Sacramento Bee,* October 7, 1911, p. 10.

68. Bell, letter to Jordan, 4.

69. Adolphus Knopf, "Why I Believe in Woman Suffrage," *California Outlook,* August 26, 1911, p. 7.

70. "Woman Is Wanted in Politics," *Los Angeles Herald,* September 24, 1911, p. 4.

71. "Judicial Review of Suffrage Question," *Los Angeles Herald,* October 5, 1911, p. 4.

72. Many of these men, like many women, were bound by the notion that women's greatest public contributions would center on health, family, and moral issues.

73. Paula Baker, "The Domestication of Politics: Women and American Political Society, 1780–1920," in Ellen Carol DuBois and Vicki L. Ruiz, eds., *Unequal Sisters: A Multicultural Reader in U.S. Women's History* (New York: Routledge, 1990), 82.

74. "Vote 'Yes' on the Equal Suffrage Amendment," *San Francisco Call,* October 4, 1911, p. 6.

75. "League Secretary Expresses His Views," *Pasadena Star,* September 3, 1911, p. 6.

76. "Suffrage," *Santa Monica Daily Outlook,* August 8, 1911, p. 4; *Daily Palo Alto Times,* October 7, 1911, p. 4.

77. *San Francisco Call,* October 8, 1911, p. 17.

78. Clifford Howard, "Why Women Should Be Given the Vote," *West Coast Magazine,* October, 1911, pp. 33, 40.

79. Clinton White, *Sacramento Bee,* October 5, 1911, p. 4.

80. Charles Willard, "Woman's Inherent Right to the Ballot," *California Outlook,* October 7, 1911, pp. 7–8.

81. Leaflet published by the Equal Suffrage Club, April 11, 1911, in California Woman Suffrage Archive, Bancroft Library, UCB.

82. Howard, "Why Women Should Be Given the Vote," 41–42.

83. "Women Will Exercise Uplift in Politics," *Los Angeles Herald,* October 4, 1911, p. 4.

84. Estelle Lawton Lindsay, "Woman Suffrage in California," *West Coast Magazine,* July 1912, p. 435.

Chapter Thirteen

The "Flabby American," the Body, and the Cold War

Robert L. Griswold

John F. Kennedy's "The Soft American," which appeared in the December 26, 1960, issue of *Sports Illustrated,* began the president-elect's campaign to reinstill physical vigor (a favorite Kennedy word) in the American people. He praised the Greeks' conviction that physical excellence and athletic skill were "among the prime foundations of a vigorous state" and then suggested that intellectual ability could not be separated from physical well-being: "But we do know what the Greeks knew: that intelligence and skill can only function at the peak of their capacity when the body is healthy and strong; that hardy spirits and tough minds usually inhabit sound bodies."[1]

Tough minds lodged in tough bodies were now at risk, undermined by America's material success. And the young, the nation's future, seemed imperiled: "A single look at the packed parking lot of the average high school," wrote Kennedy, "will tell us what has happened to the traditional hike to school that helped to build young bodies." Nor were cars alone to blame. Prosperity had reshaped the American body: what had once been "hard" was now "soft," what had once been full of vigor could now scarcely bestir itself from the car seat or the television chair. Modern life itself was the culprit: "The television set, the movies and the myriad conveniences and distractions of modern life all lure our young people away from the strenuous physical activity that is the basis of fitness in youth and in later life."[2] America's destiny, Kennedy feared, was sinking beneath a sea of flab.

With the *Sports Illustrated* article, Kennedy hoped to jump-start the fitness program established by President Dwight D. Eisenhower in July

1956. The first President's Council on Youth Fitness had experienced energetic leadership under its director, Shane MacCarthy, but the Kennedy administration wanted more action and less talk, more pushups and fewer conferences. Thus, the new administration launched a school-based program that soon had millions of children exercising the prescribed minimum of fifteen minutes per day—sometimes to the strains of the popular exercise song, "Chickenfat." They also took a battery of tests that stretched abdominals, flexed biceps, and challenged lung capacity in the six-hundred-yard run. The stakes could not be higher, for behind the fitness campaign were concerns about American morality, postwar consumerism, masculinity, and even the survival of democracy itself. Americans could choose vigor or torpor, put their bodies in action or invite perilous risks. As Kennedy later wrote: "We are, all of us, as free to direct the activities of our bodies as we are to pursue the objects of our thought. But if we are to retain this freedom, for ourselves and for generations yet to come, then we must also be willing to work for the physical toughness on which the courage and intelligence and skill of man so largely depend."[3]

The words have that familiar Kennedy ring—"freedom," "toughness," "courage." His own hard body shaped on the playing fields of Hyannisport, Choate, and Harvard and tested in war in the Solomon Islands, Kennedy called his troops to their stations by first summoning their bodies to action.[4] In his *Sports Illustrated* essay, Kennedy noted that young American men have always been willing and able to fight for freedom but warned that the strength and stamina needed for battle did not come easily: "These only come from bodies which have been conditioned by a lifetime of participation in sports and interest in physical activity." He then invoked a common man's version of Wellington's famous dictum—"our struggles against aggressors throughout our history have been won on the playgrounds and corner lots and fields of America"—and warned that "our growing softness, our increasing lack of physical fitness, is a menace to our security."[5]

How, Kennedy seemed to be asking, could we "pay any price, bear any burden, meet any hardship, support any friend, oppose any foe" if we were too weak to defend freedom? Thus, the fitness crusade of the Kennedy administration focused cultural discourse on the body. A critical look at this effort helps us explore important dimensions of American culture, clarify the body as a cultural symbol, reveal how cultural anxieties are written onto the body, and expose conflicting conceptions of gender. The fitness crusades of the Kennedy and Eisenhower administrations suggest that the body of youth—especially male youth—became the repository for a host of cultural anxieties about Cold War America and men's place within it. The concern for physical fitness, at its core, set about redeeming manhood, reenergizing masculinity, and restoring force, dynamism, and control to males in a culture full of doubts and contradictions about men's future.[6]

I say *manhood* for this reason: although the fitness campaign included both boys and girls, the great preponderance of the discourse focused on boys, and it did so because flabby boys—and ultimately a flabby, defenseless, "womanlike" manhood—was the target of cultural concern. The physical fitness movement arose at a time of great cultural anxiety about the future of American manhood. The wartime psychiatric disorders of fighting men, cultural anxieties about the absence of fathers during the war, and postwar adjustment problems of veterans were all recent history. Sociologists struggled to find a place for men in the contemporary family and worried incessantly about conformity and the loss of manly character, while pundits like Philip Wylie and experts like Edward Strecker feared that mothers had simply overwhelmed the family and had rendered manhood impotent. Work offered no salvation. C. Wright Mills believed that corporate life transformed men into "cogs in a business machinery." One of the most celebrated plays of the postwar era, Arthur Miller's *Death of a Salesman,* depicted the failure of middle-class men—through the character of Willy Loman—who were burdened with responsibilities they could not meet and expectations they could not fulfill. Even Hollywood had its say, especially in a series of *noire* films filled with images of male paranoia, senseless violence, and ubiquitous failure.[7]

Men's gender failure could be far more troubling than that of poor Willy Loman. The *Kinsey Report* on male sexuality in 1948 shocked Americans with its revelations about homosexuality, and the homosexual "menace" became one of the key anxieties of the age. The McCarthy era saw redoubled efforts to search out and punish "gender inverts." Targets abounded: "Egg sucking phony liberals," East Coast intellectuals, and emasculated "pinks, punks, and perverts" were all part of a government that was, in the words of one of McCarthy's aides, "a veritable nest of Communists, fellow travelers, homosexuals, effete Ivy League intellectuals and traitors." Even Adlai Stevenson did not escape such bashing: the *New York Daily News* called him "Adelaide" and

ridiculed his supporters as "Harvard lace cuff liberals" to whom Stevenson spoke in a "fruity" voice. In the midst of such rhetoric, a sex-crimes
panic swept America in the late 1940s and early 1950s and led to lurid
press reports, mass meetings of outraged citizens, beefed-up security
programs at schools, and the establishment of fifteen state government
commissions to study the threat to children posed by "sexual degener-
ates." For their part, psychiatrists and government officials denounced
overbearing mothers and passive fathers as the root of the problem and
urged teachers, clergymen, and police to keep a sharp eye out for boys
who were effeminate and to direct such youth to guidance centers for
psychiatric counseling.[8]

Looming over all of these fears was the Cold War itself and the belief
that America was on a collision course with the Soviet Union. "Brinks-
manship," "throw weight," "massive retaliation," "flexible response,"
and a host of other phrases symbolized the anxieties of the age. The
fitness campaign occurred within this context: it was an effort to rescue
manhood by rescuing the body, to teach boys, as one theorist put it, to
use the body in "forceful and space-occupying ways." Such bodies are
crucial to the development of male identity; to learn to be a male is to
learn to project a physical presence that speaks of latent power.[9] Promoters of physical fitness hoped to do as much for American boys and,
in so doing, to revitalize manhood so that it could better meet the
Communist threat to national survival. Cold Wars could not be fought
with soft bodies.

The Roots of Softness

Promotion of physical fitness began in the mid-1950s, when John Kelly,
a Philadelphia businessman, one-time Olympic sculler, and long-time
advocate of physical fitness, learned that in every category the physical
fitness of American boys and girls lagged far behind their European
counterparts. Kelly, who had been United States Director of Physical
Fitness during World War II, brought his concerns to Senator James H.
Duff, who, in turn, contacted President Eisenhower. These contacts led
to a White House luncheon, out of which came the establishment by
presidential proclamation of the President's Council on Youth Fitness
and the President's Citizens Advisory Committee on the Fitness of American Youth. By July 1956 the fitness crusade was underway.[10]

In defending the need for a fitness program, authorities explored the causes of the bodily weakness of American youth. Their explanations turned the body itself into a metaphor of American life. Just as American culture once had been disciplined by sacrifice and hard work, so had the body. Now, just as the culture had become morally corrupt and a prisoner of materialism and technology, so too had the body. Americans once had been a group of sturdy pioneers, living the simple life, diligently working in fields and shops in the countryside and in small towns. Sadly, their descendants had become a soft-bodied society of weaklings, living in complex environments, pushing buttons in the glass towers of downtown skyscrapers or sitting mindlessly in front of television sets in the affluence of their suburban homes.

This vision of declension appeared in many places, but none more clearly than in the speeches of Dr. Shane MacCarthy, executive director of Eisenhower's Council on Youth Fitness. MacCarthy had served in the CIA, spoke frequently on juvenile delinquency and the evils of Communism, and, more than anyone else, promoted the fitness movement during the Eisenhower era.[11] In his view, America had moved from a "rugged, primal" society that naturally built muscles to an industrial one where "the tendency is to put first the aspect of ease and soft enjoyment."[12] Many others shared his belief that technology and automation had become enemies of the body. A public health educator saw a general softening of the culture: "It seems difficult to avoid the conclusion that our motorized, mechanized, 'effort-saver' civilization is rapidly making us as soft as our processed foods, our foam rubber mattresses, and our balloon tires."[13] The very forces that had made America the envy of the world, that had expanded leisure and eliminated so much drudgery, were literally devouring the bodily strength of its citizens. MacCarthy feared the worst. Labor-saving devices sapped bodily strength that could only be restored by a conscientious, vigorous exercise program.[14] Otherwise, the "self, the person, the individual may well be lost in a mass accumulation of mechanical might."[15]

If technology was the driving force, materialism comprised the visible manifestation of the body's decline. The condition of the body mirrored the condition of the culture. John Friedrich, a Michigan physical educator, decried the flabbiness of Americans and attributed it to materialism run amok. "Living in the lap of luxury and enjoying a state of affluence induced by our high level of prosperity has resulted in a sapping of the vigor of the people of this nation."[16] Worst of all, wrote a New Mexico official, Americans seemed utterly complacent about their situation: "The movies took us away from home, the radio brought us back, and television glued us there," but despite admonitions to exercise, Americans resisted any effort to interfere with the "comfortable and pleasant process of physical deterioration."[17]

The bodies of children were especially vulnerable to material excess. Over-indulgent parents in over-heated homes carted children off to school in over-sized cars, and the results were now mirrored in the over-sized bodies of the young. Whereas schools once worried about "the gangling, underweight child and set up special milk periods for him," now the problem was one of obesity and weakness, of youth who "were overfed, spent too much time watching TV, and seldom walked farther than from their house to the car in the garage."[18] Critics lambasted television, the emblematic consumer product of the age, for destroying bodily vitality. Bert Nelson, publisher of *Track and Field News,* harshly criticized the "the idiot box" and parents who "allow their kids to grow bird brains and big fannies before the television set because junior next door gets to watch it six hours a day." Many others voiced similar concerns and deplored the fact that young children watched television more than thirty hours per week.[19] Critics also targeted automobiles, the other emblem of the age, for eroding vitality. Even the venerable game of baseball, wrote one businessman, had succumbed to the car culture. "The act of running has become so exhausting to some teen-agers that they are playing a new form of baseball called 'car ball,' in which players run the bases in cars instead of on foot."[20] Another commentator concluded that, physically, "Americans are going downhill—in a hot rod."[21]

Morality, Gender, and the Body

Ultimately, the body had been victimized by more than automation, cars, or televisions. Its flabbiness, inability to pull itself over the chin-up bar, and exhaustion at the end of six hundred yards of running signified something more troubling. Written on the bodies of the future adults of America, inscribed on the flaccid muscles and the potbellies of youth, were doubts about American society and its manhood. The body had taken on the sins of the culture; its problems were ultimately moral and reflected profound doubts about the self-indulgent world of postwar consumerism.

A sense that the body's physical decline reflected the country's moral deterioration was widespread. Eisenhower had faced the issue squarely in his State of the Union message in 1960: "A rich nation can for a time, without noticeable damage to itself, pursue a course of self-indulgence, making its single goal the material ease and comfort of its own citizens." But comfort and ease begat "internal moral and spiritual softness," which would lead to economic and political disaster. Such a path repudiated the hard-spirited history of the nation. "America did not become great through softness and self-indulgence," Eisenhower warned. "Her miraculous progress in material achievements flows from other qualities far more worthy and substantial."[22]

Without a commitment to "total fitness," America would continue to drift in a sea of "inactivity, apathy, disuse, erosion, and resultant decay and atrophy."[23] Amid the softness of postwar life, fitness leaders lamented that the "inevitable national diseases of 'do-it-easy-ism' and 'do-nothing-ism' make it difficult for the younger generation to avoid drifting into a state of internal anarchy."[24] This anarchy might well induce the "rebels without a cause" among the middle class and the duck-tailed, hip-swiveling Elvis imitators among the working class to slide into juvenile delinquency and sexual excess: "All will agree," averred MacCarthy, "that well-rounded fitness programs involving mental alertness, moral straightness, and physical keenness can help forestall the sexual impulses from monopolizing and taking priority in the emotional life of the adolescent."[25]

These oversexed, overindulged, and all-too-often delinquent adolescents were walking metaphors of cultural and moral decline. One survey offered up a veritable catalog of moral shortcomings that were now inscribed on the pudding-like bodies of the young. A track coach at the University of Pennsylvania thought America's softness came from a loss of the "pioneer spirit," while the sheriff of Los Angeles County suggested that "apathy and the absence of self-discipline" created flaccid physiques.[26] Some singled out government paternalism as the cause, while others blamed the family. The director of Los Angeles County Juvenile Delinquency Programs ascribed "softness" to "too many working mothers and homes without guidance of fathers."[27] To Father Michael Montoya, an educator and "fighter against juvenile delinquency," weak muscles signified weak morality: "Softness is due to the low ebb of morality. . . . The glorification of sex, the desecration of the human body where there is little respect or care for it."[28]

Montoya was not alone in seeing a clear link between bodily disorder and juvenile delinquency and in hoping that a renewed commitment to the body would stem youthful crime. The belief that health, hygiene, and exercise promoted moral development has deep roots within American culture, and leaders in the 1950s and 1960s drew on this heritage in arguing that disciplined bodies and disciplined minds were inextricably linked, that improving one improved the other. In launching the fitness program, Eisenhower and Vice President Richard Nixon had held out just such hope, and the American Association of Health, Physical Education and Recreation commended exercise and sports not only for containing youthful energy and allowing a boy to "express his aggressive tendencies," but also for sublimating "anti-social tendencies" and containing "turbulent urges."[29]

As symbols and carriers of culture, as repositories of taste and preferences, the bodies of the young were fraught with meaning, a message that many in the mid-1950s and early 1960s found deeply troubling. Almost every cultural anxiety of Cold War America had found its way onto the bodies of the young: materialism, conformity, maternal overprotection, parental neglect, government paternalism, moral corruption, and sexual excess had sent the body, now free of the regimentation and discipline of earlier generations, out of control. The result was perilous for social order, manhood, and national security, a point made by Attorney General Robert F. Kennedy in a speech in January 1961 at the "Coach of the Year Dinner" in Pittsburgh. Since the end of World War II—a war in which "we had proved we had the mental genius, the moral certitude and the physical strength to endure and conquer"—America had been on a precipitous downward moral and physical slide.[30] American prisoners of war in Korea evidenced this decline, as did television quiz show scandals and political, labor, and corporate corruption.[31] Kennedy saw a direct correlation between this moral blight and the rot of the body. "Has there been a connection," he asked, "between the facts that I have just mentioned and our physical fitness?" Indeed there was. Moral decline had brought with it a physical slide, as evidenced by a 40 percent rejection of draftees for moral or physical deficiencies and the fact that American youth lagged far behind European children in physical fitness. To arrest such trends, Kennedy praised the coaches who could "exert a tremendous influence for good in this country. . . . You, who participate in football, who have played well and have trained others to play well, symbolize the needs of the Nation."[32]

Making Bodies Hard

Robert Kennedy's praise of football, the quintessentially male sport, was no accident. Although champions of fitness included girls from the beginning, the cultural discussion focused overwhelmingly on the bodies of boys and young men.[33] Given the doubts about manhood in the postwar years, a rough sport like football helped to establish a hierarchy of competing masculinities that favored the sturdy athlete over his limp-wristed counterpart, the heterosexual linebacker over the homosexual fop. What the celebration of physical prowess ultimately brought was a cultural message that celebrated one kind of masculinity over another. Physical force and toughness were woven together to produce what theorists call "hegemonic masculinity," a masculine bearing that projects strength, power, aggressiveness, morality, and superiority while "inferiorizing the other," that is, females and less manly men.

This process of "inferiorizing the other" is clear in the physical fitness crusades. To fitness authorities, sports and exercise had different meanings for girls and boys. For boys, fitness leaders emphasized competition: winning the game, running the fastest, doing the most sit-ups, or joining the elite fitness group in one California high school that entitled students to wear distinctively colored gym shorts.[34] For girls, experts underscored participation, friendship, good health, and sexual attractiveness. Dr. Benjamin Spock, for example, did not oppose exercise for girls but doubted whether they liked competitive athletics. Sports he said, were "really invented by boys, for boys."[35] Other authorities focused on the way fitness enhanced girls' attractiveness to young men. Although some conceded that girls might try some of the easier physical tests, their fitness "involvement" might also include watching the physical performances of boys. They might, as one writer put it, "admire the boys for their [physical fitness] achievements."[36] Girls could also use sports as a way to boost their contact with the opposite sex, a point made by *Seventeen* magazine in suggesting that girls might try to walk a mile in eleven minutes, an ordeal made more palatable if accompanied by "a boy from the track team!"[37] A movie sponsored by the American Dairy Association and the President's Council on Physical Fitness made clear that fitness, drinking milk, and sexual attractiveness went hand-in-hand, and a newspaper publisher hoped that fitness "will make teen-age girls appear glamorous to teen-age boys."[38] Ultimately, fitness might even enhance a girl's true destiny by creating "healthful, vital, feminine women who can mother a vigorous generation."[39]

None of these matters figured prominently in the fitness campaign. The focus remained on the bodies of males. Although the fitness crusaders praised everything from calisthenics to bicycling, many authorities hoped that manhood would be reborn on the playing fields of the nation's communities. Sports—"rough sports"—would toughen bodies, teach boys to endure pain, and ultimately redeem masculinity itself. Colliding bodies hardened the flesh and the spirit and could serve as a viable substitute for the ultimate maker of men: "Except for war," Robert Kennedy averred, "there is nothing in American life which trains a boy better for life than football. There is no substitute for athletics—there can be no substitute for football."[40] Even the American Medical Association recognized "that a fractured ankle may leave less of a scar than a personality frustrated by reason of parental timidity over participation in contact sports."[41] Fitness advocates supported contact sports precisely because they involved challenging fear and accepting the inevitability of pain. The chair of the Illinois Athletic Commission, for example, praised boxing for fostering toughness, aggression, and courage among young men.[42]

Although boxing lay on the fringe of respectability, football was at its center. More than any other sport associated with the fitness movement, football captured the attention of politicians and the public alike. Here was a sport with unlimited ability to turn boys to men. Senator John Cooper of Kentucky saw it as "one of the great builders of men in our country, in our time," and former football coach Clipper Smith described the sport as "a virile game. It demands the 3-D's . . . DIRT, DRUDGERY, and DISCIPLINE." Chester LaRoche, head of the National Football Foundation, praised the game for instilling in boys "stamina, courage, competition, teamwork, sportsmanship, [and] self-reliance," while General Douglas MacArthur elevated it to iconic status: "The game has become the symbol of our country's best qualities—courage, stamina, coordinated efficiency."[43]

Fitness and athletic competition taught a boy to "disguise or hide his feelings of fear," restrain his impulses, and "reject being 'babied.' "[44] In essence, the fitness movement hoped to remold the male body, to remasculinize it, to restore the strength, resilience, and toughness that had been elided by modernity. So remade, the boy could place his body at the service of his country. After noting the dismal fitness level of American youth, Robert Kennedy told a New York City audience that sports and athletic competition were crucial to the country. They were fun to be sure, but they also built healthy bodies and promoted "stamina, courage, unselfishness and most importantly, perhaps, the will to win." And without the will to win, added Kennedy, "we are lost."[45]

Hard Bodies and Cold Wars

Kennedy's martial rhetoric was not idle after-dinner chit-chat. He, his brother, and a host of others believed and hoped that physical fitness would ready the male body for war. Nothing less than national survival was at stake: the body had become a visible manifestation, a flesh-and-blood repository of national decline and weakness, and to restore the male body's strength and vigor was to restore the nation's power and vitality. America could fulfill its commitment to freedom and secure its national survival only if a vigorous fitness program could first transform the body. If the program succeeded, indulged bodies would be replaced by disciplined bodies that would work with disciplined minds to defend liberty against Communism.

Transforming the body thus became an important element in America's Cold War. In the midst of this global conflict, the dangers of affluence, technology, and overindulgence took on new meaning and, although Eisenhower had started the fitness program, John Kennedy—the Cold Warrior and crusader—gave it more prominence. Shaped by Harvard's long commitment to virile manhood, steeled by the trials of World War II, and convinced that America faced perilous threats from the Soviets, Kennedy believed that the struggle with Communism needed to be waged more aggressively. These experiences and beliefs led him to escalate the rhetoric of physical fitness and bring the Cold War into thousands of homes, schools, and communities and into the lives of millions of children and youths.[46]

In part, fitness crusaders in the Eisenhower and the Kennedy administrations were driven by the fear that flabby American bodies could not possibly survive if pitted against the rough bodies of Russian and Chinese foes. Shane MacCarthy worried that Americans' love of comfort and ease might make them vulnerable "to subjugation of tougher races, even though these races knew a far lower standard of living."[47] Many commentators voiced similar concerns, including a reporter who warned that Americans "had better become plenty tough too if we are to survive such enemies."[48] Military expert and Pulitzer Prize–winner Hanson W. Baldwin put the matter even more starkly: "Can American man—after years of protective conditioning—vie with the barbarian who has lived by his wits, his initiative, his brawn? Will he retain the will to fight for his country?"[49] He was not optimistic. American virility had been replaced by a boyhood and manhood enfeebled by "sedentarianism, push buttonitis and indoorism. . . . From all this emerges a picture—not of an American who can lick any two or three enemies, but of a slow-witted, vacuous adolescent with an intellectual interest keyed to comic books and a motivation conspicuous by its absence."[50] Soft-bellied American boys could not stand up to hard-muscled Communist youth, a point made by one medical expert who feared that Americans could either rebuild their bodies or become "spineless physical and moral molluscs" who might as well "give up right now, enjoy a nice farewell dinner, and go home to our easy chairs and T.V. sets."[51]

These were not isolated sentiments. Fitness officials warned that soft living "may seal our doom because weakness is not prone to beget strength and fragile youth can hardly grow to strong manhood."[52] Pressing for the inclusion of money for physical fitness in the National Defense Education Act, Senator Hubert H. Humphrey argued that the younger generation must be fit and ready to serve anywhere for the sake of national survival: "We Americans must train our people to do the impossible because if we don't, it is not going to be possible to do anything."[53] Disparities in military hardware might be dangerous, but deficiencies in bicep circumference could well prove fatal. Bodies unsuited for military combat had no place in the Cold War world. "For the indubitable muscle gap between us and those who would bury us," opined the old radical turned conservative Max Eastman, "may well in the long run prove more disastrous than any alleged missile gap ever will be."[54] Two public service announcements from the President's Council on Physical Fitness made the same connection. One warned that "it may be no coincidence that *as our muscles get softer . . . our missiles* [sic] *race becomes harder*"; the other praised fitness leaders in Muskogee, Oklahoma, for achieving the "Muskogee Miracle" by dramatically improving schoolchildren's fitness scores. The text began, "Someday Muskogee, Oklahoma may be famed as 'the town that closed the muscle gap.' "[55]

Military leaders shared these sentiments and voiced ongoing concern about the physical deterioration of young men and the threat this physical corruption posed to the future of the nation. Their opinions were especially important; in linking fitness and freedom, they provided steady support for an aggressive physical fitness program capable of producing fighting men. Colonel Frank J. Kones, director of physical education at the Military Academy, feared that without a fitness program, "our children will certainly become a race of eggheads walking around on bird-legs," an anatomical anxiety shared by Brigadier General S. I. A. Marshall, who told a congressional committee that "we're a nation that has become flabby in the legs" and that physical weakness inevitably brought with it a decline in "moxie."[56] Americans needed courage to fight foes who were, in the words of the surgeon general of the Army, Leonard Heaton, "primitive, rugged, and relatively unaffected by the ease and prosperity in which we live." In the face of such foes, national survival required a high level of fitness.[57]

But it was John and Robert Kennedy who most determinedly drew the connection between the fitness program and the Cold War. The "muscle gap" and the "missile gap" were central elements in Kennedy's effort to wage the Cold War at a higher level. In the fall of 1961, President Kennedy called on American educators to do their duty in the fitness crusade. The long shadows of America's international commitments now fell across the nation's schools. Kennedy became convinced that administrators and teachers had a vital role to play in preparing the nation to meet obligations that would sorely test the loyalty, stamina, determination, and preparedness of all Americans. He considered his school-based fitness program to be "the decisive force" in equipping young Americans "to serve our nation in its hours of need."[58] Physical strength had spelled the difference for American soldiers in the past and had made the nation "history's mightiest defender of freedom." Strong bodies would defend freedom in the present and ensure America's greatness in the future. "In our own time, in the jungles of Asia and on the borders of Europe, a new group of vigorous young Americans helps to maintain the peace of the world and our security as a nation."[59]

National softness threatened to make vigorous young men a scarce resource. Kennedy explained what flabbiness meant to American security: "To get two men today, the United States Army must call seven men. Of the five rejected, three are turned down for physical reasons, and two for mental disabilities." In a crisis, such high levels of rejection caused unwanted delays and inefficiencies: "To get the 196 thousand additional men that we need for Berlin, the Government had to call up, therefore, 750 thousand men." To make matters worse, the rejection rate continued to rise.[60] Ultimately, tyranny would grow where fitness failed to flourish. The number of men who might have joined the armed services had they been fit represented "more soldiers than we now have stationed in Berlin and West Germany ready to defend freedom." President Kennedy could not have been clearer on the real dangers of the "flabby" American: "By failing to provide proper physical activity for our youth, we have put more than 18 Army divisions on the sidelines."[61]

Robert Kennedy sounded the same alarm and assured school physical education teachers of the administration's commitment to fitness. Although science, engineering, and mathematics education needed improvement, such efforts would redound to no one's benefit if American youth lacked the bodily strength to make use of their education. After all, Kennedy made clear, even technological warfare required American soldiers and technicians to walk to the silos to push the buttons: "if we are sick people; if we are people that have difficulty walking two or three blocks to the engineering laboratory, or four or five blocks to the missile launching site, we are not going to be able to meet the great problems that face us in the next ten years."[62]

Robert Kennedy concluded by praising Americans as a "tough, viable, industrious people" who do not "search for a fight" but are "prepared to meet our responsibilities." Seemingly innocuous pull-ups, sit-ups, and sprints in school gym classes the nation over were the first line of defense in the Cold War. "We cannot afford to be second in anything—certainly not in the matter of physical fitness." Before it was too late, Kennedy urged Americans to adopt a nationwide, systematic program that would stem the physical deterioration of the young, a "program that, in the defense of our freedoms, will enable them to pass any test, any time, any place in the world."[63]

Much like efforts at the turn-of-the-century to resuscitate a floundering manhood, the fitness crusade that began in the 1950s tried to rescue youth, especially male youth, from the sins of immorality and technological excess that were now inscribed on the flabby physiques of America's children. The threat to the body was not inconsequential; the future of manhood and of the nation itself hung in the balance. In a culture struggling with profound changes in race, work, and community, in a society vexed by fears of male homosexuality and women's changing position, the male body and the symbolic weight it carried were matters of grave importance. Bodily strength is the bottom line of male dominance, the ultimate proving ground of manhood, and in the late 1950s and early 1960s that body seemed to be at risk: hence the obsession with restoring its vitality and place as a cultural marker.

Ultimately, even more was at stake. The Cold War profoundly shaped the early years of the fitness campaign. Boys' bodies would be rebuilt not only to reassert the power of men over women and less manly men, but to stand against the threat of the age. On the chinning bar and in athletic competition, boys would learn to be men and men would ultimately learn to be warriors. The body redeemed would be the body at war, and it would not be long until American foreign policy would bear out this truth.

The Body of the Future

The martial rhetoric of the early fitness advocates did not last, but the movement itself did. The Vietnam War rendered the overheated diction of fitness crusaders both naive and callous. Schoolyard pull-ups were an insufficient and inappropriate preparation for what was happening in Hue and Da Nang. Instead, the message that evolved in the late 1960s and after drew on an alternative discourse—muted though present from the beginning—that equated the fit body with a healthy body that would help individuals realize their full potentials. From this perspective, the body was a source of freedom and pleasure, albeit one distinctively shaped by the formidable powers of a burgeoning consumer culture.

What gave the fitness campaign staying power, in fact, was this early recognition that fitness could be linked to deeply held ideas about individualism, to popular ideas about human potential and self-esteem, and to the twin lures of sexuality and consumption. Kennedy recognized these connections early on and boosted the cultural meaning of strong bodies into the realm of democratic theory and the meaning of civilization itself. Fitness promoted the health and vitality of free people, qualities "essential if each American is to be free to realize fully the potential value of his own capabilities and the pursuit of his individual goals." Healthy and vital bodies, Kennedy concluded, were the sine qua non of individualism, and individualism was the core of American life. "In the final analysis, it is this liberation of the individual to pursue his own ends, subject only to the loose restraints of a free society, which is the ultimate meaning of our civilization."[64]

Even as President Kennedy fused physical fitness with America's traditional commitment to individualism and democracy, others concocted less high flown, more prosaic rationales for fitness. A 1963 pamphlet argued that a fit body enhanced energy, enthusiasm, longevity, and ultimately one's sense of selfhood: "Its primary aim is to help every American realize his full potential by being physically fit."[65] This "full potential" quickly caught the eye of businessmen, media consultants, and moviemakers, who connected fit bodies to leisure opportunities, consumerism, and sexual allure. Fitness expert Julian Smith believed that the judicious use of free time would enhance "self-expression," and businessman Robert Hoffman urged an audience of parks, education, and recreation leaders to sell fitness to youth as a product to enhance their sense of well-being: "We must convince them [teenagers] that it is the most desirable thing in the world, that they can't live without it, that it is the most important purchase of their entire lives." A fit body, Hoffman implored, must be marketed as a commodity: "We must make them want fitness the way every teenager yearns for a blue convertible or a swimming pool." Packaged properly, fitness would be irresistible: "We must make it beautiful and safe and warm and wonderful."[66]

And so it has become. Business quickly saw the potential marketability and financial profit of fitness. As early as 1959, Athletic Institute President Theodore Banks urged industry to study the youth fitness movement to enhance sales. A year later, the publisher of *Sports Illustrated* praised the fitness campaign for boosting profits: "Thanks to Youth Fitness and the President's council, we have more readers, more editors, more departments."[67] Other corporations quickly answered the call. General Mills, the Milk Industry Foundation, the Bicycle Institute of America, Coca-Cola, Pepsi, U.S. Rubber, and a host of others threw their weight behind fitness. Building bodies would also build sales: young athletes needed Wheaties and milk, and thirsty competitors needed Coke and Pepsi.

It would not be long until fitness became big business, and the fit body a passport to all that American capitalism had to offer. A sign of things to come appeared in a 1960s movie sponsored by the American Dairy Association that equated fitness with improving sex appeal and one's ability to compete with other girls for the attention of boys. Milk drinkers, the movie implied, had a head start on the competition.[68] From here it was a short step to constructing a body that mirrored a highly sexualized consumer culture—a toned, vibrant body that celebrated fashion, cosmetics, sports equipment, travel, and leisure. Fitness opened doors to the good life of cycling, skiing, tennis, golf, backpacking, surfing and, ultimately, to sex.

In the 1970s and beyond, this commercial, eroticized view of the fit body would dominate and the Cold War rhetoric of the Eisenhower and Kennedy years would be consigned to *Rambo* movies and the magazine pages of *Soldier of Fortune*. But the promotion of physical fitness, launched in the 1950s and given a boost by the Kennedy administration in the early 1960s, has had remarkable durability. The bodies of youth, and the cultural anxieties written onto their bodies, continue to fascinate and to trouble. For every person worried that boys are becoming video-addicted drones, there is another extolling the sports prowess of youthful athletes; for every citizen worried that girls are becoming anorexic Kate Moss look-a-likes, there is another convinced that Kerri Strug's Olympic vault exemplifies all that is right and true about American youth. The body remains a key signifier of gender and an important locus of cultural debate. The anxiety about youthful bodies has taken new shape, but we continue to see our aspirations and doubts, our ideas of manhood and womanhood, written on the bodies of the young. The body is, after all, a mirror of our hopes and fears, our needs and desires.

NOTES

1. John F. Kennedy, "The Soft American," *Sports Illustrated* 13 (December 26, 1960): 16.

2. Ibid., 13.

3. Pamphlet, *The President's Council on Physical Fitness* (Washington, D.C.: Government Printing Office, 1963), 1. Douglas Zingale offers a brief history of the Eisenhower and Kennedy administrations' involvement in physical fitness in "A History of the Involvement of the American Presidency in School and College Physical Education and Sports during the Twentieth Century" (Ph.D. diss., Ohio State University, 1973).

4. Kennedy's lifelong engagement in physical activity had been his salvation when faced with the ultimate test of manhood—war. As one writer put it, "If it had not been for his skill as a swimmer and for a hardiness of body and toughness of spirit developed through rough-and-tumble games, he probably

would not be alive today. His gallant role in rescuing crewmen after his P.T. boat was splintered by a ramming Japanese destroyer in the Solomons is one of the fine stories of courage in World War II." See "Salt-Water Notes for a Sportsman's Biography," *Sports Illustrated* 33 (December 26, 1960): 23.

5. Kennedy, "The Soft American," 16.

6. A good starting point on theory and the study of the body are the essays in Mike Featherstone, Mike Hepworth, and Bryan S. Turner, eds., *The Body: Social Process and Cultural Theory* (London: Sage Publications, 1991). For an introduction to the literature on the history of the body and a useful bibliography, see Roy Porter, "History of the Body," in Peter Burke, ed., *New Perspectives on Historical Writing* (University Park: Pennsylvania State University Press, 1991), 206–32. Especially useful for this essay was Mike Featherstone's "The Body, Culture and Sport," a paper prepared for the North American Society for the Sociology of Sport Conference, Milwaukee, Wisconsin, November 1991.

7. On these points, see Robert L. Griswold, *Fatherhood in America: A History* (New York: Basic Books, 1993), 185–218; Michael Kimmel, *Manhood in America: A Cultural History* (New York: Free Press, 1996), 223–58.

8. Kimmel, *Manhood in America,* 223–58. On the sex crime panic, see George Chauncey, Jr., "The Postwar Sex Crime Panic," in William Graebner, ed., *True Stories from the American Past* (New York: McGraw-Hill, 1993), 161–78; Estelle Freedman, " 'Uncontrolled Desires': The Response to the Sexual Psychopath, 1920–1960," *Journal of American History* 74 (June 1987): 83–106.

9. David Whitson, "Sport in the Social Construction of Masculinity," in Michael Messner and Donald Sabo, eds., *Sport, Men, and the Gender Order: Critical Feminist Perspectives* (Champaign, Ill.: Human Kinetic Books, 1990), 19–28. In this collection, also see chapters by Lois Bryson ("Challenges to Male Hegemony in Sport"), M. Ann Hall ("How Should We Theorize Gender in the Context of Sport"), and Bruce Kidd ("The Men's Cultural Centre: Sports and the Dynamic of Women's Oppression/Men's Repression").

10. John B. Kelly, "Are We Becoming a Nation of Weaklings?" *American Magazine* 161 (March 1956): 28–29, 104–7. Kelly was the father of actress Grace Kelly. On Duff's involvement, see National Affairs Special Report, "Are We Becoming 'Soft'? Why the President Is Worried about our Fitness," *Newsweek* 46 (September 26, 1955): 35–36. See also the Papers of Frederic Fox, Box 13, Eisenhower Library, Abilene, Kansas; and Robert H. Boyle, "The Report that Shocked the President," *Sports Illustrated* 3 (August 15, 1955): 30–33, 72–75. The comparative tests sparked debate. Some experts thought the tests gave an unfair picture of American youth; see *New York Times,* August 13, 1961, p. 54; and Boyle, "Report that Shocked the President," 72–73. Some found the differences easily remediated and therefore not important, while others noted that Americans were bigger, healthier, better fed, and living longer than

ever before; "Are We Softies or Supermen?" *Senior Scholastic* 69 (December 6, 1956): 16. Perhaps the most sustained critique appeared in A. T. Slater-Hammel, "Some Comments on an Article," *Physical Educator* 14 (March 1957): 3–6. On the whole, however, most authorities accepted the general findings, in part because they aligned so well with cultural anxieties about affluence and the Cold War.

The complete story of the fitness crusade—the countless conferences, workshops, movies, magazine articles, "fitness weeks," and pilot programs—can be found in the monthly reports of the President's Council on Youth Fitness; see, for example, "Ninth Monthly Report," May 16–June 15, 1958, Bureau of the Budget, Box 14/MS 79-32, "President's Council on Youth Fitness #4," Kennedy Library, Boston.

11. MacCarthy became the Executive Director of the Council on Youth Fitness on September 6, 1956. A native of Ireland, MacCarthy became a naturalized citizen in 1935 and later worked in various capacities at the State, Labor, and Interior Departments and as chief orientation officer of the Central Intelligence Agency. On MacCarthy, see *New York Times,* September 7, 1956, p. 10; *Concord Daily Monitor and New Hampshire Patriot,* November 28, 1956, in White House Central Files, General File, Box 1055, File 134-J-1 (1), Eisenhower Library, Abilene, Kansas; Hugo Autz, "U.S. Fitness Director Pledges Early Action," reprinted from *The Sporting Goods Dealer,* White House Central Files, Official File, Box 845, File 156 A-6-B (2), Eisenhower Library; and a one-page biography, likely for press releases, in White House Central Files, Official File, Box 845, File 156 A-6-B (2), Eisenhower Library, Abilene, Kansas.

12. The text of MacCarthy's speech before the Bicycle Institute of America can be found in "A Missionary for Youth Fitness," Bureau of the Budget, Box 14/MS 79-32, File: "Youth Fitness, Council on," Kennedy Library.

13. Jean Mayer, "Muscular State of the Union," *New York Times Magazine,* November 6, 1955, p. 17; for similar views, see Fred J. Hinger, "If We Are to Survive," *Educational Leadership* 20 (March 1963): 364; Robert N. Irving, Jr., "Why All the Fuss about Fitness?" *Educational Leadership* 20 (March 1963): 376; "Are We Softies or Supermen?" 15; Charles "Bud" Wilkinson, "In a Dangerous World, Is American Youth Too Soft?" *U.S. News and World Report* 51 (August 21, 1961): 76; *New York Times,* January 21, 1961, p. 16.

14. Shane MacCarthy, "Forward with Fitness," *Physical Educator* 15 (October 1958): 83; see also G. Ott Romney, "The What, Why, and How of Youth Fitness," *Physical Educator* 16 (December 1959): 123, 127.

15. Shane MacCarthy, "Fitness and the Future," in *Fitness of American Youth: A Report to the President of the United States on the Fort Richie Meeting* (Washington, D.C.: Government Printing Office, 1958), 29. For similar sentiments, see Martha Allen, "Sociological Fitness," in *Fitness of American Youth: Planning to Involve Youth in Fitness: A Report to the President of the United*

States on the Air Force Academy Meeting (Washington, D.C.: Government Printing Office, 1959), 50 (Allen was national director of the Camp Fire Girls, Inc.);
Ted Forbes, "Physical Fitness and Our Youth," *Bulletin of the National Association of Secondary-School Principals* 46 (March 1962): 157–58; Ray O. Duncan and Wincie Ann Carruth, "Basic Issues," *Journal of Health, Physical Education, and Recreation* 33 (March 1962): 8; George W. Hawks, "Some
Comments on 'Comments on an Article,' " *Physical Educator* 14 (October
1957): 100; Darrell J. Smith, "Physical Education: Trends in Secondary School,"
Educational Leadership 20 (March 1963): 372.

16. Dr. John A. Friedrich, "Physical Education in Michigan," *Michigan Educational Review* 40 (September 1, 1962): 10.

17. Fred J. Hinger, "If We Are to Survive," *Educational Leadership* 20
(March 1963): 364.

18. Pamphlet, *The President's Council on Physical Fitness* (Washington,
D.C.: Government Printing Office, 1963), 2; *New York Times,* April 28, 1962,
p. 27; "America's Youth: Fit or Unfit?" *Senior Scholastic* 76 (April 27, 1960):
12. Senator Hubert H. Humphrey voiced similar views in "A Five-Point Fitness
Program," *Journal of Health, Physical Education, and Recreation* 33 (October
1962): 22.

19. On television and fitness, see Dr. Stephan A. Seymour, "The Soft American: Problems and Solutions," in the President's Office Files: Departments and
Agencies, Box 94, File: "Council on Youth Fitness—The Soft American,"
pp. 12, 15, 29, 30, 34, 40, Kennedy Library, Boston; Jack Lentz, "How to Improve Our Children's Physical Fitness," *Today's Health* 39 (September 1961):
87; Don A. Bailey, "Sputnik and Us," *Physical Educator* 15 (March 1958): 31.
On television statistics, see Dr. John A. Friedrich, "Physical Education in Michigan," *Michigan Educational Review* 40 (September 1, 1962): 10.

20. Kelly, "Are We Becoming a Nation of Weaklings?" 105. See also
MacCarthy, "Fitness and the Future," 30; "From Here and There," in *Fitness
in Action,* May 1959, 31 in Box "Operation Fitness," Archives of the American
Alliance for Health, Physical Education, Recreation, and Dance, Reston, Virginia.

21. R. M. Marshall as told to William Gill, "Toughening Our Soft Generation," *Saturday Evening Post* 235 (June 23, 1962): 13.

22. *New York Times,* January 8, 1960, p. 10. See also Ray W. Howard,
"Our Number One Defense Line," *Journal of Health, Physical Education, and
Recreation* 32 (September 1961): 25.

23. Memo from Louis E. Means, Director of Special Projects of the American
Association for Health, Physical Education, and Recreation, to Clarence L.
Strum, Lions International President, September 1, 1959, in Box "Operation
Fitness," Archives of the American Alliance for Health, Physical Education, Rec-
reation, and Dance, Reston, Virginia.

24. Shane MacCarthy, "Focus on Fitness," in *Fitness of American Youth: Planning to Involve Youth in Fitness: A Report to the President of the United States on the Air Force Meeting* (Washington D.C.: Government Printing Office, 1959), 4–5. A California physical educator was more direct: "The fact is that youth are physically soft. Philosophers, historians and sociologists through the ages have admonished that the companion of physical softness is moral laxity." See Smith, "Physical Education," 372.

25. MacCarthy, "Focus on Fitness," 13.

26. See Seymour, "The Soft American," 4, 13, 20, 34, 37, 42. For other examples of respondents who singled out the impact of affluence on "softness," see pp. 4, 13, 19, 20, 25, 27, 31, 40, and 41; on conformity and "softness," see p. 40; on self-indulgence and "softness," pp. 14, 21, 34, 37; and on laziness and greed in relationship to poor fitness, pp. 6, 31, 33, 36, 40–41. The Seymour report is comprised of 105 personal interviews with politicians, entertainers, sports officials, athletes, publishers, and educators and asked respondents why Americans were "soft" and what could be done about it.

27. Ibid., 9, 10, 12.

28. Ibid., 39.

29. On Eisenhower, fitness, and juvenile delinquency, see "Is American Youth Physically Fit?" *U.S. News and World Report*, August 2, 1957, 66. John Kelly, who instigated the fitness effort, strongly agreed that sports could curtail juvenile delinquency; see Kelly, "Are We Becoming a Nation of Weaklings?" 106; on Nixon, see "Closing Remarks of the Vice President of the United States," *Fitness of American Youth: A Report to the President of the United States on the West Point Conference* (Washington, D.C.: Government Printing Office, 1957), 45. The recreation leaders' position is in "Athletics in Education," *Journal of Health, Physical Education, and Recreation* 33 (September 1962): 25–26. See also letters and telegrams on sports and juvenile delinquency in the Eisenhower Library, Abilene, Kansas—for example, Herman Fagel to Eisenhower, August 14, 1955, and Reverend C. E. Stoney Jackson to Murray Snyder, Assistant Presidential Press Secretary, July 11, 1955, in White House Central Files, General Files, Box 1055, 134-J (1), File: "President's Conference on Physical Fitness"; and Joe E. Landry to Murray Snyder, September 20, 1955, White House Central Files, General Files, Box 1055, 134-J (2).

30. Kennedy's untitled speech is in the Kennedy Library, Boston, White House Staff Files, Papers of Timothy J. Reardon, Jr., Box 11, File: "Youth Fitness Speeches," 1961, pp. 2–3.

31. Ibid., 5–6.

32. Ibid., 1, 8.

33. Nixon reminded fitness leaders not to forget about girls in "Closing Remarks of the Vice-President," 39. On the inclusion of girls in the program, see also, for example, President's Council on Youth Fitness, *Sports for Fitness:*

Workshop Report No. 7 (Washington, D.C.: Government Printing Office, 1960), 11; "Conference Recommendations," in *Fitness of American Youth: Planning to Involve Youth in Fitness: A Report to the President of the United States on the Air Force Academy Meeting* (Washington, D.C.: Government Printing Office, 1959), 88; pamphlet, *The President's Council on Physical Fitness* (Washington, D.C.: Government Printing Office, 1963), 3; Virginia E. Hawke, "Girls Need to Be Fit, Too!" *Physical Educator* 16 (October 1959): 92; Wilkinson, "In a Dangerous World," 75, 79.

34. On elite gym classes, see Stanley Gordon, "La Sierra High Shows How America Can Get Physically Tough," *Look* 26 (January 30, 1962): 49. Charles "Bud" Wilkinson praised the La Sierra program and thought it would help to "make America's youth as agile and physically tough as any in the world."

35. Benjamin Spock, "Are Our Children Getting Enough Exercise?" *Ladies Home Journal* 77 (June 1960): 36.

36. Gordon, "La Sierra High," 50.

37. "How Do You Shape Up?" *Seventeen* 21 (November 1962): 20.

38. *Girls Are Better than Ever*, a movie by the American Dairy Association in cooperation with the President's Council on Physical Fitness and Lifetime Sports Foundation, ca. 1967, American Archive of the Factual Film, Iowa State University; Joseph Kingsbury-Smith, "An Action Program for Youth Fitness," in *Communications Media Forum, Magazine Forum, Broadcasting Forum: Workshop Reports Nos. 2, 3, 4* (Washington, D.C.: Government Printing Office, 1960), 10.

39. In addition to vital motherhood, the fitness program would also promote "active, healthful, vital, masculine men." See Shane MacCarthy, "Enjoy Keeping Fit," *American Recreation Society Bulletin,* May 1957, p. 6.

40. White House Staff Files, Papers of Timothy J. Reardon, Jr., Subject Files, Box 11, File: "Youth Fitness Speeches, 1961," Kennedy Library, Boston.

41. American Medical Association quotation in *Fitness of American Youth: Planning to Involve Youth in Fitness: A Report to the President of the United States on the Air Force Academy Meeting* (Washington, D.C.: Government Printing Office, 1959), 10.

42. Frank B. Gilmer, "Should the Sport of Boxing Be Discontinued? No!" *Physical Educator* 14 (December 1957): 133. See also Lawrence Sciacchetano, "Wrestling for Younger Boys," *Physical Educator* 23 (May 1966): 56.

43. All except the Clipper Smith quotation are from remarks by Senator John Cooper on the National Football Foundation's intention to build a hall of fame. See the Appendix to the *Congressional Record,* 86th Congress, 2nd session, July 2, 1960. The Clipper Smith quotation is from Seymour, "The Soft American," 32, emphasis in original. See also Arthur H. Steinhaus, "Some Larger Aspects of Fitness," *Physical Educator* 14 (October 1957): 86.

44. "Athletics in Education," 25. In the same document, the professional physical educators also praised sports for promoting tolerance of all kinds (25). Others praised athletics for teaching fair play, good sportsmanship, teamwork, and loyalty, qualities "characteristic of a good citizen." See J. E. Rogers, "Citizenship and Physical Education," *Physical Educator* 14 (December 1957): 122; G. Ott Romney, "The What, Why, and How of Youth Fitness," *Physical Educator* 16 (December 1959): 125.

45. White House Staff Files, Papers of Timothy J. Reardon, Jr., Subject Files, Box 11, File: "Youth Fitness Speeches, 1961," Kennedy Library, Boston. See also James F. Kelly, *Sports for Fitness* (Washington, D.C.: Government Printing Office, 1960), 6.

46. On Harvard and manhood, see Kim Townsend, *Manhood at Harvard: William James and Others* (New York: W. W. Norton, 1996).

47. Shane MacCarthy, "The Junior Chamber Faces the Challenge of Youth Fitness," *Future,* February 1958, p. 12. This article is among the papers of James M. Lambie, Jr., Special Assistant in the White House, Box 45, File: "President's Council on Youth Fitness, 1958," Eisenhower Library, Abilene, Kansas. For similar sentiments, see Wilkinson, "In a Dangerous World," 76; Edward L. R. Larson, D. D., minister of the National Presbyterian Church of Washington, D.C., "Youth Fitness in Today's World," in *President's Council on Youth Fitness: Workshop Report No. 5: Religious Group Leaders* (Washington, D.C.: Government Printing Office, 1960), 5–6.

48. Dr. David Goodman, "Are Children of U.S. Too Soft?" *Bergen Evening Record,* December 26, 1958, in White House General Files, Official File, Box 844, File 156 A-6-A (3), Eisenhower Library, Abilene, Kansas. Theodore Banks, head of the Athletic Institute, noted that the Russians "are involved in youth fitness to an nth degree." Whereas the Soviets could mandate youth fitness programs, in America "business and industry must help encourage fitness since we do not want to adopt the Soviet model." See Banks, "What Can Be Done to Involve Youth in Fitness in Business and Industry," in *Fitness of American Youth: Planning to Involve Youth in Fitness: A Report to the President of the United States on the Air Force Academy Meeting* (Washington, D.C.: Government Printing Office, 1959), 74. On the Soviet fitness program, see Ray W. Howard, "Our Number One Defense Line," *Journal of Health, Physical Education, and Recreation* 32 (September 1961): 25; John B. McLendon, Jr., "The Soviet Union's Program of Physical Culture and Sports," *Journal of Health, Physical Education, and Recreation* 33 (April 1962): 28, 54; "Physical Education in Russia," *Physical Educator* 15 (December 1958): 137. Bud Wilkinson admitted that in matters of fitness, Russian youth "probably are far, far ahead of us," a sentiment shared by Max Eastman. See Wilkinson, "In a Dangerous World," 75; Eastman, "Let's Close the Muscle Gap," *Readers' Digest* 79 (November 1961): 124.

49. Hanson W. Baldwin, "Our Fighting Men Have Gone Soft," *Saturday Evening Post* 232 (August 8, 1959): 82.

50. Ibid. Baldwin offered a sweeping indictment of the "softness" of the U.S. military and suggested that mechanization, automobiles, affluence, juvenile delinquency, family breakdown, crime, venereal disease, "Big Government," the welfare state, equality, conformity, high taxes, excessive civilian influence, and racial integration had undermined the fighting abilities of U.S. troops. Senator Humphrey warned that Communist hardness came from organized fitness programs: "One thing is certain—each day, each week, each year—the Soviet Union and its captive nations are increasing their efforts for the physical fitness of their populations." See Hubert H. Humphrey, "A Five-Point Fitness Program," *Journal of Health, Physical Education, and Recreation* 33 (October 1962): 74.

51. This quote is from Wilhelm Raab, a professor of experimental medicine at the College of Medicine, University of Vermont. The text of his speech to the President's Citizens Advisory Committee on the Fitness of American Youth is in the papers of the Bureau of the Budget, Box 14/MS 79–32, File: "Youth Fitness, Council on," Kennedy Library, Boston.

52. MacCarthy, "Junior Chamber Faces the Challenge of Youth Fitness," 12. On MacCarthy and national survival, see also, for example, "Fitness: Key to Survival," White House Central Files, Official File, Box 845, File 156-A-6-B (2), Eisenhower Library, Abilene, Kansas; MacCarthy, "Fitness and the Future," 33.

53. Hubert H. Humphrey, "American Youth Must Do the Impossible," *Journal of Health, Physical Education, and Recreation* 34 (June 1963): 14. Bud Wilkinson sounded the same alarm: "Fitness is vital to the future because in today's world we will survive only if we are fit to survive." Jack Lentz, "How to Improve Our Children's Physical Fitness," *Today's Health* 39 (September 1961): 88; see also Charles "Bud" Wilkinson, "How Does Your Child Rate in Fitness?" *Parents Magazine* 36 (October 1961): 148. Wilkinson also worried about Army rejection rates among draftees and the subsequent lowering of physical standards: "If this trend continues for, say 50 more years, we may face an insurmountable problem." See Wilkinson, "In a Dangerous World," 76. See also Howard, "Our Number One Defense Line," 25.

54. Eastman, "Let's Close the Muscle Gap!" 125.

55. "What Makes Sammy Walk?" in Box "Operation Fitness," archives of the American Alliance for Health, Physical Education, Recreation, and Dance, Reston, Virginia. "Sammy" refers to Uncle Sam. On Muskogee, see the papers of Timothy J. Reardon, Jr., White House Staff Files, Subject Files, Box 11, File: "Youth Fitness, 1962–1963," Kennedy Library, Boston.

56. Kones spoke before 1,800 delegates of the New York State Association for Health, Physical Education, and Recreation and is quoted in the *New York*

Times, January 21, 1961, p. 16. Marshall's comments are in George A. Silver, "Fits over Fitness," *Nation* 194 (June 9, 1962): 516.

57. Military leaders quoted in James Torpey, "A Conditioned Body and Survival," *Physical Educator* 18 (May 1961): 65.

58. Kennedy quoted in Ted Forbes, "Physical Fitness and Our Youth," *Bulletin of the National Association of Secondary-School Principals* 46 (March 1962): 161.

59. John F. Kennedy, "The Vigor We Need," *Sports Illustrated* 17 (July 16, 1962): 12.

60. A copy of the Kennedy speech is in the Papers of Timothy J. Reardon, Jr., White House Staff Files, Subject Files, Box 11, File: "Youth Fitness Speeches, 1961," Kennedy Library, Boston. For a report on the speech, see *New York Times,* December 6, 1961, p. 61.

61. "President John F. Kennedy's Message to Schools at the Beginning of the 1961–62 School Year," September 5, 1961, in the Papers of Timothy J. Reardon, Jr., White House Staff Files, Subject Files, Box 11, File: "Youth Fitness Speeches, 1961," Kennedy Library, Boston.

62. Excerpts of Kennedy's July 30, 1962, speech at the Conference of Local School Leaders in Health, Physical Education, and Recreation in "Excerpts from Speeches," Bureau of the Budget, Box 14/MS 79–32, File: "President's Council on Youth Fitness, #8, 1962," Kennedy Library, Boston. One educational consultant complained that too many parents and teachers emphasized academic achievement at the expense of physical education. See Robert N. Irving, Jr., "Why All the Fuss about Fitness?" *Educational Leadership* 20 (March 1963): 377.

63. Robert F. Kennedy, "First Things First," *Journal of Health, Physical Education, and Recreation* 33 (October 1962): 82. Senator Humphrey hoped that fitness and sports programs would make young Americans "tough in the finest sense of the word. Tough, not in the sense of cruelty or carelessness, but tough in that we do not cringe or whimper before the test or the challenge of any adversity." See Humphrey, "American Youth Must Do the Impossible," 14.

64. John F. Kennedy, "The Vigor We Need," *Sports Illustrated* 17 (July 16, 1962): 14.

65. Pamphlet, *The President's Council on Physical Fitness* (Washington, D.C.: Government Printing Office, 1963).

66. Julian Smith, "Leaders for Living," *Journal of Health, Physical Education, and Recreation* 33 (April 1962): 61; Robert M. Hoffman, "Telling and Selling the Fitness Story," in *President's Council on Youth Fitness: Recreation Planning for Fitness: Workshop Report No. 8* (Washington, D.C.: Government Printing Office, 1961), 18–20. See also Banks, "What Can Be Done to Involve Youth in Fitness," 71.

67. Banks, "What Can Be Done to Involve Youth in Fitness," 73; Sidney L.

James, "The Editor and Editorial Writer Considers Youth Fitness," in *President's Council on Youth Fitness: Communications Media Forum, Magazine Forum, Broadcasting Forum: Workshop Reports Nos. 2, 3, 4* (Washington, D.C.: Government Printing Office, 1960), 18.

68. "Girls Are Better than Ever," ca. 1967, American Archive of the Factual Film, Iowa State University.

Chapter Fourteen

Making Room for Fathers
Men, Women, and Parenting in the United States, 1945–1980

Jessica Weiss

In the fall of 1993, when the Houston Oilers penalized offensive lineman David Williams for choosing his family over his job, the nation took notice.[1] Williams had skipped a football game to be with his wife and newborn child. The *Los Angeles Times* suggested Williams receive a father-of-the-year award; but the Oilers saw no reason why, after delivery, he had not rushed back to join his teammates in time for the kickoff. With sympathetic headlines that proclaimed "Football Player Fields Role as Dad Like a Champ," "Family over Football," and "Hold a Baby or Hold that Line," reporters and columnists presented his conflicting responsibilities in the context of a national dilemma over fatherhood: work versus family.[2] Williams, many columnists insisted, symbolized the "new dad." They cast the episode as a sign of a new age in family life that portended change in the American workplace.

In an America where until recently fatherhood has been defined by breadwinning, men who take parental leave or co-parent alongside their wives become exemplars of a brave *new* form of fatherhood. Commentators have attributed the "new" 1990s father, active in his children's nurture and care, to the 1970s feminist critiques of gender roles and family dynamics and the increasing participation of married women and mothers in the labor force, which brought long-held notions of fatherhood and motherhood into question. Yet concerns about fathering and hopes of reinventing it are not so new. The roots of involved fatherhood predate "second-wave feminism" and accompanied rather than followed postwar shifts in American family life. By attempting to incorporate fathers into everyday life, the baby-boom-era families of the 1950s laid the foundations for today's emerging pattern of "daddy tracking" and co-parenting.[3]

Although the problem of defining men's family role beyond that of breadwinner has engaged experts since the turn of the century, during the 1950s experts and ordinary couples grappled with the issue, convinced they were shaping a new fatherhood particularly suited to postwar conditions. Family professionals summoned men to partake in raising children.[4] What is unique about the mid-century debate over men's role in the family is that it took place not just in the pages of magazines and advice books, but in middle-class homes across the United States.

The 1950s were a flash point for fatherhood. After two decades of disruption, fathers returned to their "rightful" place in the family. During the baby boom years, 1946–1964, Americans turned to the family as a refuge from a frightening Cold War world. "Togetherness" defined a modern ethos of family sharing and companionship in an era where postwar consumption and affluence contrasted with prewar deprivation. The stage was set for a reinvigorated middle-class family in which experts hoped men would play a greater role.[5]

Historians who have studied women's rush back into the home following World War II have not recognized that the call for domesticity extended to fathers as well as mothers. Americans attempted to define male contributions to home life in addition to that of providing. In the process, they carved out a permanent space for fathers in the home. Yet attention to fatherhood posed a dilemma for men as they sought to balance work and home demands.

A survey of family-oriented magazines from the 1950s paired with decennial interviews with couples who married in the 1940s and 1950s exposes the often painful struggles women and men waged within themselves and each other over the twin demands of fatherhood—parenting and providing. Focusing on both prescription and behavior allows us to explore the complex ways in which ideals for fathers filtered into middle-class homes. For the most part, postwar hopes for a fatherhood that harmoniously blended men's conflicting responsibilities went unrealized. Nonetheless, the ideals and experiences of the first generation to raise children in the postwar era began a transformation in gender roles within the middle-class family that continues today.

To investigate postwar family patterns, I analyzed three detailed sets of intimate interviews that were part of a more than fifty-year longitudinal study housed in the archives of the Institute of Human Development (IHD) at the University of California, Berkeley. In the 1930s, IHD psychologists began studies of infant and child development that, fortunately for historians, were continued as the participants aged. As adults, several hundred subjects were interviewed in the late fifties (1957–62), the late sixties (1968–71), and the early eighties (1980–83).[6]

Unlike cross-sectional analysis of census data, which provides one-time statistical snapshots, this study follows the same group of individuals from youthful marriage to retirement, permitting a "moving picture" of changes in American family life. My discussion here draws from one hundred IHD subjects and their spouses, selected on the basis of their continued participation at all three adult interviews.[7] IHD questions focused on issues of individual psychological development, but they reveal a great deal about the social milieu and historical events experienced by this generation.[8] A close reading of these interviews provides a fascinating journey into the inner life of middle-class Americans over the entire family cycle.

Born during the 1920s, IHD subjects came of age and wed in the 1940s and 1950s. Most lived out their lives within fifty miles of their childhood homes in the East Bay, but postwar mobility dispersed a few. They are representative of the prewar East Bay population migration that transformed the region's ethnic and racial make-up. Nearly all study participants—90 percent—were middle-class by the time they married. Working-class women attained middle-class status through marriage and working-class men through GI Bill education and home loans.[9] Participants in the IHD study, then, represent a significant slice of the middle-class experience in the second half of the twentieth century and an excellent source for the exploration of changing views of fatherhood.

The Ideal Postwar Father

Family experts in the 1950s did not invent concern about fathers; they inherited it from turn-of-the-century advisors. By 1900, declining family size, suburbanization, and a shrinking work week had begun to redefine family life for Americans. Increased income and leisure made family time a realistic goal for middle-class men, and concern about men's daily absence from family life generated calls for more involved fatherhood.[10]

Interwar professionals who hoped to improve family life included fathers in their reform efforts and encouraged them to be companions and role models for their children. Psychologists linked fathers to the sex role development of their offspring, adding urgency to concerns about men's role in rearing children. Yet, these prescriptions left unquestioned the central role men continued to play as breadwinners.[11]

The Depression increased experts' anxieties about the man's position in the American family. How would American men and their families withstand widespread unemployment? Studies such as *The Unemployed Man and His Family* sought to measure the impact of joblessness on family and marriage.[12] The prospect of men denied the breadwinning role by economic crisis worried social scientists. The Depression, which disrupted so many American families, heightened the association of fatherhood with breadwinning even as it accelerated the demand for active male parenting.[13]

World War II allotment checks and employment opportunities restored American men's status as family wage earners. But the war also raised new questions about the psychological and social ramifications of fathers' absence from the home. With so many men serving in the armed forces, Americans wondered what impact this separation from fathers would have on very young and adolescent children.[14]

After the war, parenting experts reemphasized the importance of father-child relationships—for the good of children, family, and American society. Psychologists, doctors, social workers, and journalists preached a doctrine of domestic fatherhood. They found a ready audience among the youthful and prolific parents of the baby boom. This family pattern was the backdrop for renewed concern about the role of men in the American family.[15]

The middle-class family was perhaps at its most "nuclear" at the dawn of the atomic age. Suburban developments proliferated in the 1950s, and young couples bid a not-always-fond farewell to the crowded urban housing of the war years, leaving behind an extended family and community that had long been a source of advice and support. Postwar men and women married younger, started families sooner after marriage, and had more children in a shorter span of time, all of which led to the boom in births.[16]

Isolated from traditional family wisdom on child rearing, young parents sought alternative sources of authority and advice. A veritable army of experts commanded their attention, chief among them the calming voice of pediatrician Dr. Benjamin Spock. Spock's 1946 *Common Sense*

Book of Baby and Child Care was immensely popular; it was revised the first of five times in 1957.[17] His advice generated letters of thanks from suburban parents, one of whom demonstrated both her considerable affluence and a substantial appetite for expert advice: "I've got a copy in the living room, a copy in the bedroom, a copy in the kitchen, a copy in the bathroom."[18] Spock's book was only one volley in a barrage of child-rearing advice that confronted insecure baby-boom parents.

Articles on fatherhood proliferated. Popular magazines discussed such topics as "Father as Family Man" and "What Children Need from Dad."[19] Breadwinning alone, experts proclaimed, was no longer enough; parenting was a "man's job too."[20] "Today Dad finds families function best on a partnership basis," noted a writer for the *New York Times,* "He shares in the daily care and companionship of small fry—all sizes. As for discipline, he's replaced the 'woodshed' with a do-it-yourself workshop where everyone has fun."[21] Such statements reveal the key features of fifties fatherhood, at least as the family advisors would have it. Fathers had a place alongside mothers as partners in child raising, but the chief components of fatherhood were friendliness and fun.[22]

Eager for men to parent actively, experts insisted that in no way would parenting tasks feminize a man. As the ever-popular Dr. Spock assured, "A man can be a warm father and a real man at the same time." O. Spurgeon English and Constance J. Foster, authors of *Fathers Are Parents Too,* criticized the mistaken patterns of the past wherein men deemed infants' care solely a "woman's department."[23]

The flurry of attention surrounding father's place in family life betrayed a discomfort with the organization of American domestic life. The division between home and work was a central organizing feature of the American family in the 1950s. Family professionals sought to temper what they saw as the most grievous problem—nearly complete female control over child rearing and male distance from the domestic sphere. They attempted to address this imbalance without tampering with family structure or with a corporate culture that insisted that the American workplace was a male preserve. According to experts, fathers present in the home would provide an essential counterweight to mothers' potentially overwhelming feminine influence. Play was a father's entrée into the family.

Advisors believed that fathers would benefit from their efforts at child rearing as much as children. Experts prompted dads who wanted good relationships with their kids to participate during nightly feedings and provide bedtime stories. English and Foster wrote, "Early-fathered children will be better companions to Dad when they enter their teens because they learned to be pals on the night shift over a midnight bottle or a colic pain." "Reading a bed-time story" or "pulling down training panties for the toddler" paved the way to friendship with children. The father who neglected care at the early stages, the experts warned, could never be a buddy to his children as they matured.[24]

The work men did to support their families posed both the problem and the potential for fatherhood, according to experts. Work had kept old-fashioned fathers from parenting properly by removing them from the home. But, at the same time, what a man did outside the home provided stimulus to the isolated world of mothers and children. Play would help bridge this gap, experts predicted. English and Foster called dad the "exciting courier," full of information and stories of the adult world with which to instruct his youngsters. One journalist suggested that fathers could infuse a "little adventure" into daily life, whereas mothers often were too overburdened with the drudgery of homemaking to be creative.[25] Providing connection with the wide world outside the home was a man's special contribution. Yet, fathers needed to connect with their children at home in order to do so. Father's play injected excitement and adventure into the isolated middle-class domestic world, but advice-givers freighted his antics with even greater cultural importance.

When rhapsodizing about the effects of more fathering on the family, parenting authorities focused on the contributions of a masculine presence to child rearing. Comforting a colicky baby took on different meaning when a man's arms embraced the infant: "Father's arms are strong and the child who experiences the security they give him grows up with a warm regard for some of the best qualities of masculinity—tenderness, protection, and strength."[26] By focusing on fathering, experts claimed tenderness and nurturing as male qualities, staking out a new terrain for "real" men and, they hoped, fostering this revitalized masculinity in the next generation.

With balance between mother and father restored, experts theorized that children would learn proper sex roles. A heavy dose of psychoanalytic theory permeated the descriptions of father's importance in the development of little girls and boys. From this perspective, dad was daughter's first boyfriend and a masculine model for his son. English, Foster, and their peers worried that without men's active participation in their children's upbringing, children would miss crucial lessons in male and female traits. According to advisers, active fathering safeguarded the future of American marriage by instilling appropriate gender behavior in the nation's children.[27]

Play, then, in the experts' vision, had many purposes. And, as the limits of fifties-style fatherhood illustrate, play was a duty added to the main job men expected to perform—earning the money to support the family. Fathers who returned home from work too tired for horseplay and bedtime stories were criticized for falling down on the job. Play became the proving ground for future friendships with and proper sexual identification of their young children. But if father's function was play, mother's was by extension its complement, work. Father brought excitement to the family room, while mother kept it in order and ensured his little pals were clean, rested, and sweet-smelling for his arrival. In short, the fifties version of fatherhood did little in practice to lessen women's load and in some aspects increased it.

The emphasis on fun and friendship in these formulas belied one other unchanging element in the construction of home life for men: Ideally, home was, and would remain, a haven for exhausted breadwinners. Experts anticipated that this function would continue and that involved fatherhood would enhance it. Rough-housing with the children on the family-room floor provided a respite from a taxing job, while leisure time spent in the company of family in a comfortably appointed home provided a rationale for a long, hard day at the office and restored dad for the next one.[28] Here the limits of the postwar paternal ideal became apparent: Experts sold fathering as a rejuvenating tonic to the work-a-day office world.

Few practical suggestions accompanied predictions for great changes in child rearing. Fathering advisors took for granted that work would absorb most of a man's time, but suggested that men interact with their children when they were at home. Experts coached fathers to pal around with their kids, only occasionally pitching in with the messy work involved in caring for two, three, or four young children.[29] For example, the influential Dr. Spock advised fathers never to push themselves beyond their limited endurance. He permitted them to play with the kids for fifteen minutes and then unfold the evening paper after a hard day at the office.[30]

Significantly, prescriptive literature about fatherhood targeted women as well as men, placing a good deal of the burden of father's participation on mother. Bashful, hesitant fathers, Spock surmised, "just need encouragement" from their wives. If men eschewed participation in parenting, articles hinted, women should make sure they were allowing them to try. Mothers, writer Selma Lentz Morrison maintained, could influence the tenor of a father-child relationship; they could "foster it, stunt its growth or completely destroy it." Experts feared that too many women mistakenly believed that child rearing was solely their responsibility and failed to include their husbands in the joint venture of parenthood. Worse yet, according to English and Foster, were women who discouraged a "man's interests in his children because unconsciously they want to derive all their emotional satisfaction from keeping the youngsters dependent on them." They advised wives to encourage and guide fatherly interest in children. If a husband did not measure up to new standards, English and Foster insisted, "It will pay you to do a little soul-searching, and see whether, without realizing it, you have been doing some of the things that make a man retire behind his newspaper or play golf instead of enjoying his youngsters and taking a sharp interest in home and all of its doings." As important as fathers were to the fifties conception of family life, women were ultimately responsible for and regulated the ability of men to father. If mom performed her role correctly, dad would be cavorting cozily with the kids. It followed that his detachment from his children became evidence of her failure.[31]

The ideal postwar father, then, read advice books with his wife, stepped in to help out with the occasional diaper or bottle when she was exhausted, and played and conversed with his children as much as his schedule allowed. Shared care for children, according to experts, should be subordinate to fun and companionship; both, however, had to fit on the periphery of work life. Experts suggested that dad get the most out of the few hours he had available after fulfilling work obligations. Yet, without promoting fundamental alteration of the division of labor in the middle-class nuclear family, experts did broaden the boundaries and increase the permeability of this division. In practice, middle-class men and women attempted to find flexibility within the parameters of work and family and the prescriptive ideals of mothering and fathering.

Parenting in Practice

Prescriptions for play and an enhanced paternal role made their way into middle-class expectations for family life, where they met with similar sentiments and concerns already fermenting. In IHD interviews from the late 1950s, young fathers articulated a desire to be involved with their children's upbringing, but few knew how to put these urges into practice. Mothers of young children expected their husbands to participate in child rearing and complained if they did not. In practice, for men who saw themselves as family men, providing proved central to fatherhood on the one hand, and an obstacle to it on the other.[32]

The new ethos of parental sharing is evident in many of the 1950s interviews. Dean Lawrence, a father of six, described his more active role:

> I think it's better for the children to have two parents—to say nothing of the relief to my wife. When I take over the discipline, she's the comforter. When she does, I'm the comforter. . . . We think it's unwise for one parent to have exclusively one role . . . it's not fair to the parents or wise for the children.[33]

The Lawrences saw many reasons for Dean's increased participation, including not only the children's development, but his wife's respite as well. Many young fathers made a conscious effort to "bond" with their children. First-time father Adam Walker vowed, "My daughter isn't going to grow up with a father who is a stranger."[34] As these men set out to distinguish themselves from the remoteness of their own fathers, they placed a high premium on involvement with their children. Some men expected parenthood to be a joint endeavor.

For most fathers, however, the ideal remained simply that. Many who were aware of new demands on men believed they did not measure up. As Malcom McKee put it, "I feel that I don't spend enough time with the children. . . . Sometimes I feel I neglect them. The old style of father is what I am."[35] Among the men from the late fifties examined here, there was an almost universal litany of "I should spend more time with my kids." So many expressions of the same feeling suggest that the period's fatherly ideal was both widely disseminated and narrowly practiced. What prevented these dads from putting the experts' ideas into action? One acknowledged that he simply wanted to relax when he got home. Dale George confessed, "I don't make the effort. I don't go out to play with them."[36] Others left the house too early in the morning and returned too late at night to see their children on weekdays. Providing, in short, often won over active parenting.

If not all middle-class men had fully adopted the edicts of involved

fatherhood propagated by the media, most middle-class women clearly
had. They praised their husbands' involvement with the children. Kay
Patterson said with satisfaction:

> There's not a day that passes that he doesn't spend some portion . . . with
> each individual in his family. If it isn't building a fort, it's helping with
> homework, trying to get them to raise a grade, maybe teasing Francine
> about the cute boy she was walking with or telling her she looks sharp in
> this outfit.[37]

Wives read the advice books and articles in *Parents* and other magazines,
bringing the professionals' advice into their homes to support their requests for more help from their mates. Although experts and dads were
no doubt satisfied that postwar fathers played more with their children,
mothers were not. Dad's new playtime with his youngsters only highlighted the difference between men's and women's parenting experiences.
Young mothers who prodded and persuaded their husbands to join in
child care responded to another impulse. In baby-boom households,
where there could easily be three or four children under the age of six,
there were simply too many meals, baths, and diapers for one parent to
handle alone. The harried mother who had one child barely walking,
another barely talking, and one more on the way, expected a contribution from her partner. Necessity convinced mothers of the need for an
additional pair of hands at midnight feedings and evening bathings more
effectively than the urging of experts alone could have.

In fact, women often instigated changes in paternal habits that cut
deeper than the palliatives offered by advice columnists. The syndicated
columnist Erma Bombeck described the deal she struck with her husband
while her children were infants. At first her husband's only role was to
ensure that there was "strained squash" on the table by bringing home
a paycheck. Annoyed by his leisure at home while she labored on,
Bombeck recalled, "My hours were getting longer and my job description kept growing." To save herself from exhaustion, she divided the
tasks of feeding and bathing their child—allocating the "top half" to
him while she continued to handle messy diaper detail, "the bottom
half." Postwar women like Bombeck pressed their husbands to take up
parental duties.[38]

Not only did wives urge their husbands to pitch in, they also criticized
their husbands when they did not. Claudine Meadows complained that
her husband's contribution to their son Johnny's care was limited to

putting the boy to bed.[39] For Scott Meadows, what may have represented a considerable advance from his own childhood still left his wife feeling she shouldered too much of the burden. The inequity of their household arrangements frustrated these postwar mothers and left them exhausted. May Perkins wished she had more help from her husband with their two children. She explained, "Dennis is tired at night, and he doesn't want to deal with the kids. He only thinks of himself."[40] Wives, still primarily responsible for the labor and minutia of child rearing, added their voices to the clamor for more paternal involvement, but they wanted more than a new playmate for their children. They encouraged their husbands to take the children for the day, put them to bed, or share in the troubles of disciplining. Moreover, they spoke up when fathers failed to join in the work of parenting.

Middle-class women stretched the fatherly ideal of the 1950s, urging their mates to partake of both the problems and the pleasures of raising the baby boomers. While women hoped their husbands would share the tasks of parenting and invited them to do so, many men focused instead on the financial rewards their hard work brought the family.

For the fathers of the baby boom, providing remained the key to fatherhood. Those men who devoted themselves to work hoped that the material benefits of their salaries would make up for their absence from the home.[41] "My most important function as a father," asserted Edward Martin, "is to earn the money the family needs."[42] Fathers might worry about the hours they spent at work and away from their families, but they took pride in supporting their wives and children financially. By their own and their wives' accounts, most men resolved the conflicting pulls of home and work in favor of the latter. Whichever side of the equation men chose, however, they viewed family and work as competing spheres that siphoned energy from each other. Ken Harris summed up the male dilemma: "I would like to spend more time with my kids I guess. But I like my work. . . . And I feel that I must do that in order [to] in the long run help them and in the short run help myself." Work was a compelling responsibility as well as a rewarding one. Harris could reap personal satisfaction and material comfort from his devotion to his career, benefits that overshadowed attentive fathering.[43]

The experts' often superficial emphasis on play restricted the impact of the new version of fatherhood, as did the continued expectation that men earn the family living. In addition, the corporate culture in which men worked offered little opportunity to put desires for fuller involvement at home into practice. Thus, fathers of the 1950s felt torn between the demands of work—their aspirations for financial security and professional success—and their longings for greater connection with their children, as well as their wives' demands for parenting partners.

As a result, by the early 1970s, when their children were grown, most men felt detached from the intimacy their wives and children shared. Two decades of career commitment and limited involvement with now teenaged or grown children left hopes for fatherly intimacy stillborn. Burt Hill spoke for many when he described himself as "a stranger in the midst" of his family.[44] John Thompkins, who had three daughters, perhaps best encapsulated the paternal view of his generation. With a mixture of sadness and pride he said, "I've been just as affectionate and close to my daughters as my business or my time would allow."[45] His occupational commitment and success curtailed his parenting experience.

Wives were resentful of their husbands' limited contributions. Jane Mills said, "I would have liked someone to take more interest in the, you know, the raising of the family . . . I've had to do all that myself." Claire Reilly said, "I think so far as I've had basic[ally] good children, I've always had a husband that's been wrapped up in his work, and not time. He's never had time for his children." She could take the credit for raising good children, but she would have preferred to share both the task and the pride with her husband. For women, the hopes behind this generation's unsuccessful attempts to enlist men in shared parenting lingered long after the children were grown.[46]

But men felt the effects of these unrealized ideals even more poignantly. The fathers of the baby boom could take pride in the economic support and opportunities they bestowed on their families. Yet, in order to fulfill the longstanding expectation to provide, fathers had sacrificed closeness with their children, failing at even the fatherly friendships the experts had promoted. When work had wound down and the children had grown, the true ramifications of choices made in youth became apparent. Empty-nest fathers could only hope to develop closer ties to adult children or forge friendships with young grandchildren. Upon retirement, Greg Fox hoped to "perhaps be available more over the coming decade for the kids and for other members of the family." The postwar male life course placed men out of sync with the baby-boom family cycle, making paternal participation most difficult when it was most necessary, and returning men to the family only when their children were off starting families of their own. The irony of the male life course did not escape the men of this generation. Looking back from the age of sixty, Andrew Sinclair observed, "I don't think any father is as close as they should be. . . . The span of our life is upside down. . . . It should absolutely be reversed. When you're young and you're raising a family, you're so intent on making ends meet at whatever social level, that takes priority." Grant Thornton, prompted to reexamine the familial consequences of career commitment, expressed his regret poignantly: "When I was young and started out, I presumed that my work was essentially more important than that of my wife who would shape our children. . . . I have subsequently concluded that, in terms of my satisfactions . . . hers is a more lasting and useful and meaningful job than was mine."[47]

The twin demands of career advancement and parental involvement fell heavily and simultaneously on young men and eased concurrently as they aged. When fathers returned to the family nest upon retiring, they often found it empty.

The 1950s ideal, which experts so optimistically promulgated, had inherent limitations. The postwar workplace made few concessions to men's family lives, and the calls for involved fatherhood planted seeds that American corporate culture prevented from bearing fruit.[48]

Postwar fathers were united by the desire to do more for their children than their own fathers had done for them. They hoped to take a more active interest in their children. But they found it difficult to measure signs of success in this endeavor. The benefits fell into indefinable categories of affection and emotional closeness. The breadwinning role, in contrast, bestowed time-honored and easily gauged rewards. Fathers who experienced the Great Depression as boys and managed to ensure material comfort and college educations for their children reaped deep satisfactions from this achievement. As young fathers, few dared risk failure as providers for the intangible rewards of participatory child rearing.

Proponents of postwar fatherhood emphasized companionship over care and nurture. Experts and ordinary men struggled to make fathering compatible with men's unchanging role as breadwinners; at the same time, middle-class women yearned for parenting partners. The formulation of fatherhood in the 1950s, both as prescribed and as experienced, represented an enhanced but still limited vision of parental sharing. Only after the parents of the baby boom moved through the family cycle did profound changes in American society permit a truly new perspective on fatherhood and greater opportunities to put it into practice.

American families have paid a price for the inflexibility of the workplace. Increasingly, however, men have chosen to forge close relationships with their children, despite the professional repercussions, and to show a greater willingness to sacrifice career for family goals. For many in the early 1990s, football player David Williams symbolized this willingness. These sacrifices hold the key to corporate change. The demands of male and female employees equally committed to both children and careers may yet reshape American business and family life.[49] But long before a family-oriented football player placed the dilemma on the pages of the nation's newspapers, it was the original "organization men" and their wives who internalized the ideal of involved fatherhood, grappling with the push and pull of home and work for men. In practice, providing for their families failed to supply the emotional and psychological satisfactions that this generation of men craved and left women resenting the extent to which they had parented alone. The emotional legacy of fathering ideals from the 1950s echoes in families today, as contemporary parents attempt to understand their own fathers and to fashion more equitable parenting roles for themselves.[50] These attempts to involve men in family life are laudable and essential, but they should not obscure the efforts of the 1950s and 1960s. The parents of the baby boom framed work and family as a dilemma for men and demanded a space for men in parenting, subtly yet permanently altering American families in the process.

In 1993, the public responded with anger, but not surprise, to the Houston Oilers' decision to dock Williams's pay for the missed game. By the 1990s, Americans criticized the workplace's resistance to concessions to middle-class employees' family lives. The Oilers' owner attempted to defend himself against the accusations of insensitivity that bombarded the team like so many blitzing linebackers.[51] Perfectly in accord with Williams's decision to be present at the birth of his child, he argued that once the infant was safely swaddled, it was time for Dad to go to work. By staking a claim to be there not only for his son's birth, but also during the precious first hours afterwards, David Williams announced his full involvement on a new playing field. A father and self-defined family man, he was not just an observer, but a full-fledged member of the family team. The Williams case captured national attention, but most Americans failed to recognize the hidden actors in this headline-making drama—the postwar men and women whose parental hopes and experiences continue to shape family patterns today.

NOTES

1. This chapter is based on a paper, "Make Room for Fathers: Fatherhood and Family Life, 1947–1980," delivered at the Second Carleton Conference on the History of the Family, Carleton University, Ottawa, Canada, May 1994. For their suggestions and insights on earlier versions of this essay, I would like to thank Laura McCall, Donald Yacovone, Jesse Berrett, Karen Bradley, Sue Grayzel, Robert Griswold, Beth Haiken, Vlad Luskin, Mary Ryan, Julia Rechter, and Tina Stevens. Barbara Burek at the Institute of Human Development was extremely helpful during the research phase of this project. The Mellon Dissertation Fellowship and the Eugene Irving McCormac Fellowship provided essential financial support.

2. Robin Abcarian, "Football Player Fields Role as Dad Like a Champ," *Los Angeles Times,* 24 October 1993, E1, 5; K. S. (Bud) Adams, Jr., "Don't Call the Oilers Insensitive Bosses," *New York Times,* 31 October 1993, S8, 11; Samantha Stevenson "Family Over Football: Williamses in their Own Words," *New York Times,* 24 October 1993, S8, 11; Sam Howe Verhovek, "At Issue: Hold a Baby or Hold that Line," *New York Times,* 20 October 1993, A1, B10.

3. Each generation of fathers, it seems, sees themselves as breaking with the past. Sociologist Ralph La Rossa comments, "While it may be gratifying for men in the late twentieth century to believe that they are the first generation to change a diaper or give a baby a bath, the simple truth is that they are not." Ralph La Rossa, *The Modernization of Fatherhood: A Social and Political History* (Chicago: University of Chicago Press, 1997), 3.

4. By family professionals and experts, I mean the battalions of sociologists, physicians, psychologists, educators, and journalists who disseminated advice on family life in the 1950s.

5. For a thorough discussion of the Cold War's impact on 1950s family life, see Elaine Tyler May, *Homeward Bound: American Families in the Cold War Era* (New York: Basic Books, 1988). For an overview of American family history and postwar family change, see Arlene Skolnick, *Embattled Paradise: The American Family in an Age of Uncertainty* (New York: Basic Books, 1991). Otis Stiese, "Live the Life of McCall's," *McCall's Magazine,* May 1954, p. 27. The link between togetherness and consumption was explicit. One ad for *McCall's* told readers, "And when there are things to be bought, *togetherness* determines the kind of car or cake mix." Advertisement, *Harvard Business Review,* January–February 1946, p. 129. Historian Marty Jezer links family atomization to

the concept of togetherness in *The Dark Ages* (Boston: South End Press, 1982), 222. For more on "togetherness" and its impact on American marriage, see Jessica Weiss, "To Have and to Hold: Marriage and Family in the Lives of the Parents of the Baby Boom" (Ph.D. diss., University of California, Berkeley, 1994). Thanks to Karen Bradley for sharing with me the advertisement in *Harvard Business Review*.

6. Glen Elder's work on the Great Depression and John Clausen's studies of adolescent competence and of women's work lives are also based on the IHD studies. Glen Elder, *Children of the Great Depression* (Chicago: University of Chicago, 1974); John A. Clausen, *American Lives: Looking Back at the Children of the Great Depression* (New York: Free Press, 1993); John A. Clausen and Martin Gilens, "Personality and Labor Force Participation across the Life Course: A Longitudinal Study of Women's Careers," *Sociological Forum* 5, no. 4, 595–618; See also Dorothy Eichorn et. al., *Present and Past in Middle Life* (New York: Academic Press, 1981).

7. Two of the IHD's three longitudinal studies are part of this case study. The Berkeley Guidance Study surveyed every third child born in Berkeley between January 1928 and June 1929 whose parents agreed to participate, resulting in 252 subjects. The Oakland Growth Study (OGS) began in 1931 to study adolescence by selecting 215 ten-year-olds slated to attend Claremont Junior High School in Oakland. Long-term, continuous cooperation with the IHD was a necessary criterion for selection, in order to take advantage of the longitudinal potential of these sources. The IHD lost track of two-fifths of its subjects over the years. Those who withdrew or were lost tended to be from working-class backgrounds or to have experienced family disruption, especially those who left as youths. Thus, I chose my sample from a group that was overwhelmingly middle class and disproportionately committed to contact with the IHD. The demographic profile of the IHD study as a whole closely matches the national norms for most features. Of the study members queried in 1979, the mean age of marriage for women was twenty-one and for men, twenty-four. Most women had their first child two years after marriage and their last child at the median age of thirty-one. They bore an average of 3.4 children in this short time. See Arlene Skolnick, "Married Lives: Longitudinal Perspectives on Marriage," in Eichorn et al., *Present and Past in Middle Life*, 272; Janice B. Stroud, "Women's Careers: Work, Family, and Personality" in ibid., 388.

8. Although the regular therapeutic interaction does set these study members apart from others in their generation, in the postwar years therapeutic solutions to human emotional problems grew more prevalent in the United States, blurring the distinctiveness of the IHD experience. On "psychological gentrification," see Skolnick, *Embattled Paradise*, 16–18; May, *Homeward Bound*, 187, 191. Of the limitations and richness of the IHD material Clausen writes, "If our data are somewhat deficient in showing the relationship of the individual to the larger

society, however, they are much more adequate in depicting relationships among individuals, especially in the family." Clausen, *American Lives,* 12.

9. Thirty percent of the Berkeley families and 40 percent of the Oakland families were working class when the study began. The Berkeley study was 97 percent white, and the Oakland study was entirely white at a time when Oakland's population was 92 percent white. My sample contains two African-American couples. Clausen, *American Lives,* 28–33.

10. Historian Margaret Marsh dubs this development "masculine domesticity." Margaret Marsh, *Suburban Lives* (New Brunswick, N.J.: Rutgers University Press, 1990), 76.

11. Griswold, *Fatherhood in America,* 94–98; La Rossa, *Modernization of Fatherhood,* 39, 40.

12. Mirra Komarovsky, *The Unemployed Man and His Family: The Effect of Unemployment upon the Status of the Men in Fifty-Nine Families* (New York: Dryden Press, 1940).

13. Elder, *Children of the Great Depression,* 196; May, *Homeward Bound,* chap. 2.

14. For more on men's family roles in the early twentieth century, see Griswold, *Fatherhood in America,* 88–98, 121–37; Elaine Tyler May, *Great Expectations: Marriage and Divorce in Post-Victorian America* (Chicago: University of Chicago Press, 1980), 137–55. For a discussion of the war's impact on children whose fathers served, see William M. Tuttle, Jr., *"Daddy's Gone to War": The Second World War in the Lives of America's Children* (New York: Oxford University Press, 1993), esp. chaps. 3 and 12.

15. As Griswold shows, fatherhood in the fifties and sixties was linked to correcting youth and social problems. Griswold, *Fatherhood in America,* 186.

16. The average age of marriage for young men fell from twenty-six before World War II to twenty-two after the war. The age for women, similarly, dropped from twenty-three to twenty. For my sample, the average age at first marriage for women was 21.84 and men 24.44. For a broader discussion of the origins of the baby boom, see Steven Mintz and Susan Kellogg, *Domestic Revolutions: A Social History of American Family Life* (New York: Free Press, 1988), 177–94.

17. Benjamin Spock, M.D., *The Common Sense Book of Baby and Child Care* (New York: Pocket Books, 1946). For an admiring and insightful overview of Spock's contributions to postwar family life, see Ann Hulbert, "Dr. Spock's Baby: Fifty Years in the Life of a Book and the American Family," *New Yorker,* May 20, 1996, 82–92. As of 1976, Spock's book had sold over 28 million copies. See Nancy Pottisham Weiss, "Mother, the Invention of Necessity: Dr. Benjamin Spock's *Baby and Child Care,*" *American Quarterly* 19 (winter 1977): 520.

18. Hulbert, "Dr. Spock's Baby," 83.

19. O. Spurgeon English and Constance J. Foster, *Fathers Are Parents Too* (New York: G. P. Putnam and Sons, 1951); M. Robert Gomberg, "Father as Family Man," *New York Times Magazine*, 6 September 1953, p. 34; Andrew Takas, "What Children Need from Dad," *Parents Magazine*, May 1953, p. 77.

20. Harold Justin, "It's a Man's Job, Too!" *Parents Magazine*, September 1951, p. 165.

21. Gomberg, "Father as Family Man," 34; Ruth Newburn Sedam, "Who Wants to Go back to the Good Old Days?" *Parents Magazine*, October 1956, p. 38.

22. For a discussion of the meanings of fatherly play in the nineteenth century, see Stephen M. Frank, "A Frolic with Father: Play and Paternal Identity in Nineteenth-Century Midwestern and New England Homes," paper delivered at the Second Carleton Conference on the History of the Family, Carleton University, Ottawa, Canada, May 1994.

23. Benjamin Spock, *The Common Sense Book of Baby and Child Care* (New York: Duell, Sloan, and Pearce, 1957), 18 (all subsequent references are to this edition); O. Spurgeon English and Constance J. Foster, "How to Be a Good Father," *Parents Magazine*, October 1950, p. 86.

24. English and Foster, "Father's Changing Role," *Parents Magazine*, October 1951, p. 44; English and Foster, "How Good a Family Man Is Your Husband?" *Parents Magazine*, September 1952, p. 81.

25. English and Foster, "How to Be a Good Father," 87; Lloyd W. Rowland, "Father's Role," *New York Times Magazine*, 31 July 1949, p. 27. For a similar sentiment, see also Edward Streeter, "Have Fathers Changed?" *New York Times Magazine*, 9 May 1954, p. 14. Rowland's reference to the "exciting courier" bears a curious similarity to earlier twentieth-century discussions of men as "mysterious travelers" in the world outside the family. See Ernest R. Groves and Gladys H. Groves, *Parents and Children* (Philadelphia: Lippincott, 1928), 127–28, cited in Griswold, *Fatherhood in America*, 93.

26. English and Foster, "How to Be a Good Father," 84.

27. English and Foster, "Father's Changing Role," 45.

28. May, *Homeward Bound*, 175–77. "For men . . . the home was a source of relative solace," 185.

29. Griswold writes, "Men's belief in the sanctity of the division of labor and the ideology of male breadwinning precluded sustained involvement in daily housework and the less appealing aspects of child care." Griswold, *Fatherhood in America*, 194.

30. Spock, *The Common Sense Book of Baby and Child Care*, 314.

31. Ibid., 18; Selma Lentz Morrison, "Father Needs Your Help," *Parents Magazine*, October 1950, p. 32; English and Foster, "Father's Changing Role," 44; English and Foster, "How Good a Family Man," 77.

32. Although my data is drawn from a study of middle-class family life, it should not be assumed that the goal of enhanced fatherhood was solely a middle-class phenomenon in the postwar years. As social scientist John Snarey shows, working-class fathers also sought and found involvement in the rearing of their children. John Snarey, *How Fathers Care for the Next Generation: A Four-Decade Study* (Cambridge: Harvard University Press, 1993), 313, 314.

33. Lawrence, IHD Archives, 1958, S-P, p. 2. I have assigned pseudonyms to Lawrence and all other IHD subjects named in this chapter. Any similarity to actual names is purely coincidental.

34. Walker, IHD Archives, 1959, I-2, p. 71.

35. McKee, IHD Archives, 1959, I-3, p. 16.

36. George, IHD Archives, 1959, I-3, p. 5.

37. Patterson, IHD Archives, I-6, 1959, p. 22.

38. Erma Bombeck, *A Marriage Made in Heaven, or Too Tired for an Affair* (New York: HarperCollins, 1993), 43, 51.

39. Meadows, IHD Archives, 1958, S-S, pp. 6, 11.

40. Perkins, IHD Archives, 1958, S-S, p. 3.

41. Forty-seven percent of those responding to a 1968 IHD survey worked more than fifty hours a week; 47 percent worked between forty and fifty hours a week; only 5 percent worked less than a forty-hour week.

42. Martin, IHD Archives, 1970, p. 9.

43. Harris, IHD Archives, 1970, p. 13.

44. Hill, IHD Archives, 1970, p. 9.

45. Thompkins, IHD Archives, 1970, p. 27.

46. Mills, IHD Archives, 1982, p. 25; Reilly, IHD Archives, 1982, p. 30.

47. Fox, IHD Archives, 1982, p. 19; Sinclair, IHD Archives, 1982, p. 34; Thornton, IHD Archives, 1982, p. 10.

48. Married women and mothers began to enter the labor force in increasing numbers in the 1950s and 1960s. For a discussion of the impact of women's employment on the postwar family, see Weiss, "To Have and To Hold," chap. 2.

49. Michael Kimmel, "What Do Men Want? Fatherhood, Recession and Corporate Upheaval Redefine What Work Means." *Washington Post,* 31 October 1993, H1, H6. Sociologist Kathleen Gerson suggests that "when parenthood becomes as costly to men's work and careers as it is to women's then men too will have a stake in reducing the economic and social penalties for taking care of children." Kathleen Gerson, *No Man's Land: Men's Changing Commitments to Family and Work* (New York: Basic Books, 1993), 288.

50. Psychologists now study the problems of "absent fathers and lost sons" and set up support groups for the "wounded daughters of distant fathers." Guy Corneau, *Absent Fathers, Lost Sons: The Search for Masculine Identity* (Boston: Shambhala, 1991); flyer posted in Berkeley, California, 1992.

51. I am grateful to Jesse Berrett for his tutelage in football similes.

Contributors

Mark C. Carnes is professor of history and chair of American Studies at Barnard College, Columbia University. He is the author of several books on the history of gender. His most recent work is *Mapping America's Past* (1996), coauthored with John A. Garraty. He is now working on a book about visual perception and gender in the nineteenth century.

Joan E. Cashin, associate professor of history at Ohio State University, has written *A Family Venture: Men and Women on the Southern Frontier* (1991) and *Our Common Affairs: Texts from Women in the Old South* (1996). Her chapter is a revision of an article that first appeared in the *Journal of the Early Republic.*

Patricia Cleary, associate professor of history at California State University, Long Beach, published a study of businesswomen in colonial Boston in *Entrepreneurs: The Boston Business Community, 1700–1850,* edited by Conrad Edick Wright and Katheryn P. Viens (1997).

Richard Godbeer, associate professor of history at the University of California, Riverside, is the author of *The Devil's Dominion: Magic and Religion in Early New England* (1992) and numerous articles on Colonial America. He is currently writing a book on attitudes toward sex in early American society. The essay reprinted here from the *New England Quarterly* received the Colonial Society of Massachusetts's 1994 Walter Muir Whitehill Prize.

Robert L. Griswold, professor of history at the University of Oklahoma, has published widely on the history of gender and the family, including *Family and Divorce in California, 1850–1890: Victorian Illusions and Everyday Realities* (1982) and *Fatherhood in America: A History* (1993).

Anya Jabour, assistant professor of history at the University of Montana, is completing a book-length study of the marriage of Elizabeth and William Wirt for Gender Relations in the American Experience series, published by Johns Hopkins University Press.

Jane Kamensky, assistant professor of history at Brandeis University, is the author of *The Colonial Mosaic: American Women, 1600–1760* (1995) and *Governing the Tongue: The Politics of Speech in Early New England* (1997). Her chapter originally appeared in *Gender and History.*

Laura McCall, professor of history at Metropolitan State College of Denver, is currently preparing a book-length manuscript entitled "Symmetrical Minds: Literary Men and Women in Antebellum America." She is also conducting research on women who engaged in violent acts on the early American frontier.

Kevin P. Murphy, a Ph.D. candidate in American history at New York University, is completing a dissertation entitled "The Manly World of Urban Reform: Homosocial Desire and the Politics of Class in New York City, 1886–1917." He is also a member of the *Radical History Review* editorial collective.

Katherine M. B. Osburn, assistant professor of history at Tennessee Technological University, contributed to *The American Indian: Past and Present,* 4th edition, edited by Roger L. Nichols (1991), and is the author of *Southern Ute Women: Autonomy and Assimilation on the Reservation, 1887–1934* (1998).

Eric Dwyce Taylor, a Ph.D. candidate in American history at the University of California, Davis, is completing a dissertation on the history of gender in the public sphere.

Elizabeth R. Varon, assistant professor of history at Wellesley College, originally published her chapter in the *Journal of American History.* It is based on her book, *"We Mean to be Counted": White Women and Politics in Antebellum Virginia* (1998).

Jessica Weiss teaches U.S. and women's history at the University of California, Berkeley, and California State University, Hayward.

Lisa Wilson, associate professor of history at Connecticut College, is the author of *Life after Death: Widows in Pennsylvania, 1750–1850* (1991). Her next book is tentatively entitled *"Domestick Concerns": The Private Life of Men in Early New England* and is forthcoming from Yale University Press.

Donald Yacovone, associate editor at the Massachusetts Historical Society, is the author of *Samuel Joseph May and the Dilemmas of the Liberal Persuasion, 1797–1871* (1991) and *A Voice of Thunder: The Civil War Letters of George E. Stephens* (1997). He is also editing *The Letters of Robert C. Winthrop.*

Index